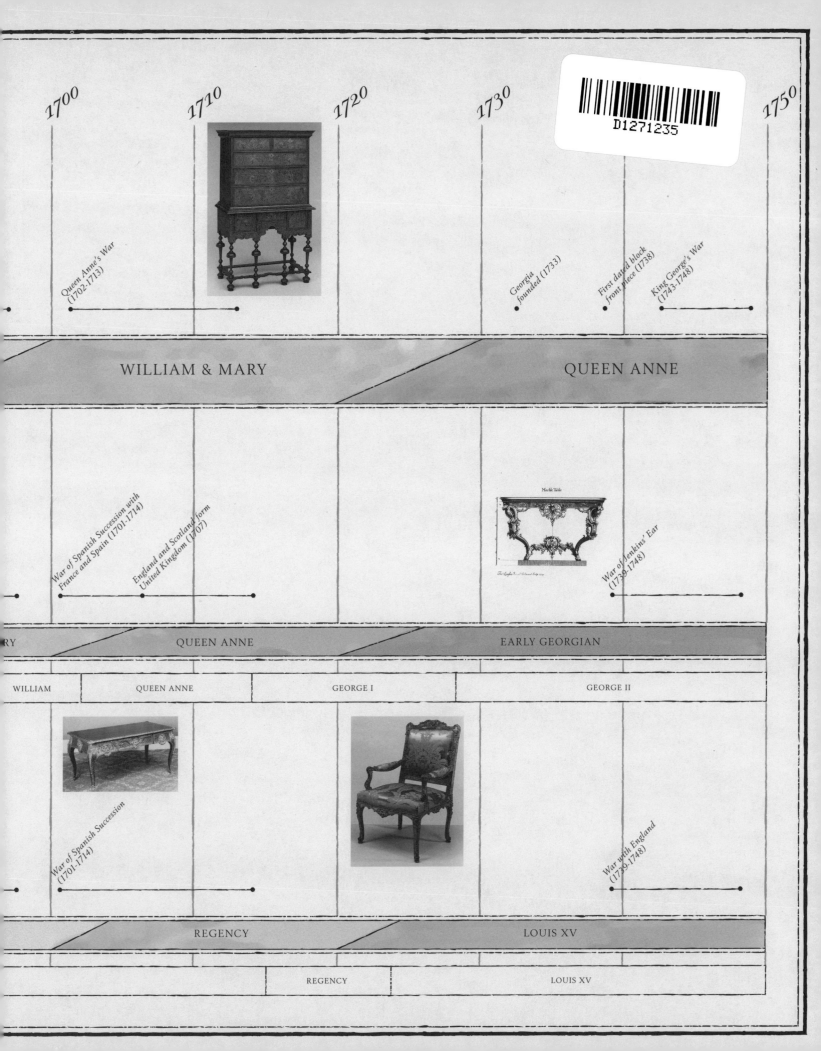

1700　1710　1720　1730　1750

Queen Anne's War
(1702-1713)

Georgia
founded (1733)

First dated block
front piece (1738)

King George's War
(1745-1748)

WILLIAM & MARY

QUEEN ANNE

War of Spanish Succession with
France and Spain (1701-1714)

England and Scotland form
United Kingdom (1707)

War of Jenkins' Ear
(1739-1748)

Marble Table

RY　QUEEN ANNE　EARLY GEORGIAN

WILLIAM　QUEEN ANNE　GEORGE I　GEORGE II

War of Spanish Succession
(1701-1714)

War with England
(1739-1748)

REGENCY　LOUIS XV

REGENCY　LOUIS XV

AMERICAN FURNITURE

of the
18th CENTURY

AMERICAN FURNITURE
of the
18th CENTURY

Jeffrey P. Greene

The Taunton Press

Cover photo: *Scott Phillips*

Back-cover photo: *Courtesy Yale University Art Gallery,
The Mabel Brady Garvan Collection*

Time-line art (end papers): *Scott Bricher*

for fellow enthusiasts

First printing: 1996
Printed in the United States of America

A FINE WOODWORKING Book

FINE WOODWORKING ® is a trademark of The Taunton Press, Inc.,
registered in the U.S. Patent and Trademark Office.

The Taunton Press, 63 South Main Street, PO Box 5506,
Newtown, CT 06470-5506

Library of Congress Cataloging-in-Publication Data
Greene, Jeffrey (Jeffrey P.)
        American furniture of the 18th century / Jeffrey Greene.
            p.   cm.
        Includes index.
        ISBN 1-56158-104-6
        1. Furniture—United States—History—18th century.   2. Furniture—
        United States—History—19th century.   I. Title.
NK2406.G74   1996   96-12859
749'.213'09033—dc20   CIP

To Christine and our wonderful daughter Hayley,
for sharing an aspiration and helping to achieve it.

Special thanks to:

Alan Lotterman, a friend whose passionate enthusiasm
for eighteenth-century American furniture is inspirational,

and

John W. McAlister, Jr., a gentleman and cabinetmaker, who suggested
this undertaking and whose encouragement helped bring it to fruition.

ACKNOWLEDGMENTS

*Sincere thanks to all those who
gave generously of their time and knowledge
to help in this endeavor.
They include:*

Judy Anderson and the Marblehead Historical Society

David Barquist, Yale University Art Gallery

Linda Eppich, Rhode Island Historical Society

Oliver and Elizabeth Greene

Daniel E. Kiernan III and the Wethersfield Historical Society

Jean Landry

Arthur and Mr. and Mrs. Israel Liverant, Nathan Liverant and Son,

Colchester, Connecticut

Thomas S. Michie and Jayne Stokes, Museum of Art, Rhode Island School of Design

Albert Sack and Deanne Levison, Israel Sack, Inc., New York

Daniel Snydacker and the entire staff of the

Newport Historical Society

Bud Steere Antique Tools, North Kingstown, Rhode Island

Steve Stenstrom, Museum of Fine Arts, Boston

Philip Zea, Historic Deerfield

*Thanks also to the museum staff members, archivists
and photograph and slide librarians
who researched and provided many of the photographs
used throughout this book.*

CONTENTS

INTRODUCTION

American furniture of the 18th century stands as one of the pinnacles of human creativity. In a newly settled land, often torn by political and economic strife, one would not expect the design and construction of household furnishings to advance to such a high state of refinement as to be considered among the greatest of artistic achievements. What occurred in America in the 18th century was a rare combination of resources, tradition, inspiration and determination. The forms and structures that resulted remain as standards of design and construction for all furniture that followed.

During this amazing century, furniture design seemed to awaken from a long post-medieval slumber and literally burst onto the world stage. The 18th century was witness to four totally new design styles: William and Mary, Queen Anne, Chippendale and Neoclassical. These styles followed one another in rapid succession, each a reaction to, or an advancement on, the previous style. The designs were a reflection of the changing world at the time. Commerce, politics, social structure and economics all contributed to the new designs.

Antiquarians, furniture historians and furniture makers have often approached the subject from different points of view. To these groups, 18th-century furniture is art, artifact or craft, but rarely a combination of all three, and that is reflected in the literature. Every museum and major collection has a catalog that documents its holdings in great detail, and includes as much of their historical background as possible. For those of us who have a strong interest in period furniture, these books are valuable resources. Without them, few of us would have been exposed to the full depth and breadth of American furniture. In addition, a number of superb furniture-history books have been published that painstakingly trace the development of styles and place them in context with trends in interior design and social and political movements. The two landmark books by Albert Sack, *Fine Points of Furniture* (New York, 1950) and *The New Fine Points of Furniture* (New York, 1993), are among the few that address the artistic merits of originals and define their value to collectors. Within the last 30 years, books dedicated to the craft of furniture making have proliferated. The methods and techniques that were once the secrets of the apprentice system are now available in print. These books illustrate some of the classic designs, provide measured drawings and often give step-by-step descriptions of the building process.

What seemed to be missing from the literature was a work that sought common ground between art, artifact and craft: a book that presented the viewpoints of the connoisseur, historian and artisan to one another. Antiquarians and furniture makers look at the same subject matter, but with different perspectives. This book is intended to present the craftsman's art to the connoisseur and connoisseurship to the craftsman. It is not primarily meant to be a book on how to make furniture, but rather on how period furniture was made—and why.

The furniture maker's viewpoint would help antiquarians better understand the methods of work that yielded the forms of period pieces. It would also explain the evolution of woodworking techniques that enabled new styles to develop, as well as design trends that forced advances in techniques. It illustrates the limits placed on designs by materials and methods, and presents the dynamic nature of wood and its implications on structure and joinery. For example, an antiquarian could better understand the degree of development of a cabriole leg if he or she were familiar with the process of shaping one from rough stock, and could better determine the level of sophistication achieved by the original maker.

The antiquarian's view would benefit cabinetmakers by explaining the important aesthetic points of American furniture, and what differentiates a great expression of style from a mediocre one. The antiquarian's perspective stresses the importance of form in furniture, and how that form applies to the style determines its merit. Students of American furniture know that ornamentation does not make a piece great and that not everything old is worth venerating. Antiquarians have a sense for the historical evolution of design and how world events helped shape it. Similarly, they understand the effects of time and have a reverence for the color, surface and radiance that period pieces achieve over centuries.

All of this cannot be achieved without some risk. I know that exploring the area where the fields of the connoisseur, historian and craftsman converge is bound to generate some discord. For one thing, some long-cherished myths may be endangered. Folkloric explanations and romantic notions are fascinating, but practical reasons take precedence. I have also been so bold as to make aesthetic judgments. While every piece of period furniture is important for its contribution to the body of knowledge on the subject, some pieces uphold the design ideals of their era better than others. Subjective evaluations are by their very nature not quantifiable and therefore arguable, but such is the nature of the discussion of artistic achievement.

In addition, this book is full of references to the various periods or styles of furniture design that emerged over the course of the 18th century. I have noticed an increasing reluctance to use the traditional period names of Jacobean, William and Mary, Queen Anne, Chippendale, Hepplewhite and Sheraton. Being nonjudgmental can easily extend to being nondescriptive, and avoidance of "labels" can mean avoiding the fact that there have been and will continue to be preferences in popular fashions. Granted, the names that have come to be associated with some of these styles are not wholly appropriate. The names of English monarchs have only the loosest association with the designs, and the furniture designers probably wouldn't recognize much of what in America came to bear their names. However, these names do represent certain popular styles of furniture

design that were in keeping with the ideals of the day, and they are very useful for that purpose.

With each phase of 18th-century furniture design, underlying philosophical goals manifested themselves in the various styles. These styles were more likely to be part of a desirable "look," with common distinguishable attributes, than any consciously stated objectives. In each there are common proportions, elements and ornamentation that are characteristic of that trend in design, and which differentiate it from preceding and following styles. Despite the colloquial origins of the style names, they can be useful and descriptive in identifying these trends, their evolution, and the spread and duration of their popularity. Taken for their general descriptive value, style names are valuable in establishing a common ground of understanding among historians and enthusiasts.

With such a broad subject to cover, this cannot be an academically detailed history of furniture design. As a result there are some areas that cannot be explored in the detail they deserve. Among them are clocks, looking glasses and Windsor chairs. I have purposely chosen to concentrate on the main body of 18th-century American furniture and would refer the reader to sources that address these subjects in detail (see the bibliography on pp. 302-303).

As a professional furniture maker who specializes in the 18th-century American styles, I learned the subject by studying the originals in depth and by building hundreds of examples. I feel that this has given me a practical perspective on the techniques and designs of the era. Building these pieces on a daily basis imparts an insight into the way the original makers thought and worked

and adds another dimension to even the closest examination of a finished example.

If I can impart some insight into how the cabinetmakers of the 18th century thought, worked and approached their designs, I will consider this effort a success. Some of the finest furniture ever made was crafted with relatively simple hand tools two or three centuries ago, which underscores the original makers' skill as designers as well as builders. Their work verifies the fact that aesthetic achievement and technical skill are equally important, and it is a reminder that a solid foundation in design and craftsmanship is essential to the successful practice of any craft. It also speaks to the capabilities and importance of fundamental hand tools, a point that is becoming lost amidst the proliferation of modern equipment. To build furniture by traditional methods, furniture that has a soul, one has to work *with* the wood. Machining wood is just something done *to* it.

History can often be reduced to a dry series of events, and a similar view of the history of furniture can rob it of its ingenuity and spontaneity. I have come to view this history as a vibrant account of human effort and try not to forget that the people of this country two or three centuries ago were not that different from we who have inherited it. From the surviving fruits of their labor, I give the original makers great credit and respect for their efforts and ingenuity, and for their skills as consummate artists and craftsmen.

Part One

THE ORIGINS AND EVOLUTION OF AMERICAN FURNITURE STYLES

The account of how and why American furniture reached such a high level of development during the 18th century is a fascinating historical narrative. This furniture, and the extraordinary achievement it represented, was anything but the chance product of a distant colony. It was rather the logical outcome of practical requirements molded by aesthetic trends. In addition, the influences of global commerce, shifting political alignments, evolving social customs, personal preferences, market forces and an occasional spark of genius all contributed toward shaping the work of American craftsmen.

To understand 18th-century American furniture, we must look outside the 18th century and beyond the shores of America. The development of American furniture during this era had its origin deep in the previous century, and it continued well into the following century, so the narrative stretches over a span of 200 years. America was a part of the worldwide British Empire for three-quarters of the 18th century and remained closely linked with England even after the Revolution. English tastes were influenced greatly by those of continental Europe, especially the French. If American styles followed British trends, then those influences were truly global in scope. As a result, much of the discussion of American furniture of the 18th century takes place in other lands and during other times, since it was there that American furniture had its roots.

The essence of 18th-century American furniture is not easily defined, but it is clearly recognizable to those who have a passion for the subject. American craftsmen, inspired by English styles, infused a purity of line and a refined sense of proportion into their designs. Without the undue ornamentation or uninspired appearance that plagued most European work, American furniture of the period had a spirit and clarity that was missing from the English pieces on which it was based. To what degree this resulted from the conservative and practical dictates of the American market or the independent spirit of the American craftsman is arguable, but the results are apparent. The 19th-century essayist John Ruskin summarized the effect in stating, "No architecture is so haughty as that which is simple."

The thread of refined simplicity runs through 18th-century American furniture design, but simplicity of design should not be confused with simplistic design. Refined simplicity denotes an optimized form, while simplistic designs are undeveloped. Without an aristocracy, American cabinetmakers had to achieve more with less. Cost was an object, and American tastes were more restrained than those of the wealthy English elite. Early in the century, American cabinetmakers developed a distinctive style based on refined and well-proportioned forms. Their furniture was never just a platform for ornament, and they were wary of short-lived stylistic trends. Even the more highly ornamented American pieces have at their core carefully proportioned and optimized designs. As the important style periods of the 18th century evolved and ebbed, American artisans kept pace with the changes and breathed their own refinements into the designs.

1

Prelude to Change

THE JACOBEAN PERIOD
(1607–1690)

The 17th century was a period of profound transition in Europe, and nowhere more so than in England. Colonization, expanding commerce and governmental upheaval brought a change in the patterns of daily living and in England's role among the nations of the world. With an increasingly global network of trade came an infusion of new ideas and goods. The rising affluence of the merchant middle class fueled a demand for consumer products, which was answered by a growing number of skilled artisans. These artisans functioned as the manufacturers of their day, choosing from the increasingly diverse supply of raw materials to produce finished goods, including furniture, for both domestic consumption and export to the English colonies. This combination of commercial prosperity and new cultural influences invited a dramatic change in taste and design, which began in earnest with the Restoration of Charles II.

This detail from *A Lady at Her Toilet*, c.1660, by the Dutch painter Gerard Terborch (1617–1681), illustrates some of the northern European tastes that were among the many global influences converging in England after the Restoration of Charles II.

This prosperity extended beyond England itself. By mid-century the recently settled colonies in America were well established and thriving. During the 1630s, 60,000 Englishmen left for America, and 20,000 of them settled in New England. In 1634, colonist William Wood wrote of the need for "an ingenious Carpenter, a cunning Joyner, a handie Cooper, such a one as can make strong ware for the use of the countrie." A popular English song of the day was entitled *Summons to New England*. Skilled craftspeople and people from all walks of life came to America and brought with them their traditions, trades and a desire to carve out a new world.

The Restoration of Charles II

In May 1660, Charles II returned to England from the mainland of Europe. He had left England after the execution of his father, Charles I, in 1649. The execution had been preceded by six years of war, and was followed by eight years of Puritan rule under Oliver Cromwell. The Puritan regimen had brought what was left of the arts to a grinding halt and imposed a strict moral order that reduced daily living to an unending effort to avoid damnation. The restoration of the monarchy came as a great liberation from the burden of Puritan rule and the two years of virtual anarchy that had followed.

With the Restoration came a resurgence of art and culture. The ten years that Charles II had spent in Europe influenced the prevailing court tastes of the period. Two years after taking the throne, Charles married a Portuguese princess, Catherine of Braganza, whose dowry included the privilege of free trade with Portuguese possessions.

England had been languishing in a cultural depression and stylistic slump for nearly two decades. Its internal strife had kept its attention focused inward, in stark contrast with the commercial exuberance that characterized the first half of the century. With the Restoration, England was

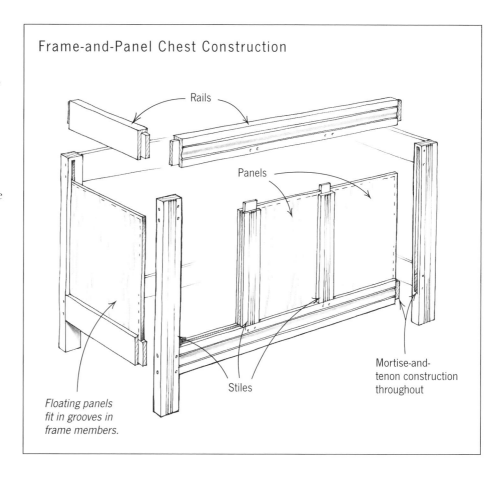

Frame-and-Panel Chest Construction

Rails

Panels

Mortise-and-tenon construction throughout

Stiles

Floating panels fit in grooves in frame members.

able to embrace some extravagance, and it was suddenly inundated with the most fashionable tastes of the French court of Louis XIV, the Low Countries and the Portuguese and all their trading partners.

Of these various influences, the Dutch influence was most important. Not only had Holland been the refuge for many loyalists during the years of Cromwell's Protectorate government, but prosperity and power were shifting from Holland to England after the Restoration. Many Dutch craftsmen were following this change by moving to England, and many Dutch furniture makers who chose to remain were exporting their finished work to England. The English furniture-making business was suddenly busy supplying the prosperous and style-conscious English, and it was even busier after the Great Fire of London in 1666, which destroyed two-thirds of the city. London furniture makers were also exporting finished furniture to Norway and Denmark in exchange for high-quality, cabinet-grade wood.

Jacobean Furniture

Before the Restoration of Charles II, English furniture was built much as it had been for centuries. The construction of these pieces was not unlike that of the timber-frame houses of the period, with a framework of straight members, square, or nearly square, in cross section. These members were joined at right angles by mortise-and-tenon joints. Whereas timber-frame houses were covered by a sheathing that became the walls and roof, the flat sides of furniture were panels let into the stiles and rails of the structure (see the drawing above).

This frame-and-panel style as it was manifested in the 17th century has come to be known as Jacobean, from the Latin "of James." James I was king during the first quarter of the century and the predecessor of the ill-fated Charles I. As with most furniture-design trends named after royalty, the style includes many aspects that were introduced outside of the years of James's reign. In this case, what has come to be called Jacobean includes the first three quarters of the 17th century.

While the frame-and-panel method of construction proved to be durable and practical, it was at the same time stylistically confining. The straight frame-work and flat panels limited the overall designs to severe rectilinear forms. Within this system of building there was no practical way to incorporate sweeping curves or gentle contours, even though they would have made the furniture more comfortable to the user. Decoration was limited to surface carving of the panels, applied geometric shapes or half-turnings.

CAROLEAN FURNITURE

The Late Jacobean, or Carolean period, refers to the period from the Restoration until the ascendancy of William and Mary in 1689. This period includes the rule of Charles II, and the brief reign of James II, which lasted from 1685 to 1688.

Chests of drawers, cabinets on stands, tall case clocks and fall-front writing cabinets were among the newer forms that flourished after the Restoration. Walnut began to replace oak as the wood of choice for fine furniture, because of its warm color, attractive grain and workability. Scrolled legs, ball feet, extensive carving and inlaid marquetry were among the elements that were introduced from the Dutch. Brass mounts or pulls, in the familiar drop shape, and likely of Oriental design origin, replaced earlier iron hardware.

Many of the changes that were introduced in the Carolean period have come to be associated with the William and Mary style. The Carolean period is best remembered as a transitional period from the pre-Restoration Jacobean styles to the fully developed William and Mary style. During the Carolean era, external influences were having a powerful effect on English furniture design, and it was undergoing drastic changes in both structure and appearance. In America, these changes had not yet come to the fore. Throughout furniture history there was a lag in the time required for English styles to become established in America. Many of the changes that occurred in England after

CHEST, CONNECTICUT (PROBABLY NEW HAVEN), 1640–1680.
This frame-and-panel chest with a lift top typifies the structure and form of chests of the 17th century. Chests of the second half of the century frequently included one or two drawers in the bottom of the case.
[COURTESY YALE UNIVERSITY ART GALLERY]

the Restoration came to America as part of the later William and Mary style, so until the last decade of the 17th century, the English Jacobean style dominated American furniture design.

American Jacobean Forms

In America, the first furniture had come from England with the early settlers. Almost immediately, however, furniture that was needed for the use of the settlers was also made domestically. From the outset, tradespeople who came to America found their skills in demand in a new market. The Great Migration that followed the first settlers brought more specialized craftspeople, along with their methods and styles. The regional variations of England were transplanted to America. For much of the 17th century, American furniture was a continuation of the prevailing English tastes, which included the infusion of Dutch tastes and European Renaissance

influences that started to find their way into the forms after the Restoration.

CASE PIECES

One of the most familiar forms of American Jacobean furniture is the chest, which for most of the period had a lift top and often one or two drawers at the bottom. Depending on the place of origin, the exterior, and in particular the front, was either carved or decorated with applied half-turnings or geometric shapes (photo above). The stiles at the front and back corners continued beyond the bottom of the case to form the feet as well. These chests share a common structure and trace their roots to medieval pieces.

A distinction should be made between chests with drawers and chests of drawers. Chests comprised entirely of drawers, usually four, appeared later in the period and were seen in America with increasing frequency after about 1670. Documents from the time often refer to them as cases of drawers, and early 17th-century English references mention cases of drawing boxes.

The Dutch influence after the
Restoration brought about one of the more
spectacular case pieces of the period: the
cupboard. Cupboards had an English origin
in Elizabethan designs of the previous
century, but the Dutch influences gave
them a new stature. They are visually
complicated, with strong horizontally
layered elements and exceptionally bold
turnings. As is the case with chests, these
turnings and half-turnings are usually
ebonized. Ebonizing involves painting
these parts a strongly pigmented black to
make them stand apart from the lighter
colored case (see pp. 194-195). The use
of contrasting light and dark colors, not
unlike the paintings of the Dutch masters,
is a theme that runs through much of
Jacobean-era design.

Cupboards were made to stand in the
most important room of the house, and
were a reflection of wealth and social
standing. Needless to say, only the very
wealthy owned them, since the complexity
of these pieces made them prohibitively
expensive. Apart from its role as a symbol
of refinement, the cupboard's primary
function was to store linens. Textiles
were very valuable in the 17th and 18th
centuries, and many important pieces were
dedicated to their storage and protection.
Jacobean cupboards are categorized today as
either press cupboards, which have their
lower portion enclosed, or court cupboards,
which have the bottom part open.

TABLES

Stylish tables of the period featured turned
legs and stretchers, and were similar to
English examples. They were made in a
range of sizes from about 3 ft. to over 6 ft.
in length and served a variety of purposes.
Their primary requirement was their
functionality, so they were usually built
without as much decoration as other pieces.
In addition, trestle-type tables were in use,
sometimes of the variety that was easily
disassembled for storage. Another variety
was the chair-table, the hinged top of which
allowed it to be converted from table to
chair. With space at a premium in many
early houses, tables that folded or
disassembled were not uncommon.

CHAMBER TABLE, SALEM, MASSACHUSETTS, 1690.
Chamber tables functioned as dressing tables. This
table is one of the few 17th-century pieces to move
away from the low horizontal Jacobean format.
(COURTESY WINTERTHUR MUSEUM)

JOINT STOOL,
MASSACHUSETTS,
1690–1715.
Joint stools with turned
and splayed legs were
made in great quantity
for use as seating
furniture into the early
18th century.
(COURTESY YALE UNIVERSITY
ART GALLERY)

One very unusual form that survives
from the 17th century is the chamber table
(top photo at left). A chamber table is best
described as a small lift-top chest with one
drawer beneath, but built on tall turned
legs with decorative stretchers. The
construction is frame and panel with
mortise-and-tenon joinery throughout. Its
purpose was to hold personal effects in the
bedroom, and the interiors of the drawer
and case were divided by partitions. In this
way, chamber tables fulfilled much the
same purpose as dressing tables or lowboys
did during the 18th century. The personal
nature and intricate design of the originals
suggest that they may have been built, and
perhaps given as gifts, to mark important
events like marriages or the coming of age.

SEATING FURNITURE

One of the most commonly used pieces of
seating furniture of the Jacobean period
was the joint stool (bottom photo at left).
Joint stools are comprised of four turned
and splayed legs joined by an apron and
stretchers, with a board top. Structurally,
they have more in common with tables
than with chairs, and when needed they
could double as small tables. Joint stools
were the most affordable and common type
of seating furniture of the period. In a
household that may have had only one or
two regular chairs, the remaining family
members would use joint stools for dining
or sitting near the fire. An elongated
version of the joint stool, called a form,
was more like a bench and could seat two
or more people. There was a certain
practicality to the use of joint stools,
considering both the bulkiness of winter
clothing and the practice of rearranging
the furniture in a room according to the
activity going on there.

Among the more conventional chairs
were a number of standard designs.
Wainscot chairs were built with the frame-
and-panel method of construction. The
ornamentation of these chairs was
primarily surface carving of the panels and
frame members. Turned chairs were
comprised of elements that were all turned
on the lathe. This method allowed for the
component parts to be turned to decorative

WAINSCOT ARMCHAIR, CONNECTICUT, 1640–1680.
Frame-and-panel wainscot chairs are highly rectilinear in form. As on chests, the flat panels and frame members were decorated with shallow moldings and carving. This Connecticut example has turned front legs.
(COURTESY CONNECTICUT HISTORICAL SOCIETY)

TURNED GREAT CHAIR,
EASTERN MASSACHUSETTS, 1640–1680.
This striking armchair, made contemporaneously with wainscot chairs, is comprised entirely of turned elements. Chairs of this type with vertical spindles below the seat are often referred to as Brewster chairs.
(COURTESY THE METROPOLITAN MUSEUM OF ART)

TURNED ARMCHAIR, SOUTHEASTERN
MASSACHUSETTS, 1640–1680.
Similar to the turned great chair, this turned armchair (or Carver chair) from the same period has no vertical spindle turnings below the seat.
(COURTESY COLONIAL WILLIAMSBURG FOUNDATION)

profiles, and resulted in visually interesting chairs. Because turned chairs are comprised of spindles rather than panels, they can be looked through as well as at. The beauty of turned chairs is in their silhouette, while that of wainscot chairs is on their surface. Turned chairs are sometimes categorized as either Brewster or Carver chairs, after William Brewster, an original chair owner, or John Carver, the first governor of Plymouth. Brewster chairs have vertical turned spindles under the seat, whereas Carver chairs do not. It was customary to use a separate upholstered cushion on the hard seat panels of Jacobean-era chairs.

Another form of chair, sometimes called a Cromwellian chair, is a very rectilinear form of joined chair. These chairs appeared in the last quarter of the century, well after the others. Rather than having inset panels, the backs were either upholstered in fabric or leather, or colonnaded with vertical spindles. In either case, they are usually without arms (to accommodate the bulky dress of the day) and have a large space between the seat and the back. The stark

CROMWELLIAN CHAIR,
MASSACHUSETTS, 1670–1700.
Side chairs of this rectilinear design were made in quantity in Boston in the last quarter of the 17th century. This example retains its original 'Turkey work,' a European imitation of Middle Eastern upholstery fabric.
(COURTESY THE METROPOLITAN MUSEUM OF ART)

SIDE CHAIR, PHILADELPHIA, 1680–1705.
Similar in form to the Boston chairs, this Philadelphia version has twist-turned stretchers and spindles, an English design element from after the Restoration.
(COURTESY WINTERTHUR MUSEUM)

plainness of some of these chairs belies their age and association with the Jacobean period. Existing examples show that those with a New England heritage are upholstered in leather or fabric with marsh-grass stuffing and have ball-turned stretcher and leg details. An elongated version with arms is the basis for an early couch. An unupholstered Philadelphia chair from during or after the 1680s shows the twist-turned spindles and stretchers that had come into fashion in London after the Restoration (see the bottom right photo on p. 11). In a slightly different style, the Dutch tradition of using horizontal slats across the backs of turned chairs continued in the regions that they populated, namely the New York and New Jersey coastal areas.

BEDSTEADS

During the 17th century, the term "bed" referred to the mattress itself, and the bedstead was intended as both a frame for the rope suspension and the bed hangings. With the inherent cold and draft of early houses, it was essential that the bed be well off the floor and surrounded by curtains. Though none survive, it is known through documentary evidence that there were frame-and-panel bedsteads with turned posts. Another type of bedstead, called a French bed, was a light frame of a simple style that held the mattress and hangings. This form probably evolved into the common pencil-post bed of slender proportions in the 18th century. Examples of a third type of bed, with low posts and turned elements, are reminiscent of the Brewster and Carver chairs (see the photo at right).

Jacobean Structure

Because it was built from stout frame members, American Jacobean furniture was rugged enough to withstand heavy use. As in England, oak was a favorite wood. In New England, oak and ash were in abundant supply, and they were the woods with which most immigrant joiners were experienced. Furthermore, these woods were strong and durable, and without the brittle characteristics of fruit woods. Frame members and panels were easily split from short logs with a froe and dressed to final dimensions with a hand plane. Compared to sawing, this method was quick and easy. The mortise-and-tenon joinery and floating panels were seemingly impervious to the ravages of climatic extremes and constant use.

Relatively few tools were required to make the structural elements of Jacobean furniture. Joiners, as furniture makers of the 17th century were known, needed only an auger, saw and chisels to make a snug-fitting joint. Higher levels of sophistication or decoration required a more extensive array of tools. There was a certain modularity to this kind of construction. The same kind of elements that made up a chest also made a wainscot chair or a cradle. The same tools and techniques were used to make the elements of each, but the dimensions were varied to fit the piece.

The mortise and tenon was a basic and universal joint during this time, and the joiner's skills were employed in more than just furniture making. Joiners often doubled as housewrights, wagon builders and general repairmen as well. Since nearly everything was made out of wood and the joiner was the primary tradesman of the medium, he often wore many hats.

Parts of furniture that couldn't be joined by mortise and tenon were usually nailed. Until the end of the 18th century, nails were hand-wrought. The multifaceted head gave them the name "rosehead." Chest

TURNED BEDSTEAD, NEW ENGLAND, 1670–1710.
With the exception of the rails, this bedstead is made up of turned elements. The use of turnings and the profiles of the spindles are reminiscent of the turned chairs of the mid-17th century.
(COURTESY MUSEUM OF FINE ARTS, BOSTON)

17th-Century Drawer Construction

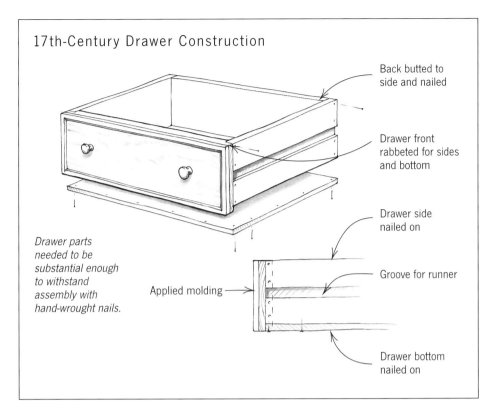

Back butted to side and nailed

Drawer front rabbeted for sides and bottom

Drawer side nailed on

Groove for runner

Applied molding

Drawer bottom nailed on

Drawer parts needed to be substantial enough to withstand assembly with hand-wrought nails.

Side-Hung Drawer

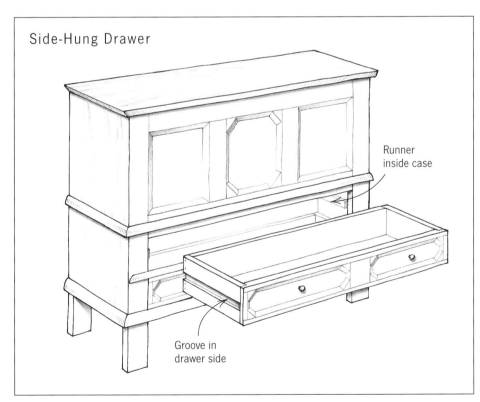

Runner inside case

Groove in drawer side

bottoms and backs were often nailed in place, as were hinges and any other hardware that was attached. Until near the end of the century, drawers were also nailed together (see the top drawing at left). The sides were nailed to the front and back, and the bottom was nailed on as well.

The standard method of suspending a drawer in a case was to have a groove cut along the center of the drawer side from front to back, which rode on two runners nailed to the inside of the case. These are known as side-hung drawers (see the bottom drawing at left). To accommodate the grooves and the nails, the drawer parts needed to be thick. Some examples have drawer parts as thick as 1 in. Since the wood of choice was usually oak, the drawers were very heavy.

The mass of these thick drawers, along with that of frame-and-panel construction, did not facilitate the building of tall or delicate furniture. By its very structure, Jacobean furniture was obliged to maintain the low, solid and horizontal format that was indicative of the style.

Seventeenth-Century Decoration

The solidity and practicality of early Jacobean pieces did not preclude them from being handsome, decorative and well proportioned. With a simple lathe, the joiner could produce turnings for table legs and stretchers as well as chair and bed parts, and thereby add some decorative embellishment to otherwise utilitarian forms. The flat panels of Jacobean pieces were also well suited to shallow carving, a style of decoration used widely during the period.

TURNINGS

Seventeenth-century turnings are noted for being robust, often bordering on stout, though some turnings of great delicacy and refinement appeared as ornamentation on chairs and bedsteads. Half-turnings were applied to chest and cupboard surfaces as an alternative or addition to carved panels. The distinctive shapes of turnings differentiate the work of various craftsmen and regions, and are important details in determining the origin of pieces.

By their very nature, turnings are inherently decorative. Woodturning comprised an important subset of woodworking that had developed as a field in itself. In areas that had the population density to support full-time turners, joiners often purchased their turnings from these specialists. While most joiners owned lathes, economy often dictated that repetitive or elaborate turnings be bought from specialists. Throughout much of American furniture history, turners were a group separate and apart from joiners and later cabinetmakers. The two groups enjoyed a parallel development and their paths crossed continually. Not only did turners supply joiners with turned elements, but they also developed their own kinds of furniture, most often chairs. In the American Jacobean period, joiners built their wainscot chairs from square or rectangular members with panels incorporated into them. The joinery was the pegged mortise-and-tenon joint used on a variety of pieces. Turners' chairs were the Brewster and Carver chairs, made entirely of turned pieces and put together with round turned tenons and round drilled mortises.

CARVING

Carving had been an important part of ornamentation for millennia, and, besides turnings, was the predominant method of embellishing the flat surfaces of frames and panels. Most of the carving on 17th-century American furniture was botanical in nature and derived from Renaissance designs. As with most ornamentation, each region had an identifiable set of designs.

The very first American chests were stylized with scratch or shadow moldings (top photo at right). These shallow profiles were literally scraped lengthwise into the stiles and rails to give some visual relief to an otherwise plain frame-and-panel facade.

The most recognizable kind of carving was the shallow relief carving of panels, often done in conjunction with the use of half-turnings (bottom photo at right). One

CHEST, CONNECTICUT RIVER VALLEY OF MASSACHUSETTS, 1685–1700.
This oak chest is clearly of frame-and-panel construction. Like many chests of the 17th century, its only ornamentation is the shallow shadow moldings on the stiles and rails.
(COURTESY HISTORIC DEERFIELD)

CHEST WITH DRAWERS, WETHERSFIELD, CONNECTICUT, 1675–1710.
This chest is attributed to Peter Blin of Wethersfield. The design, including the shallow relief carving of the sunflower and the use of half-turnings, is nearly identical to several other chests attributed to him.
(COURTESY WETHERSFIELD HISTORICAL SOCIETY)

of the most prolific practitioners of this style was Peter Blin of Wethersfield, Connecticut, who was working during the last quarter of the century. Blin carved the panels with the sunflower (or perhaps marigold) and tulip design that became a signatory detail of that region. A consummate craftsman, Blin planned his carving carefully and stayed within the confines of the panels. On the North Shore of Massachusetts at about the same time, Thomas Dennis and William Searle were

carving in a similar way, but including more free-flowing ornamentation, scrolls and references to more medieval designs. Some chests of coastal New England origin have applied geometric designs on the panels and drawer fronts, which was another influence of Dutch taste on the English styles.

Some of the most interesting examples of carved ornamentation come from farther north in the Connecticut River Valley, namely the Hadley, Massachusetts, area. Although the structure of the furniture from this area was nearly the same as elsewhere, its proportions were somewhat lighter and its carving was remarkable. The fronts of Hadley-area chests are covered with all sorts of fanciful carvings in very shallow relief (see the photo on the facing page). At first glance the designs appear to be a whimsical kind of folk art, but the style is consistent among a number of pieces and shows a high degree of sophistication. The designs include all kinds of botanical subjects, stylized animals and figures, and geometrical and compass designs. The carvings know no bounds and extend all over the front of these chests. Despite their exuberance, the carvings are arranged in an orderly manner and are consistent within their respective frame member or panel. On close examination they are like no other kind of carving, and, despite their magnificence, the observer cannot help but wonder how their creators were inspired.

CHEST OVER DRAWER, CONNECTICUT RIVER VALLEY OF MASSACHUSETTS, 1670–1710.
This painted Hadley chest has the characteristic shallow relief carving of stylized botanical elements.
Over 125 original chests with this type of ornament exist, and nearly half of them are of this form.

(COURTESY YALE UNIVERSITY ART GALLERY)

PAINTS AND STAINS

Carved pieces were very often painted as well. The entire spectrum was to be found highlighting the carvings or coloring the ground between raised portions. Deep reds, blues, greens and ivory are frequently seen colors on surviving examples. While it was to be another two centuries before commercially produced paints were available, a number of naturally occurring pigments could be ground with linseed oil from flax seed to make a very good paint. Some of these pigments were available locally, and others were imported. In urban areas there was enough of a demand for paint and decoration to support a separate profession by the end of the century.

It is not known for certain what kind of stains (if any) were used in 17th-century America. Based on the sophistication of the furniture, it is probable that the builders of the period would have used some kind of tinted wash to impart at least an even tone if not darken the wood. Any number of plant materials, like bark, roots or nut shells, could be boiled in water to extract their dye. Throughout the 18th century, water-based dyes continued to be among the formulae for colorants.

Any colorants were likely sealed into the wood with a top coat of boiled linseed oil or wax. Both linseed oil and beeswax were readily available, and they could be applied alone or in succession to give a protective finish with a nice luster. Both materials are rubbed in and buffed off, making them very easy to apply. With either finish, the oxidation of the surface deepened the color of the wood in time. Almond and walnut oil were also used as furniture finishes in early America. It has been suggested that some of these pieces were not originally finished, and that their present surface is a result of centuries of use. This seems highly unlikely, since raw wood quickly becomes dirty when handled, and it is even more improbable that a piece would be handled all over to give it the patina we see today. The original makers were trained and skilled craftspeople, and applying an oil or wax finish would have protected and enhanced their work. (For more on period finishes, see Chapter 12.)

The spirited decoration of 17th-century American furniture, while seemingly in contrast to the strict moral values of a Puritan society, was a holdover from the Renaissance and the jubilance of Elizabethan England. While there was sin in public overindulgence, there was no limit in indulging in fancifully decorated furniture. Owning a highly decorated piece was a way of showing one's wealth or importance in society, since most households had few pieces of furniture and the forms of the pieces were fairly uniform. The Puritans did not frown on success, and the decorative arts were a measure of it. According to Puritan ethics, material success could be considered a reflection of one's goodness in the eyes of God. As a practical point, at a time when most people had relatively few possessions and houses were poorly lit, it seems natural that brilliant colors and extensive carvings would be in fashion. Just as spinning and weaving were winter work for women, elaborate carving and painting were likely indoor pastimes for men, especially in isolated rural areas. Many of the pieces of the period show evidence that they were carved after they were built, suggesting that the decorative work was taken up when there was time for it.

Historians all too often attempt to find serious reasons for every aspect of early American life, as if these were dour souls who needed a solid reason for every action. Like all people they could appreciate a bold design and some bright colors. After all, these designs were rooted in their recent English history, and the long New England winters called for something to brighten them up. To deny these people their spontaneity robs their surviving work of some of the creativity and individualism that is inherent in any handcraft.

2

The Century of Cabinetmaking Begins

THE WILLIAM AND MARY PERIOD
(1690–1725)

The many influences that converged in England after the Restoration of Charles II combined to form a new style that began a century of rapidly changing furniture design. The new style was uniquely English, but American craftsmen added their own refinements of design and proportion, based on the tastes and needs of the flourishing colonies. The American interpretation of the English designs imbued them with a distinctive spirit that was to continue as a hallmark of American design.

Foreign Influences and Baroque Ideals

With the ascendancy of William and Mary in 1689, the Dutch influences that had arrived in England with the return of Charles II were further reinforced. Both the Dutch and Portuguese were trading extensively with the Orient, and their tastes were colored by cultures far different from their own.

Cabinetmakers to the court were instrumental in incorporating the new foreign influences and helping to synthesize a new style. One of the leading cabinetmakers of the day was Gerreit Jensen, a craftsman of Flemish and Dutch origin who

The Tea-Table is an engraving by an unknown English artist published in London about 1710. In addition to showing cane-back chairs and a gateleg drop-leaf table in the William and Mary style, it documents the relationship between increasing prosperity and leisure time and the growing importance of furniture as the centerpiece of social gatherings.
(COURTESY BRITISH MUSEUM, LONDON, ENGLAND)

was a cabinetmaker to the Crown from 1680 to 1715. He was skilled in marquetry and lacquerwork and worked under Charles II, James II, William and Mary and Queen Anne. His skill and versatility were instrumental in keeping the royal families supplied with furniture of the latest tastes. An influential craftsman best known for his

carving technique was Grinling Gibbons (1648–1720). Gibbons was born in Rotterdam but had moved to England shortly after the Restoration. He is known for his deep, airy and fluid style of carving of both architectural details and furniture. His style permeated Late Jacobean ornament, and set a standard in carved design that continued into the William and Mary style.

The revocation of the Edict of Nantes in 1685 led many French Huguenot craftsmen to flee France for other European countries and America. One of these French Protestants was Daniel Marot (1662–1752). Marot was an architect and a designer of both furniture and ornament. He fled to Holland and then came to England with William III. Marot served as King William's architect before returning to Holland in 1698. He brought with him a decidedly French taste in the style of Louis XIV, and introduced some details that were to become synonymous with the William and Mary style. Among these are cross stretchers and the turned leg in the trumpet and inverted cup shape.

THE BAROQUE STYLE

Apart from the stylistic influences brought to England by trade, monarchs or their spouses, and foreign craftsmen, the emerging designs were also the manifestation of the Baroque style. The Baroque is a term that is used to describe the artistic style prevalent in Europe from about 1600 through 1750. It spread northward from Rome and did not come into vogue in England until after the Restoration. While Renaissance design was refined but static, the Baroque was intended to be dynamic. In addition, work was to be done with a flourish and everything was to appear effortless. There is an increased sense of drama and flair in the furniture designs of the period, in keeping with the Baroque idea that artists and scientists were, according to art historian Helen Gardner, "brilliant performers" and "virtuosi proud of their technique and capable of astonishing quantities of work." The difference is evident when comparing the solid, rectangular forms of the best Renaissance-inspired Jacobean style with the complexity and bold undertaking of William and Mary designs.

Furniture met the Baroque ideals by becoming more vertical and more ornate. By Baroque standards, one of the best ways to create an impressive piece of furniture was to make it tall. Court furniture makers were building taller and taller pieces to fill the increasingly cavernous interiors of

palaces that were being built at Versailles and elsewhere. Chests became nearly square and were full of drawers. Some chests were placed on top of stands (see the photo above). Chairs became taller and were crowned with ornate carved designs. In addition, case pieces were given the flourish of elaborate moldings at top and bottom. Legs became excuses for showing off dramatic turnings. Aprons and stretchers became decorative as well as functional, and wildly grained veneers were everywhere. Those of the old school must have shaken their heads in disbelief.

At the same time that Baroque design was encouraging dramatic results, Enlightenment ideals were demanding logic and order. The two were not at odds in the William and Mary designs, and in fact they merged nicely. The new style was a very orderly display of drama. Pieces were designed to be impressive, and part of this was in the logical arrangement of their component parts and the great attention paid to symmetry and order. In subtle ways, the vertical mass of these pieces was made apparent. Feet and bases were designed to show that they carried weight. It was as if Enlightenment logic sought to make it evident that designers went to great lengths to achieve Baroque drama.

As with most styles, it is impossible to trace the lineage of the emerging design of furniture, which would come to be known as the William and Mary style, to any one place or person. It is instead the sum of many global influences and the willingness of the enlightened English aristocracy to embrace them. The William and Mary name is a modern one, and like the names of other periods, it is not entirely accurate. In England the style had started to develop under Charles II, in the so-called Carolean period, and the prevailing tastes during his reign actually had more to do with the fundamental development of the style than the influences brought by William and Mary's ascension nearly 30 years later.

As with all other furniture periods named after royalty, the monarchs were usually gone by the time the styles became popular in America. William and Mary's joint rule ended with her death in 1694, and William III ruled alone until 1702, just as the style was emerging as an important trend in American design. Like most emerging styles, what we now call the William and Mary period in retrospect was simply called the "new furniture" or the "latest English style" in its day. In American furniture, the William and Mary style first appeared toward the end of the 17th century and dominated the first quarter of the 18th century, roughly from 1690 to 1725.

The Convergence of Design and Technique

Some details of the William and Mary style can be traced to specific origins. Spanish feet, delicate turnings and the colonnaded bases of high chests were Moorish in nature, and indicate the influence of England's connections with Portugal. Scrolled legs, trumpet and ball turnings, and inverted cup-shaped turnings used for legs can be traced directly to Dutch and earlier French designs. Distant trading partners like Africa, India, Ceylon and China inspired the use of exotic burled and figured veneers on the faces of pieces. Decorative brass hardware such as drawer pulls and escutcheons, inspired by the Orient, added a new element of design to functionality.

THE DOVETAIL JOINT

The single most important contribution that enabled the development of the William and Mary style was the increased use of the dovetail joint. Dovetail joints made it possible to join two thin pieces of wood at right angles by cutting interlocking triangular elements into their ends. Dovetail joinery had been used by the ancient Egyptians, and occasionally by Renaissance craftsmen, but it wasn't until the 17th century that its use formed the basis for a whole system of structure.

The dovetail enabled drawers to be built of very thin wood, because they no longer needed to be nailed together. Case pieces could be dovetailed together as well, superseding the frame-and-panel method that had been the basis for Jacobean pieces. The lighter construction facilitated by this joint enabled chests to be taller and allowed for the design trends that were synonymous with the Baroque.

Dovetails had started to show up in American furniture long before the William and Mary style arrived in America. Toward the end of the 17th century, dovetailed drawers were becoming more frequent in frame-and-panel cases. At first the dovetails were large and crude, perhaps only one or two on a drawer corner, but as time progressed they became smaller and more closely spaced and the drawer parts became thinner. While it is true that William and Mary designs would not have been possible without the advent of dovetail joinery, furniture makers did not seem to be at an impasse for want of better joinery. With the exception of a handful of late-17th-century pieces made with long legs or stands (see the photo below), there

CHEST-ON-STAND, PROBABLY BOSTON, ABOUT 1700.
Standing less than 3 ft. tall, this chest-on-stand is among the few pieces of American furniture built with frame-and-panel construction that rose above the horizontal Jacobean format.
(COURTESY MUSEUM OF ART, RHODE ISLAND SCHOOL OF DESIGN)

are no existing pieces that indicate a conscious effort to move to a more vertical format while using frame-and-panel construction. Dovetails were one of the many innovations in technique and design that converged at the time and enabled the development of the William and Mary style as we know it today.

The William and Mary Style in America

Since the first settlers had arrived in New England in 1620, there had been a constant influx of new craftsmen and new ideas in design from overseas, primarily from England. It stands to reason that the major seaports would have been the first to receive new trends, and that the new fashions would work their way inland over time. The local tastes, skills and available materials would alter the purity of the imported design as the style found acceptance farther inland from the coast. As the 17th century was drawing to a close, the most important points of entry for new furniture designs were Boston, New York and Philadelphia. Through those bustling ports were coming a new sense of design and a new approach to furniture making.

Just as England was ready to embrace new designs following the Restoration of Charles II, so was New England ready to accept the William and Mary style some 30 years later. The tide of the Great Migration had been stemmed in the 1640s with the outbreak of war between the forces of the Crown and those of the Puritans and nonconformists. New Englanders found themselves somewhat isolated, without frequent infusions of new ideas and struggling to hold onto Puritan ideals while becoming increasingly prosperous. They held onto fashions and manners that had long since passed out of style in England. As late as 1689 an English visitor wrote that they were "very home-bred" and "exceedingly wedded in their own way." As their prosperity and commerce increased, however, so did their appetite for new fashions.

The acceptance of William and Mary furniture in America was based on an American desire to remain stylistically competitive with England. By the last two decades of the 17th century, travelers between New England and England were primarily engaged in government or private business. The colonies had become stable trading partners and were enjoying a prosperity of their own making. Government officials and merchants were in frequent contact with London, and anything unavailable in America could easily be imported. To the most affluent colonists, the latest and most stylish designs in furniture and other goods were readily available.

By 1700, the William and Mary styles had captured the imagination of style-conscious buyers in the major American seaport cities. American furniture makers, quick to capitalize on their affluent customers' desire to keep pace with both London and their neighbors, took up the new style wholeheartedly. Human nature dictates that when one successful family received new furniture, others would soon follow. "Equal or Superior to the Most Fashionable London Styles," or a variation thereof, was a phrase that was found in the advertisements and labels of American furniture makers for another hundred years.

William and Mary Forms

Because of the changes in structure brought about by the use of the dovetail joint, William and Mary pieces were able to take on forms that were not possible with earlier frame-and-panel construction. Generally, the use of the dovetail joint allowed for several levels of drawers to be stacked in one case, and for cases to be tall or placed upon stands. Seating furniture, while not affected by the new methods of construction, followed the Baroque trend for greater height and ornamentation.

CHESTS

The design possibilities enabled by the use of the dovetail joint gave a new impetus to case pieces such as chests. Drawers had proven to be very practical, and with dovetail joinery drawers and their cases could be made light and strong. Chests evolved to include more drawers, and chests-on-frame and tall chests continued the shift toward the vertical format.

Chests of drawers

During this period, chests took on nearly square proportions (see the photo above). While the earlier fashion of a lift-top chest with one or two drawers underneath

HIGH CHEST OF DRAWERS, EASTERN MASSACHUSETTS, 1695–1720.
The earliest American high chests used the standard form of chests of drawers on low bases with turned legs and stretchers.
(COURTESY HISTORIC DEERFIELD)

HIGH CHEST OF DRAWERS, MASSACHUSETTS, 1700–1725.
In its most developed form, the proportions of the William and Mary high chest became more refined and better expressed the Baroque ideals of height and order.
(COURTESY MUSEUM OF FINE ARTS, BOSTON)

continued in America through the first quarter of the 18th century, the coastal style centers were building chests with four drawers as early as 1670. As with every stylistic change, the transition from one period to another is best described as an evolution. The horizontal forms evolved into the familiar square form, and this style spread out from the urban centers of design. Many of the early 18th-century chests that were built with drawers and lift tops were made to look like the more stylish examples with four drawers. Rectangular legs, which had been the extension of the vertical corner stiles in frame-and-panel construction, were phased out in favor of plump turned ball feet. Simple, bold

moldings graced the top and bottom of the case, adding definition and flair. Half-round moldings on the case front, either alone or in pairs and called arch or double-arch moldings, surrounded the plain drawer fronts.

High chests

By placing a chest of drawers on a stand, a new form of furniture came to America in the early 18th century. The high chest (or highboy as it came to be known in the late 1800s) was a form that had been known in late Renaissance Europe (see the photo on p. 17) and had come into fashion after the Restoration in England. American high

chests, first seen about 1700, were initially little more than chests standing on bases with turned legs, stretchers and perhaps one wide drawer (photo at left above). Early bases show legs that were twist-turned, sawn from flat stock in the shape of Flemish scrolls or turned in familiar inverted-cup or trumpet-shaped profiles. As the style developed, the design of the chest and the base became more integrated and the proportions of the piece as a whole became more refined (photo at right above). As with any other chest, the high chest was intended for the storage of clothing or linens.

High chests were the most impressive pieces of furniture in their day, as the cupboard had been in the previous century.

As such, the maker and his customer could maximize their impact by building a piece that embodied all the maker's talent and exhibited his customer's good taste. Thus high chests tend to be some of the best examples of William and Mary design and technique and show the full breadth of design elements and decorative methods in use at the time. High chests exemplify the period so well that a separate discussion of their design is taken up later in this chapter (see pp. 30-32).

DESKS

Another form that was new to America during the William and Mary period was the slant-front desk (photo below). Previously, the function of desks to store papers had been given to document boxes, sometimes with sloping lids, that were portable and used on tabletops. The new desk was an integration of a chest of drawers with a slanted front that folded down to become a writing surface. It is likely that the slant-front desk evolved from a small number of bureau-cabinets that were made before the turn of the century. These pieces were cabinets of many small

BUREAU-CABINET, PHILADELPHIA, 1707.
The case and fall-front writing surface of turn-of-the-century bureau-cabinets were forebears of the familiar slant-front desk.
(COURTESY COLONIAL WILLIAMSBURG FOUNDATION)

compartments and drawers, fronted by a panel that folded down to double as a writing surface (photo above). The base of the cabinet was a case of drawers, with the usual William and Mary detailing (flush-fitting drawers, surrounding moldings and ball feet).

Freestanding cabinets that concealed drawers and compartments behind doors or panels had been popular in England, but were not practical enough to warrant widespread use in America. In the case of the American bureau-cabinet, the upper cabinet could be of a shallow depth, but the base needed to be as deep as a chest of drawers for stability. The slanted lid proved to be an elegant way to make the transition between the two halves. The substitution of a bookcase top yielded the desk bookcase form that would continue to evolve through the century (photo at right). The base alone, with the slanted lid on top and drawers below, was able to stand on its own as a complete piece.

DESK, BOSTON, 1700–1725.
William and Mary desks used most of the same ornamental and construction details as chests of the period.
(COURTESY HENRY FORD MUSEUM AND GREENFIELD VILLAGE)

DESK BOOKCASE,
CONNECTICUT OR NEW YORK, 1700–1730.
The inclusion of a bookcase top was the beginning of an important form that would continue to develop over the rest of the century.
(COURTESY YALE UNIVERSITY ART GALLERY)

TABLES

The William and Mary period brought a
proliferation of tables for various purposes.
Dressing tables, for use in the bed chamber,
evolved from the chamber table. Tea and
tavern tables were made in great number as
tea drinking, card playing and other social
pastimes became important. Large tables
with drop leaves came into use and
combined ample dining surfaces with an
ease of storage.

Dressing tables

Dressing tables (or "lowboys," as they came
to be called in the late 1800s) served a
function similar to that of the chamber
table of the previous century, in that they
were bedroom pieces that held jewelry and
personal effects. Since they were usually
used in the same room as a high chest, it is
not uncommon to find dressing tables and
high chests that were made as a matching

set. Structurally, dressing tables are very
similar to the bases of high chests, except
for the inclusion of the tabletop.

A typical William and Mary dressing
table has four turned legs, whereas high
chests usually had six. While their apron
designs are similar, dressing tables often
have two turned drop finials below the
apron where a high chest would have had
two front legs. It was also customary to
strengthen the legs by connecting them
with cross stretchers just above the foot.
Frequently a third finial, pointing up, is
located at the intersection of the stretchers.

Tea or tavern tables

A number of other tables from this period
survive, and they document a blossoming of
the form in the early 18th century. Small,
multipurpose tables with turned legs and
stretchers abounded. These are called tea
tables or tavern tables, but, in fact, they

were used any time a compact horizontal surface was needed. Within this one group there is a wide variation of shape and detail. Rectangular, oval and octagonal tops can be found, and the bases vary from rectilinear forms with gentle turnings to splayed-leg examples with deep and robust leg profiles.

Drop-leaf tables

The drop-leaf gateleg table reached its zenith during the William and Mary period. Used primarily as a dining table, its gatelegs swung out from a central frame to support two leaves (top photo at right). When not in use, the table was easily folded to about one-third of its fully opened width and moved out of the way. The vast majority of gateleg tables are round or oval, and about 4 ft. or 5 ft. long. Some of the most spectacular examples of this form appeared early in the century. They feature robust turned legs and stretchers that make the base as visually interesting as any other piece of William and Mary furniture.

Another type of drop-leaf table used folding wings to swing out in support of the leaves (bottom photo at right). This variety is generally known as a butterfly table. Without the fully swinging leg, these tables were not as stable as gatelegs, and thus were usually somewhat smaller. Both butterfly and gateleg tables often have drawers in the end of their bases. Drop-leaf tables, in one form or another, remained in use throughout the entire 18th century. Their flexibility and functionality were well suited to the demands of space and utility to which life at that time subjected them.

SEATING FURNITURE

In keeping with Baroque ideals and the practical considerations of comfort, seating furniture took on a distinctive William and Mary style. Chairs continued the theme of a vertical format and were ornamented in a more fluid style than their predecessors. Fully upholstered easy chairs, most often used by the aged or infirm, came into widespread use. Couches, based upon the prevailing designs of chairs, served as furniture for both sitting and reclining.

DINING TABLE, BOSTON AREA, 1715–1735.
The drop-leaf dining table was a form that was to continue for most of the century. William and Mary drop-leaf tables have bold turnings and stretchers and often include a drawer at one end.
(COURTESY MUSEUM OF ART, RHODE ISLAND SCHOOL OF DESIGN)

TABLE, CONNECTICUT, AFTER 1710.
Butterfly tables were small drop-leaf tables, usually with splayed legs for increased stability, which featured hinged wings to support the leaves.
(COURTESY WADSWORTH ATHENEUM, HARTFORD)

Chairs

Although chairs were not subject to much structural change, they underwent a transformation to conform to the Baroque ideals of the day and embody many of the important elements of William and Mary design. Dramatically turned legs and stretchers were incorporated along with gracefully curved arms with scrolled ends (photo at left below). In comparison to Jacobean forms, these chairs were much taller, sometimes more than 4 ft. tall. The backs of the chairs, while still straight, were slanted back from the vertical at a noticeable angle (no doubt a small concession to those who had to sit in them). The backs consisted of two vertical stiles, continuations of the back legs, with either vertical banisters or a narrow panel of caning or leather upholstery. The crowning of any of these chairs was a tall and elaborately carved crest rail. These rails, while taking many forms, carry the eye

upward and emphasize the height of the chair. Most crest rails are about half as tall as they are wide, and rise to an apex in the center (see the photo on p. 28). In the Philadelphia area, arched crest rails over vertical banisters were in favor. In New England, the designs were based on Flemish scrolls, and the rails were pierced and deeply carved. As if to counterbalance the ornate crest rails, carved Spanish feet were usually used on the front legs of the best New England chairs.

A subset of the chairs of the period are those with caned back panels and seats (center photo below). Caning was quite fashionable in London at the start of the 18th century, and the style found its way to Boston shortly thereafter with the importation of some English chairs. Rather than caning the entire back of the chair, American craftsmen built a vertical frame inside the rear posts and caned that. This left tall narrow spaces on either side of the

caning, and allowed the rear posts to be turned. The arrangement as a whole emphasizes the vertical better than some of the English imports, and creates an effective contrast of solids and voids that lends the design a lively vigor. These caned chairs date from the first quarter of the century.

Another important subset of William and Mary chairs is a leather-upholstered design that is called a Boston chair (photo at right below). These chairs were in vogue starting about 1715 and were made for about another 35 years. Boston chairs used turned front legs and stretchers, Spanish feet and vertical proportions like other chairs, but the narrow back panel and seat were upholstered in leather fastened with decorative round-headed brass tacks. At the time, leather was less expensive than either cane or fabric. In its most common form, the crest rail is of a simple cyma-curve shape, rising to a flat plateau at the center, though variations exist. The rear posts are

SIDE CHAIR, BOSTON, 1710–1725.
Imported English chairs with caned seats and backs were fashionable at the turn of the century, which spurred Boston chair makers to adopt the style for their own use over the next two decades.
(COURTESY HISTORIC DEERFIELD)

ARMCHAIR, COASTAL NEW ENGLAND (PROBABLY MASSACHUSETTS), 1700–1720.
The dynamic flourish of Baroque ornament is evident in the turnings, arms and crest rail of this Massachusetts-area banister-back chair. The canted back provided a great improvement in comfort over earlier chairs.
(COURTESY MUSEUM OF FINE ARTS, BOSTON)

SIDE CHAIR, BOSTON, 1720–1750.
'Boston chairs,' upholstered in leather, were made in quantity for sale outside of New England. Their cyma-shaped rear stile and back shape were innovative and foreshadowed the later evolution of chair design.
(COURTESY COLONIAL WILLIAMSBURG FOUNDATION)

flat faced with beading at either side, a profile that carries through the crest.

Boston chairs are important for two reasons. First, when viewed from the side, the back of the chair has the shape of a gentle S or cyma curve, making the chair actually comfortable to sit in. In literature of the period, these chairs are often called crooked-back chairs. Stylistically, they were a great departure from the straight-backed chairs that had preceded them. Rather than being turned on a lathe, the curved elements could only be shaped and molded by hand from solid material. As a result, even leather crooked-back chairs were three or four times more expensive than common banister backs. Second, this design was a forerunner of the Queen Anne style in the second quarter of the century.

Boston chairs were made in great numbers and exported to New York and Philadelphia, much to the chagrin of the indigenous furniture makers. In both those cities, resident craftsmen were forced to compete with the Boston imports by offering lower prices or better style, but the imports continued to do well. This example demonstrates the extent of intercolonial commerce in existence early in the 18th century, completely debunking the idea

that furniture making was a relaxed business catering to a local clientele. In the urban areas it was as much of a large-scale business as any other, and its owners sought to capture as much of the market share as possible. Business concerns were very much a part of the trade.

Upholstered pieces

Fully upholstered easy chairs, known today as wing chairs, also made their debut in the William and Mary period. These were the first pieces of seating furniture to be enveloped in permanently attached upholstery. Like other pieces of the period, they employ bold turnings as stretchers and front legs, and they have Spanish feet. The known original examples have horizontal arm rolls at the arms and vertical rolls over the front legs. The ends of the two rolls are connected by a sweeping curve (photo at right). The folkloric explanation for the wings is that they were protection from drafts, which seems plausible enough. The original upholstery padding is known to have been quite full, and the seat cushions were thick and full of down, in keeping with a long history of thick cushions for unupholstered chairs. Springs were not used during the 18th century, and

EASY CHAIR, BOSTON, 1710–1725. Fully upholstered easy chairs first appeared in the William and Mary period. The upholstery on this chair is an accurate reconstruction of the appearance of the original. The seat cushion is thick because springs were not used in 18th-century upholstered pieces. *(COURTESY MUSEUM OF FINE ARTS, BOSTON)*

upholstered pieces were dependent on stretched webbing or fabric and a variety of stuffings for comfort and support. Peculiar to the period is the shaped and upholstered front rail. Textiles were expensive in the 18th century, and thus easy chairs represented a considerable investment. They are known to have been bedroom pieces at the time, and were not used in the main room of the house.

Couches, today known as daybeds, are a variation on William and Mary chair designs. They have most of the same design elements as unupholstered chairs of the period, but have dramatically different proportions. Their backs are shorter, and the seats can be more than 5 ft. long (photo at left). The stuffed cushions are separate. Couches were made for reclining, and the backs are frequently hinged and adjustable to any angle. The extra length necessitated as many as eight legs and a host of turned stretchers to connect them.

COUCH, BOSTON AREA, 1710–1730. Couches are stylistically linked to the chairs of the period and share many similarities in their backs and turnings. The back of this example is hinged for reclining. *(COURTESY MUSEUM OF FINE ARTS, BOSTON)*

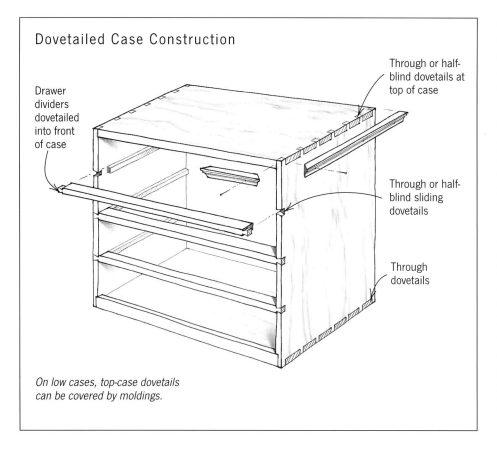

Dovetailed Case Construction

Drawer dividers dovetailed into front of case

Through or half-blind dovetails at top of case

Through or half-blind sliding dovetails

Through dovetails

On low cases, top-case dovetails can be covered by moldings.

William and Mary Structure

The structure that is the basis for William and Mary pieces revolutionized the way furniture was to be built for the rest of the 18th century and beyond. As discussed earlier, the dovetail joint had rendered the frame-and-panel method of construction obsolete. The lightness of drawers and cases afforded by dovetail joinery allowed for the more vertical forms of the William and Mary period.

CASE CONSTRUCTION
The cases of chests, including the upper half of high chests and desks, shared similar structures. In each of these examples, the cases consisted of two sides, a top and a bottom. The beginnings of these cases resembled a vertical box without a front or back. Rather than being a panel set inside a frame, each of the parts was one wide board or two glued side to side. They were joined to each other at the corners by a row of

dovetail joints, as shown in the drawing above. Since the grain ran along the length of each piece, they all expanded and contracted in unison with changes in humidity. The resulting case was very light, strong and easily built.

Drawer dividers were let into the front of the case with sliding dovetail joints that often extended through the sides to the outside of the case. Runners to support the drawers were nailed to the inside of the case behind the dividers, sometimes in shallow dadoes to hold them in position. The back of the case consisted of thin boards of secondary wood nailed into rabbets in the back of the case. The moldings at the top and bottom were nailed in place on the sides and front. Ball feet, if they were included, were fastened with a round tenon, turned as part of the foot, glued and inserted into a hole drilled into the case bottom.

The use of attached parts, like moldings and feet, seems to reflect an increased acceptance of glue and nails, which were no doubt more readily available and of better quality than they had been in the previous

century. In Jacobean forms, both moldings and feet tended to be built into the structure of the piece, which limited their use as visually important components of the overall design.

The cases of dressing tables and high-chest bases were structurally similar but differed from those of chest and desk cases. In these cases, the grain ran horizontally on the four pieces that comprised the sides, front and back (see the top drawing on p. 140). The pieces were dovetailed at all four corners, with the row of dovetails running vertically. The bare case was essentially a horizontal box with no top or bottom. Like chest cases, the components expanded and contracted together, allowing the joinery to retain its integrity. For aesthetic reasons, the dovetails were usually half-blind, that is, they did not extend through the case sides. Runners and guides for drawers were mortised into the front and back. As with other case pieces, horizontal and vertical drawer dividers were dovetailed in place.

This light case construction did not provide a convenient place to attach the turned legs used on dressing tables and high chests. Therefore, large blocks were glued inside the corners of the cases, which were then bored to receive the tenons of the turnings. Since the legs were not an integral part of the case, and since William and Mary turnings were very thin in some places, flat stretchers connecting the legs, just above the feet, were structurally necessary.

DRAWER CONSTRUCTION
Drawer construction saw a great evolution during the William and Mary period. At the beginning of the 18th century, drawer components were thick, heavy and joined by a few large dovetails. The drawer bottoms were nailed in place. By 1725, the components were light, thin and elegantly joined by a series of finer dovetails. Drawer bottoms were glued and nailed into a rabbeted drawer, or slid into grooves from the back. Drawer development was a microcosm of construction techniques as

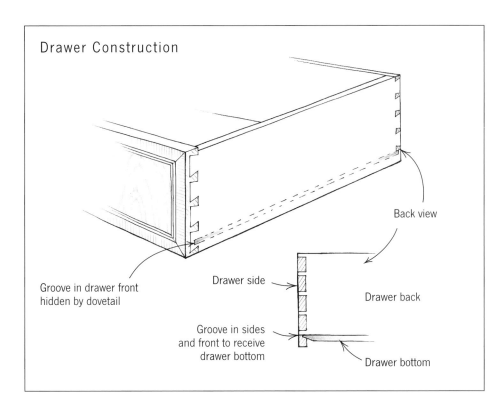

Drawer Construction

Groove in drawer front
hidden by dovetail

Drawer side

Drawer back

Back view

Groove in sides
and front to receive
drawer bottom

Drawer bottom

Turnings were important decorative focal points for many case pieces and offered a simple and effective method of ornament for a variety of other pieces. Moldings, previously integral to frame-and-panel construction, were now added to dovetailed cases, offering a new flexibility in their design and placement.

FIGURED VENEERS

Figured veneers were the primary surface decoration of the period. The use of veneers superseded the Jacobean penchant for intricate but shallow surface carving on the front face of case pieces. The very word "veneer" has become a pejorative term from its use in the late 19th and 20th centuries. It implies a thin layer of high-quality material over a base of inferior quality, and it earned a poor connotation when it was used for that purpose.

a whole. It represented the introduction of a new method of joinery and the evolution that ensued to optimize the details of the new furniture forms.

TABLES AND CHAIRS

Tables and chairs continued to be made with mortise-and-tenon construction, since most were comprised of turned or narrow elements. With the notable exception of dressing tables, table aprons were tenoned into the legs. Like the turnings on case pieces, the legs required stretchers to tie them together. On chairs and tables, these stretchers were usually turned to familiar William and Mary profiles and tenoned into leg mortises.

Decorative Elements

The decorative details of William and Mary designs fall into three main categories: the use of figured veneers, deep carving and dramatic turnings. Figured veneers allowed the cabinetmakers of the period to achieve striking surfaces but necessitated the use of varnishes to protect and enhance the wood. Carving, in the manner of Gibbons, became an important embellishment for chairs.

HIGH CHEST OF DRAWERS, NEW ENGLAND, PROBABLY MASSACHUSETTS, 1700–1725.
The highly figured veneer of this piece is its most important decorative element. To extend the effect, the cabinetmaker simulated the figured pattern with paint on the turned legs of the base.
(COURTESY WINTERTHUR MUSEUM)

In the case of William and Mary originals, the use of veneer has no negative implications. Veneering a piece was a labor-intensive process requiring hard-to-find materials, but it gave a high level of sophisticated decoration to a piece. There are some strictly practical reasons for applying figured wood as a veneer. Burled or figured wood is not easy to come by, and by sawing it into thin sheets, the yield of well-figured wood is increased. Because of its swirling grain, it lacks strength for structural purposes and would be nearly impossible to work with in solid form. Sawing highly figured wood into veneer is the only practical way to use it, and since it is applied to the surface, the joinery and structural work can be done in more easily worked material, like pine or maple.

Consecutive sheets of veneer have nearly identical grain, and they can be opened and applied to a surface to give a perfectly symmetrical, or bookmatched, grain. This kind of symmetry was important to William and Mary design and exemplified the logic and order that accompanied Enlightenment ideals. It is not uncommon to see four or even eight bookmatched veneers across a drawer front, dividing it evenly into identical, symmetrically grained sections. This pattern was repeated on every drawer and on the front of the case itself. Four sections of veneer, symmetrical about the center point, were used to decorate larger areas like desk lids and dressing-table tops. In most examples, veneered panels

and drawer fronts are framed with a border of contrasting veneer—often a herringbone border consisting of two veneer strips cut at 45° to the orientation of the grain. A cross banding, a strip cut at 90° to the grain, was sometimes used in conjunction with the herringbone inlay.

The veneers of the period were much thicker than modern veneers—as much as ⅛ in. thick. They were sawn from a solid block of figured stock with a frame saw, and ⅛ in. was probably about as thin a veneer as that method would allow. The substrate to which the veneer was to be applied was prepared by roughening its surface with a finely toothed plane to improve the adhesion of the glue. The veneers were glued in place with a hide glue, and held in place until the glue cured. Documentary evidence from the period shows that the veneers were held in place by weights or clamped between boards. (For more on period veneering, see Chapter 10.)

These highly figured pieces required a finish that would enhance the grain, protect the wood and impart a nice luster to the surface better than the oils and waxes of the previous century. William and Mary pieces required the use of varnishes, which at the time encompassed all kinds of clear, hard finishes. Like many aspects of William and Mary furniture, the raw materials for these finishes came from extensive foreign trade. There were a number of different tree resins from Africa and the Orient that

could be dissolved in alcohol (distilled from wine) or sometimes oil, to make a hard, glossy finish. It was long thought that shellac, refined from the deposits of the Asian lac insect and dissolved in alcohol, was the primary 18th-century finish. Recent analysis has disproven this, however, and shellac did not come into widespread use until the next century. A number of other resins, principally sandarac, were soluble in alcohol and no doubt were similar in application and appearance. Another resin, copal, was soluble in hot oil. Although it was more difficult to prepare, it is known to have been used throughout the century, but especially after 1776 when the formula and procedure for making it were published. (For more on period varnish resins, see Appendix III on p. 296.)

CARVING

Carving took on a new sense of purpose during the William and Mary period. The primary focus of the carver's attention was chairs, which were well suited to this kind of decoration. Whereas Jacobean carving was a thin surface treatment that included Renaissance and medieval botanical, strapwork and geometric motifs, the carving of William and Mary chairs was mostly of Baroque Flemish design, and was more integrated into the form of the piece. These carvings were deep, bold and dramatic. The carving of components of William and Mary chairs defined those components, not just decorated them.

CREST-RAIL DETAIL, ARMCHAIR, PROBABLY MASSACHUSETTS, 1700–1720.
The bold carving of period chairs followed the standards set in post-Restoration England by such craftsmen as Grinling Gibbons.
(COURTESY MUSEUM OF FINE ARTS, BOSTON)

TABLE, CONNECTICUT, 1700–1735.
This table has spindle turnings of simple vasiform profile that are symmetrical about their midpoint.
(COURTESY WADSWORTH ATHENEUM, HARTFORD)

The crest rails of chairs were frequently comprised of two or more Flemish scrolls, a C-shaped scroll with volutes on either end (see the photo on the facing page). They were of considerable depth, and the wood was cut and pierced to silhouette them. Similar cut and pierced scrolled elements were used as front stretchers on a number of Boston examples, a detail seen on English chairs of the period. The arms of armchairs, or elbow chairs as they were then called, were themselves long sweeping curves terminating in tight carved volutes.

The other carved element in chairs and occasionally small tables was the Spanish foot. Spanish feet were of Portuguese origin and were not as sculptural as Flemish carved details. These feet are square in cross section and have a simple flared, brushlike profile. The only carving on them is a few simple flutes shaped to follow their curve.

TURNINGS

Turnings became an important part of the decorative and structural aspects of William and Mary furniture. As with carvings, their use was more an integral part of the design and less a superficial decoration. Turnings of the period fall into three categories depending on their use and design.

Spindle turnings, which are found on table legs and stretchers, are inherently thin and of shallow profile (top photo at left). Their turned designs are frequently symmetrical about the midpoint and include rings and greatly elongated vasiform shapes.

Chair and gateleg-table components show a greater degree of sophistication with deeper turned profiles and more complicated shapes (top photo at right). These shapes could be a combination of any number of elements from a standard group that includes beads and rings, vase shapes, cylindrical cups and tulip forms. They are seen stacked in a variety of combinations, often alternating with a square section of the stock. As with many other details of design, these turned elements show regional characteristics that are helpful in determining origins.

By far the most notable turnings of the period are those used as legs on dressing tables and high chests (bottom photo at right). They too are assembled from a basic

lexicon of shapes, but they are very different elements from those described previously. These turnings were recent transplants from Flemish and French court furniture, and they were free from the practical considerations of functioning as chair or table legs. They were the legs of expensive and conspicuous pieces, and their styling was not intended to be restrained. Among the elements included in these turnings are inverted bowl and cup forms, ball and vase shapes, flared trumpet profiles and the familiar flattened ball foot on a tapered pad.

The drama in these turnings is in their extreme variation in diameter at various points. They are turned from stock that is at least 3 in. square, and the diameters range from 3 in. to less then 1 in. at the narrowest points. The design of the turnings makes them look even more dramatic. The largest diameter and mass is about three-quarters of the way up the leg, giving the leg an inherently dynamic quality. This shaping imparts to them an upward, almost fountainlike appearance. The mass is counterbalanced, seemingly anchored, by the large diameter of the foot. The mass of the case and the unifying effect of the stretchers are needed to put these legs in context and have them make sense in relation to the whole. The spectacular effect of the legs would be wasted if they were used in a context other than to support case pieces.

MOLDINGS

Moldings should also be mentioned as an important part of ornamentation beginning in the William and Mary period. Visually, moldings played an important role in finishing off the extremities of case pieces in the absence of case frame members. The cove, cyma and torus moldings that became part of a standard repertoire of profiles, all had their origins in classical architecture and had been resurrected in the late Renaissance with the designs of Andrea Palladio (1508–1580), among others. Palladio was a Venetian architect whose designs drew on those of ancient Rome, and, through his published work, he had a

lasting influence in England and America for nearly two centuries after his death. The influence of architectural details can be attributed in part to the massive rebuilding of London necessitated by the Great Fire of 1666, just a few years after the Restoration and the marriage of Charles II, and at a critical time in the development of the new styles.

Logic, Order, Proportion and the Baroque

The inception of William and Mary furniture designs came at a time when Baroque trends were requiring stylistic theatrics, and the Age of Reason was prompting a search for the underlying order of the physical world. The William and Mary style found a way to integrate the two seemingly opposed aims into a well-structured grandeur. Since the high chest embodies more of the design philosophy than any other piece of the period, it is a good piece to analyze (see the photo on the facing page). The insight revealed by the careful consideration of a such a piece is quite astounding, and it makes one appreciate the sophistication of the design and its creators all the more.

Studying the form of the piece reveals a very logical and precise approach to its design. The upper case, for example, is nearly square. The drawer heights are graduated in an arithmetic progression, meaning that each drawer is larger than the one above it by an equal amount. This arrangement gives the visual suggestion of height and, from a practical aspect, puts the smaller and lighter drawers at the top of the case. It was standard form to have two or three small drawers in the top row, which could be removed from the case to view the contents.

The base of the high chest is somewhat more complicated. The case itself is in proportion to what would have been the next drawer down from the upper case, and therefore continues the arithmetic

progression from the top. The vertical drawer dividers align with the centerline of the two inner legs. The two outside drawers echo the same proportion as the entire base. The center drawer is roughly half the height of the outer ones and relates visually to the smaller drawers in the top row. The three large spaces across the front, those that are bounded by the legs and apron, are of the same proportion. Although the space between the two center legs is greater than the spaces on either side, the apron height is taller to maintain the proportionality. The shape of the apron is echoed in the shape of the stretchers (a fact that is more readily apparent when you see the piece in person than in a photograph). Finally, the massive, large diameter on the legs is balanced and visually stabilized by the mass of the ball foot that is squarely connected to the ground.

Each of the drawers is divided into two or four equal sections by the bookmatched veneers and the placement of the brass pulls and escutcheons. Their positioning is deliberately mathematical. Each drawer is bordered by veneer bands set in a herring-bone pattern, and each drawer opening is framed by a double-arch molding. The veneer on the apron is bookmatched to be perfectly symmetrical about the center, and even the left and right drawers, at both the top and bottom, have matched veneers to maintain symmetry.

Looking at the piece as a whole, the high chest has three strong and nearly equally spaced horizontals: the cornice molding, the midmolding and the stretchers. These three elements extend all the way around the piece, making them all the more strong when viewing the piece in person. Although the high chest is quite tall, these three horizontals are unifying elements that also emphasize the top, the bottom and the meeting point of the two cases. The horizontals are countered by the strong vertical lines of the legs and feet.

The Baroque considerations are not as easily quantified as the logical proportions, but rather rely on the movement that the various elements imply. The most noticeable effect of Baroque design is the vertical

Strong cornice, midmolding and
stretcher horizontals are balanced
by bold vertical lines of base.

Upper case is nearly square.

Each drawer is bordered
with veneer banding.

Each drawer opening is framed by
double-arch molding.

Drawer heights are graduated in
arithmetic progression. All drawers
are divided evenly by placement
of brasses and bookmatched veneer.

Center drawer relates visually
to top-row drawers.

Lower case is in proportion
to upper-case dividers.

Outside drawers echo same
proportion as base.

Vertical drawer dividers are
aligned with turned legs.

Case veneers maintain symmetry.

Apron shape is repeated in
stretcher shape.

Three front spaces, though
different sizes, are in proportion
to one another.

High placement of mass
on legs is balanced by massive foot
with large contact area to ground.

HIGH CHEST OF DRAWERS,
MASSACHUSETTS, 1700–1725.
(COURTESY MUSEUM OF FINE ARTS, BOSTON)

format of the piece. A typical William and Mary high chest is more than half as tall as it is wide. This is a dramatic change from the horizontal Jacobean forms. Second, the piece is up on legs. To have something as massive as a chest of drawers perched on legs is a spectacular departure from the earlier norm. The lifted mass was intended to be noticed. This piece is held up by six legs, which emphasizes the mass of the upper case. The ornate profile of the turned legs draws attention to their number and function. The eye-catching stretcher emphasizes that the legs are supporting a great mass, and the flattened ball feet testify to the weight of that mass. Everything about the base of this piece is meant to overemphasize the structural considerations of achieving a vertical format. It was to be evident to all that the designer had put a great mass at a great height.

While making this quite clear, the designer also sought to give the piece an inherent lift of its own. There are a number of elements that draw the eye up and out, visually reinforcing the height of the piece. Just having the cases floating on fountain-like turnings exhibits the greatest display of designed lift. The legs themselves exhibit this upward and outward flair, six times in a row, to stress an internal feeling of lift. The apron shapes arch up above the space between legs. The drawers march upward in orderly progression. The midmolding, and especially the cornice molding, echo this progression with a flourish. Often a simple but well-flared cornice molding can cap off the square upper case with just the right spirit. On some examples, the cornice molding is so dramatic that it becomes the dominant element in the piece. In either case, the eye is drawn up the length of the legs, across the expanse of highly figured, but well-ordered case fronts, and out through the top by way of the crowning moldings.

The seemingly contradictory needs for Baroque extravagance and Enlightenment logic coexist in a design that simultaneously espouses lift while emphasizing its own mass, and does it all within measured proportions. That is a remarkable design achievement.

The Advent of the Cabinetmaker

The design and construction of William and Mary furniture marked a radical departure from all that had preceded it, and it required very different techniques from those employed by the traditional joiner. The use of dovetail joinery, decorative veneers and extensive turnings called for more specialized skills than frame-and-panel construction. This development marked the emergence of a field dedicated to this new kind of furniture making, that of the cabinetmaker.

Joiners continued in their role as tradesmen in wood, but cabinetmakers were fine-furniture specialists. Joiners who did not make the transition to the newer styles of furniture making still had their work in utilitarian furniture, carpentry and repairs, all of which were important aspects of their work even before the William and Mary style.

In rural areas, where there was not the population density to support specialists, joiners were the cabinetmakers, carpenters and repairmen for the local clientele until late in the century. Account books from the period show that rural cabinetmakers built coffins, renovated and built buildings, made wagon parts and sometimes did a little farming in addition to cabinetmaking. Building furniture was only part of their work, which is another reason why the newest designs of the period took a while to come into vogue in outlying areas.

THE APPRENTICE SYSTEM
The apprentice system in America was a continuation of the longstanding English system. An apprenticeship provided the practical training that a young man needed to learn a profession. Both urban and rural cabinetmakers took on apprentices for more than the proliferation of their trade. In a time before the Industrial Revolution, apprentices were often the power equipment of their day. Much of the cabinetmaker's work was labor-intensive, and apprentices were expected to take care of most of the drudgery. Some of this would include sawing stock, planing sawn boards flat and to an even thickness, turning the great wheel of a lathe, stacking lumber, cleaning up and running errands. As the apprentice grew older and learned more skills, his work would include the finer aspects of the trade, such as joinery and finishing. As apprentices progressed, new ones would take up the menial work.

When the terms of the apprenticeship had been fulfilled, the apprentice became a journeyman and was free to continue in the paid employment of the shop master or seek employment elsewhere. Many journeymen worked in a number of shops and eventually opened their own, and in that way learned a number of different aspects of the trade. History records many journeymen cabinetmakers as being somewhat transient, moving from shop to shop and town to town in the employment of established cabinetmakers. However, the term journeyman derives from the French *journée,* meaning a day's work, rather than from any idea that these men were willing or able to travel.

Apart from the journeymen who did travel, the apprentices who continued in the employment of their shop masters or who set up shop in the area propagated the styles and methods of the master. Given this linear system of passing on skills, it would be expected that the cabinetmakers of one region would develop a set of characteristics in their work that would differentiate their work from that of others. As the 18th century progressed, these regional variations became more numerous and pronounced.

3

Elegance and Refinement

THE QUEEN ANNE STYLE
(1725–1760)

As Americans prospered during the second quarter of the 18th century, a distinct social hierarchy became more pronounced. Successful families and civic leaders recognized their role in shaping civilization in America, and their surroundings and furnishings became important reflections of their refinement. In England, the taste in furniture had shifted toward an elegant, refined style that exemplified grace and comfort. What eventually came to be known as the Queen Anne style was well suited to American tastes.

The Growing Prosperity of America

American pursuance of a genteel society and the interest in a refined style in the decorative arts were made possible by the peace and prosperity of the era. In both England and the colonies, a growing merchant middle class fueled an interest in the products of tradesmen and artisans.

With the end of the Spanish War of Succession in 1713, England, under stable leadership, emerged as the dominant European power. The Navigation Acts, a series of laws passed beginning in 1650 to

The refinement and grace that underscored the lifestyle and furnishings of the second quarter of the 18th century are portrayed in *Tea Party at Lord Harrington's House*, a 1739 oil on canvas by English painter Charles Philips.
(COURTESY YALE CENTER FOR BRITISH ART)

protect English industry, encouraged the colonies to build merchant fleets and established shipbuilding and shipping as businesses that accelerated American prosperity. As early as 1676, Boston was home port for 230 vessels, and by 1748 that number had reached 491, with another 131 ships sailing from neighboring Salem. Similarly, there was a growth in commercial fishing, iron smelting and the production of agricultural products such as flour, cotton and tobacco for both domestic markets and export.

With prosperity came improvements in the standard of living and the standards of aesthetics, as personal possessions and homes reflected that success. The prosperity enabled the decorative arts to continue to thrive and evolve. For any such evolution there needs to be a market both to demand and afford it, and such was the case in the early part of the 18th century. There was always a desire on the part of the Americans to remain stylistically competitive with England. Anything that was needed from England could easily have been imported, but American preferences in furniture were diverging from those of the English.

Early in the 18th century, Americans were showing their interest in light, exuberant designs that captured what could only be called a unique American spirit: a spirit inherent in the colonial designs, but not seen in English pieces. The desire to remain competitive did not manifest itself in increasing English imports, nor were English pieces copied wholesale to any great extent. From the American pieces it is evident that their makers wanted to maintain a separation in style but an equal level of sophistication, as if to make clear they were part of a separate but equal American culture that was following a parallel path of its own making.

THE EMERGENCE OF A SOCIAL HIERARCHY

The beginning of the 18th century marked the start of a more pronounced stratification of American society. A wealthier upper class was rising from among the colonists, and the wealthy formed their own social network. Within this group, civility and refinement indicative of status differentiated its members from those of lesser means. The successful people of the 18th century were expected to be part of a polite society that exuded grace, charm, self-confidence and poise—and all without apparent effort. This extended to their furnishings as well, which were chosen to reinforce and testify to the refinement of their owners. Fine furnishings were less a display of wealth than the accouterments of an elegant life.

It should be noted that America in the 18th century was a very rural place. Less than 5% of the population lived in cities, and by mid-century only five cities—Philadelphia, New York, Boston, Newport and Charles Town (South Carolina)—had populations in excess of 7,000 (see the chart below). The other 95% were spread out in smaller towns, most of them farming and pursuing various small businesses. Apart from neighborly gatherings and church activities, there were few cultural events and the arts were slow to progress. Throughout the history of American furniture there is a distinction between urban and rural styles of furniture design and construction. The urban areas, with the greater concentration of wealth, had both the demands of a sophisticated clientele and the skilled craftsmen to carry them out. Here, new designs were introduced and evolved in their purely American style. Once established, they served as standards for the cabinetmakers and customers of smaller towns. The designs emanated, with adaptations and variations, inland from the coastal cities, sometimes taking decades to gain acceptance.

Origins of the Queen Anne Style

With its height, ornamentation and vertical emphasis, William and Mary furniture had marked a dramatic departure from earlier styles. The Queen Anne style was a continuation of that same trend to an even loftier Baroque standard, but with some mid-course corrections. As if in a final departure from the heavy and solid furniture of the past, Queen Anne designs balanced mass with space, making the size and shape of the space between components as important to the overall design as the components themselves. Queen Anne furniture was made to be seen and to be seen through. Equally important to the style was the more complete integration of the cyma curve into furniture. The shallow S-shaped curve was in favor with late Baroque designers as an essential element in all things beautiful, and it was incorporated in Queen Anne furniture in curved pediments, apron shapes and, most important, cabriole legs.

The Queen Anne style as we know it originated in England, but it was inspired by trends in mainland Europe and even the Orient. Two decades before the death of Louis XIV in 1715, there began a relaxation of the tremendously ornate Baroque standards that had been set at Versailles. Louis XV became king at age five, but

POPULATION OF AMERICAN CITIES					
	1690	1720	1743	1760	1775
BOSTON	7,000	12,000	16,000	16,000	16,000
PHILADELPHIA	4,000	10,000	13,000	23,750	40,000
NEW YORK	3,900	7,000	11,000	18,000	25,000
NEWPORT	2,600	3,800	6,200	7,500	11,000
CHARLES TOWN	1,100	3,500	6,800	8,000	12,000

NOTE: For comparison, the population of London grew from about 685,000 in 1690, to 725,000 in 1740, to an estimated 800,000 in 1775.

BUREAU PLAT, PARIS, C.1700.
Cabinetmaker André-Charles Boulle was instrumental in introducing gently curved elements into French court furniture in the 1690s, signaling a relaxation of Baroque standards and inspiring English furniture designers. This bureau plat, or writing desk, is likely from the Boulle workshops and is veneered in ebony with inlaid boullework of tortoiseshell and brass.
(COURTESY THE WALLACE COLLECTION, LONDON)

Phillipe, Duke of Orleans, served as Regent for eight years. The high Baroque had reached a peak in furniture design, and the coronation of a new, young monarch offered the court designers an opportunity to explore more practical, comfortable and graceful designs.

THE INFLUENCE OF BOULLE
André-Charles Boulle (1642–1732) was a French cabinetmaker to the court who gave his country's furniture a style of its own beginning in the 1690s. Prior to this time, French furniture had been some combination of Dutch and Italian styles, but with a full complement of Baroque ornamentation. Boulle is best known for his marquetry of tortoiseshell, brass, silver, horn, ivory and mother of pearl, which came to be called *boullework* (see the photo above). He also used ormolu (gilded bronze) mounts both as decorative elements and as a means of fastening inlaid panels. More important, he introduced curved shapes to furniture forms, including the gentle cyma-

CHAIR, CHINA, C.1700.
Chinese objects were of interest to Europeans throughout the 17th and 18th centuries. The simplicity of design was inspirational after the excesses of the Baroque.
(COURTESY DOVER PUBLICATIONS)

curved leg, which was the forerunner of the cabriole leg. His protégé, Charles Cressent (1685–1768), continued his styles under the Regent, where he had a leading role in developing the less ornate and more graceful court furniture and established what was to become the Louis XV style. References often cite Thomas Hogarth, the English designer and painter, as a leading proponent of the cyma curve since he extolled its virtues in his book, *Analysis of Beauty*. His praise was in retrospect, however, since the book was published in 1753, more than half a century after Boulle began to use the cyma in France.

The Flemish Baroque had run its course in England as well. Since the restoration of Charles II in 1660, the style-starved aristocracy had embraced the Flemish and Moorish styles and the extravagances of the Baroque. The intricate ornamentation of the post-Restoration trends, culminating in the William and Mary style, was abandoned in favor of more reserved designs, since, as one historian noted, "although they periodically succumb to 'foreign excesses,' the English are inherently adverse to extravagant design." In 1712, Lord Shaftsbury wrote of the trend to subdue the drama of the Baroque: "In short we are to carry this remembrance still along with us, that the fewer the objects are beside those which are absolutely necessary in a piece, the easier it is for the eye by one simple act, and in one view to comprehend the sum or whole." It seems clear that the English were never quite comfortable with the busy nature of the Baroque.

THE INFLUENCE OF CHINA
Imported Chinese furniture also played a key role in shaping the emerging Queen Anne style. Chinese furniture had been imported to Europe in the late 17th and early 18th centuries. Chinese objects were of great interest to Europeans since they were both exotic and aesthetically pleasing. The furniture had a simplicity of form and

elegance of line that was admired and emulated by European designers at many points in history. As the Baroque ideals of exuberance were being modified to lessen the grandiose ornamentation of furniture, Chinese pieces served as quiet inspiration for more conservative designs.

THE INFLUENCE OF ARCHITECTURAL DESIGN

The architectural books of Palladio and the designs of Inigo Jones (1573–1652), who followed in the Palladian style as architect to James I and Charles I, had been influential in England (especially in the rebuilding of London after the fire of 1666), and had been inspirational during the William and Mary period. Through the start of the next century there was a continuing interest in architectural design as an appropriate pastime for the English aristocracy, and it contributed to the development of a quieter Baroque style in furniture. The classic molding profiles were revisited with an eye toward their beauty and clean lines. Palladio's drawings of vasiform balusters presented another cyma-based form that was well-suited for inclusion in the new style. The parallels between the Queen Anne style at its inception and as it evolved and those of Palladian and Georgian architecture are numerous.

CABRIOLE LEGS

The graceful curves of the new French styles and the simple elegance of Chinese pieces combined with remnants of the Flemish scrolled legs of the Baroque to yield the familiar cabriole leg in about 1700. The cabriole shape is based on that of an animal's leg, and the name derives from the Greek *kapros,* meaning wild boar, or the Latin *capreolus,* meaning goat or roebuck (a small European deer). The use of a stylized animal leg was not a new concept; the form had been seen repeatedly since at least the Egyptian Third Dynasty (2650 B.C.). The style originated on the Continent, was further developed in England and saw acceptance in other parts of Europe as part of the spread of English tastes early in the second quarter of the century.

Early English legs terminated in cloven doe (*pied de biche*) and horses' hoofs, which evolved into flatter pad feet, sometimes called Dutch feet. Animal claw feet, especially ball and claw feet of Chinese origin, were of interest in England, and the French had a preference for whorl feet, which were scrolled volutes. It was in England and its colonies that the cabriole leg found an enduring reign of popularity as a basic element of the Queen Anne style, a characteristically English style that thoroughly suited the English need for restrained elegance. (Cabriole legs are discussed in detail in Chapter 9.)

Queen Anne Design Goals

Even though the new trend in English design was very different from the preceding William and Mary period, it still represented a continuation of Baroque ideals. Queen Anne furniture retained the Baroque preference for visually impressive pieces, usually through the use of height, but it did so with a reliance upon grace rather than ornamentation. Queen Anne pieces continued the shift of format to the vertical and increased it to even loftier heights.

One important aspect of the style is its intention to disguise the mass of furniture.

**HIGH CHESTS OF DRAWERS,
(ABOVE) MASSACHUSETTS, 1700–1710,
(RIGHT) CONNECTICUT, 1740–1760.**
The many powerful legs of the William and Mary high chest (above) ensure that the accomplishment of a raised mass does not go unnoticed. The graceful cabriole legs of the Queen Anne design (right) loft the mass without apparent effort.
(ABOVE: COURTESY MUSEUM OF FINE ARTS, BOSTON; RIGHT: COURTESY THE BROOKLYN MUSEUM)

Soaring vertical pieces look even more so if they appear to be light. William and Mary pieces had pioneered the vertical format by raising the mass, but it was not to go unnoticed. A William and Mary high chest, for instance, was supported by six powerful legs, the design of which emphasized their weight-bearing role (see the photo above). Queen Anne designs replaced the busy colonnaded base with four slender and gracefully curved legs that appeared to loft the upper case with style and ease (see the photo at right). William and Mary chests and desks were supported by ball feet that seemed to be bulging under the strain. Queen Anne counterparts were supported by short cabriole or bracket feet that performed their task without apparent effort. Like their owners, American Queen Anne pieces were to exude an effortless grace.

**DESK AND BOOKCASE,
BOSTON, 1730–1750.**
An exaggeration of the
vertical emphasis of the
period is exemplified by
this desk and bookcase,
which is just under
30 in. wide but stands
88 in. tall. The soaring
pediment, arched
paneled doors and
straight legs further
enhance the effect of
the tall proportions.
*(COURTESY MUSEUM OF FINE
ARTS, BOSTON)*

There were other design changes that furthered the aim of making Queen Anne furniture seem light. The proportions of case pieces were stretched taller than the still somewhat squat shape of many William and Mary pieces (see the photos above). Features that emphasized the surface, such as expanses of highly figured veneer and extensive carving, were replaced by smooth surfaces of plainer wood, with carving used quite sparingly. Curved pediment tops and finial ornaments further exaggerated the height of tall case pieces, and visually drew the eye upward so the height couldn't be overlooked. The emphasis had changed from a visual interest directed toward the surface to a visual interest in the shape, and the result was lofty furniture with an ethereal quality, seemingly unencumbered by its mass.

The role of mass and space in Queen Anne furniture is so important that it warrants closer examination. As the Queen Anne pieces were made to belie their mass and emphasize their shape, the spaces between shaped components became more prominent and visually important in themselves. In a design trend that stressed curved shapes, the spaces left by them increasingly became part of the design. There could be no better way to lighten a piece than to design it with space as well as with material. Thus the balance of solid and void was used to further the aim of reducing the apparent mass of a piece.

In Queen Anne examples, this balance is exhibited in two ways. In chairs of the period, there is an interplay of solid and void throughout the composition, and its rendering requires more skill than one may at first imagine. Some very minor changes in the thickness of components, as little as ⅛ in., could make the chair appear either too spindly or too stout. By adhering to the proper balance of solid and void, the chair has the appearance of strength with grace and neither the elements nor the spaces they leave dominate the composition. Of particular interest in Queen Anne chairs is the way the central splat is designed in conjunction with the voids on either side of it. Makers purposefully shaped vasiform splats to leave bird-shaped voids (see the photo below). Although working in solid wood, the makers were working as much with the space left by its absence.

The other use of the balance of solid and void is to give case pieces and tables "lift." In Queen Anne furniture, lift is the attribute of achieving a light appearance in the body of the piece by giving it a stance that contradicts its mass. This gives Queen Anne pieces their "perching" quality, a

SQUARE TEA TABLE,
NEW ENGLAND,
1740–1760.
'Lift' is the perching quality of Queen Anne furniture that gives it a light appearance through the use of a high apron and gracefully shaped legs.
(COURTESY THE METROPOLITAN MUSEUM OF ART)

characteristic exhibited by better examples of the period that is much sought after by connoisseurs. Good lift was achieved by the use of long, slender and gracefully shaped legs, along with a high apron of a sweeping curved profile (see the photo above). The result lifted the mass of the piece high off the ground, reinforcing the height and weightlessness of the piece. The large space left under the piece allowed the shape of the legs to be seen without distraction, and the shape of the apron spanning the void became an important element in the overall design. With this kind of stance, Queen Anne furniture does not seem intended to stand statically on the floor. Outstanding examples seem poised to go *en pointe*.

The Queen Anne Style in America

Queen Anne, Mary's younger sister, assumed the throne after William III's death in 1702. Although she reigned until only 1714, the style that was given her name had only its most fundamental beginnings during her reign. The style first emerged in America about 1725, and over the next decade came to dominate furniture design. The style continued to evolve and remained popular until about 1760. In some areas

outside of the style-conscious cities, the Queen Anne style was peaking in certain forms as late as the 1780s. The cabinetmakers of the Deerfield, Massachusetts, area had their own distinct style and produced some of the finest examples of Queen Anne pieces after the Revolution when the style had long since passed out of favor elsewhere. Throughout American furniture history, styles are more important then dates, and references to certain eras or periods pertain more to the stylistic trends than to particular times. Commercial success, routes of travel and trade, social customs and local preferences, skills and materials all contributed to the way styles changed or were retained.

While all Queen Anne designs descended from an English origin, American pieces varied in their degree of direct influence. In some cases, pieces were clearly copied from English examples. Many cabinetmakers emigrated from England and brought their methods and designs with them. On the other hand, many American pieces show just the influence of new English styles applied to existing American pieces. Of course, those existing pieces were essentially English themselves, but with a history of American interpretation. The fact that some aspects of furniture design remained in fashion for decades, often

SIDE CHAIR, NEWPORT AREA, 1735–1750.
The careful balance of solid and void and the use of open space as a design element yield forms that are to be looked through as well as at.
(PRIVATE COLLECTION)

coexisting with earlier and later styles, indicates that the Americans held onto the familiar designs they liked but were open to newer styles if the change was warranted. This approach speaks to a certain quality of practicality and frugality inherent in colonial Americans and their desire to have fashions that were influenced rather than dictated by the mother country.

EARLY GEORGIAN STYLE

American furniture styles between 1725 and 1760 are often referred to as Queen Anne and Early Georgian, and some explanation of the latter is in order. Early Georgian refers to the reign of George I, 1714–1727, and George II, 1727–1760. Subsequent Georges III and IV were on the throne until 1830. In America, the Early Georgian was not a separate style, but rather the later evolution of the Queen Anne. In England the difference was more distinct. The first Queen Anne forms were seen in the first decade of the 18th century, and during the reign of George I the English style came to include more carved decoration, mostly restrained shells and foliage, and began to assume somewhat stouter proportions. This phase is sometimes called the Decorated Queen

SIDE CHAIR, BOSTON, C.1730–1740.
In the Early Georgian style, furniture proportions became stouter and the use of carved ornament increased, as evidenced by this Boston example that closely followed English tastes. Chairs of this style were previously thought to be of New York origin but have recently been shown to have been made in Boston for shipment to other colonial cities.
(COURTESY MUSEUM OF FINE ARTS, BOSTON)

Anne style. William Kent (1684–1748) was an architect in the Palladian style and a decorator who introduced late European Baroque ornamentation; he was influential from 1725 until about 1740. His furniture designs for Palladian mansions were encrusted with shells, fruit, foliage, eagles and dolphin carvings. Although furniture in the Kent manner was not for everyone in England, his designs were influential in steering English tastes toward more opulent carving (see the illustration below). Given Kent's architectural background and the strong interest in architectural design among the aristocracy, elements of architecture continued to be an important part of both the form and its decoration throughout the Early Georgian period.

The increased use of ornament in the Early Georgian period coincided with a change in material. Since shortly after the Restoration and through England's Queen Anne period, walnut was the wood of choice for cabinetmakers. Most of the walnut used in England was imported from France, but by 1720 it was in short supply. To reduce its depletion and to maintain their domestic supply, the French banned its export. The following year England reduced its high import duties on wood

DESIGN FOR A MARBLE TABLE BY THOMAS LANGLEY, LONDON, 1739.
The Palladian style represented the uppermost limit of European Baroque ornament that could be applied to furniture of Queen Anne-era design. The style was advanced by the architect William Kent and was influential in creating a movement toward more opulently carved surfaces.
(PRIVATE COLLECTION)

from the American colonies and the West Indies, and imported mahogany began to replace walnut in English furniture. The change in material was for the better. Dense West Indian and Central American mahogany was better suited to the increasing amount of carving, and it could be finished with a deeper and richer surface. In 1733 England repealed the import duty on mahogany, allowing for its nearly exclusive use over the next three decades.

American trends in design were running a decade or two behind the English, and Americans were selective in what they chose to include. The American Queen Anne style was just starting as the English were entering the Early Georgian phase of ornament. Pad feet were the norm for American cabriole legs at the outset, but ball and claw feet were later used on pieces of particular importance beginning in the 1740s, some 20 years after they became popular in England. The extravagances of William Kent were not adopted in the American colonies. They were not in keeping with American tastes, and there was no aristocracy with either the palatial homes or the unlimited wealth required for such furniture. The use of an occasional, well-placed shell was in keeping with the American view of Queen Anne, and gilding those shells was the limit of acceptable flamboyance. The architectural aspect of the Early Georgian period was influential in America, since design books were plentiful and inspirational for craftsmen. Before the Revolutionary War, at least 85 different architectural guide books were known to have been available, and most all of them followed the Palladian precepts. As the style progressed, more fluted pilasters, plinths, arched pediments and architecturally rendered moldings found their way into furniture designs.

American Queen Anne Forms

The shift to the more reserved style of Queen Anne, along with the continued influence of the Baroque, yielded some new forms and brought the evolution of some old ones. Case pieces, while maintaining most of their structural details, were modified to include cabriole legs or bracket feet, improved drawers and arched pediment tops. Tables with bold turnings and stretchers were simplified to four cabriole legs. Chairs underwent a thorough redesign leaving them quite unlike their predecessors. Across the board, intricate turnings and elaborate carvings gave way to the sweeping lines and smooth surfaces of the relaxed Queen Anne designs. As the standard of living improved, social interaction and pastimes increased, and new forms of furniture with specialized purposes proliferated throughout England and its colonies.

CHESTS

Chests with drawers had proven their practicality with the William and Mary designs, and their evolution continued into the second quarter of the century. High chests and chests-on-frame were well suited to the Queen Anne style, and American cabinetmakers advanced the development of those pieces beyond that of English examples.

Chests of drawers

The chest of drawers changed only cosmetically with the Queen Anne style, since its structure had been established during the William and Mary years. The evolution from lift-top chests to those comprised entirely of drawers was mostly complete as the new style came into vogue. Chests that combined lift tops over drawers continued to be made in more rural areas into the second half of the century, but they had long since passed out of favor in urban areas, where chests of drawers were the

CHEST OF DRAWERS, ATTRIBUTED TO JOHN TOWNSEND, NEWPORT, C.1750.
The use of bracket feet, delicate moldings and a more refined graduation of lipped drawers brought case pieces into the Queen Anne period.
(PRIVATE COLLECTION)

HIGH CHEST OF DRAWERS, CONNECTICUT, C.1730.
Early American Queen Anne high chests continued many of the proportions of earlier high chests.
(PRIVATE COLLECTION, COURTESY NATHAN LIVERANT AND SON, COLCHESTER, CONNECTICUT)

HIGH CHEST OF DRAWERS, CONNECTICUT, 1750–1780.
As the style progressed, high chests assumed more vertical proportions and lost the vestigial remains of earlier styles.
(PRIVATE COLLECTION)

CHEST-ON-FRAME (AFTER AN ORIGINAL), NEWPORT, 1730–1760.
An important form for the period, the chest-on-frame had many of the same endearing qualities as Queen Anne high chests.
(PRIVATE COLLECTION)

standard. Modernizing the chest of drawers entailed replacing its decorative elements. Ball feet were replaced by bracket feet, giving the piece a more stable stance and a foot that was better integrated into the overall design. The arch moldings that had surrounded the drawers were eliminated as drawers came to have overlapping lips. The drawer lips featured delicate bead moldings cut into the drawer fronts, which cleaned up the appearance of the piece by covering the space between the drawer and its case. Top and bottom case moldings were given a new refinement in keeping with the quieter style, and more attention was paid to the graduation of drawer sizes to aid in creating the appearance of height.

High chests

High chests and chests-on-frame underwent a more obvious change in design than did chests of drawers. (Chests-on-frame are generally distinguished from high chests by

the absence of drawers in the base.) In both examples, the bases were changed drastically by replacing their numerous and bold legs and stretchers with four graceful cabriole legs. The effect was immediate and profound and represented a stylistic leap forward. The early chests-on-frame and high chests retained the case proportions of the William and Mary period, but they increased in height as the style evolved. Similarly, the early bases retained apron details from the previous era, and pairs of drop finials sometimes appear as the vestigial remains of what had been the two center legs (photo at left above). As the style progressed, the apron designs came to include more flowing curves to span the

HIGH CHEST OF DRAWERS, CONNECTICUT, 1750–1770.
At the apex of Baroque aesthetic, the arched pediment top contributes to the ethereal goals of the period.
(COURTESY HENRY FORD MUSEUM AND GREENFIELD VILLAGE)

distance from side to side (top photos at center and right on the facing page).

In keeping with the continuing vertical thrust, the familiar arched pediment top for high chests emerged later in the Queen Anne style (see the bottom photo on the facing page). The pediment profile represented the purest form of the cyma curve, and it added height and visual interest to the case top. In combination with the sweeping curves of the cornice moldings, central and side finials were intended to draw the eye upward through an impressive design.

DESKS

Desks followed a similar development through this period, and shared most of the advancements of other case pieces. As with chests of drawers, bracket feet and overlapping drawers became the norm, and when they were equipped with upper bookcases those cases were sometimes given the same arched pediment tops as high chests (see the photo at right). Short cabriole legs, called bandy legs, were used on chests but were most frequently seen on desks of the period.

Part of the splendor of Queen Anne desks was in the complexity and sophistication of their interiors. Behind the slanted lid, the interior drawers and compartments were as carefully designed as the piece as a whole, and represented an area of both utility and focus. A dazzling array of drawers and doors, complete with shaped and carved fronts and secret compartments, made for an impressive desk. It was the perfect place for a cabinetmaker to exhibit consummate skill and a client to show exquisite taste. The same idea was extended to the upper bookcase, if the piece was so equipped, by revealing carved shells behind the arched doors, and extensive and elaborate partitioning.

TABLES

As with case pieces, the use of the cabriole leg drastically altered the appearance of tables in the Queen Anne era. Busy, turned-leg bases gave way to gracefully curved legs. The continuing prosperity and the increase

in available leisure time gave rise to a number of tables in the Queen Anne style to serve a wide range of specific purposes.

Dressing tables

Dressing tables continued into the Queen Anne era with most of the same changes as the bases of high chests. The turned legs and stretchers gave way to cabriole legs, and apron profiles took on more sweeping curves (see the photo at right). With prosperity must have come vanity, because dressing tables had more drawers during the Queen Anne period. While most William and Mary dressing tables had three drawers, Queen Anne designs frequently added a shallow drawer of full width over the others. Some Boston examples have six drawers arranged in two rows of three. Either way, a slight increase in the height of the case was necessary.

DRESSING TABLE, MASSACHUSETTS, 1735–1750.
Queen Anne dressing tables share structural and design similarities with the bases of high chests, and the two forms were often made *en suite*.
(PRIVATE COLLECTION, COURTESY ISRAEL SACK, INC., N.Y.C.)

TEA TABLE, BOSTON, 1755–1765.
A standard form for Boston rectangular tea tables, this example has a molding on the top and a gently scrolled apron that flows into the legs.
(COURTESY THE SOCIETY FOR THE PRESERVATION OF NEW ENGLAND ANTIQUITIES)

TEA TABLE, NEWPORT, 1750–1780.
The Newport version of the rectangular tea table features slipper feet and a more austere apron.
(COURTESY MUSEUM OF ART, RHODE ISLAND SCHOOL OF DESIGN)

MIXING TABLE, BOSTON AREA, 1735–1745.
Mixing tables are stylistically similar to tea tables, but feature ceramic tile or marble tops to prevent damage from alcohol.
(COURTESY WINTERTHUR MUSEUM)

Tea tables

Tea tables deserve special recognition as a new form that developed in conjunction with a new social trend. The drinking of tea was one of the English customs that became very fashionable in the 1720s, and all the implements required to serve it—porcelain, silverware and the furniture—were a focus of attention and had to be in the best of taste. William and Mary tables, with turned legs and stretchers, had functioned as occasional pieces and had been used wherever and whenever needed. Queen Anne tea tables served a more dedicated purpose, and, being so central (both literally and figuratively) to the service of tea, they developed as some of the most refined examples of the style.

One of the most familiar forms of the Queen Anne tea table is the rectangular shape, with a shallow apron and slender cabriole legs. This family of tea tables has the top set into or on top of the frame, with no overhang, but with an applied molding giving it a raised outer edge (see the photos at left and center above). Very often an applied molding runs along the bottom edge of the apron, connecting the knees of the legs, and this molding is shaped with a curving profile. Many examples include extension slides on either end that increased the serving area.

Since the top has no overhang, the legs are at the outermost corners of these tables, and they show an exceptionally stable stance. It is the short height of the apron, the scrolled apron profile and the slender nature of the legs that maintain the delicacy and lightness that are so essential to the period. Since tea tables were small and relatively simple pieces, cabinetmakers were able to modify their designs and adjust the balance of the components. Because tea tables could be built quickly and were not technically difficult, more attention could be paid to the subtle points of their design. As a result, the maker's skill as a designer and the aims of the Queen Anne period in general are exhibited in these pieces.

Mixing tables

As with any universally popular form, there is a wide range of variation in small elegant tables. One subset of cabriole-leg tea tables used delft ceramic tiles as the top surface, while others used marble instead of wood for the tops. Tables with these tops are generally referred to as mixing tables since their surfaces are well suited for the mixing of alcoholic beverages (see the photo at right above). The period finishes of other tea tables were subject to the ravages of hot tea pots and water, but alcohol called for a more impervious surface.

Informal tea tables

Informal tea tables have turned tapered legs that end in pad feet and overhanging tops of various shapes. Being somewhat less expensive, these tables were very common in their day and a great many have survived to the present. Most of these tables have either an oval or porringer top measuring about 2 ft. by 3 ft. Porringer tops are rectangular with protruding rounded corners, and were a common form in the Rhode Island area (see the top photo on the facing page). The shape was probably inspired by Boston gaming tables that used the shape as an extension of a three-quarter-round corner turret on the apron from

TEA TABLE, NEWPORT, 1740–1770.
Less formal tea tables enjoyed widespread use, with regional variations in shape and detail. The porringer-corner shape of this table is indicative of the Newport area.

(COURTESY MUSEUM OF ART, RHODE ISLAND SCHOOL OF DESIGN)

took hours to make, and they had to be cut from more expensive 3-in. stock. The entire table could be built in one-quarter to one-third of the time required for a cabriole-leg table. Although these tables were less formal, they were not rural interpretations of city pieces. Some of the leading cabinetmakers of the day made them in quantity, but the simplicity of their design allowed less sophisticated makers in outlying areas to build them with good results.

Folding tea tables

Another variation on the tea table was one that could fold flat and be stored away when not in use. Sometimes called "tuckaway" tables, these tables featured very slender cabriole legs attached to an X-shaped frame that was hinged at the center to fold flat (see the photo below). The top, usually about 28 in. in diameter, was attached to

the frame with hinges so it swung to a vertical position. The folded table was only 5 in. or 6 in. thick and could be tucked away anywhere.

These tables were mechanically clever, and their aesthetics often exhibited a high level of sophistication. Examples have slender but well-formed cabriole legs, and they frequently have dished tops where an outer molded edge is left by dishing out all but the edge of the top. Both features are expensive to produce and require considerable skill. The fact that they are sophisticated but storable implies that they were not the primary tea table in the home, but rather an extra tea table that was brought out on occasion when needed. Folding tea tables were once common, especially in the northern colonies where interior space was often at a premium. They have become exceedingly scarce, and those of exceptional form are greatly sought after.

which the leg extended (see the top photo on p. 47). On porringer tables it was primarily a decorative treatment, though the corners do suggest a convenient and out of the way place for candlesticks or saucers. Oval tops had universal appeal and were used throughout the colonies. Variations in top shapes, including rectangular tops, round tops and some with incised corners, were seen regionally.

The base of these tables was very simple, but nonetheless elegant. The legs were turned off-center to a delicate ankle, below which extended a dainty pad or Dutch foot. The apron, which was tenoned into the leg to form the frame, had only its profile shape for ornament. Along with the overhanging top, the design was quite pleasing and had all the grace and style that the period demanded.

These tables were less formal and less expensive than those with cabriole legs. Since the legs were turned, each leg could be made in minutes from 2-in. stock. Cabriole legs were much more involved and

FOLDING TEA TABLE, NEW HAMPSHIRE, 1740–1760.
With a hinged X-shaped frame and a hinged top, this table folds to less than 5 in. in thickness.
(COURTESY MUSEUM OF FINE ARTS, BOSTON)

Tripod tables

Candlestands in the tripod form had been known since Jacobean England, but they found a resurgence in beauty and usefulness in the Queen Anne period. These small tables, originally made to hold a lighting device, had existed in a more utilitarian form during the William and Mary era. The tripod design was well suited for cyma-curved legs and an architecturally inspired turned center, and thus came to assume a well-developed form. Because of their simplicity and usefulness, regional variations and degrees of sophistication abound.

Larger versions of the tripod design were used as tea tables and, in some cases, were designed to allow the top to turn to aid in serving. The tops were hinged so they could be tipped vertically, allowing the table to be put aside when not in use. These are commonly known as tip-top tables, which is a modern appellation, but to early American cabinetmakers they were known as round tea tables. Earlier English examples were descriptively called pillar and claw tables, denoting the use of claw

feet, and snap tables, since the latches snap shut in the horizontal position. Tip-top tables were an enormously popular form of table throughout the colonies. Philadelphians were especially fond of the form and would later take it to a high level of development. The tripod form, with stylistic changes, remained in common use well into the next century.

Side tables

Side tables were a new form for the Queen Anne period. Usually about 4 ft. long and without drawers, they were the forerunner of the sideboard and were intended to stand along a wall as a secondary piece for serving food or drink. The fact that many side tables have marble tops is indicative of their function, and explains why later versions came to be known as "slab tables." Side tables have all the attributes of Queen Anne tea tables, but their size and design speak to their specialized role. Since they are large and were used in serving, they would have belonged to the wealthier segment of society, and original examples are few in number. The term "console table" is often used erroneously; console tables came at a later date and were mounted to the wall.

Card tables

As increasing prosperity brought more leisure time and social interaction, another popular activity, besides tea drinking, was card playing. The gambling craze had started in France, spread to England, and eventually come to America. While their Puritan forebears would have been dismayed, whist and other card games became pleasant social pastimes among the well-to-do. The elite could afford to have tables built specially for the purpose, based upon the latest English designs. Like formal tea tables, they were the centerpieces of the evening's activity and had to be of the best style. Many featured needlework playing surfaces, dished pockets for chips or counters and recesses for candlesticks or beverages (see the top photo on the facing page). While they were made in several shapes, English examples with four corner turrets, from which the legs extended, were the most practical because the legs were well out of the way of the sitters' knees. Furthermore, their tops followed the same shape, giving them increased surface area and room for the wells. This is the shape that seems to have inspired the familiar porringer top.

An important feature that was established by early card tables was a top that folded in half on itself, or opened to be supported by swinging legs. When not in use, the table could stand against a wall, taking up half the space. By folding the top in half, the playing surface was protected

CARD TABLE, BOSTON, 1730–1750.
This card table features turreted front corners and a needlework top surface. The rear legs open outward to support the folding top.
(COURTESY MUSEUM OF FINE ARTS, BOSTON)

CARD PLAYING

While the Puritans frowned on them, amusements and pastimes abounded in 18th-century America. Taverns were popular establishments where cards, billiards, backgammon, shuffleboard, dice games and even bowling augmented the primary activity of drinking. Among the favorite card games of the day were *whist, lanterloo, put, piquet, cribbage* and *all fours*. The chips or counters for these games were called "fish" and were made of bone in the shape of discs, stars or fish. The upper level of society also enjoyed cards, but since they did not frequent taverns, they had private gatherings of friends at home. The domestic gaming tables of the day were made with pockets for the counters, and their needlework playing surfaces often depicted cards, counters and money.

and as a result many still have their original needlework in excellent condition. After 1730, some of the English examples featured rear legs that swung out on a hinged accordion-like frame, which gave the tables full aprons and a nicer appearance when open. The folding card table was a new form for the period, but it established a precedent that card tables would follow well into the next century.

Drop-leaf tables

The drop-leaf gateleg table of the William and Mary period had proven to be versatile and practical, and its design was carried into the Queen Anne era with some modification. The elaborate assemblage of legs and stretchers was replaced by four cabriole legs, two of which swung out on hinged frame members to support the leaves. Table tops were either oval or rectangular when opened. The drawer on the end of some William and Mary examples was not seen in Queen Anne pieces. Some examples from the middle Atlantic states have six legs, with the swing (or fly) legs positioned just behind stationary ones so as to increase the table's sturdiness and stability.

Queen Anne dining tables saw the first widespread use of the rule joint in joining their leaves. This joint concealed the steel leaf hinges by placing them within a quarter-round molding that ran the length of the joint and fit into a corresponding cove molding on the underside of the leaf. The rule joint required quite a bit of skill to make accurately, but the result was a table with a much neater appearance. Rule-joined

DINING TABLE, MASSACHUSETTS, 1740–1780.
The drop-leaf table was an elegant and practical form of table, well suited to the needs of 18th-century life. The Queen Anne version had cabriole legs, two of which swing to support the leaves, and a gently shaped apron.
(COURTESY COLONIAL WILLIAMSBURG FOUNDATION)

SIDE CHAIR, CONNECTICUT OR MASSACHUSETTS, 1720–1740.
The 'splat-back' chair retains stretchers and front legs of an earlier style but has a back design similar to later Queen Anne chairs.
(COURTESY THE SOCIETY FOR THE PRESERVATION OF NEW ENGLAND ANTIQUITIES)

SIDE CHAIR, BOSTON AREA, 1735–1760.
The classic New England Queen Anne chair developed in Boston about 1730 and evolved with regional variations over the next three decades.
(COURTESY THE SOCIETY FOR THE PRESERVATION OF NEW ENGLAND ANTIQUITIES)

SIDE CHAIR, PHILADELPHIA, 1740–1760.
A Philadelphia chair shows the greater propensity for sculptural elements and carved details outside of New England.
(COURTESY MUSEUM OF ART, RHODE ISLAND SCHOOL OF DESIGN)

leaves became the standard method of attaching leaves for all subsequent drop-leaf tables. Cabinetmakers' account books of the period often refer to these as rule tables, and they are priced by the foot according to the length of the frame or, as they called it, the bed.

A small version of the drop-leaf dining table was known as a breakfast table and was approximately 36 in. in diameter. This table functioned much like a folding tea table; it could be used when needed and stored away in little space when not in use. It was for occasional use, and its name is not indicative of its only purpose. These tables have all the same elements as full-size dining tables and required nearly as much labor to make. That much effort for a table of this size made them quite a bit more expensive than a common tea table and limited their numbers. Their diminutive size and scaled-down detailing make them endearing little tables. When well executed, they are gems of Queen Anne design.

SEATING FURNITURE

The Queen Anne style brought a great advance in the design of chairs. Most chairs before this time were composed of straight elements, which limited both comfort and aesthetics. In the early part of the century, Boston chairs had been the first American chair design to use the cyma curve in the back profile while retaining William and Mary elements elsewhere (see pp. 24-25). This design was a preview of things to come, as the fully developed Queen Anne chair kept the curved back and included all the new design elements as well.

Splat-back chairs

An important and widely used New England chair that developed after the Boston chairs was an early Queen Anne design first seen in the 1720s. This design incorporated a vasiform, or baluster-inspired, curved splat. The top of the splat was met by a double-arched crest rail that carried the shape of the splat over to meet

the molded shape of the vertical stiles. The base of the splat was secured by a distinctive horizontal rail a few inches above the seat (photo at left above). This yoke-shape crest included a scooped saddle on the crest above the splat, which was to continue as a standard form in Queen Anne chairs. To differentiate these chairs from other varieties, they are often called splat-back chairs.

More than a purely transitional or rural version of a higher style, this design shows the New England penchant for combining the new Queen Anne elements with existing designs. Some variations of these chairs used block-and-turned front legs with either ball or Spanish feet, while others employed the cabriole shape. Existing examples include some with rush seats and others with loose seats and over-the-rail upholstering.

This style enjoyed a widespread and long-lived acceptance, which accounts for its many variations. Examples date from the early part of the second quarter of the century and continue until the time of the Revolution in some areas. While splat backs were superseded by more stylish designs in the major cities in the 1730s, they remained in favor elsewhere as locally produced examples of the Queen Anne aesthetic.

Queen Anne chairs

The Queen Anne side chair, in its best known form, is comprised of curved back stiles, arching through a crest rail to meet a splat of the familiar vasiform shape (see the center photo on the facing page). The bottom of the splat joins the seat rail through a molded shoe. Cabriole legs, well rounded in cross section, support either a square seat or a rounded compass (sometimes called balloon) seat. Each of these shapes would have held a slip seat, a separate upholstered seat frame that drops into place. The front and back legs are joined by block and turned stretchers, and two swelled turnings form the rear and medial stretchers.

This style of chair, in its American form, is known to have developed in Boston no earlier than 1730, and it soon became a standard for New England Queen Anne chairs. While all the design elements are from the English Queen Anne, the design evolved by applying those elements to existing American chairs rather than directly copying English examples, since English chairs did not have the same vertical proportions.

Regional variations of the form appeared as its popularity spread. Newport versions were nearly identical to the standard form, but with subtle differences in the delicacy of the elements that gave the chair a lighter appearance (see the photo at bottom on p. 39). Farther south, in New York and Philadelphia, Queen Anne chairs had shorter and wider proportions (more like the English style), and they were likely to incorporate more dynamic sculptural elements in the rear stiles and splat shape, along with a more extensive use of carving (see the photo at right on the facing page). Once the style had been established in each city, the variations grew as each developed in accordance with local tastes.

The divergence between Philadelphia and New England style becomes apparent in the Queen Anne designs and is typified in the chairs. At first glance, the conservative restraint of New England makers is obvious in comparison to the relatively daring flamboyance of their Philadelphian counterparts. A more subtle point is the growing stylistic kinship between Philadelphia and London, while New England maintained a separate identity. Whereas the Philadelphia makers and their clientele were readily willing to embrace the latest English designs, the New England market was more comfortable in applying the influence of those designs to existing pieces. Part of this had to do with the growth rate of both regions. The populations of New York and Philadelphia were starting to skyrocket, while in New England growth was much more modest. During the third quarter of the century, the population of New York and Philadelphia roughly doubled while the growth rate in

Boston was flat. By the time of the Revolution, Philadelphia had a population two and a half times that of Boston. Most of those who swelled the population of Philadelphia, including indentured servants and tradespeople, came directly from England. With them came both the appetite for and the designs of the latest English furniture.

Upholstered pieces

Fabrics and shape were both important elements in Queen Anne design, so upholstered pieces in the forms of easy chairs and sofas were well in keeping with the style. Textiles were expensive (a locally woven coverlet was close to a simple tea table in value), and the finest and most stylish fabrics were imported. The prosperity of the times and the accompanying pursuit of creature comforts made upholstered pieces more available and desirable.

Easy chairs made a smooth transition from the William and Mary style into the

EASY CHAIR, BOSTON, OR POSSIBLY RHODE ISLAND, 1740–1770. Easy chairs have a more relaxed stance than those of earlier eras and share leg and stretcher designs with other chairs of the period. *(COURTESY YALE UNIVERSITY ART GALLERY)*

SOFA, PHILADELPHIA, 1740–1750.
Sofas were still quite rare before mid-century because of the cost of upholstering and their space requirements. In keeping with the Queen Anne aesthetic, they share stylistic similarities with easy chairs.
(COURTESY WINTERTHUR MUSEUM)

Queen Anne. In keeping with the design philosophy of the time, they became broader and more relaxed in shape, losing some of the vertical thrust that had characterized the earlier styles. Easy chairs assumed most of the attributes of other Queen Anne chairs, with cabriole legs and simplified turned stretchers.

Sofas were a new form for the period, having evolved from a combination of earlier settees and fully upholstered easy chairs. Since most houses of the period had limited space, and since the amount of fabric required to upholster a sofa was prohibitively expensive, they were only affordable to the very wealthy. As a result, American Queen Anne sofas are exceptionally rare. When they were made they followed the conventions of the style, with cabriole legs, arm rolls and serpentine backs that were harmonious with the designs of easy chairs.

Couches, or day beds, continued in the Queen Anne style, but their popularity was waning as sofas became more desirable. The need for a large upholstered piece was becoming more important for social reasons rather than for purposes of repose, and sofas were a more useful and elegant solution. Couches increasingly became bedroom pieces as they were displaced by sofas.

TALL-POST BEDSTEAD, RHODE ISLAND, 1735–1750.
The primary purpose of bedsteads was to hold the mattress and bed hangings. Little of the structure is seen except for the front posts, which here feature cabriole legs.
(COURTESY WINTERTHUR MUSEUM)

BEDSTEADS

Bedsteads continued to be frames for the purpose of holding a mattress, and tall-post beds were designed to support bed hangings as well. In that regard, they were valued more for their function than for their aesthetics. Nonetheless, they were made in keeping with the Queen Anne style, with cabriole front legs and a gently arched headboard. When fully equipped with bed hangings, only the front posts and legs and the top of the headboard remained visible, so most of the bedsteads of the period have a concentrated emphasis there. Low-post beds were the norm for those of more modest means, but they too show the attributes of the styling of the period.

Queen Anne Structure

William and Mary pieces owed much of their design to their structure since widespread use of the dovetail joint had fundamentally changed the way furniture was built. The Queen Anne style brought an aesthetic evolution to that structure, and a refinement to its method of construction. In some cases, the changes were improvements in technique that came with continued practice, and in other cases the

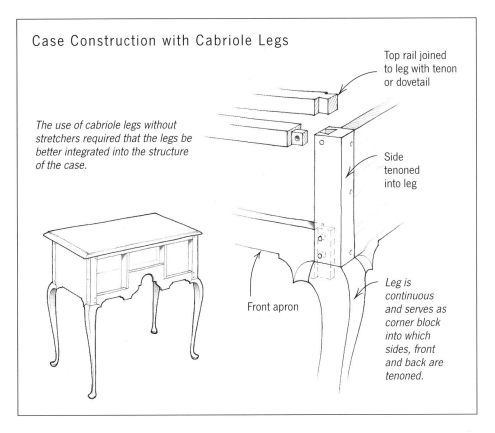

Case Construction with Cabriole Legs

The use of cabriole legs without stretchers required that the legs be better integrated into the structure of the case.

Top rail joined to leg with tenon or dovetail

Side tenoned into leg

Front apron

Leg is continuous and serves as corner block into which sides, front and back are tenoned.

The redesign entailed dropping the idea of dovetailing the case edges, and instead tenoning the case parts into the extended leg block of the cabriole (see the drawing at left). This method made the legs an integral part of the case rather than a later attachment, and gave the piece solidity and unsurpassed durability. The one drawback was the inability of the tenoned components to expand and contract freely across the grain, and some cracking of case sides resulted. Nonetheless, this method was vastly superior to the former, and it became the universally accepted method of building these pieces. The one notable exception was in Newport, where cases continued to be dovetailed at the edges, with the cabriole-leg blocks attached to the inside corners. This method of construction proved to be very practical with high-chest cases. The legs could be positioned in the case with attached blocks that left the legs free to slide out, and they could then be removed for shipping.

changes were necessitated by the new components that made up the Queen Anne style.

Case pieces remained structurally unchanged from the previous era, but the construction techniques of cabinetmakers became more refined. Dovetails increased in number and precision as methods were perfected. Components like drawer parts and case panels became thinner, as cabinetmakers learned that bulk was not a requirement for strength. Besides purely aesthetic and stylistic improvements, such as more delicate case moldings, bracket feet and improved proportions, Queen Anne case pieces continued the construction methods established with William and Mary pieces, but with two notable exceptions: the structure of dressing tables and high chest bases, and the use of lipped drawers.

CASE CONSTRUCTION

The cases of dressing tables and the bases of high chests had consisted of four sides, dovetailed together along their four vertical edges. The turned legs were tenoned into interior corner blocks, which were glued in

place (see the top drawing on p. 140). This was not an ideal method of construction, but given that the turned legs were numerous (six in the case of a high chest) and tied together by stretchers, it proved adequate for the William and Mary period. In the Queen Anne style, where there were only four legs and no stretchers, their attachment required some redesign if they were expected to endure.

LIPPED DRAWERS

The other notable change in the structure of case pieces involved the use of lipped drawers. Drawers with a lip at the top and sides covered the space between the drawer and its case and gave the piece a neater appearance. Single- and double-arch molding on the case surrounding the drawer opening fell out of favor in the Queen Anne aesthetic, but delicate bead moldings, less than $1/4$ in. wide, took their

DRAWER DETAIL, 1730–1750.
Lipped or overlapping drawers covered the space between the drawer and case and made for a better appearance. A quarter-round bead on the edge was used universally.

place in outlining the drawer. Drawers were not lipped along the bottom edge, since this lip would have quickly broken off if the drawer was removed from its case and placed on a table or floor. (Hard-to-reach top drawers were likely removed from the case and put on a tabletop as a matter course.) Otherwise, the construction of drawers continued with refinements in component thickness and the delicacy of dovetailing. As part of the evolution, drawer bottoms came to be installed by sliding them into place from the back, into grooves cut in the front and sides, and they were held in position by a small nail or two. Earlier methods of nailing them to the bottom of the drawer components became obsolete.

CHAIR CONSTRUCTION

With the divergence of styles between New England and Philadelphia came a divergence in construction methods, which is most evident in chairs. Philadelphia makers learned that they could do without stretchers between the legs, and did so, while northern makers continued to use them. The Philadelphia makers extended the tenon of the side seat rail through the rear leg, where it stopped flush with the surface (see the drawing at right). The strength of this very substantial joint allowed them to build chairs without stretchers. New England makers used shallower mortises that did not extend through the leg.

The seat construction of compass-seat chairs also varied between the two regions (see the drawing on the facing page). Philadelphia makers made the seat rail as a unit by tenoning the curved sides directly into the curved front rail with horizontal tenons. The cabriole legs were then attached to the underside of the seat rail by a single round tenon on the leg glued into a large hole in the rail. The lip to hold the slip seat was attached separately after the seat-rail assembly was complete. New England makers tenoned the curved seat-rail components into the blocks of the front legs, and then shaped the blocks to conform to the seat curve. The material inside the

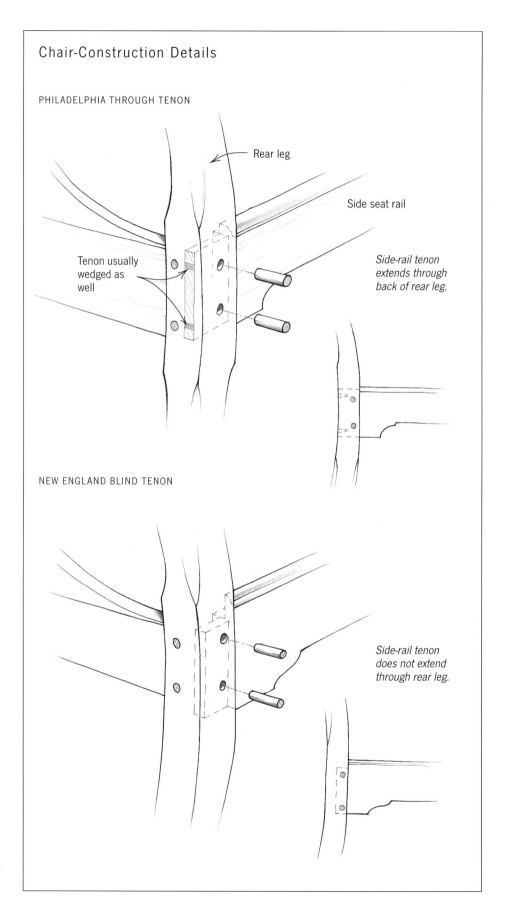

Chair-Construction Details

PHILADELPHIA THROUGH TENON

Rear leg

Side seat rail

Tenon usually wedged as well

Side-rail tenon extends through back of rear leg.

NEW ENGLAND BLIND TENON

Side-rail tenon does not extend through rear leg.

Compass Seats

PHILADELPHIA COMPASS SEAT

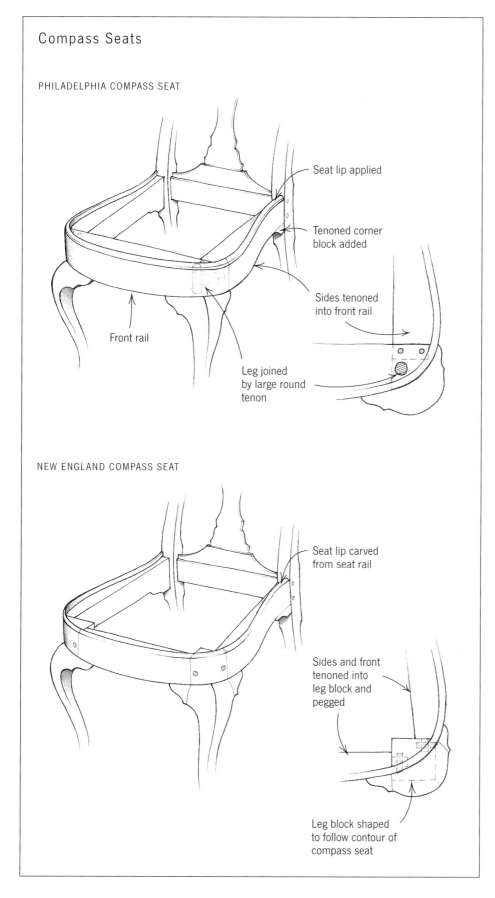

Seat lip applied

Tenoned corner block added

Sides tenoned into front rail

Front rail

Leg joined by large round tenon

NEW ENGLAND COMPASS SEAT

Seat lip carved from seat rail

Sides and front tenoned into leg block and pegged

Leg block shaped to follow contour of compass seat

seat rail was cut away to provide the recess for the slip seat. This method was identical to that used for a square, straight-sided seat. Structurally, the New England method of building compass seats was superior since the Philadelphia technique was dependent on the integrity of the glued joint.

Interestingly, the Philadelphia method of chair construction found a niche in the heart of New England. A style of simple and unadorned compass-seat chairs came to be a common form in the Connecticut River Valley. They were made just before mid-century for the Porter family, and now are referred to by that name. Porter chairs have all the construction characteristics of the best Philadelphia Queen Anne chairs but none of the ornament (photo below). They have pad feet, a plain crest rail and no stretchers. Of further interest is the fact

SIDE CHAIR, CONNECTICUT, 1740–1760.
Though made in Connecticut, 'Porter' chairs of this type have structural similarities with Philadelphia Queen Anne chairs.
(PRIVATE COLLECTION)

that many are made of walnut, the wood of choice for high-style cabinetmakers in the cities but not the usual choice for cabinetmakers in the Connecticut River Valley, where cherry was the predominant medium. The possible scenario of a Philadelphia-trained cabinetmaker bringing his style to the area is tantalizing and not without parallels in furniture history.

Other pieces continued to be built with mortise-and-tenon construction, since there were no other acceptable methods. As with all pieces, the precision of the joinery became increasingly important as the structural members became more delicate and the use of reinforcing stretchers diminished. Throughout the period, the designs and their structures continued in this process of optimization.

Decorative Elements

Queen Anne decorative elements are by definition few, or at least they were in the earliest and purest versions of the style. The reaction to Baroque extremes ensured that beauty was designed in and not added on. As the style progressed in England, designers added increasing degrees of ornamentation until they arrived at Queen Anne forms dressed out in the full regalia of the Italianate Baroque, but the purity of the unadorned Queen Anne style had an innate appeal to the Americans. They used ornamentation sparingly, to augment the design of the piece but not overpower it. American furniture was never a vehicle for ornament.

Apart from the role that the cyma curve played in replacing intricate turnings and severe lines with cabriole legs, gentle turnings and sweeping curved lines, other decorative elements were used with restraint. Veneer, usually walnut in the early decades of the style, continued to be used on the fronts of better high-style case

**HIGH CHEST OF DRAWERS,
CHARLESTOWN, MASSACHUSETTS, 1739.**
The Baroque shells, here gilded on the Hartshorn high chest, represented the acceptable limit of ornament for American tastes before mid-century.
(COURTESY MUSEUM OF FINE ARTS, BOSTON)

pieces, but it was intended to appear rich, rather than wild. Inlay, usually of cross-banding or herringbone design, was used to border drawer fronts and panels, but it was not as bold or contrasting as it had been previously. The surface was not intended to be the sole focus of attention. Many pieces were finished in a light color, increasing the visual appearance of size. The Queen Anne ideal was to have furniture of lofty grace, with expanses of smooth warm wood, interrupted only occasionally by restrained carved embellishment.

CARVINGS

Shells and fans on American Queen Anne pieces were inspired by the English obsession with them, and the English in turn had borrowed the motif from Italian, French and Dutch decorative styles. American makers of the period were careful to use carvings in proper proportion and number to the rest of the piece, with an eye toward only enhancing the design (see the photo on the facing page). Their carvings were also well integrated into the overall form of the piece, and gave the impression of being designed in from the outset, rather than added on later.

Carvings were used more extensively later in the period to enliven familiar forms, differentiate new pieces from earlier ones and feed an increasing appetite for opulence. The complexity and extent of carving varied according to local tastes and the price a customer was willing to pay. Philadelphians began to show a preference for more elaborate and detailed carving, which was to continue into the next era of furniture design. Following London styles, carved ball and claw feet appeared on Boston pieces as early as the 1730s and grew more widespread after mid-century.

ARCHITECTURAL DETAILS

As mentioned previously, architectural elements found their way into furniture as a result of the enduring popular interest in architecture and the natural evolution of the style. In the absence of furniture-design books, architectural guides were often the only source of fashionable styles available to designers and cabinetmakers. Decorative

HIGH CHEST OF DRAWERS, CONCORD, MASSACHUSETTS, 1755–1775.
The use of architectural details is evident in the upper case of this high chest attributed to Joseph Hosmer, himself a housewright. More formal pieces also reflected the influence. Note the architectural styling of the entablature and the pulvinated base and capital of the fluted pilasters.
(COURTESY THE SOCIETY FOR THE PRESERVATION OF NEW ENGLAND ANTIQUITIES)

features including fluting (especially of pilasters), molding profiles, plinths and finials, and arched pediments were used widely. The infusion of these elements was strong in England, where Palladian influence continued to be felt, especially after the leading proponent of Baroque ornament, William Kent, published the work of the leading proponent of Palladian architecture in *The Designs of Inigo Jones* in 1727.

In America, architectural design books proliferated, but Batty Langley's 1740 publication of *The City and Country Builder's and Workman's Treasury of Designs* was widely consulted. Langley's book helped reinforce existing architectural details and infused new ones into American furniture. It stands to reason that a region that was growing and building at the rate of the colonies would see an architectural impact on its furniture design. More of these elements would be included in the later part of the century.

JAPANNING

The ongoing merchant trade with the Far East kept alive a fascination with Oriental design that had been strong since the late 17th century. So different were Oriental designs and so distant was their origin that they had a mysterious and exotic allure. Of particular interest was Chinese lacquerware, usually chests of many compartments, covered with strange scenes and finished to perfection. Many were imported to Europe and England and put on twist-turned bases of local origin. European cabinetmakers and decorators were soon simulating the finish on pieces of their own making, a process known as "japanning." England experienced a great deal of exposure to the Oriental work from Portuguese trade with the east,

from the relation through marriage that Charles II had with Portugal, and from the Dutch East India Company by way of William of Orange. In 1688, John Stalker and George Parker published their *Treatise of Japanning and Varnishing*, in Oxford, England, and for a while japanned decoration became a fashionable pursuit of young women, not unlike needlework. It was all the rage, much to the dismay of the classicists who were touting the purity of classical architectural design at about the same time.

In America, japanning first took hold in Boston. Boston experienced the most rapid growth in the colonies just before the start of the 18th century, and it was home to the most affluent merchants who wanted the newest London styles. Soon Boston cabinetmakers and decorators were making their own version of Oriental lacquer, and applying it to the standard furniture forms. The first evidence of japanning being done in Boston was in 1712 and it continued to be fashionable until the middle of the century. New York also took up the decorative treatment, but its acceptance and duration trailed that of Boston by about a decade. Japanning was not an inexpensive treatment; the time required to japan a piece could easily exceed the time required to build it. Since it was to be shown off, it was usually done on impressive pieces, like high chests or tall case clocks, though some dressing tables and looking-glass frames were also japanned.

During this period about a dozen japanners worked in Boston; the best known three (Robert Davis, Thomas Johnson and William Randle) were born and trained in England. Fewer than three dozen Boston japanned pieces remain, two dozen of which are high chests. The period during which this decoration was applied overlapped the William and Mary and

Queen Anne eras of design, and examples of both styles were japanned. Of the known japanned Boston high chests, seven are William and Mary, and seventeen are Queen Anne.

Like Oriental lacquerwork, japanning consisted of gold figures and designs in raised relief on a black or mottled background. Pieces that were to be japanned were built of a hard pine or maple, since the wood wouldn't show. The japanner would draw the design on the bare wood of the piece and build up the figures with gesso, a thick paintlike mixture made from whiting and glue. The entire piece would be given a base coat of reddish-brown pigment in oil, and when that had dried it was given a similar coat of black. While the black paint was wet, it could be daubed or brushed to allow a hint of the base color to show through, giving the paint the mottled effect of tortoiseshell. The figures that had been raised with gesso were then gilded either with leaf or gold powder paint, and additional detailing was added over that in black. The entire piece was given several coats of a varnish and rubbed to a glossy finish. (For more on the technique of japanning, see Chapter 12.)

The many layers of dissimilar materials, their varying degrees of adherence to one another and the sometimes brittle quality of gesso made japanned decoration very delicate, and few original pieces have survived with their decoration intact. Japanning is especially intolerant of extremes of temperature and humidity, and the expansion and contraction of the underlying wood loosens or cracks the gesso. Eighteenth-century homes offered poor conditions for the well-being of japanned pieces, but modern climate controls can at least prevent further deterioration.

4

Opulence and Stately Presence

THE CHIPPENDALE STYLE
(1760–1785)

Refined grace evolved into a stately elegance with the Chippendale-era designs, and the attention to opulent detail is evident in the side chair in *The American School*, a 1765 oil by Matthew Pratt (1734–1805).

The increased stratification of the American social structure after mid-century led the wealthy elite to continue their quest for elegant surroundings. What had previously been expressed through elegance increasingly became defined with opulence. In an effort to infuse a richness into their furnishings, Americans embraced the English styles propagated by Thomas Chippendale: Grace gave way to strength and understatement yielded to bold presence.

The Rise of an American Aristocracy

In the absence of inherited titles and the European system of class structure, social status was determined primarily by wealth. The prosperity of the colonies had enabled the merchant families to amass considerable wealth, and most used it to expand their holdings. Their earnings enabled them to buy property and invest in business ventures that people of lesser means were unable to do. In the 100 years before the Revolution, the most wealthy 15% of Bostonians went from owning one-half of the city's assessable assets to owning two-thirds. The concentration of wealth (and poverty) was proportional to the size of the city. Throughout colonial America, the larger cities had a greater percentage of their assets under the control of the wealthiest few, and they had a larger percentage of poor.

Within the cities, occupations were numerous and diverse. The Boston tax and probate records for 1780 show that, among those who were taxed, 36% were artisans and 29% were engaged in shipping and trade. Professional men accounted for 4%, and the rest were laborers, servants, clerks and mariners. Philadelphia tax lists for 1769 show that at least 25% were artisans, though many more were employed as artisans but did not have taxable assets. Given that artisans like tailors, silversmiths and cabinetmakers were the manufacturers of their day, these high numbers are not surprising.

Social status and class distinctions became more pronounced as the century progressed, and so did the accompanying privileges and trappings of wealth. The image of opulence that surrounded the emerging American aristocracy is portrayed in this description of Bostonian Peter Faneuil (1700–1743), a very successful merchant trader and accomplished smuggler:

> We see him on Sundays, splendid in his snuff-brown velvet suit and full bottomed wig, crossing the street from his residence to King's Chapel and entering to take his accustomed seat. His mansion he inherited from his uncle Andrew Faneuil, and he lived sumptuously with his Negro slaves, his silver plate, his coach and chariot, and his fine English horses. (Justin Weaver, ed., *Memorial History of Boston*, 1880–1881)

One can be certain that Peter Faneuil had the latest and most fashionable furniture that could be imported from London or made in the colonies. His belongings, like those of other very wealthy members of society, were rich and opulent reflections of his wealth and status.

DESIGN FOR A CARTOUCHE, HENRY COPELAND, *A NEW BOOK OF ORNAMENTS* (LONDON, 1746). The designers of Rococo ornament abandoned Baroque standards of symmetry and order to create unusual asymmetrical designs using free-flowing scrolls and foliage.
(COURTESY THE METROPOLITAN MUSEUM OF ART)

In England, where a true aristocracy existed, the need for elegant furnishings was stronger than ever. Governmental power had increasingly come into the hands of the third estate (the merchant or business class) and a powerful and competent (though thoroughly corrupt) prime minister who kept England peaceful and prosperous until the middle of the century. Free from most of the unpleasant details of ruling, the nobility concerned itself with architectural pursuits and intellectual discourse, and availed itself of luxuries and furnishings of the very best style.

Origins of the Chippendale Style

English Queen Anne furniture had become increasingly ornate as a result of the desire for increased opulence. The trend had reached its zenith with the designs of William Kent, whose Italian Baroque ornamentation was used to great excess on the furniture of Palladian mansions and estate houses. His Palladian style had an influence on the furniture of less grand houses as well, and lingered through the 1740s. By mid-century the Palladian style was yielding to something quite different: the Rococo.

THE ROCOCO

The Rococo is more a style of ornament than a style of furniture design. It is based on natural forms—foliage, flowers, fruit, shells, streams of water and waves—arranged to appear loose, casual and relaxed in form. Baroque ornament used many of the same motifs arranged with order and symmetry, but the most notable feature of the Rococo ornament was its asymmetry. Scrolling leaf fronds and natural curves were arranged and joined to yield unusual new shapes that were asymmetrical and lopsided, and lacked the stability of shape of conventional designs. The inverted pear shape was one of these shapes, and it defied the usual norms of design by being larger on the top than the bottom. The looseness of the ornament and the peculiar shapes it inspired were in marked contrast to the orderly nature of Baroque design.

Grottoes were a popular feature of formal gardens at the time, and many of the natural elements in Rococo design were inspired by their ornament. The word *rococo* derives from the French *rocaille*, meaning rock work, possibly with a contraction of *coquillage*, or shell work. It was first used as a pejorative term in the late 1790s, when designers looked back on the style and coined the term to portray it as an antiquated and overly ornate trend that exemplified bad taste. But the term was descriptive, and it eventually lost its bad connotation as the ornament came to be better understood and appreciated.

Like most English styles, the Rococo was transplanted from France, where it had been developing as a form of ornament since the death of Louis XIV in 1715. Two decades previously, the high standards of the Baroque were relaxed with the designs of Boulle. This trend was continued by Cressent during the French Régence. (The period's name comes from the years between 1715 and 1723, when Phillipe,

Duke of Orleans, served as Regent until Louis XV reached age 13 and was considered old enough to take the throne.) Even before the turn of the century the French designers had introduced the cyma-shaped leg, but not until the reign of Louis XV did the flowing curves that characterized the French Régence reach their full development. The remaining classical elements of design were supplanted by undulating curves, swelled shapes and swirling ornament.

Rococo ornament became synonymous with the Louis XV style, though the extent of its use varied through the years. It reached its peak during the 1730s and declined until the mid-1750s, when the Louis XV style faded from fashion. Young English noblemen who made the Grand Tour of European cities as part of their cultural education were no doubt exposed to the height of the Rococo style, but it was not until Kent's Palladian style

had waned that the English took up the new trend.

Once again, English furniture design had gone completely to an extreme and needed to be reigned in to something that was more comfortable and practical. Kent's designs had become monumental and massive, and were made more for show than for use. The relaxed, delicate and graceful designs of French furniture that had been developing in France since 1715 offered a refreshing change. The English began to take up aspects of the French style in the 1740s, and it remained in vogue through the 1760s. Whereas the French had spent over three decades in developing the style, the English merely took up the aspects of it that they liked, especially the dynamic and unrestrained nature of Rococo ornament. French Huguenot goldsmiths who were working in England had started to use some Rococo ornament during the 1730s, as did engravers, illustrators and ceramists. After 1740, some French ornament, like carved ribbons and cabochons, began to be

included in some existing forms of English furniture, but it was not until several design books were published that the style came to the fore.

Design books
The ornate and fanciful nature of Rococo design made design books necessary for the propagation of the style, and they were popular and interesting as well. Illustrated books proliferated during this time and came to be an important part of the design business from then on. One of these works was by Matthias Lock, a carver and proponent of the Rococo in England. His work, *A New Book of Ornaments with Twelve Leaves*, was published with Henry Copeland in 1752 and presented Rococo designs of girandoles (elaborately ornamented wall-hung mirror frames, often with candleholders), some of which included Chinese motifs.

THE ALLURE OF THE ORIENT
A travel book had been published in 1735 that had rekindled European interest in China. Europe's fascination with chinoiserie had endured since the end of the previous century, and upon the rejection of yet another overly ornate style, its simple grace once again beckoned. The 1757 publication of Sir William Chambers' *Designs for Chinese Buildings and Furniture* kept the interest alive. The mysterious allure and exotic nature of the Orient were in keeping with the Rococo in an unusual way. Chinese design elements were admired in part because they were fanciful and wholly foreign to the English. They evoked images of strange places where the people, architecture and landscape seemed unworldly.

The proponents of chinoiserie, most of whom had never left Europe, took their own liberties with Oriental decoration and offered fanciful interpretations of Chinese design. Rococo ornament had no connection with Chinese motifs, but it appealed to the same kind of fascination with fantastic designs. There were no rules as to symmetry, balance or stability, and the most interesting Rococo designs were the most fanciful. Both styles broke all the existing rules, and neither was confined to a

According to the present prevailing whim, everything is Chinese, or in the Chinese taste; or, as it is sometimes more modestly expressed, *partly after the Chinese manner.* Chairs, tables, chimney-pieces, frames for looking-glasses, and even our most vulgar utensils are all reduced to this new-fangled standard; and without doors it has spread, that every gate to a cow-yard is in Ts and Zs, and every hovel for the cows has bells hanging at the corners." (From *The World*, London, 1753)

new set of rules. The imaginative nature of Rococo and chinoiserie could be combined to represent scenery that came from pure fantasy, and the stranger it was, the better.

GOTHIC REVIVAL

Another style that emerged at mid-century was a Gothic "revival." It was championed by the author Horace Walpole (1717–1797), who furnished his entire home in the Gothic style. Walpole had a small following that was committed to introducing Gothic elements in architecture and furnishings. Their interest in the Gothic was spurred by Batty and Thomas Langley's *Ancient Architecture* of 1742. As was the case with Rococo and Chinese designs, the adherence to actual Gothic designs was loose at best. Designers in the Gothic style borrowed pointed arches, trefoils, cinquefoils, tracery and cluster columns and worked them into existing forms wherever they would have the most dramatic effect. Some of the most fashionable houses would later have a

"Gothick" room, but the trend never grew much beyond its cult status. As with the other trends of the period, it was a fanciful interpretation based on exotic imagery. Like the Rococo and Chinese designs, it evoked an intriguing mood that was far removed from the designs of classical antiquity. The movement did lead to the literary form of the Gothic novel, replete with all the pointed arches and dungeons Gothic enthusiasts had failed to introduce into English manor houses.

Thomas Chippendale

Thomas Chippendale (1718–1779) is credited with having combined French style, Rococo ornament, Chinese design and the passing interest in the Gothic into a furniture design book that captured the imagination of anyone interested in the latest fashionable styles. That book was *The Gentleman and Cabinet-Maker's Director*, published in April 1754. The *Director* ushered in a new era in furniture design and forever changed the way furniture designs evolved and were disseminated.

THE LIFE OF CHIPPENDALE

Little is known of Thomas Chippendale before the publication of the *Director*, but what is known is quite telling. He was born into a family of joiners in the Yorkshire town of Otley in 1718. The next record of Chippendale does not appear until 1747; it is an entry in an account book noting that Chippendale had been paid by the Earl of Burlington, presumably for supplying furniture for one the Earl's mansions. Tradition has Chippendale working at other manor houses (Nostell Priory and Harewood House), and by 1748 he was in business in London. Over the next six years he moved his business four times, on each occasion to a more fashionable location, eventually occupying three houses in St. Martin's Lane. There he was in partnership with James Rannie, an established cabinetmaker and upholsterer. Chippendale's shop was directly across from Old Slaughter's Coffee House, a favorite gathering spot for enthusiasts of the new Rococo style, and very near St. Martin's Lane Academy, where prominent artists

including William Hogarth taught. Chippendale was well positioned for the publication of the *Director* in early 1754. Since having been established in London, the firm had grown continually and is known to have employed at least 22 workmen by 1755.

Thomas Chippendale's meteoric rise to prominence and his many moves to more prestigious locations demonstrate his intention to evaluate the needs of the market and position his firm to provide for them. His location in St. Martin's Lane, at the heart of the developing styles, was valued at ten times that of his first London address only six years earlier. The move to St. Martin's Lane and the publication of the *Director* were each large undertakings, yet they were done simultaneously. Although virtually nothing is known of his schooling or early years in the trade, his rapid rise to success, his demonstrated business acumen and his ability to work for and with demanding aristocratic patrons all indicate that he was a man with unusually adroit entrepreneurial skills and an extraordinary personality.

The publication of *The Director* helped make Thomas Chippendale the best-known cabinetmaker of the era, and he has acquired a legendary (and usually over-romanticized) status as a result.
(FROM THE BOOK OF KNOWLEDGE, *1933)*

THE

GENTLEMAN and CABINET-MAKER's

D I R E C T O R :

Being a large COLLECTION of the

Moſt ELEGANT and USEFUL DESIGNS

O F

HOUSEHOLD FURNITURE,

In the Moſt FASHIONABLE TASTE.

Including a great VARIETY of

CHAIRS, SOFAS, BEDS, and COUCHES; CHINA-TABLES, DRESSING-TABLES, SHAVING-TABLES, BASON-STANDS, and TEAKETTLE-STANDS; FRAMES for MARBLE-SLABS, BUREAU-DRESSING-TABLES, and COMMODES; WRITING-TABLES, and LIBRARY-TABLES; LIBRARY-BOOK-CASES, ORGAN-CASES for private Rooms, or Churches, DESKS, and BOOK-CASES; DRESSING and WRITING-TABLES with BOOK-CASES, TOILETS, CABINETS, and CLOATHS-PRESSES; CHINA-CASES, CHINA-SHELVES, and BOOK-SHELVES; CANDLE-STANDS, TERMS for BUSTS, STANDS for CHINA JARS, and PEDESTALS; CISTERNS for WATER, LANTHORNS, and CHANDELIERS; FIRE-SCREENS, BRACKETS, and CLOCK-CASES; PIER-GLASSES, and TABLE-FRAMES; GIRANDOLES, CHIMNEY-PIECES, and PICTURE-FRAMES; STOVE-GRATES, BOARDERS, FRETS, CHINESE-RAILING, and BRASS-WORK, for Furniture.

AND OTHER

O R N A M E N T S.

TO WHICH IS PREFIXED,

A Short EXPLANATION of the Five ORDERS of ARCHITECTURE;

WITH

Proper DIRECTIONS for executing the moſt difficult Pieces, the Mouldings being exhibited at large, and the Dimenſions of each DESIGN ſpecified.

The Whole comprehended in Two HUNDRED COPPER-PLATES, neatly engraved.

Calculated to improve and refine the preſent TASTE, and ſuited to the Fancy and Circumſtances of Perſons in all Degrees of Life.

By THOMAS CHIPPENDALE,

CABINET-MAKER and UPHOLSTERER, in St. Martin's Lane, London.

THE THIRD EDITION.

L O N D O N :

Printed for the AUTHOR, and ſold at his Houſe, in St. Martin's Lane; Alſo by T. BECKET and P. A. DE HONDT, in the Strand.

MDCCLXII.

TITLE PAGE OF *THE GENTLEMAN AND CABINET-MAKER'S DIRECTOR*, 3RD ED. (LONDON, 1762).
The first edition of Chippendale's *Director* contained 160 plates illustrating a wide variety of furniture. A second edition was published the following year. A third edition consisting of 200 plates, the title page of which is shown here, was issued between 1759 and 1762 in weekly installments and finally as a complete volume.
(COURTESY DOVER PUBLICATIONS)

Chippendale's skills are legendary, but although there are many pieces that have been traced to the firm, there are none that are authenticated to him personally. He was, however, unusually adept at gathering talent around him, and effectively marketing the exceptional skills of his firm in furnishing the interiors of the grand houses of the day, whole rooms at a time.

THE *DIRECTOR*

The publication of *The Gentleman and Cabinet-Maker's Director* of 1754 was Chippendale's most important contribution to furniture design, but it was important for more than the designs it contained. Previous to the *Director*, architectural guide books proliferated, and they sometimes touched on the design of furniture, especially when it was designed to complement the buildings. The *Director* was the first guide of its kind to acknowledge the importance of furniture design as a field in itself.

The *Director*, as the first in a long series of furniture-design books (see Appendix II on pp. 294-295), also served to popularize furniture design. A century earlier, furniture styles had their development and evolution within the court and among its selected artisans. Then as the nobility took a greater interest in their houses and furnishings, they increasingly turned to outside craftsmen. Commercial cabinet-making proliferated, but its direction had to filter down from court designs. The revolutionary idea of publishing designs put the latest and most desirable styles into the hands of anyone who wanted to buy them. The local artisans in outlying areas were now as aware of the latest trends as those in St. Martin's Lane. The styles no longer spread by word of mouth, sketch or memory, so they were not subject to changes and influences in their dissemination. From then on, pieces were built more as their original designers envisioned them.

Chippendale's book also served to move the authority in furniture design from the Crown to the cabinetmakers. Styles were now presented by the leading designers and makers of the day, and the success of each was determined by the market rather than

DESIGNS FOR TWO CHAIRS, DETAILS OF PLATES XXI AND XI, CHIPPENDALE'S *DIRECTOR* (LONDON, 1754).
Chippendale's Rococo designs were based on French (left) and prevailing Georgian (right) forms with the addition of Rococo ornament. The Georgian forms, with their distinctly anglicized version of the Rococo, found wide American acceptance.
(COURTESY DOVER PUBLICATIONS)

Chippendale's designs

Chippendale's Rococo designs, which he called French or Modern, have their basis in form in French and English furniture (see the illustrations at left). Those with smooth flowing lines are based on French Louis XV designs. Others with more rectilinear shapes are based on established English designs of the Early Georgian era. During the later part of the Early Georgian period, many of the English designs had started to show an increased delicacy and lightness. Chippendale continued the Early Georgian forms, adopted the French forms, and integrated into both a suitable amount of Rococo ornament to make them stylish. The result was a distinctly anglicized Rococo with varying degrees of adherence to the original French movement.

Chippendale's Chinese furniture imposed geometric Chinese fretwork and motifs on rectilinear European pieces (see the illustration below). The designs included a number of obvious Chinese elements, such as pagoda-shaped roofs and depictions of fanciful Oriental scenes, but

by the whims of the court. Being in more of a free market, furniture designs became subject to refinement through comparison and competition. The *Director* was also important for the way it presented a thorough overview of the styles. Previous furniture publications had been little more than pamphlets and were limited in their scope. The new designs were shown applied to a wide variety of furniture forms, and the *Director* gave the entire line a better sense of unity than some earlier styles.

Often an effort to please everyone satisfies no one, but such was not the case with the *Director*. Chippendale included something for everyone, and in a market looking for direction, his work was well received and history has proven him successful. The *Director* was the only authoritative work on the three new styles (Rococo, Chinese and Gothic), and it allowed cabinetmakers who were out of the mainstream of design to be immediately in the vanguard. For want of a definitive explanation of the new styles, Chippendale's renderings became the standard.

DESIGN FOR A CHINA CASE, DETAIL OF PLATE CXXXII, CHIPPENDALE'S *DIRECTOR* (LONDON, 1754).
Chippendale's design for a china case in the Chinese style imposed Oriental ornament on rectilinear forms.
(COURTESY DOVER PUBLICATIONS)

bore no resemblance to actual Chinese furniture. It was, however, new, different and mildly exotic, and fulfilled the English appetite for Chinese designs.

The Gothic designs are much the same, but with the Gothic lexicon of pointed arches, trefoils and cinquefoils standing in for all the Chinese design elements (see the illustration above). They too were fanciful, completely nonacademic, and bore little likeness to actual medieval furniture, but like the Chinese furniture they evoked the feeling of a distant time and place. Interestingly, few of the Chinese or Gothic designs escaped having at least some French Rococo ornamentation added.

The nature of the ornament had a strong bearing on the form of Chippendale pieces. Chippendale's Chinese ornament was mostly geometric fretwork, and the Gothic elements were all derived from architecture. Both types of ornament required straight, rectilinear forms. Neither type could be worked into the English cabriole leg, so simple straight legs were adopted. For example, a Chippendale Chinese chair would have a straight square leg with a fretwork pattern cut into its length, and the same straight leg could have a Gothic fretwork motif or be carved to a straight bundled column shape. In either case, a strong geometric style of furniture form had arisen as a response to the need for using this type of ornament. Its rectilinear forms are in sharp contrast to the curvaceous lines of the French designs. Rococo ornament was perfectly suited for the French designs, and it was easily adapted to the English Georgian designs that had carried over. Thus the Chippendale style included two completely different kinds of forms, but that is just one of the peculiar contrasts that characterize the era.

Mahogany was the wood of choice at this time. It was a good medium for carving, and could be finished to the desired level of richness. The leading makers of the day, Chippendale's firm and others, went well beyond lustrously finished mahogany. Many of the Chippendale designs, such as girandoles, were intended to be gilded. Side tables and sets of chairs for the grandest houses very often received the same treatment. The Rococo color scheme called for pastel colors with gilt ornament, so it was not uncommon to find pieces in pale blue or yellow. Chinese designs were often painted in bolder colors; deeper blues and bright reds were in keeping with Chinese lacquerwork.

Chippendale's firm was one of many that was catering to the new tastes, and many of his competitors were also in St. Martin's Lane. William Vile and his partner John Cobb operated from 72 St. Martin's Lane. Vile was a cabinetmaker to the king, and his pieces are generally regarded as being of superior design and more skillful execution than most. William Hallet was situated next door to Vile, and his pieces were considered to be the most fashionable at the time. In addition, there were the well-established cabinetmakers, such as Benjamin Goodison, William Bradshaw and Giles Grendey, among others, who had been masters of the Early Georgian period, and who also worked in the new styles. Chippendale was one of many, but the success of the *Director* ensured that his name would forever be associated with the style.

The Chippendale Style in America

American design trends had always run a decade or more behind those of London, but the *Director* and the similar books that it inspired enabled the latest English designs to reach America without the usual delay. While the Americans were still exploring the possibilities of the Queen Anne style, most notably those that included Georgian architectural elements, the English had moved into the mid-Georgian phase of anglicized French forms with increasing amounts of Rococo ornament. This movement had started in England in the 1740s, a decade before the *Director* was published, but it did not have time to establish itself in America before Chippendale's book arrived. In England, the *Director* was a summation of the trends

CHIPPENDALE AND THE LAW

French furniture was considered prestigious, and English cabinetmakers frequently imported it. To avoid import duties, they would often disassemble it in France and ship it in as "lumber." The alternative was to undervalue the items being imported. In 1768, Chippendale shipped a crate of five dozen chairs across the Channel, and listed their value at £18. The customs officers were suspicious and impounded the chairs. In cases like these, the customs service purchased the impounded items for 10% over their declared value, paid the duties, and later resold the undervalued goods at a handsome profit, which they kept.

Other cabinetmakers, including John Cobb of 72 St. Martin's Lane, had brushes with the law for moving things in and out of the country in diplomatic bags. Customs officials made occasional raids on cabinet-makers' shops to find illegally imported goods, and in the 1770s Chippendale was found to have a large quantity of Indian chintz. Its importation had been made illegal to protect English manufacturers. The chintz actually belonged to a client, for whom Chippendale was making an "Oriental" bedroom, but she blamed him for its seizure and took the opportunity to criticize everything the firm had done for her over the previous six years.

of the day, presented in a clear and concise manner, but in America, the designs were quite new. Like previous trends, it was accepted in varying degrees throughout the colonies.

The Chippendale style offered the opulence that the upper echelon of the American market wanted. Their homes were becoming increasingly palatial, and they were accustomed to having the most fashionable clothing, rich European and Oriental textiles, delicate Chinese porcelain and sparkling silver and glassware. The majestic appearance of the new furniture, intricately carved in rich mahogany and finished to a glossy luster, fit perfectly in their world.

The *Director* sold well in Philadelphia, where the growth rate was so fantastically high and the inhabitants were eager to adopt some definitive English styles. New York was also a good market for the book. Boston sales were disappointing, however. The city's growth rate was flat, and cabinetmakers there had traditionally opted to include new features into existing designs rather than taking up whole new ones. Furthermore, the ornamentation shown in the *Director* was not in keeping with the restrained tastes of most New Englanders. Sales in Newport were low, since the leading cabinetmakers were pursuing their own evolution of design, but they did incorporate much of the Chippendale style in their work over the next three decades.

As reflected in the sales of the *Director*, the Chippendale period marked the greatest point of divergence in style between New England and Philadelphia. In general, American tastes rejected most of the French designs, those of curvilinear shape inspired by the Louis XV style. Americans were already familiar with the forms and construction of the Georgian designs, and these became the basis for American Chippendale furniture. Philadelphia, with its growing wealth and influx of English immigrants, eagerly accepted the ornamental aspects of the Rococo. Philadelphia pieces embodied the strength and presence of the period and are noted for exceptionally well-rendered carvings, equaling those of London in their

design and execution. Philadelphia cabinetmaking shops, like those of Thomas Tufft (c.1738–1788), Thomas Affleck (1740–1795), William Savery (1720–1787) and Benjamin Randolph (1721–1791), supplied a wealthy clientele with furniture in the full spirit of the Chippendale designs. New York furniture followed the same trend, though not to the same level of ornament as Philadelphia.

The leading Boston cabinetmakers, Benjamin Frothingham Sr. (1708–1765), Benjamin Frothingham Jr. (1734–1809) and George Bright (1726–1805), worked in a more restrained style. Their work put an emphasis on strong stature with less reliance on Rococo carved ornament. Philadelphia-trained Eliphalet Chapin (1741–1807), working in East Windsor, Connecticut, combined Philadelphia proportion and technique with the New England taste for restrained ornament in the tradition of independent Connecticut cabinetmakers. Newport cabinetmakers John Goddard (1723–1785) and John Townsend (1733–1809) continued a style unique to Newport that paralleled the period's precepts of stately furniture.

The Chinese aspects of the Chippendale style were of great interest to the Americans. Not only was there an ongoing merchant trade with the Orient, but the simple geometry of the designs also appealed to them for the same reasons that the French designs did not. The designs were pure and elegant in their simplicity and conveyed just enough of an exotic nature to make them interesting, but not foreign. The Gothic style, which had a small following in England, was of little interest to the Americans.

As interpreted by the Americans, the Chippendale designs retained most of the forms of the previous era, but with a more stout and solid set of proportions. The light and ethereal qualities of American Queen Anne evolved to have a more robust and massive appearance, more like the English Georgian style. Rococo ornament was applied, but rarely to the extent that it was in London. Graceful curves with smooth surfaces and only occasional carving became rich surfaces resplendent with ornate carving. Beauty of line was supplanted by the intricacy of ornament. The ethereal became stately, and restraint was abandoned for presence.

The mid-Georgian style of American case pieces meant that their cases were taller and their legs were correspondingly shorter and stouter. Chair designs were patterned after the Georgian Chippendale forms but with a more restrained use of ornament. The simplicity of the Chinese Chippendale chair form was appreciated by the Americans who adopted the form without the Chinese decoration in many cases. Very often, only proportion and a few decorative details separate one era from another in American furniture. A slant-top desk, for instance, built in 1770 may differ only in its more stately proportions from one built 20 years previously. Similarly, a drop-leaf table built during the American Chippendale era may differ from an earlier one only by the substitution of ball and claw feet and a simplified apron for pad feet and a scrolled apron.

BALL AND CLAW FEET

In England, ball and claw feet were used in the Queen Anne and Early Georgian styles, spanning the period from about 1710 to the 1740s, peaking in popularity in the 1720s. They faded from fashion in the 1740s as interest grew in the French Rococo style with its scroll or whorl feet. Ball and claw feet were gaining acceptance in America as they were falling out of favor in England and were first seen in Boston furniture in the 1730s. Their use peaked simultaneously with the Chippendale style and became an integral part of the American interpretation. Ball and claw feet were not illustrated in the *Director*, yet they were perfectly in keeping with Chippendale-era ideals of grandeur, powerful presence and richly carved detail.

The ball and claw motif was of Chinese origin, exemplifying the balance between the opposing forces of good and evil as represented by a dragon's claw clutching a pearl. The pearl, a perfect sphere representing purity, wisdom and truth, is guarded by the dragon from the forces of

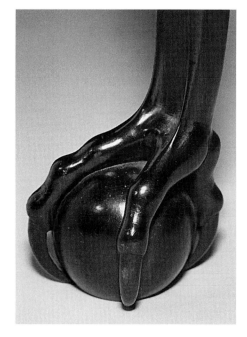

Ball and claw feet were first seen on American pieces during the 1730s and remained in style through the 1770s, their peak of use coinciding with the American Chippendale period. This example of an open-talon ball and claw foot is by John Goddard of Newport.
(COURTESY RHODE ISLAND HISTORICAL SOCIETY)

evil. The symbolism appealed to Western interest in order, balance and symmetry growing from Enlightenment ideals and exemplified by the William and Mary designs. The ball and claw had been seen in Chinese porcelain imported to Europe in the 16th and 17th centuries and is known to have been adopted for use by London silversmiths as early as 1581. The claws that appear on furniture in both England and America closely resemble the raptorial feet of birds of prey, such as eagles, hawks and falcons. (The term "eagles foot" is commonly used to describe these feet in mid-century Boston inventories.) Given the scarcity of dragons, there is no doubt that the claws were modeled after these familiar birds. A related foot, the hairy paw, derives from similar mythology. These feet are inspired by lions' paws and are sometimes depicted in statuary with the sphere as a powerful protector of integrity.

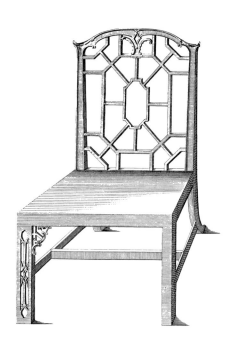

(LEFT) DESIGN FOR A CHINESE CHAIR, DETAIL OF PLATE XXVII, CHIPPENDALE'S *DIRECTOR* (LONDON 1754).
(RIGHT) SIDE CHAIR, PORTSMOUTH, NEW HAMPSHIRE, 1760–1790.
The simplicity and rectilinear lines of Chippendale's Chinese designs were inspirational to those who rejected the French forms and the ornate character of Rococo decoration.
(LEFT: COURTESY DOVER PUBLICATIONS; RIGHT: COURTESY THE SOCIETY FOR THE PRESERVATION OF NEW ENGLAND ANTIQUITIES)

American Chippendale Forms

Many of the American forms of the Chippendale era were revisions of earlier Georgian pieces, updated to the latest standards. Others were quite new in form and marked a departure rather than an evolution from earlier styles. As the society changed, some pieces found increased popularity, while others fell out of favor.

CHESTS

With stateliness being of prime importance to the ideals of the era, case pieces and chests were good forms to embody the new style. The decorative elements that marked American Chippendale case pieces tended to be designed into, rather than added on to existing forms. Queen Anne case pieces were generally of plain case construction, with the ethereal qualities of the period concentrated in long legs, delicate feet and soaring pediments. The swelled fronts of Chippendale's French designs inspired American makers to move away from straight fronts and experiment with serpentine, block-front and bombé cases, which will be examined in greater detail later (see pp. 77-79).

The curved fronts of these pieces precluded the use of overlapping drawers and necessitated the use of flush-fitting drawers with surrounding cockbeading (see the bottom photo at right). The cockbeading, a half-round astragal bead about ⅛ in. wide and protruding about ¹⁄₁₆ in., was either attached to the edges of the inset drawer or cut from the solid of the case and drawer dividers. Different regions and makers had their own preferences. Either way, the surrounding cockbead outlined the drawer and disguised the space between the drawer and the case.

Case pieces in general assumed a more solid appearance and were usually larger than their earlier counterparts. Strong ball and claw feet or solid ogee feet testified to the substantial nature of the pieces. To achieve this look of substance, the makers made the pieces look powerful rather than heavy. Less formal pieces saw the change as

CHEST OF DRAWERS, BOSTON, 1750–1780.
Case pieces, like this block-front chest of drawers, took on an air of stately presence in the Chippendale era. A rich and visually interesting surface, a solid stance and bold brasses all contribute to the effect.
(COURTESY DALLAS MUSEUM OF ART)

When curved case fronts made lipped drawers impractical, small astragal moldings called cockbeads were used to surround the drawer. The bead is either cut from the case or attached to the drawer.

HIGH CHEST OF DRAWERS, PHILADELPHIA, 1755–1790. Philadelphia cabinetmakers and their clients readily embraced Rococo ornament and followed closely the prescripts of Chippendale. *(COURTESY YALE UNIVERSITY ART GALLERY)*

HIGH CHEST OF DRAWERS, NEWPORT, 1760–1785. New England cabinetmakers adhered to the fundamental importance of form and proportion to achieve a stately appearance, with well-integrated carved detail remaining secondary in importance. *(COURTESY THE NEWPORT HISTORICAL SOCIETY)*

HIGH CHEST OF DRAWERS, EAST WINDSOR, CONNECTICUT, 1760–1790. Connecticut's Eliphalet Chapin combined the bold proportions of Philadelphia pieces with the restrained use of ornament favored in New England. *(COURTESY WADSWORTH ATHENEUM, HARTFORD)*

well, as even simple bracket feet changed from trying to belie mass to supporting it with a more forthright stance.

High chests

High chests continued much in the earlier tradition but were updated to the new style. They evolved to be wider and more massive in appearance, with less space below the bottom of the case. Their legs became shorter and more powerful. Pediment tops continued in either arched or straight shapes, but more for grandeur than loftiness. High chests did not lend themselves to shaped fronts, so they remained flat-fronted, with overlapping drawers, and relied on Rococo ornament more than other pieces.

More than any other region, Philadelphia furniture embodied the decorative aspect of the Rococo. Though still restrained by European standards, the flowing carved details on the pediment, cartouche and base are the primary decorative elements of the massively proportioned chest shown in the photo at left above.

Newport cabinetmakers maintained a reliance upon the fundamental importance of form and the secondary importance of ornament. Their designs showed little influence of the Rococo, but through bold design and well-integrated carved details they satisfied both the ideals of stately presence and their own market's tastes (center photo above).

Connecticut's Philadelphia-trained Eliphalet Chapin combined the proportions and construction techniques of Philadelphia with the New England preference for restrained ornament (photo at right above). The result was his own distinctive and original style of American Chippendale design.

Chests-on-chests

Chests-on-chests were the most massive of case pieces, having the bases of chests and the upper cases of high chests (see the photo at left on the facing page). They could be built with some of the curved-front attributes that could not be applied to high chests with long legs. They were thoroughly useful, being entirely drawers, but were not

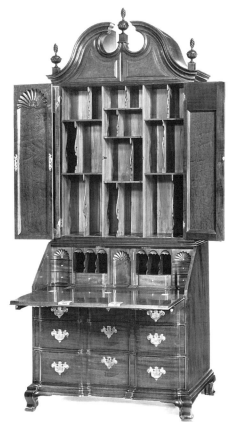

CHEST-ON-CHEST, NEWPORT, 1760–1785.
Chests-on-chests, such as this one by John Townsend, were among the most massive pieces of the era.
(COURTESY THE NEWPORT HISTORICAL SOCIETY)

DESK AND BOOKCASE, NEWPORT, 1755–1790.
Goddard or Townsend desk and bookcases went beyond their functional role to stand as milestones of achievement in design and cabinetmaking.
(COURTESY YALE UNIVERSITY ART GALLERY)

DESK AND BOOKCASE, NEWPORT, 1760–1785.
As evident in another Newport example, the interior of the desk and bookcase is equally impressive. This piece features a blocked set of small drawers in the desk and movable, shaped vertical partitions in the bookcase.
(COURTESY MUSEUM OF ART, RHODE ISLAND SCHOOL OF DESIGN)

limited to use in bedrooms. Pieces with the stature of chests-on-chests could just as easily have stood in a parlor or drawing room as a testament to the owner's refinement. Interestingly, chests-on-chests had become a popular form in England in the Early Georgian period, but none are shown in Chippendale's *Director*.

The American chest-on-frame disappeared from general use. Its function was given to either high chests or other case pieces. Although it had been both useful and popular in the first half of the century, it was not an ideal form for Chippendale grandeur, and it fell from favor among the style conscious.

Desks
Desks and desk-bookcases followed all the changes that chests underwent in entering the Chippendale period. They too were sometimes rendered in serpentine, block-front and bombé forms and went through a similar increase in stature. As the literal and figurative centers of family businesses and fortunes, they were subject to the greatest amount of aggrandizement. They also presented many opportunities for using complex details since they were so much more intricate than other pieces. The maker of a desk bookcase had the chance to incorporate the features of both chests and high chests into the base and top, and the opportunity to develop intricately detailed

interiors in both. It is little wonder that desk bookcases of the high Chippendale design are considered the apex of 18th-century American furniture making.

TABLES
The trend toward more varied forms in tables, which had started at the turn of the century, continued unabated into the Chippendale era. Even within groups of tables intended for specific purposes, such as tea tables, popular regional styles added to the diversity of designs being built. Tables related to dining, such as side tables

DRESSING TABLE, EAST WINDSOR, CONNECTICUT, C.1760–1790.
Dressing tables, like the bases of high chests, developed taller cases and correspondingly shorter legs in the era of Chippendale design. This Connecticut example is by Eliphalet Chapin.
(COURTESY CONNECTICUT HISTORICAL SOCIETY, HARTFORD)

TEA TABLE, NEWPORT, 1763.
This tea table by John Goddard exemplifies Newport cabinetmakers' interest in using shape as ornament in itself.
(COURTESY WINTERTHUR MUSEUM)

and drop-leaf tables of all sizes, proliferated in the Chippendale style as dining became an increasingly social activity.

Dressing tables

Dressing tables and high chests were very often built as matched sets, and the former followed the evolution of the high chest toward a taller case with shorter legs. Dressing tables continued to be flat fronted, with overlapping drawers, and were ornamented just like the base of high chests. The height of the case had made the dressing table more of a case piece by this point, having evolved away from the original form of a table with drawers since the start of the century.

Tea tables

Tea drinking continued to be the important social activity that it had been earlier, and the evolution of the tea table progressed. The rectangular tea table adopted more Rococo features in Philadelphia but continued with Baroque trends in northern cities. Sometimes the change was so slight that it involved substituting ball and claw feet for slipper or pad feet (see the photo at left). Two important subsets of the rectangular tea table are the China table and the turret-top table. Their importance lies in their designs more than their popularity, since neither was made in great number.

China tables are tea tables in the Chinese manner and were inspired by a plate from the *Director* (see the illustration and photo on the facing page). They have straight molded legs, a shallow apron and an inset top. Their most notable features are a pierced gallery around the top, corner fretwork brackets and decidedly Rococo cross stretchers that sweep upward to support a center finial. China tables are associated with Portsmouth, New Hampshire, and seven examples survive from there. Their regional popularity is attributed to Robert Harrold, an immigrant English cabinetmaker working in Portsmouth from 1765 to 1792, who patterned these after English examples.

(LEFT) DESIGN FOR A CHINA TABLE, DETAIL OF PLATE LI, CHIPPENDALE'S *DIRECTOR*, **3RD ED. (LONDON 1762).**
(RIGHT) CHINA TABLE, PORTSMOUTH, NEW HAMPSHIRE, 1765–1775.
China tables, with fretwork galleries and reverse curve stretchers meeting in a central finial, are a subset of tea tables that relate directly to a similar design in Chippendale's *Director*.
(LEFT: COURTESY DOVER PUBLICATIONS; RIGHT: COURTESY SMITHSONIAN INSTITUTION)

The turret-top tables, of which only six are known to exist, trace their origin to the Boston area. While they have the spark of the American Chippendale style, their predominant ornament, the repeated use of turrets, is essentially Baroque in nature. This treatment is associated with the corner turrets of the early Boston card tables, which were from English examples. Some of the turret tops have 14 turrets, while others have only 12. Only two are similar enough to have clearly been made by the same hand, and all have varying amounts of molding detail and carving. Being so unlike other designs yet so spirited and stately in their form, they are notable examples of American design capabilities.

TEA TABLE, BOSTON, 1750–1775.
This example is the most refined of the turret-top tea tables, with a small amount of Rococo carving over the knees and a top dished from a single piece of mahogany.
(COURTESY MUSEUM OF FINE ARTS, BOSTON)

TEA TABLE, PHILADELPHIA, 1760–1790. Carved ornament is masterfully incorporated in this round tea table in the pillar and claw form, but the crowning glory is the bold patter of the 'piecrust' top. The top is a single piece of mahogany, 32 in. in diameter, from which the molded edge has been carved from the solid.

(COURTESY MUSEUM OF ART, RHODE ISLAND SCHOOL OF DESIGN)

Pedestal tables

Tip-top tables, with tripod pedestal bases, had been a universally popular form, but came to their highest level of development in Philadelphia during the Chippendale years. Their legs and pedestals were carefully carved, and the legs terminated in ample ball and claw feet. One of their most sought-after attributes is a molded scalloped edge to the table top, often called a "piecrust" edge. Like all dished tops of the period, the center surface of the table was cut away to leave the edge molding. Better examples are equipped with a "bird-cage" mechanism, which allows the top to rotate on the center pedestal and tip up for storage. Since they were the focal point of Philadelphia tea service, pedestal tables were built and ornamented to the highest standards of the day. Smaller pedestal tables for occasional use and for candlestands continued in their roles.

Side tables

Side and pier tables progressed in development as homes became larger and more stylish. Side tables continued in their use as secondary serving pieces for dining rooms, with marble tops, or as hall pieces. Chippendale presented several plates of designs for slab tables in the *Director*. American side tables followed all the prevailing conventions, with an increase in carving and ball and claw feet. Their

greatest change was in adopting some of the curved-front characteristics that were seen in other pieces, and they were often made with curved or serpentine fronts and tops.

Pier tables are similar, but are intended to be more ornamental. Of all the forms of furniture, pier tables bear the closest relationship to the development of architecture, as they were often situated in front of the piers between large windows (hence the name) or as side pieces in grand rooms. When architects ventured into furniture design, as William Kent had done, they considered the design of pier tables well within their purview.

SLAB TABLE, PHILADELPHIA, 1750–1780. Side tables functioned as serving pieces or ornamental pier tables. This slab table (with marble top) is one of a pair that were made to stand in either a formal dining room or parlor.

(COURTESY MUSEUM OF ART, RHODE ISLAND SCHOOL OF DESIGN)

Card tables

Like tea tables, card tables were important social centerpieces, and their development followed similar lines. Many Philadelphia pieces continued the English form of using corner turrets integrated into cabriole legs (top photo at right), but northern makers were dropping the turrets and including more complex shapes in their aprons. Boston and Newport makers employed recessed shapes, reminiscent of blocking, and New York makers produced numerous tables with serpentine forms (bottom photo at right). One or both legs were hinged at the table frame and swung out to support the folding top. This design became the norm after some earlier experimentation with accordion-like leg-extension mechanisms. New York tables frequently had a fifth leg to swing out and support the top, which folded next to one of the rear legs when the table was closed.

Drop-leaf tables

American drop-leaf tables continued much as they had previously, but with the inclusion of ball and claw feet and stylistic improvements to the aprons. While they were made with both oval and square tops, some of the most stately examples of the style have square leaves, almost as wide as the table is high and nearly reaching the floor when they are down. Square tables could seat more people, and two could be put together to seat larger parties.

CARD TABLE, PHILADELPHIA AREA, 1760–1770. Philadelphia makers were fond of turreted front corners on their card tables, an English design that had inspired earlier Boston card tables.
(COURTESY YALE UNIVERSITY ART GALLERY)

CARD TABLE, NEW YORK, 1770–1780. New York card tables often feature serpentine fronts and a fifth fly leg to support the open top.
(COURTESY WINTERTHUR MUSEUM)

DINING TABLE, MASSACHUSETTS, 1750-1780. Drop-leaf dining tables were updated to the Chippendale era with the addition of ball and claw feet and stylistic improvements to the apron.
(COURTESY MUSEUM OF ART, RHODE ISLAND SCHOOL OF DESIGN)

**PEMBROKE TABLE,
NEWPORT, 1760–1780.**
Pembroke or breakfast
tables are small drop-
leaf tables. This example
by John Townsend is in
the Chinese style and
measures 33½ in. long.
*(COURTESY WINTERTHUR
MUSEUM)*

SEATING FURNITURE

Chippendale seating furniture fell into two types: that which was based on the Early Georgian use of cabriole legs, and that of Euro-Chinese inspiration which used straight legs. There were also differences in chair form and a further refinement of upholstered pieces during this period.

Chairs

Chippendale chairs are fundamentally different in form from the previous Queen Anne style (see the drawing below). When viewed from the side, their back legs and stiles were no longer of a reverse curved cyma shape, but were now one continuous curve, arcing from the crest rail, into the seat, and outward to form the rear leg. The splat, which had also been cyma-shaped, was now flat or gently arched with intricate pierced designs. The crest rail, previously yoke-shaped to flow smoothly into the vertical stiles, now merged with the stiles in upward and outward facing "ears." These changes were all part of the mid-Georgian design changes that preceded Chippendale's influence but arrived in America with the *Director* and other books. As evidenced in the *Director*, mid-Georgian chairs with cabriole legs were built without stretchers, but straight and simple

Pembroke tables

The term "Pembroke" refers to a small table with drop leaves about 3 ft. across when open; it is particularly descriptive of a family of small drop-leaf tables of the Chippendale period that developed at mid-century. They were the continuation of what had been called the breakfast tables of the Queen Anne period, but they generally had a square top, often with a drawer at one end, cross stretchers between straight legs, and hinged supports on the table frame to hold the extended leaves. Chippendale illustrated similar tables in both Chinese and French styles, which undoubtedly influenced the Americans. The earlier style of breakfast table, differentiated by swinging legs to support the leaves, continued with the inclusion of ball and claw feet and updated details.

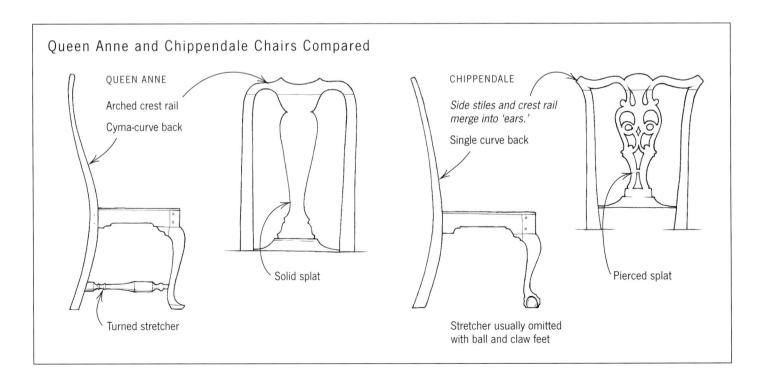

Queen Anne and Chippendale Chairs Compared

QUEEN ANNE

Arched crest rail

Cyma-curve back

Solid splat

Turned stretcher

CHIPPENDALE

Side stiles and crest rail merge into 'ears.'

Single curve back

Pierced splat

Stretcher usually omitted with ball and claw feet

SIDE CHAIR, NEWPORT, 1765–1790.
Rectilinear chairs, showing the influence of
Chippendale's Chinese designs and usually made with
simple stretchers, are an important subset of American
Chippendale design. The form was extended to include
easy chairs and sofas with straight legs and stretchers.
*(COURTESY THE SOCIETY FOR THE PRESERVATION OF NEW
ENGLAND ANTIQUITIES)*

SIDE CHAIR, PHILADELPHIA, 1760–1780.
The Gothic element of Chippendale's designs made
little impact in America, but its influence can be seen
in some chair backs that feature interlaced pointed
arches, as in this example by Thomas Tufft.
(COURTESY WINTERTHUR MUSEUM)

SIDE CHAIR, PHILADELPHIA, 1755–1780.
Philadelphia chairs exhibit the closest adherence to
London designs in both form and ornament. The
proportions of this chair are close to those of English
examples of the period.
(COURTESY MUSEUM OF ART, RHODE ISLAND SCHOOL OF DESIGN)

stretchers were specified on those of
Chinese inspiration. That convention was
continued in American pieces (see the
photo at left above).

The prominent design element in
Chippendale chairs is the chair back. The
crest rail and splat design flow together as
an integral unit, and their designs can often
be traced directly to the designs of
Chippendale or Robert Manwaring, who
published *The Cabinet and Chair-Maker's
Real Friend and Companion* in 1765. The
scrolled splat shapes are usually of a Rococo
design, but interlaced pointed arches are
Gothic in nature, and are perhaps the only
significant influence the Gothic style had
on American pieces (center photo above).
The elaborate nature of the carved detail on
Chippendale chairs varies regionally, with
Philadelphia pieces showing the most
carving and the closest adherence to the
London designs (photo at right above).

EASY CHAIR, BOSTON, 1760–1790.
Chippendale easy chairs changed little from their
earlier Queen Anne counterparts, with the exception of
decorative details like ball and claw feet and carved
knees. New York and Philadelphia easy chairs were
often built without stretchers.
(COURTESY THE METROPOLITAN MUSEUM OF ART)

Easy chairs

Although there are examples of easy chairs
in the curvaceous French style, most
American makers applied the new design
elements to existing forms. This usually
meant giving the piece a more majestic look
by including ball and claw feet and
updating the shape to include a serpentine
back. Stylistically, easy chairs remained very
similar to the earlier style. The ample and
relaxed posture of the Queen Anne chairs
needed only cosmetic changes to fit the
Chippendale ideals. Furthermore, the
nature of the piece was influenced by the
upholstery material as much as by its
design, and upholstering an easy chair in a
rich damask accomplished as much for its
character as any redesign.

SOFA, PHILADELPHIA, 1765–1780.
The shapes of the period's sofas show less restraint than earlier versions. This example has the straight molded legs and stretchers deriving from the Chinese aspect of the Chippendale designs.
(COURTESY WINTERTHUR MUSEUM)

Sofas

Upholstered sofas reached a stylistic peak during the Chippendale era, and the most spectacular came from Philadelphia. They went quite beyond Chippendale's inspiration to become sculptural works in their own right. American designers used serpentine fronts and backs and sweeping arm rolls to build an elegant form on which to display vast stretches of the finest imported fabrics. Some have ball and claw feet on cabriole legs, and others have straight molded legs with or without square block feet called Marlborough legs. Sofas were still very expensive, but those who could afford them wanted to be sure they would be the focal point of any room. By the Chippendale era, couches, or day beds, had fallen out of fashion in favor of more luxurious upholstered pieces.

TALL-POST BEDSTEAD, PROBABLY MASSACHUSETTS, 1760–1790.
Most of the designs for beds in the *Director* have Marlborough legs, but Americans, still fond of ball and claw feet half a century after they had peaked in England, used them into the fourth quarter of the century.
(COURTESY COLONIAL WILLIAMSBURG FOUNDATION)

BEDSTEADS

Bedsteads became the subject of renewed interest during the Chippendale era. As homes became larger and their furnishings more extensive, bedrooms became more than just places to sleep. In the more elegant homes of the period, one would read, write or take tea or breakfast in one's room, and the bedstead accordingly became more stylish and less utilitarian.

Chippendale illustrated a number of bedposts in the *Director* that were inspirational to American makers in their quest for suitable designs. Tall-post beds with luxurious hangings were the style of the day. Most of Chippendale's designs had Marlborough legs, which saw wide acceptance through the second half of the century. Ball and claw feet on stout cabriole legs were also made in America, but they did not enjoy the lasting popularity of Marlborough legs.

DESIGN FOR A DOME BED, DETAIL OF PLATE XLIII, CHIPPENDALE'S *DIRECTOR* (LONDON, 1754). Chippendale's designs for beds were far too elaborate for American tastes, but they show the importance of the bed and its hangings during the period.
(COURTESY DOVER PUBLICATIONS)

Chippendale illustrated 15 elaborately canopied beds, indicating the importance that the bed and its hangings had at the time. His more flamboyant designs have carved and gilded cornices supported by the pillars, or posts, and for one plate he notes that the legs are not intended to be covered. He also notes that the hangings may be tied up like a drapery or drawn across on a rod, and one design mentions pulleys to hoist up the hangings. It was clear that according to the tastes of London, the bed was to be throne-like in its majesty and to be the cabinetmaker and upholsterer's joint *tour de force*.

Chippendale Structure

American Chippendale structure was a continuation of that of the Queen Anne designs. Apart from their proportions and ornamentation, the forms were nearly identical and the methods of construction

carried from one style into the next. There were the inevitable improvements in joinery, such as finer and more delicate dovetails, and greater precision in joints to ensure strength in delicate members. There had also evolved improved methods of attaching feet and tops, which, while not major structural changes, better allowed for the expansion and contraction of wood without sacrificing strength. These improvements were simply the natural progress of refinement in the newly developed methods of dovetail-based construction methods.

Decorative Elements

Aside from the decorative elements of carving, which accounted for the majority of the ornament on Chippendale-era pieces, more sublime elements were designed into

the form of these pieces. Of particular note are the curved-front treatments arising from the French influence, some of which were illustrated in the *Director*. These treatments include the serpentine front, the block front and the bombé shape, all of which emphasize the substance of the piece.

SERPENTINE FRONTS

Serpentine chests have a double-reverse curve-front profile, convex in the center and concave at either side (see the photo below). The style is thoroughly French, having come from commode-bureaus as illustrated in the *Director*. There were limits to what could be done to stylize a chest of drawers, and making a serpentine front was a relatively simple way to give the piece the impact that was associated with the era. Higher-style examples included a carved

CHEST OF DRAWERS, MASSACHUSETTS, 1760–1790. Serpentine case fronts added visual impact to pieces that were boxlike and otherwise difficult to ornament.
(COURTESY COLONIAL WILLIAMSBURG FOUNDATION)

vertical panel or pilaster at the outer edges of the case, set at a 45° angle to the front and sides. This design, too, was from French examples, and it extended ornament to the sides of the chest. The angled-corner shape was carried through to the top and down through the base and feet as well. Other American pieces have a reverse serpentine shape, where the center is concave and either side is convex. In both cases, American makers cut the serpentine drawer fronts from solid wood, and they cut a corresponding shape on the inside to give drawer fronts a uniform thickness.

BLOCK FRONTS

Block-front designs differ from serpentine fronts in that their shaping is not a continuous flowing curve. On a typical block-front piece, the front is divided into three vertical panels, with the center area depressed and the outer two panels raised

BUREAU-TABLE, NEWPORT, 1785–1790.
This piece by John Townsend exemplifies the Newport cabinetmakers' integration of the block front with both form and ornament.
(COURTESY YALE UNIVERSITY ART GALLERY)

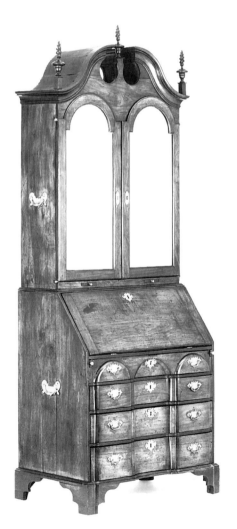

DESK AND BOOKCASE, BOSTON, 1738.
The Job Coit desk and bookcase is the earliest dated piece of block-front furniture.
(COURTESY WINTERTHUR MUSEUM)

about ½ in. or ¾ in. The earliest dated example of American block-front furniture is the Job Coit desk and bookcase, made in Boston and dated 1738 (see the photo at left). It is thought to have derived from English and perhaps earlier Dutch or German designs, since there are no clear parallels in French pieces. The design has no basis in the Rococo and in fact has a distinctly Baroque flavor. This first American example predates the *Director* by 16 years, making block fronts, like ball and

claw feet, coincidental but important aspects of the American style. In the Coit piece, the blocking ends in half-round shapes on the upper drawer, but extends down onto geometric bracket feet.

Block fronts were used on desks and chests all along the coast from Portsmouth to New York, but no one developed the style as highly as did the cabinetmakers of Newport. The Goddards and Townsends worked sophisticated curved-ray shells (see pp. 164-166) into the upper terminus of the blocking and carried it downward through ogee feet to end in tiny scrolled volutes. Their refinement of the style gave it a permanent place of prominence in furniture history, and their style was emulated in other cities. Newport cabinetmakers, however, had an unsurpassed mastery of the style, which they applied to desks, desk bookcases, chests and bureau-tables or kneehole desks. Like serpentine-front drawers, block-front drawers are cut from the solid. The exception is the convex shells, which were usually carved separately and applied. Skilled makers would carve them from the next board in sequence so the grain and patterning would match the drawer front exactly.

BOMBÉ CASES

The third decorative shape is the bombé family of furniture. *Bombé* is French for "bulged" or "swelled" and refers to the chests, desks and desk bookcases that have the pear-shaped bulging lower sides and fronts. The most arresting examples combine the bombé shape with a serpentine front to yield fronts that curve in all directions.

The earliest dated American bombé piece was built in 1753 by Benjamin Frothingham Sr. of Boston, predating the *Director* by one year. The style had come to London from France, and at least one piece from London was known to have been imported to Boston. The style remained unique to the Boston and North Shore area and was still fashionable well into the 1780s, some two decades after passing out of style in London. The French shape as recorded by Chippendale was more of an inverted pear shape, with the greatest bulge at the top of the case, just the inverse of the shape that was popular in Boston. The lower bulge was an English adaptation, since no trace of it is to be found on the European mainland. American makers shaped the curved sides and drawer fronts from the solid. In Europe, where thick cabinet-grade wood was scarce, the curves were built up from pieces of secondary wood, shaped and veneered over.

All three of these front profiles seem to have been ornate enough for the American taste without undue carving or extra ornamentation. As a result, American examples with these shapes are remarkably restrained in their ornament. Where it does occur, it is worked into the design of the

CHEST OF DRAWERS, BOSTON AREA, 1760–1785.
The bombé form was in vogue in Boston from 1753 into the 1780s. The curved sides are shaped from the solid. In combination with a serpentine front, the visual effect is arresting.
(COURTESY MUSEUM OF ART, RHODE ISLAND SCHOOL OF DESIGN)

piece, as are the Newport curved-ray shells, rather than added as an afterthought. The Americans were aware that excessive ornament on such powerful forms ran the risk of appearing superficial and could diminish the desired stateliness of the Chippendale style.

HARDWARE

An important decorative element for case pieces was the use of large polished-brass pull plates and escutcheons. They were generally much larger than their Queen Anne counterparts and became an important part of the opulent look that was in demand. Sometimes the brasses were pierced for added effect, and very special pieces had imported ormolu brasses of high Rococo design. On pieces of more rural origin, where earlier styles lingered for decades, original brasses of a Chippendale character are sometimes the key in determining when the piece was built. Given the American propensity for letting one style evolve into the next, it is often the brasses that define a piece, identifying it as having been made in one era while its overall design is a continuation of earlier ones.

CHEST-ON-FRAME, CONNECTICUT RIVER VALLEY, C.1786.
Historic Deerfield's well-known Mary Hoyte chest-on-frame, with its distinctive scalloped top, has many of the attributes of a Queen Anne piece. The bold brasses, which are the full height of the top drawer, indicate a later date.
(COURTESY HISTORIC DEERFIELD)

5

Designs for the New Republic

THE FEDERAL PERIOD
(1785–1810)

The last third of the 18th century witnessed yet another remarkable change in European and American furniture design. As had happened so often before, a new style was emerging that was the antithesis of its predecessor. Throughout the century, the prevailing tastes had swung from classicism to the exotic, and ornament had changed from the restrained to the outrageous and back again several times. The latest trend was a rejection of the Rococo and a return to designs inspired by the classic art and architecture of ancient Greece and Rome. In what was later to be known as the Federal period, the Neoclassical influence of Greek and Roman design came to bear on furniture design as it had in the government of the new republic.

The sparse orderliness of Neoclassical design pervaded furniture of the Federal era and also extended to the arrangement of pieces within a room. This plate from Hepplewhite's *Cabinet-Maker and Upholsterer's Guide* of 1788 shows a suggested arrangement and illustrates the integration of furniture with the room architecture.

(COURTESY DOVER PUBLICATIONS)

The Neoclassical Style

Most of the renewed interest in the classical style was in response to the excavations of Herculaneum and Pompeii, which had started in 1738. During the 1750s and 1760s, many illustrated books appeared on ancient art and artifacts. Rome became a mecca for archeologists and scholars as well as for designers and architects who appreciated the purity of classic design and saw it as an antidote to the excesses of the Rococo. There was also a certain romanticism attached to the classic designs. They were a reflection of what was imagined to be a perfect and well-ordered world, where the works of artisans and architects were exalted and exuded the refined simplicity of a harmonious society. At the same time, classic designs appealed to the European fascination with the exotic, just as did the Chinese, Gothic and Rococo styles.

The renewed interest in the classics first manifested itself in the collecting of art and antiques. The English and European aristocracy collected and displayed ancient artifacts along with paintings and artwork in their grand houses. The Grand Tour of the cities of Europe, including Rome, was still part of the cultural development of the young elite.

ROBERT ADAM

The one person who was most responsible for introducing the Neoclassical taste to England was the architect Robert Adam (1728–1792). Like most inspired young designers, he went to Italy in his mid-twenties. There he visited the ruins of the Palace of Diocletian, and produced drawings of the palace in its original condition. He took exception to the Palladian trends in interior design for having been adapted from exterior architectural details of Roman temples. Murals that had been unearthed in the excavations revealed to Adam what he considered to be the true forms of classical domestic interior decoration, which he described as "all delicacy, gaiety, grace and beauty."

When Adam returned to London in 1758, his firsthand knowledge of the classic forms made him a rising star among architects. At this time, interest in the Rococo was beginning to wane, and Neoclassical trends were emerging as the newest fashion. In 1773, Adam and his brother and partner James began to issue a series of engravings depicting some of their many designs for buildings and furniture. This folio was entitled *Works in Architecture*, and it firmly established the Adam brothers as the authoritative voice on Neoclassical design and ornament. As Chippendale's book had done, *Works in Architecture* helped spread the popularity of the new style.

The Adam style brought new forms of furniture and new styles of ornament. Rococo, as practiced by the English, used Early Georgian and French-inspired furniture designs as a platform for carved

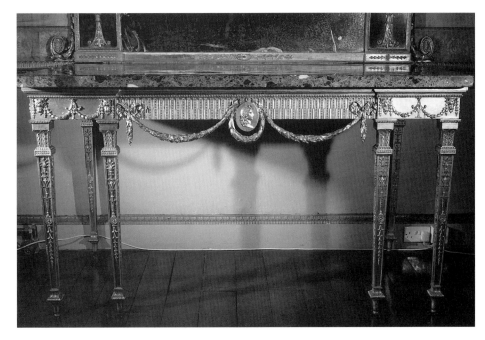

SIDE TABLE, LONDON, 1778.
This table has the delicate proportions, tapered legs and ornament in low relief of the Adam style. It was made by the Chippendale firm a year before Chippendale's death.
(COURTESY CHRISTOPHER GILBERT AND ARTLINES [UK] LTD.)

ornament. Adam was insistent on using ornament to enhance designs, not to overpower them. He realized that the beauty of design was in its lines, and that the lines were not to be obscured by decorative additions.

The Adam style

The elements of the Adam designs for furniture were clean and simple. Cabriole legs were generally replaced by slender, straight tapered legs or straight legs that ended in plinth feet, such as Marlborough legs. The swelled shapes of case pieces were simplified to be semi-circular or semi-elliptical, and sweeping Rococo aprons were straightened to more linear shapes. Elaborate moldings were simplified and reduced in size to give them a more delicate appearance. The lift and delicacy that had once been associated with the Queen Anne style had returned in a very different form.

The Adam brothers also introduced some new elements into the lexicon of furniture ornament that had been inspired by ancient artifacts. The most notable of these was the urn shape. Urns appeared on pedestals as freestanding decorative pieces,

as part of side-table sets (as knife cases or water containers), as finials and as applied composition ornament. Ovals were also a favorite shape in the Adam style. They were used for mirror frames and chair backs and as inlaid or applied panels. Small oval or round rosettes, called *paterae,* were a common applied decorative element. The classic lyre shape also found its way into designs, usually in chair backs. Another element seen often is the *anthemion*, a string of honeysuckle buds arranged in a garland. From ancient architecture came fluted legs and friezes, and in keeping with the spirit of the style swags and festoons were added.

While carving was an important part of the Rococo style, the clean geometric lines of the Neoclassical style did not lend themselves to its use. Carving was not abandoned altogether, but its decorative use was greatly diminished. When it was employed, it was used sparingly as supplemental or applied ornament.

Marquetry became the predominant form of surface decoration. Unlike carving, it allowed the surface to be ornamented without interrupting the lines of the piece.

In order to be effective, marquetry required the use of contrasting woods, so light woods like satinwood, holly and harewood were favorites. Inlaid decoration included string inlays and cross-banded borders, and oval or round central panels with favorite Neoclassical motifs of urns and flowers. Adam's own designs for clients sometimes called for decorative porcelain panels as a central ornament, supplied by such craftsmen as Josiah Wedgwood. He also used painted panels depicting Neoclassical scenes, either in soft colors or *en grisaille*, shades of gray. These painted panels were used in both his furniture and architectural details. For these, Adam lured decorative artists from Switzerland and Italy to work in London.

Painted ornament proved to be very effective, and its use was expanded to include entirely painted pieces. Muted secondary colors were in favor, and pieces were painted to harmonize with Adam's interior treatments. He often called for painted surfaces to simulate marble and made use of *scagliola*, plasterwork made to simulate stone, in both furniture and interiors.

The shift from carving to two-dimensional decoration did not occur overnight; neither did the change from Rococo to Neoclassical design. In his first few years in London, Adam's designs for furniture were very much like the existing mid-Georgian designs of the 1760s, but with his own application of classic ornament. As his own style developed and matured and popular sentiment turned away from the Rococo, the Neoclassical elements became more pronounced. By the end of the decade the transformation was complete, and by 1775, buoyed by the acclaim that *Works in Architecture* had received, Adam had perfected his style and achieved his desired delicacy of form and restraint of ornament.

The Adam brothers' designs were remarkable in their detail, for they believed there was no part of the interior that was beyond their scope. This credo extended to designing such furnishings as lighting devices, fireplace equipment, door and

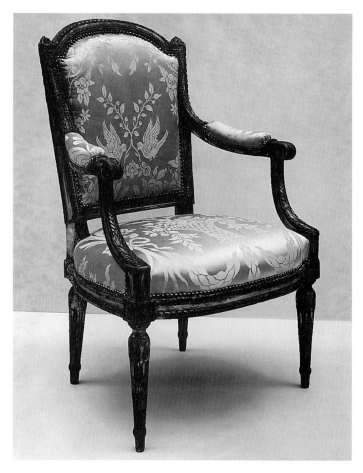

CARVED BEECHWOOD FAUTEUIL, PARIS, C.1780. The Louis XVI style embodied the French Neoclassical movement and shared many similarities of form and ornament with the Adam style. *(COURTESY THE METROPOLITAN MUSEUM OF ART)*

window hardware, silver tea services and candlesticks. The actual building of their furniture designs was contracted out to the leading cabinetmakers of the day, Thomas Chippendale's firm among them. By the end of the 1760s, the firm whose name has come to be synonymous with the English Rococo, was doing some of its finest work, but in the Adam style.

The transformation from Rococo to Neoclassical design was nearly simultaneous in France. There, the Rococo had its detractors all along, but it wasn't until the 1760s that the style was supplanted by the Neoclassical. In nearly every previous style, English fashion had followed the French, but the shift to Neoclassical in both countries was the result of inspiration from Rome. That is not to say that the development of the style in England and France was totally independent. England and France shared many ideas, but neither country copied wholesale from the other's lead. In France

the style was known as the Greek or antique style, but later came to be known as the Louis XVI style, though Louis did not take the throne until 1774.

The Adam style set the stage for the balance of the 18th century in English furniture design. Adam had introduced the Neoclassical taste that brought about the end of the Rococo era. The famous designers who followed based much of their work on the foundation established by Adam, but, as history would have it, their names would be more closely associated with the style.

George Hepplewhite

George Hepplewhite was one of the many London cabinetmakers who followed the Neoclassical style as prescribed by Adam. His cabinetmaking shop was one of those commissioned by Adam to execute his designs, which is a testament to Hepplewhite's talent. Hepplewhite's name might not have achieved a lasting place in

THE HEPPLEWHITE STYLE

Hepplewhite's designs are notable for their elegant simplicity and clean geometric forms (see the illustration at left). Adding a restrained practicality to Adam's inspirational designs, they continued the Adam preference for straight tapered legs, usually square in cross section, but sometimes round. Often the legs end in spade feet. Adam's aims of lightness and lift were continued by keeping case heights short and legs long and slender. Reflecting the mature Adam style, carved applied ornament was used sparingly and in low relief. The curved fronts of sofas, chairs and some case pieces were gentle serpentines, and other case pieces continued Adam's preference for simple plan shapes like semi-circles and semi-ellipses.

The *Guide* is surprisingly complete in conveying design and detailing in its plates. Its illustrations are far more lifelike than those of the *Director*, and they have the appearance of having been drawn from actual examples rather than from the imagination. The details of ornament are precise and realistic. The chairs and sofas show a variety of fabric patterns and give a sense of the appropriate plumpness of the period upholstery. The designs that call for decorative veneer clearly illustrate the marquetry design, so the grain direction,

furniture history had his widow not published *The Cabinet-Maker and Upholsterer's Guide* two years after his death in 1788.

THE *GUIDE*

The *Guide* is a volume of over 200 designs for household furniture. The designs are thought to be taken from drawings of pieces that Hepplewhite's firm made over the years, and therefore did not present any new designs. What the drawings do represent is an assemblage of popular Neoclassical forms as they were made in London in the 1780s.

As a cabinetmaker and not solely a designer, Hepplewhite and his firm presented a practical version of the Neo-classical in the *Guide*. Adam's furniture designs were for the great houses of the nobility, and their appearance was primary and the cost and difficulty of their execution secondary. While the Hepple-white firm built to Adam's specifications, they and other cabinetmakers built for customers of lesser means to whom style was important, but cost was a factor. The *Guide*, by illustrating practical designs that could be built by almost any skilled cabinetmaker, became the authoritative Neoclassical furniture-design book.

As had Chippendale's *Director*, the *Guide* served to popularize and disseminate the new style, but the two books had many other points in common as well. Neither book was a vehicle for introducing new designs. Each was a compendium of the most fashionable prevailing London designs, and so both were published with the hope of finding fashion-starved cabinetmakers outside the mainstream. Each publication established the author's name as synonymous with the style, though in each case the style predates the book. Neither author was the leading cabinet-maker of the day. As with Chippendale, there are no pieces known to be the personal work of George Hepplewhite, and, stranger still, there are no vestiges of Hepplewhite's business other than the name on the *Guide* and six plates included in *The Cabinet-Maker's London Book of Prices*, published in 1788.

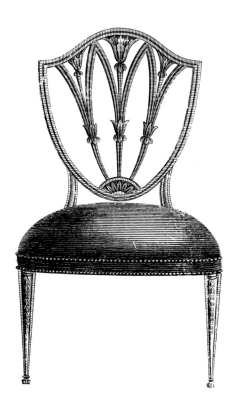

**DESIGN FOR A SHIELD-BACK CHAIR,
DETAIL OF PLATE 5, HEPPLEWHITE'S *GUIDE*.**
The Adam preference for oval-back chairs had given
way to shield-back chairs by the time the *Guide* was
first published in 1788.
(COURTESY DOVER PUBLICATIONS)

string inlays and figure of crotch and swirl
veneers are evident. The *Guide* shows a
detailed variety of cornice and base
moldings, and even includes a room plan
with wall elevations to illustrate the proper
placement of furniture (see the illustration
on p. 80).

Hepplewhite's *Guide* illustrated in part
the evolution of the Neoclassical style since
Adam's introduction of it in the 1760s.
Some 20 years had passed between the
displacement of the Rococo and the
publication of the *Guide*. Adam's
preference for oval chair backs had evolved
into shield backs, a form indicative of the
Hepplewhite style. The *Guide* also
illustrated many square-back chairs, with a
predominance of horizontal and vertical
elements, which were descended from
some of Adam's "Etruscan" chairs. One
favorite base for chests and desks used a
gently scrolled apron and outward-curved,
tapered French feet. The apron and feet are
continuous with the case, often without a

molding between. The shape of the apron
and the outward bend of the feet were one
of the last holdovers from the Louis XV
style, but the French feet finished off the
bases of case pieces in keeping with the
Hepplewhite look. The *Guide* includes one
of the first illustrations of a bow-front chest
of drawers with a simple convex front,
showing the Neoclassical preference for
simple plan shapes applied to a form that
had previously been serpentine or bombé.
Also shown are some of the first sideboards
with drawers (see the illustration below).
Previously, they had simply been sideboard
tables, but with the addition of drawers
they were becoming more like case pieces,
and are shown with shaped fronts.

Practical considerations

The practical Hepplewhite approach to
furniture design sheds light on the everyday
uses of late 18th-century pieces and shows
how the designs of architects were adapted
to the needs of everyday life. According to
Adam, no grand house of the day would
have been complete without a pair of
pedestals and urns on either side of a
sideboard table. The *Guide* illustrates and
explains that one pedestal is designed as a
plate-warming cabinet, lined with tin and
equipped with racks and a heater (see the
illustration at right). The other pedestal
serves as a pot cupboard, but one hopes it is
not the same cheerful term used in
reference to chamber-pot cupboards. The
urns are described as being knife cases or
ice-water dispensers.

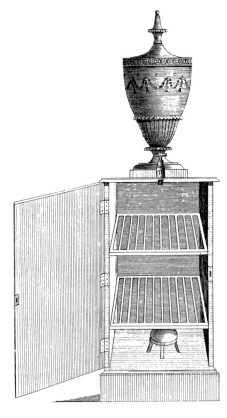

**DESIGN FOR AN URN AND PEDESTAL,
DETAIL OF PLATE 36, HEPPLEWHITE'S *GUIDE*.**
Hepplewhite's cabinetmaking experience added a
practical dimension to Adam's designs. The *Guide*
illustrated how an ornamental Adamesque urn and
pedestal could double as an ice-water dispenser and
plate-warming cabinet.
(COURTESY DOVER PUBLICATIONS)

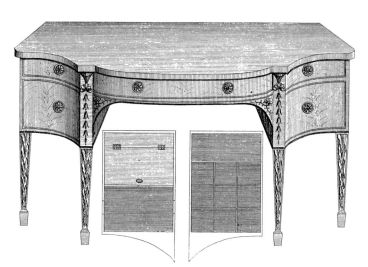

**DESIGN FOR A
SIDEBOARD, PLATE 29,
HEPPLEWHITE'S
GUIDE.**
The *Guide* was one of
the first publications to
illustrate the sideboard,
a new form for the
period. The illustration,
including details of bottle
compartments, set the
pattern of design for
American sideboards.
*(COURTESY DOVER
PUBLICATIONS)*

Sideboards are shown with built-in features such as drawer dividers to hold bottles, lined drawers for silverware and a drawer lined with lead and equipped with a drain valve to hold water for washing glasses. It is noted that they are often made to fit in a recess. The *Guide* also pictures a large number of practical pieces: dressing tables, shaving stands, night tables and pot cabinets, basin stands, bidets and wardrobes, indicating that the stylish cabinetmaker's work was not restricted to flamboyant show pieces. They were, after all, the manufacturers of their day.

Thomas Sheraton

Thomas Sheraton (1751–1806) is one of the more curious characters in furniture history. He had many interests and talents but was so unfocused that he was never very successful at any of them. At various times in his life he was a cabinetmaker, artist, inventor, author, publisher, teacher, mystic and Baptist preacher, or more often a simultaneous combination of them all. Trained as a cabinetmaker, Sheraton likely worked in the employ of others at first but looked to continue on his own path. It is not known to what extent he pursued cabinetmaking, but if it was anything like his other interests, it was sporadic at best. Throughout his life he tried to make his mark in the world, but his story is one of unfulfilled dreams and unachieved success.

THE *DRAWING BOOK*

Between 1791 and 1794 Sheraton published T*he Cabinet-Maker and Upholsterer's Drawing Book* in four parts containing a total of 113 plates. An expanded edition of 122 plates was published in 1802, followed by *The Cabinet Dictionary* in 1803. In 1805 he started to publish *The Cabinet-Maker, Upholsterer and General Artist's Encyclopedia*, which was to be issued in 125 parts. Sheraton died in 1806 having completed only 30.

Sheraton is best remembered for the *Drawing Book*, but although it was reprinted in three editions, it did not bring him financial success. He himself said that the expense of publishing it left him very little profit. Chippendale had used his book

as a means of advertising and promoting his cabinetmaking business, but Hepplewhite did not. A firsthand account of Sheraton's situation is included in the 1885 *Memoirs of Adam Black*, who in 1804 came to London from Scotland looking for work. Sheraton paid him half a guinea to spend a week cleaning and organizing his disastrously untidy shop. Black describes him as being:

> …in an obscure street, his house, half shop half dwelling house, and looked himself like a worn-out Methodist minister, with threadbare black coat. I took tea with them one afternoon. There was a cup and saucer for the host, another for his wife, and a little porringer for their daughter. The wife's cup and saucer were given to me, and she had to put up with a little porringer. Miserable as the pay was, I was half ashamed to take it from the poor man.

Adam Black went on to become the publisher of the *Encyclopedia Britannica*.

The *Drawing Book* sought to enhance the role of drawing and the rules of perspective in guide books, and the first half does so splendidly. The second half illustrates furniture designs, showing Sheraton's skill as both a designer and draftsman. The

preface is a harangue against the books that preceded it. Sheraton derides the quality of drawings and design in Chippendale and Hepplewhite's books, among others'. His critical comments cast a pall over the *Drawing Book* and suggest that his own caustic and eccentric personality may have been responsible for his failings.

Although Adam is not mentioned, his Neoclassical designs are the basis for Sheraton's *Drawing Book* pieces. If Hepplewhite represented the first practical phase of the early Neoclassical, Sheraton represents the next phase. Building upon the Adamesque foundation, Sheraton took the new taste to the next level of refinement. The similarities between his designs and Hepplewhite's are many, but Sheraton's drawings show more delicacy and a more refined use of ornament. Sheraton showed more interest in tapered turned legs of slender proportions, whereas Hepplewhite often used square tapered legs. Sheraton dropped most of the curved case fronts and replaced them with straighter facades. When he did use curved surfaces, they were very simple in form, like cylindrical desk lids or library tables with cylindrical ends. Against a backdrop of more geometric forms, he intermingled simple but elegantly curved elements in chair backs and bookcase door mullions.

DESIGN FOR A PIER TABLE, DETAIL OF PLATE 4, *APPENDIX*, THOMAS SHERATON, *THE CABINET-MAKER AND UPHOLSTERER'S DRAWING BOOK* (LONDON, 1791–1794). This pier table with turned legs shows Sheraton's refined use of ornament, including turnings, and an appreciation for very delicate proportion. *(COURTESY DOVER PUBLICATIONS)*

DESIGN FOR A FRONT LEG OF A DRAWING-ROOM CHAIR, DETAIL OF PLATE 10, *ACCOMPANIMENT*, SHERATON'S *DRAWING BOOK*.
Sheraton's carving designs were delicate enough to embellish a piece without interfering with the shape of its form.
(COURTESY DOVER PUBLICATIONS)

The fine detail of ornament was integral to the design of Sheraton pieces. Turnings inherently have more visual interest than flat square legs, and they were further enhanced with straight or spiral reeding or carved foliage (see the engraving above). The Sheraton designs show a renewed interest in intricate carved and turned detail, most of which had been stripped away during Hepplewhite's reign. Sheraton illustrated the ornament in minute detail, with the idea that it was to enhance the form but not overpower it. Adam had applied ornament to Neoclassical forms, Hepplewhite had

replaced it with inlay, and Sheraton successfully integrated both carved, inlaid and turned decoration into the form. Turnings had not been an important decorative element since the William and Mary period.

Sheraton's inventiveness is evident in a number of his designs. One of his ideas for seating furniture held heating rods. A Sheraton library table converts into library steps. His Harlequin Pembroke Table featured a case of drawers and pigeonholes that arose from the table top to convert it into a desk. One design for a circular dining table had a three-leveled turntable built into the center. A chair unfolded to become a bed, a precursor of modern convertible furniture. His Lady's Writing Table held candle holders and doubled as a vanity. With the release of a catch, a mirror rose from the back of the case, lifted by counterweights.

Sheraton's designs are classified as either early or late. The early designs, as exemplified in the first editions of the *Drawing Book*, were Neoclassical in the tradition of Robert Adam. After the turn of the century and with the publication of *The Cabinet Dictionary,* Sheraton was increasingly influenced by the French Directoire and emerging French Empire styles, and his work took on a decidedly different, sometimes bizarre flavor. The French styles were an overblown version of the Neoclassical that spoke more of imperial grandeur than the harmonious ancient societies that had inspired Adam. They included the use of carved lions, sphinxes and griffins, and adopted Greek and Roman furniture forms such as Grecian couches, *klismos* or saber-leg chairs and *curule* or cross-base chairs (see Chapter 6). The style foreshadowed the English Regency period that followed. This last phase is sometimes referred to as Sheraton's decadent period and bears little resemblance to his early designs.

Upheaval in America

The American interpretation of the Neo-classical style followed the lead of England with some modifications and delays. The last two decades before the war were prosperous for Americans, and their desire

for the rich Chippendale designs continued unabated. While English cabinetmakers were taking up the style of Adam in the 1760s, the Americans had just started to explore the possibilities of the Chippendale designs and were adapting them to their own markets' preferences. Increasingly bad relations with England and the popular dislike for Crown officials and their loyalist supporters contributed to a general American disregard for the new style.

With the outbreak of hostilities in 1775, and the full-fledged war of the following years, advancement of furniture styles stopped. The end of the war came in 1781, but it was not until 1784 that the Definitive Treaty was signed, recognizing the independence of the United States. After the war the country and its economy were in a precarious state, and in 1784 the country began a slide into depression.

Needless to say, during the war and the depression that followed, the decorative arts and furniture making were in a dormant period. What cabinetmaking existed followed the prewar styles, and it likely involved a lot of repair and replacement. Practical considerations had taken priority over fashion, and most tradesman did whatever they could to survive the hard times. Some of the new Neoclassical furniture had been built in America before the war, but it was not enough to be considered a mainstream style. With new tastes well established in Europe, a new and promising government in place in the United States and an improving economy, the 1790s were to be a decade of profound change.

The Federal Era

As the United States recovered from the war and entered an era of increased prosperity in the late 1780s, it was ready to adopt the newest fashions in the decorative arts. American furniture design had changed little since the late 1750s and saw virtually no advances through the war years. The American gratitude to the French did not extend to a widespread appreciation for their furniture. Although the United States had fought and won its political independence from England, it was still stylistically linked. What was fashionable in London was the Neoclassical, and so it was to be in America.

Because of the war and the absence of an authoritative guide book, the Adam style was not taken up in America. There had been some interest in the Neoclassical trend before the war, due to the influence of English immigrant craftsmen and the alliance with France, but it had not gained a significant foothold. The publication of Hepplewhite's *Guide* and the *London Book of Prices* in 1788 served as effective vehicles for the further dissemination of the Neoclassical style in America. It was just at that time that the economy was taking a turn for the better and style-starved customers were willing and able to consider new furniture.

The Neoclassical designs fit well with the new United States. They were a rejection of the ponderous English government as much as they were a rejection of the ponderous Chippendale style. The new government, a democratically elected representative republic, owed much of its inspiration to ancient Greek and Roman examples. Studies of ancient history and classic literature were an important part of a complete education, and furnishings that reflected classic antiquity were a sign of refined taste. As when Robert Adam introduced them to London, Neoclassical designs evoked the sense of a well-structured society. The parallels between the new republic and the early Neoclassical designs are responsible for the name of this era in American furniture: the Federal style.

THE FEDERAL STYLE

The Federal style initially followed the designs of Hepplewhite's *Guide* of 1788. Earlier examples, built from the experience of immigrant cabinetmakers, were in a similar vein. Hepplewhite's designs were buildable, and their clean lines and simplified ornamentation appealed to American tastes. American cabinetmakers and their clients took up the style whole-heartedly, rendering Chippendale designs obsolete. The use of decorative veneers was a new fashion for American makers who had been carving ornament for the previous half century. Nonetheless, they mastered

CHEST OF DRAWERS, MASSACHUSETTS OR NEW HAMPSHIRE, 1790–1810.
Following the Hepplewhite style of design, this chest has a bowed front, bold marquetry ornament and delicate French feet. The smooth surface, light stance and unfettered lines are in marked contrast to the aesthetics of Chippendale-era case pieces, yet the visual interest of the surface makes it no less impressive.
(COURTESY WINTERTHUR MUSEUM)

the art of marquetry and produced stunning examples of Hepplewhite designs.

The important centers of furniture production changed in the aftermath of the Revolution. Prosperity followed maritime activity after the war, and what had previously been secondary cities now rose to prominence. In most cases the war had taken a heavy toll on the established urban centers. Providence surpassed Newport in business activity, Salem grew as a secondary port to Boston, and Baltimore flourished in the shadow of Philadelphia. All three of these cities became important centers of Federal furniture making. Baltimore was particularly notable for achieving a high level of development in the Hepplewhite designs.

As they had done with other styles, the Americans infused a vitality into the designs and executed them with a distinctive delicacy and grace. The pared-down Hepplewhite style quickly became the look of the new country. The pieces were light, clean and sparingly ornamented. Their inlaid designs often featured patriotic symbolism or military heraldry in addition to the classical motifs. Their Hepplewhite legs were square in section and tapered over their length with a thin, delicate appearance. Curved aprons and fronts featured central inlaid ornament or a panel of figured veneer. String inlays varied in pattern, but each was a fine detail used to outline important elements of the form. The American Hepplewhite style had a

**CHEST OF DRAWERS,
MASSACHUSETTS OR
NEW HAMPSHIRE,
1810–1820.**
Made in accordance
with Sheraton precepts,
this chest has turned
legs that continue to the
top as reeded corner
columns and a semi-
elliptical shape to the
front.
*(COURTESY WINTERTHUR
MUSEUM)*

refined simplicity that relied on basic
shapes of sophisticated proportion. The
designs were a pure assemblage of curves,
rectangles and straight tapers, ornamented
in a way that enhanced the design without
interfering with the lines.

The designs of Thomas Sheraton
inspired the second half of the Federal
period in American furniture. His early
designs, as illustrated in the *Drawing Book,*
began to supersede Hepplewhite's as early
as 1795. The early Sheraton designs were
similar in proportion to Hepplewhite's but
they differed in detail. There was a logical
evolution from one style to the next. The
most notable feature of American Sheraton
pieces is the inclusion of turned and
tapered legs, often reeded, instead of the
tapered square legs. The Sheraton designs
show a shift away from sweeping curved
fronts toward more rectilinear forms. Pieces
continued to be ornamented with figured
veneers and inlays but included finely
detailed carvings in low relief in the manner
of Adam. The Sheraton designs remained
in vogue in America until about 1810,
and some vestiges of the style lingered into
the 1820s.

Federal Furniture Forms

American Federal furniture closely
followed the designs of Hepplewhite and
Sheraton. Unlike previous eras, when new
designs evolved from old, the Federal
designs were taken up without delay. Some
notable features of the new forms are
discussed below.

CHESTS

Federal-era chests of drawers, or bureaus as
they were now known, continued many of
the earlier trends for front treatments, but
were updated to Neoclassical standards.
Chests with serpentine or bowed fronts
were in keeping with the Hepplewhite style.
They were fitted with simplified bracket
or French feet (see the photo on p. 87).
Examples in the Sheraton style feature
turned reeded legs, which often extend the
full height of the case as corner columns.
The Sheraton designs included semi-
elliptical swelled fronts (see the photo at
left). In either case, the drawers continued
to be flush fitting with a surrounding
cockbead. Better chests were embellished
with a full complement of decorative
veneer. Figured-birch or maple panels in
mitered frames of mahogany veneer, and
mahogany crotch veneer were favorite
choices, and crossbandings and string inlays
were used on most designs.

The function of dressing tables, which
had become case pieces, was largely
transferred to bureaus or chests of drawers.
Some chests featured top drawers that were
partitioned into compartments, and others
held mirrors. A derivative form was the
chamber table, a piece with dimensions
similar to a bureau, but consisting of two
full-width drawers in a case supported by
long thin legs (photo below). The chamber

**CHAMBER TABLE,
PROBABLY SALEM,
1805–1815.**
Federal chamber tables
featured two full-width
drawers in a case with
long legs. This piece has
the height and width of a
small chest, and was the
Neoclassical equivalent
of earlier dressing tables.
*(COURTESY WINTERTHUR
MUSEUM)*

table had a useful top surface and two shallow drawers, but omitted larger clothing storage drawers. The form was not unlike the much earlier Jacobean form (see p. 10). Pieces with specific purposes, like basin stands and shaving stands, had become practical necessities decades before, and tables for occasional use abounded. As a result, dressing tables, or lowboys, were not continued into the Federal era.

High chests suffered the same fate. Their function was also transferred to chests of drawers or bureaus or, to a lesser extent, chests-on-chests. The form, which had been born of Baroque ideals and updated with Rococo ornament, had been in use for nearly a century and was not readily adaptable to the Neoclassical style.

In rooms where a large piece was needed for visual effect, desk bookcases were the largest and most highly ornamented pieces in general use, but visually imposing pieces were not an aim of the period.

DESKS

The Federal era saw important design changes in desks. Previously, the standard form for a desk, with or without a bookcase, was the slant front. One Federal-era revision was the introduction of a secretary drawer, a false drawer front that folded down to become a horizontal writing surface and exposed an interior bank of small drawers and pigeonholes (see the photo at left above). The secretary drawer was the top drawer in a case that was often topped by a

bookcase with glass doors, themselves a Federal innovation. A gentleman's secretary was wider, with cabinet doors flanking the central drawers and a correspondingly wider bookcase top.

A tambour desk, sometimes called a lady's writing desk, stands on long legs and usually has two full-width drawers (photo at right above). The top folds open onto sliding supports (or "lopers") to become the writing surface. In the usual form of the desk, a low case along the back contains the small drawers and pigeonholes behind flexible tambour doors that slide open horizontally. A lady's writing table and bookcase substitutes a taller glass-doored bookcase for the tambour-fronted case.

The last of the desk innovations was the cylinder desk, a desk of either conventional case form or on tall legs, with a cylindrical lid that rolled up, over and behind the desk interior to expose the writing surface and compartments (see the photo at left). It should be noted that these cylindrical lids were not flexible tambours, but solid curved panels. They were equipped with pivot mechanisms so they rotated smoothly about their central axes.

All three of these desk designs were illustrated in either Hepplewhite's *Guide* or Sheraton's *Drawing Book*. Some of their designs are quite fanciful, with spectacular combinations of cabinets, cylinders and cases. Nonetheless, they represented some of the innovative changes that furniture had undergone in England since before the Revolution.

TABLES

The Neoclassical trend toward light and elegant designs was exemplified well by the table designs of the period. Tea tables lost their prominence as a vehicle for the expression of good taste, but side tables, sideboards and new forms of card tables rose in importance in displaying the design philosophy of the day.

PEMBROKE TABLE,
NEW YORK CITY, 1785–1800.
This Pembroke table in the Hepplewhite style has an oval top, curved aprons and drawer front, tapered legs and the full complement of regional decorative inlay.
(COURTESY YALE UNIVERSITY ART GALLERY)

CYLINDER DESK AND BOOKCASE, PROBABLY MARYLAND, 1790–1800
The desk with a rotating cylindrical lid was one of the novel designs to come from English designers in the late 18th century. Sheraton was fond of such intriguing mechanisms and presented several in his *Drawing Book*.
(COURTESY WINTERTHUR MUSEUM)

Tea tables

Tea tables *per se* were conspicuously absent from the Federal furniture forms. The social custom of taking tea did not hold the same social importance or require specialized furniture as it had before the war. If tea was served in other than the dining room, it would have most likely been on a Pembroke table.

Pembroke tables of Hepplewhite design are oval drop-leaf tables, measuring about 30 in. by 40 in. when open. Their standard form includes bowed aprons, to follow the shape of the top, a drawer on one end and straight tapered legs. The leaves are held up by supports that are hinged to swing out from the frame. Pembroke tables are usually treated to the full complement of inlay, including inlaid flutes or rosettes on the top of the leg and pendant flowers and string inlay down its length. Simpler versions had square tops and frames with tapered legs. Later Sheraton examples were typically straight fronted with turned and reeded legs and had leaves of semi-elliptical shape or ovolo corners.

Pedestal tables

Tripod pedestal tables continued mostly in the form of small candlestands. Federal

CANDLESTAND, BOSTON OR SALEM, 1795–1810. The central turning of this candlestand features the Neoclassical urn motif and all the delicacy of the Federal era. The oval top has rays of satinwood and mahogany veneer.

(COURTESY MUSEUM OF FINE ARTS, BOSTON)

candlestands are noted for their delicate center turning, which usually includes the classical urn shape. Early pieces continued to use the cyma-shaped leg with snake feet, but more stylish examples reversed the curve and gave it a thin tapered shape that met the ground at a right angle with spade feet (photo at left). Tops were frequently oval with a central inlay, but other shapes were also common.

The form of the pedestal table lent itself to stylization in the Federal mode, and a wide variety of interpretations exist. Larger pedestal tables, which had been used as tea tables or as occasional pieces, were not in the vanguard of the new style, and their function was given to Pembroke tables among the most style conscious. But the form had enjoyed widespread use previously, and large pedestal tables, updated with urn turnings, were made into the Federal era.

Side tables

Pier tables, side tables and sideboards are closely related and all saw development in the Federal era. All developed from earlier side or slab tables, but each became distinct in its form and purpose.

SIDEBOARD, BOSTON AREA, 1790–1810. Sideboards were a new and important form for the Federal period. Since they were focal points in formal dining rooms, they were elegantly decorated with figured veneers and inlay.

(COURTESY DALLAS MUSEUM OF ART, THE FAITH P. AND CHARLES L. BYBEE COLLECTION, GIFT OF THE EFFIE AND WOFFORD CAIN FOUNDATION)

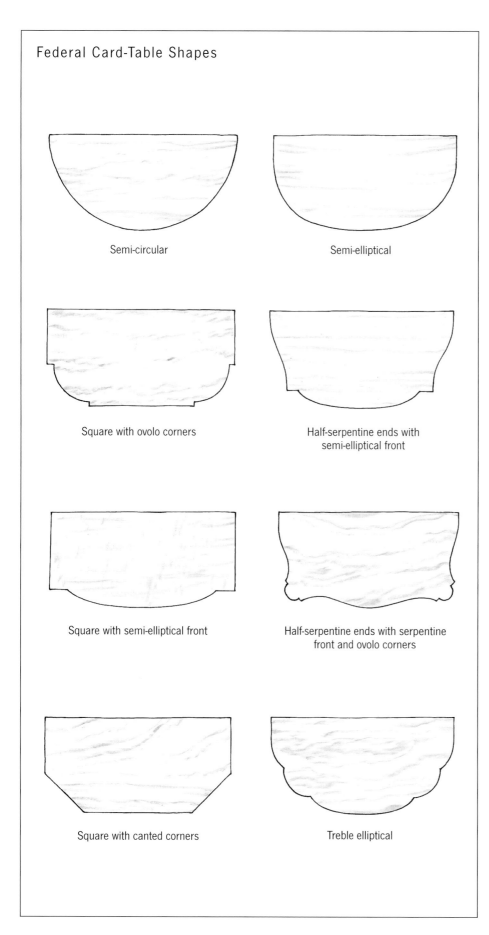

Federal Card-Table Shapes

Semi-circular

Semi-elliptical

Square with ovolo corners

Half-serpentine ends with
semi-elliptical front

Square with semi-elliptical front

Half-serpentine ends with serpentine
front and ovolo corners

Square with canted corners

Treble elliptical

Pier tables were made to stand against the narrow pier walls between tall windows. They were designed to fill the space, and as such were more ornamental than functional. Pier tables were made in the Federal period, but their role was greatly diminished as sideboards became increasingly important as dining-room pieces; and card tables, often made in pairs, could serve as ornamental side tables when not in use.

Side tables are differentiated by being more functional and usually including drawers. As side pieces, they often stood as hall tables or secondary dining-room pieces. By this time, the primary side piece in the dining room had become the sideboard.

Sideboards were one of the most important developments of the Federal era. As dining-room pieces, they were second only to the table and chairs. They were used for serving and storage of silver, linens and liquor, and traditionally have partitions for bottles in the lower right drawer following the practice established by Hepplewhite's design in the *Guide* (see the bottom illustration on p. 84).

American makers fully embraced the form and produced masterful examples. As important pieces that were the focus of attention, they were built with all the ornamental inlay of the day, and with swelled or serpentine fronts. Most sideboards averaged about 5 ft. in length, but some larger examples are known to have approached 8 ft.

Card tables

Card tables reached a peak of refinement during the Federal period, testifying to the continued popularity of card playing as the 19th century approached. Federal card tables are noted for their delicate proportions and their high level of ornamentation. They were designed also to serve as attractive side pieces when not in use.

Both Hepplewhite and Sheraton designs feature short aprons on long slender legs, giving the tables a distinctive lift and exceptionally light footprint. The aprons have the most sophisticated of decorative veneer and inlay, including oval and rectangular panels of figured wood. Popular top shapes included semi-circular, semi-elliptical, square with ovolo corners, and half-serpentine ends with a semi-elliptical front (see the drawing on the facing page). As in earlier tables, the tops folded in half onto themselves or opened to be supported by one or two hinged fly legs.

Sheraton examples differ little from the Hepplewhite designs, with the exception of the use of turned and reeded legs. Some of the better examples of the Sheraton style extended the leg turning all the way to the underside of the top by using the legs as half columns over the apron. The legs were integrated into the aprons that were half-serpentine on the ends, and serpentine on the front. The top followed the same shape and echoed the profile of the leg turning with small ovolo corners.

Dining tables

A new form of dining table developed with the Federal period that solved the age-old problem of providing a solid table that could be lengthened or shortened as

CARD TABLE, NEW YORK CITY, C.1800.
This round card table, in the Hepplewhite style with inlaid ovals and bellflowers, features square tapered legs extending from a half-round apron. The fifth fly leg is typical of New York card tables.
(COURTESY WINTERTHUR MUSEUM)

CARD TABLE, PROVIDENCE, 1800–1810.
One of a pair, this card table in the Sheraton style bears the label of Joseph Rawson and Sons. The turned legs are reeded and continue over the apron as half-columns. The front is serpentine and the sides are half-serpentine. One back leg swings out to support the folding top.
(COURTESY RHODE ISLAND HISTORICAL SOCIETY)

**DINING TABLE,
NEWPORT, 1790-1810.**
This Hepplewhite-style
dining table is in three
sections: two half-round
ends, and a center table
in the familiar drop-leaf
configuration. The
design was flexible in
size but solid in use. The
inlaid urns, stringing and
pendent bellflowers are
related to pieces by
Thomas and Samuel
Goddard, sons of John
Goddard.
*(COURTESY RHODE ISLAND
HISTORICAL SOCIETY)*

**WORK TABLE,
BOSTON, 1800–1810.**
This work table with
serpentine sides and
ovolo corners is thought
to have been made in
the Seymour shop. A
reading and writing
board ratchets up at an
angle from the opened
top drawer, and the
frame holding the
suspended work bag
slides from the right
side.
*(COURTESY WINTERTHUR
MUSEUM)*

needed. The new design actually consisted
of three separate tables: a traditional square
drop-leaf table, and two half-round tables,
each with a single drop-leaf along its
straight side. On each piece, fly legs swing
out to support the leaves. The table could
be assembled with any combination of
components and extended leaves. A table of
average leaf width could reach 14 ft. in
length. By removing the center table and
using the two half-round ends with their
leaves extended, the length could be
shortened to 8 ft. Similarly, the square
drop-leaf section could be used alone and
the ends could be used as side tables.

The best feature of these tables is their
solidity. The legs are placed along the
outside edge of the table where the support
is needed most. Even a slight amount
of "sponginess" can be annoying in a
dining table, which is a problem inherent
in later pedestal-base dining tables, but this
Federal design offered an elegant and
flexible solution.

Work tables

The term "work table" is applied to a
number of small four-legged tables, usually
with at least one drawer, used for a variety
of purposes during the Federal period.
These tables have a fabric bag suspended

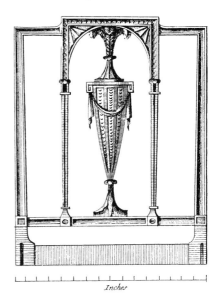

below the apron in which needlework and
sewing projects could be stored (see the
bottom photo on the facing page). The bag
was attached to the inside of a thin frame
that slid out of the table like a shallow
drawer. Tables either with or without this
feature served as occasional pieces near
sofas, chairs or beds. The form is most
highly developed in the Sheraton style, with
turned, reeded legs and highly figured
drawer fronts and aprons.

SEATING FURNITURE

Chairs of the Federal period required a high
level of skill on the part of the cabinet-
maker, since delicacy and strength, usually
exclusive of one another, had to coexist in
each design. Upholstered pieces, such as
easy chairs, sofas and a new form called a
"lolling" chair, were made to uphold similar
Federal-era ideals.

Chairs

American chairs of the Federal period
closely followed those prescribed by
Hepplewhite and Sheraton. The familiar
shield back, illustrated in both their books,
became a popular American form closely
associated with the Hepplewhite era.
Square-back chairs, more profusely
illustrated in Sheraton's *Drawing Book,*
saw increased use around the turn of the
century.

Both types of chairs established a new
level of delicacy and refinement in
ornament. The backs of both styles were

**UPHOLSTERED ARMCHAIR,
MASSACHUSETTS, 1795–1810.**
The upholstered open armchair, called a 'lolling' or 'Martha Washington' chair, has design roots in Queen Anne and Chippendale examples, but found new importance in the light and delicate aesthetic of the Federal period.
(COURTESY MUSEUM OF FINE ARTS, BOSTON)

chairs with upholstered seats and backs, which were sometimes made as bedroom or dining chairs, and the few Chippendale open armchairs were the forebears of the Federal lolling chairs. Their freestanding wooden arms connect with the front legs by way of a sweeping upright support. They are notable for their vertical proportions and clean lines. Early versions used stretchers, which were largely dropped after the turn of the century. Because they were open and less enveloping than easy chairs, lolling chairs were favorite parlor pieces. Their light appearance was very much in keeping with Federal design ideals.

Easy chairs underwent some minor revisions to bring them up to the same standards of the day. In general, they became lighter in appearance and more refined as Federal elegance replaced Chippendale opulence (see the photo below). In keeping with the changing styles, tapered square legs with straight stretchers replaced cabriole legs, as prescribed by

Hepplewhite, and later Sheraton versions used turned and reeded front legs without stretchers.

The first Federal sofas were much like the earlier versions, but with the inclusion of tapered legs. In general, the more flamboyant sofa shapes of the Rococo were toned down for the Federal period. Hepplewhite's designs predominated in sofas of this period. Besides inspiring the updated version of earlier designs, Hepplewhite presented what was called in the trade a cabriole sofa, wherein the seat was semi-elliptical in plan and the back was a gentle arch instead of the familiar serpentine "camel" back. In this design the back curves around to become the side, and the arms are light and integral (see the top photo on the facing page). The huge arm rolls of previous styles were atrophied or eliminated. The name of these sofas has nothing to do with the cabriole leg, but it is a reference to the French styles from which they derived. In this general sense, the term cabriole simply means "curved."

composed of exceptionally slender members, and their shallow carved detail was integral to their shapes. One has only to look at an example of a back ornamented with swags or plumes to see that the element and its carving are the same. Tapered square-front legs with inlay or molding were the norm, and chairs were built with and without stretchers.

Slip seats had passed out of favor, and the new chairs were designed to be upholstered over the rail. Round-head brass tacks were frequently arranged along the seat rails as part of the design, either in a straight line or in a wave pattern following the prevailing swag motif.

Upholstered pieces

"Lolling" chairs are distinctly American pieces with no clear precedent in either of the dominant design books. They have been given the name Martha Washington chairs in the vernacular, but the origin of the term is unclear. They are high-back chairs, with upholstered seats and back, but without the wings of easy chairs (photo above). Earlier

**EASY CHAIR,
NEW ENGLAND,
1790–1810.**
Easy chairs progressed into the Federal era with cosmetic changes to keep them current. Legs became straight or were turned in Sheraton examples. This chair has curved wings or 'cheeks' as shown in the *Guide*.
(COURTESY DALLAS MUSEUM OF ART, THE FAITH P. AND CHARLES L. BYBEE COLLECTION, GIFT OF MRS. JANE SANFORD BEASLEY)

**CABRIOLE SOFA,
BALTIMORE,
1790–1800.**
The cabriole sofa
differed from previous
styles in its semi-
elliptical seat plan and
continuous flow of the
back into the arms.
This Baltimore example
in the Hepplewhite style
derives from a design in
the *Guide*.
*(COURTESY WINTERTHUR
MUSEUM)*

Hepplewhite also presented designs for square sofas, with both open and closed arms (photo below). Square sofas are highly rectilinear in form, with either straight or slightly curved backs and front rails, vertical arms and a rectangular seat form. Square sofas became associated with later Sheraton-inspired Federal designs, because they usually have turned and reeded legs that extend upward to become arm supports.

Another piece of seating furniture popularized by the *Guide* was the window stool, of which Hepplewhite offered six designs. Each features a wide horizontal seat on four slender legs with scrolled arms on either end, as shown in the photo at right below. The seat and arms are upholstered. The design was directly inspired by classical forms and fit perfectly into window recesses. The window seat is another example of the Adamesque penchant for designing furniture to coordinate with architecture.

BEDSTEADS

Hepplewhite and Sheraton illustrated many beds, and in the European tradition they are largely show pieces for upholsterers. They do show in detail the designs for bed posts, which were some of the few visible

SQUARE SOFA, MASSACHUSETTS, 1800–1810.
Square sofas, which are associated with the Sheraton style, frequently feature a decoratively veneered or carved panel in the center of the back rail. The carving on this example is attributed to Samuel McIntire.
(COURTESY WINTERTHUR MUSEUM)

WINDOW SEAT, SALEM, 1795–1800.
The window seat was a new form of Neoclassical design and was illustrated in Hepplewhite's *Guide*.
(COURTESY WINTERTHUR MUSEUM)

parts of the bed structure. Both designers
featured turned and reeded posts, but
Hepplewhite tended toward square tapered
legs or Marlborough legs below the rail,
while Sheraton offered turned profiles.

American tall-post beds followed the
lead of both designers, and the sectional
shape of the foot is often the only clue as to
which style was adopted. Federal tall-post
beds fall into one of two categories: beds
with tall posts (in excess of 6 ft.) with
straight testers (canopy frames), and field
beds with shorter posts that necessitated
arched or serpentine testers. The taller
beds were the more formal of the two, and
would have been used in the main
bedrooms and equipped with the best of
bed hangings (top photo at left). Field beds,
inspired by those used by military officers
in the field, are shown by both Hepplewhite
and Sheraton (bottom photo at left).
Sheraton states that they "may be
considered for domestic use, and suit for
low rooms, either for servants or children to
sleep upon; and they receive this name an
account of their being similar in size and
shape to those really used in camps...." Low-
post beds of a less stylish nature continued
to be made as well for the purely functional
purpose of holding a mattress.

Federal Decoration and Ornament

The primary decorative element of Federal
furniture is marquetry in the form of
panels of fancy veneer or inlaid shells,
rosettes, banding or strings. Making
intricate inlay from scratch was not the
kind of work a busy commercial shop
would have done in the course of making
furniture, and most urban cabinetmakers
purchased their inlay already made. From
newspaper advertisements of the time,
some inlay is known to have been imported
from England, but most cities had a
resident inlay maker, or "ébéniste," who
supplied the local cabinet shops. Baltimore
had become one of the leading centers of
Federal furniture making, and Thomas
Barrett was an inlay supplier there. His shop
inventory of 1800 lists 1,316 "shells for
inlaying in furniture," priced from 7 to 25

cents each, and 76 yd. of banding, valued at 5 to 12½ cents. The value of each is evident when compared to the prevailing wage of $1 a day for journeymen cabinetmakers. Barrett's account books list at least 145 cabinetmakers as his customers, which along with his inventory, establishes him as a major source for inlay in Baltimore.

Other cities had their own inlay makers who supplied the cabinetmaking shops. As a result, each city came to have patterns and designs that were distinct. In the absence of a signature or label, the pattern of banding or inlaid ornament is often the only feature that can identify the origin of a piece. By the Federal era, interstate commerce and the increased use of guide books had made furniture designs more uniform from city to city. In addition, most journeymen cabinetmakers were in the employ of larger shops, rather than working in traditional family businesses. They were mobile and spread styles and methods from place to place. With imported materials, uniform designs and a mobile workforce, locally procured inlay was often the only indigenous aspect of a piece. A comprehensive view of regional variations in inlay is presented by Charles F. Montgomery in

CARD TABLE, BOSTON AREA, 1790–1810. This Hepplewhite-style card table shows both the Neoclassical and patriotic aspects of Federal inlaid ornament. The detail at far left is from the apron; the detail at left from the pilaster. *(COURTESY YALE UNIVERSITY ART GALLERY)*

The use of reeding is associated with the Sheraton style in America. The Neoclassical motif derives from the Roman *fasces*, a bundle of rods or arrow shafts symbolizing power and authority. This detail of a Sheraton card table also includes a fluted section at the top of the leg.
(PRIVATE COLLECTION)

American Furniture: The Federal Period (Viking, 1966).

The second important decorative element in the Federal period is the use of reeding, a detail closely associated with Sheraton designs. Reeding is a shallow surface carving that gives the appearance of bundled rods, each convex, as opposed to fluting, which is carved concave channels. Reeding is most often seen on turned Sheraton legs, and it was also used on curved saber legs in later styles. Reeding is purely Neoclassical in style, and is taken from the Roman *fasces*, a bundle of rods (or arrow shafts) containing an ax and bound

with a spiraling ribbon. The fasces was a ceremonial object carried before Roman officials as a symbol of their power and authority. By contrast, fluting derived from the fluted columns of classical architecture, and had been used in furniture in the Queen Anne and Chippendale periods. Fluting was largely considered dated by the Federal era.

Federal Structure

The essential structure of 18th-century furniture had changed little since the William and Mary period, and it continued with refinements through the Federal era. Over the course of the century, the trend had been toward increased delicacy and the advancement of form over the limitations of structure. Cabinetmakers continued to push the material to its limit and to minimize the number of structural elements necessary for a piece. Compare, for example, the many legs and stretchers of a William and Mary gateleg table with the spartan delicacy of a Sheraton card table. The Federal period was the peak of this trend, and the appearance of pieces seems unfettered by structural concerns. This effect made the integrity and precision of the remaining structure and joinery that much more important.

With the increased use of decorative veneer and the importance of the surface in Federal designs, some minor changes occurred in joinery. Exposed joinery or visible pegs were not to be seen on better pieces, so they were either covered or omitted. Case pieces frequently had veneered fronts, including the case fronts and drawer dividers, so the sliding dovetail joinery was covered. This trend had started in American Chippendale pieces (following the English), where the front edges of the case sides were covered with a thin applied strip from which the vertical cockbead was cut. In mortise-and-tenon joints, where pegs could not be used or hidden, large glued-in corner blocks were used to help hold the joint together. The delicate nature of Federal chairs and card tables made glue blocks an important part of their original structure that should not be overlooked.

The extensive use of veneer produced a change in how many individual elements were made. Rather than being made of one piece of shaped wood, furniture of the Federal era was more likely to include panels built up of pieces and veneered over. This method of work had been common in Europe for years, where cabinet-grade lumber was more scarce and veneering was extensively practiced. In the Federal era, it was not uncommon for the shaped front of a card table to be glued up from thin layers of a secondary wood, such as pine, which was then cut to shape and veneered. By this time, native wood was no longer in limitless abundance, and more important, commercial shops would have found a way to use what was already in their inventories. Laminating eliminated the need to stock large-dimension secondary wood. Veneering panels, such as door panels on sideboards, resolved structural concerns as well. Doors cut from the solid are free to expand, contract and warp, so it is common to find flat and curved doors built up from secondary wood as a framed panel or a panel with "breadboard" ends, which was then veneered over. The veneering of surfaces allowed for an inventive variety of subsurfaces, some of which offered structural improvements while others were merely for cost-cutting reasons.

The Changing Nature of the Business

Over the course of the 18th century, cabinetmaking progressed from a trade to a business venture, and the trend accelerated after the Revolution. While many shops continued to be family owned and may have employed a few journeymen, the trade took on a decidedly business-oriented approach in the 1790s. The war and depression that followed caused a pent-up demand for furniture, and the emergence of new styles increased that demand.

The cabinetmaker's shop was not the only place to purchase furniture. Merchants had been selling the ready-made work of cabinetmakers for most of the 18th century.

Boston chairs had been sold by merchants in New York and Philadelphia in the first quarter of the century, and Newport makers made pieces for shipment to southern coastal cities at mid-century. Many cabinetmakers sold the work of others in addition to pieces of their own making. An example would be a maker of case furniture who supplemented his offerings with looking-glasses or chairs from other artisans. Often this led the shop owner to give the cabinetmaking work over to hired journeymen, while he pursued the business of buying and selling furniture. City directories show many examples of cabinetmakers who were later listed as merchants. Shops that employed journeymen cabinetmakers making furniture in greater quantity and on speculation came to be known as manufactories. The term is now obsolete, but its roots, meaning "to make by hand," are insightful. Where major pieces were once mostly built to order, they were now commonly available for purchase right off the floor.

This shop structure led to a new kind of relationship between the employer and the employees. The shop owner no longer functioned as the shop master, and he did not even need to be a skilled cabinetmaker. The journeymen no longer had to be familiar with every aspect of the trade, since they were part of a larger group of more specialized craftspeople. The need for increased quantity and specialized cabinetmakers led to shorter apprenticeships, and it was therefore easier to become a journeyman. The new relationship put an emphasis on wages, hours, productivity and division of labor. The cabinetmaking shops in most cities came to mutual agreements concerning retail prices for goods and set the journeyman's wages for these pieces. The first such American price book, as they were known, was published in Hartford in 1792, and other cities soon followed. Journeymen were paid by the piece at a rate based on the length of time a given piece should require to build (see the sidebar below). It was not unusual for cabinetmaking shops to set prices among themselves to prevent one from undercutting the others. As early as 1756, six Providence cabinetmakers had encroached on the workings of the free market by fixing their prices.

Journeymen sometimes found themselves in adversarial positions with their employers, and as a result they banded together in "societies" that were in essence labor unions. In Philadelphia, in 1795, the Federal Society of Journeymen Cabinet and Chair Makers refused to work for certain employers who did not recognize the Society and its rules. They also refused to work with other journeymen who did not adhere to the Society's rules. In Baltimore, the Society required all cabinetmakers to become members within six weeks of working in that city or pay a fine of twice the membership dues. In 1796, the Philadelphia Society published a set of new higher rates that was rejected by employers. They opened their own "ware-room" to display and sell their work. They also made an effort to band together with other societies of craftspeople such as painters, printers, coopers, carpenters, tailors, hatters and shoemakers to present a larger united front. Eventually the employers agreed to a cost of living allowance tied to living expenses in addition to a 50% raise for all journeymen whose work they found acceptable. The strike had been effective for the journeymen, who were now guaranteed one dollar a day for working eleven hours a day, six days a week, with the additional stipulation that the employers were to supply the candles. Similar strikes occurred in New York in 1802 and 1803. The family cabinetmaking business was not what it had once been.

THE TIME REQUIRED TO BUILD PERIOD PIECES

By knowing the prevailing wages and the piecework, or labor price, for furniture, the length of time required to build a piece can be determined. Around the turn of the century, the wage of a journeyman cabinetmaker was about one dollar for an eleven-hour day. Nearly every city had a Book of Prices to establish agreeable pay rates and retail prices. The entries in the next column are from the Philadelphia and New York price books of 1796.

Chest, four drawers, veneered drawer fronts, cockbead surrounds: 8 days

Desk, four drawers, veneered fronts, cockbeaded, 3½ ft. long, fancy interior: 16 days

Dining table, mahogany: 8 days

Pembroke table: 3½ days

Square card table: 3½ days

Circular bureau: 9½ days

Clock case: 8 days

The retail prices were set at roughly three and a half times the labor price, and included material, overhead and profit.

(ADAPTED FROM CHARLES F. MONTGOMERY, AMERICAN FURNITURE: THE FEDERAL PERIOD; NEW YORK, 1966)

6

Revisiting Ancient Splendor

AMERICAN EMPIRE
(1810–1830)

The second phase of the Neoclassical movement shifted away from the classically inspired designs, like those of Adam and the Louis XVI style, toward a more realistic classical revival. This phase was a literal adoption of Greek and Roman design, where form and ornament were copied with precision from antiquity. Some

historians have described this revival as having been executed with an archeological zeal, which is a very fitting description of the passion with which the designers approached their work and the respect they felt for the designs of the ancient civilizations. This style of design followed separate but closely related paths of

development in England and France, with France providing most of the initiative.

The Greco-Roman Revival

While Neoclassicism is sometimes discussed in its entirety, the differences between its early and late phases are significant enough to be addressed separately. The early American Neoclassical, or Federal period designs, descended from the work of Robert Adam and the successive English designers who built on his work (see Chapter 5). The later Neoclassical, the Greco-Roman or Empire period in American furniture, takes its inspiration from the Directoire and Empire designs of the French. Both periods have roots in antiquity, but each followed a different path to become established in America, and each had distinct phases of evolution during its period of popularity.

The more literal adoption of Greek and Roman designs and their use in the American interior is documented in *The Tea Party*, c.1821–1825, by Boston painter Henry Sargent (1770–1845).
(COURTESY MUSEUM OF FINE ARTS, BOSTON)

DIRECTOIRE

In France, the transition period from the Louis XVI designs to the second phase of the Neoclassical was called the Directoire style. After the French Revolution, the country's governing body until 1795 was the National Convention, followed by the Directorate from 1795 to 1799. It is from the latter that the name "Directoire" is taken. The style was marked by an increase in the archeological authenticity of Neoclassical pieces. The Louis XVI style became more severe and angular and increasingly similar to actual Greek designs. This more spartan and rectilinear form was mixed with ornament that had significance to the French Revolution, such as the cap of Liberty, the Roman fasces and the tricolor of the Republic. The Directoire was in style in a continuously evolving form from 1793 until about 1804. At that time, Napoleon dropped all pretenses of running a republic and had himself made the emperor, making the Empire style more or less official.

FRENCH EMPIRE

The French Empire style was largely created for the aggrandizement of Napoleon by his two official architectural designers, Pierre Francois Léonard Fontaine (1762–1853) and Charles Percier (1764–1838). Both had studied antiquity in Rome and, after returning to Paris, were commissioned to redecorate one of Napoleon's palaces. They adhered closely to the original Greek and Roman forms, and created the look of imperial grandeur that was the hallmark of the Napoleonic years.

The French Empire style was taken from what was then known of Greek and Roman furniture. Ancient furniture often had cast-bronze or iron components, such as table legs, pedestal bases, and chair and stool frames. These parts survived, as did anything made of marble, such as thrones or temple pieces. For the most part, wooden furniture and component parts had long since been lost to the moist Mediterranean climate. The missing links that provided great inspiration to the Empire designers came from the Greek and Roman depictions of furniture in their murals, ceramics and bas-relief sculpture. The ancient scenes showed a limited number of furniture forms, but Percier and Fontaine used the style to create all the forms necessary for modern standards of living. Percier and Fontaine's designs were published in serial form beginning in 1801 under the title *Recueil de Décorations Intérieures*, which was issued as a book in 1812.

There was nothing comfortable or inviting about the French Empire style. Its geometry was sharp and severe, and its decoration was stiff and imperial. The Empire designs were nearly completely rectilinear; its form was composed of flat slabs of wood and thick square columns. The pieces could just as well have been cut from marble. There was no significant use of marquetry, very few moldings, and carving was seen only on some seating furniture. Chairs, which offered some relief from the severity of other pieces, were in the Greek *klismos* or saber-leg design, or the curule or cross-base form. The style is noted for its very strict symmetry in both form and ornament. The preferred material was a dark wood like mahogany or knot elm, stained to a deep color and finished to a high luster.

The classically inspired ornamental details of Louis XVI furniture were dropped for another set of classical ornaments. Where the earlier phase of the Neoclassical used architectural details and well-integrated applied ornament, the Empire style called for contrasting applied ornament. The primary form of Empire decoration was the application of gilded bronze (ormolu) mounts. The mounts were shallow reliefs of classical motifs and stylized emblems, including mythological figures, medallions, foliage and, a favorite of the period, wreaths. These mounts were finely detailed and quite stunning in their gilded finish, to contrast with the dark smooth surface to which they were applied.

The French Empire was also noted for the fanciful creatures that were worked into furniture designs. Gilded sphinxes, griffins, eagles, swans, dolphins and human busts were integrated into forms as columns, bases and supports. Heads, wings, paws, claws and feet were used in strange combinations with each other and as furniture components. One example of this interplay of furniture and body parts is a column motif used in many Empire designs: A square, tapered wooden column is capped with the gilt bust of a woman, and the column base is a pair of gilded human feet (see the photo on p. 107). This theme of furniture transforming in and out of human and animal shapes throughout its structure is essential to the Empire style. Although it is quite strange, it is also very imaginative and almost whimsical at times. The Empire designs were executed in a way that was very refined. They had the potential to be grotesque and could have easily crossed the line of good taste, but their makers were so skilled they made the designs work well.

Empire, like most of the French styles that had preceded it, was a court style that saw little acceptance outside the upper levels of society. Its imperial nature prevented it from being taken up by the general public, though some aspects of its appearance did enter the vernacular of furniture design. The style outlasted Napoleon and continued under Louis XVIII, who ruled from 1814 to 1824, and under Charles X, whose reign continued until 1830. This later part of the Empire style, often call the Restauration, for the restoration of the monarchy, was a more mature version than the earlier style. The later pieces had lost their initial spirit, and, as is the case in the late stages of many styles, settled into a comfortable repetition. The designs became heavy and more ornamental as successive designers added their own touches and moved the style away from its original precepts.

After 1830, France was witness to revivals of Gothic, Renaissance and Louis XIV styles, but they were poor imitations at best. Sequels are rarely as good as the originals, and these revivals were

thoroughly uninspired and unoriginal. For all intents and purposes, the end of the Napoleonic era marked the end of French innovation in furniture design for the remainder of the 19th century.

English Regency

The second phase of the Neoclassical movement in England is known as the English Regency period. The style came to the fore in the late 1790s and remained in vogue until the 1820s. The name refers to the short period from 1811 to 1820 when George, the Prince of Wales, served as Regent for his father George III. George III had reigned since 1760, but was declared insane in 1811. Upon his death in 1820, the Prince assumed the throne as George IV.

Credit for the early introduction of the style is given to English architect Henry Holland (1746–1806), who brought details of the French Directoire to the interior design of homes of the aristocracy. Thomas Sheraton's publications after the turn of the century showed the same creeping influence of the French Directoire and Empire designs on English tastes.

THOMAS HOPE

The Regency style was further advanced and ultimately defined by Thomas Hope (1769–1831). Hope was from a wealthy Dutch family and had traveled extensively in Europe and the Middle East, collecting art and antiquities and developing a passionate interest in the styles and customs of the places he visited. Among his friends was Charles Percier, designer of the Empire style. Hope settled in London in 1799, buying a house built by Adam in the 1760s, and set about remodeling the place to house his collection and to serve as a showplace for the new furniture he had been inspired to design and have built. His designs were an eclectic blend of the many styles he had seen during his extended Grand Tour. They embodied Greek, Roman, Turkish and Egyptian forms and ornament combined into one synthesized style.

Hope's designs proved to be influential, and soon poor copies of his pieces were

being made. For the sake of his own reputation he wanted these copies to be true to his original intent, so in 1807 he published measured drawings of the pieces in *Household Furniture and Interior Decoration*. His book became the standard for the new style that would later be called the English Regency.

Household Furniture

The designs presented in *Household Furniture* are not unlike those of the French Empire style. They are of classical Greek and Roman form, and are severe and rectilinear. This effect is increased by the way they are depicted in the plates of the book. Each piece is shown in line drawings in front and side elevations, without perspective. Hope used many of the same design elements as the French designers: Sphinxes, griffins and winged lions appear often, and indeed it would be hard to differentiate the two styles at first glance. The English designs also show a more regular use of Egyptian elements, which were added to the Greek-inspired repertoire after the 1802 publication of *Voyage dans la Basse et la Haute Egypte (Voyage in Lower and Upper Egypt)*. That book illustrated numerous examples of ancient Egyptian art in the aftermath of Napoleon's 1798 campaign there.

Hope's designs are more of an honest tribute to ancient cultures than a statement of imperial grandeur. Hope enjoyed surrounding himself with ancient artifacts so much that he devoted three rooms in his house to the display of classical vases. His furniture designs were intended to give the aura of antiquity to all the furnishings in the house. *Household Furniture* was intended to extend it to the houses of others.

REGENCY STYLE

Like the French Empire style, the Regency called for dark woods, in this case mahogany and rosewood. The use of satinwood was held over from the earlier phase of the Neoclassical, but it soon passed out of favor. Regency designers used bronze mounts, but with more restraint than the French. Their metalwork was not as carefully detailed as

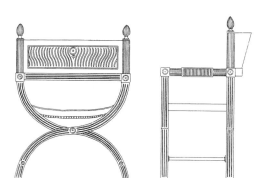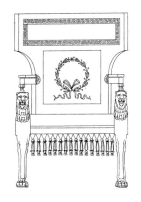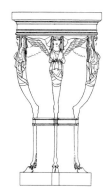

DESIGNS FOR TWO CHAIRS AND A TRIPOD TABLE, DETAILS OF PLATES XX AND XXII, THOMAS HOPE,
***HOUSEHOLD FURNITURE AND INTERIOR DECORATION* (LONDON, 1807).**
Hope's English Regency designs included the curule or cross-base chair, an armchair with rear saber legs and griffin arm supports, and a tripod table like some unearthed at Pompeii.
(COURTESY DOVER PUBLICATIONS)

the French, and they employed a different lexicon of ornament. Among the favorite English mount designs were waterleafs, rosettes, wreaths, female faces and lion masks. Caryatid figures (female figures used as columns) were also used widely. Lion masks with ring handles became a standard element of the Regency, as did brass animal feet or paws with casters for use on saber legs. Brass also came into use as an inlay into the dark wood, both in fretwork designs and as a string inlay. This was a feature that Sheraton spoke fondly of in his later publications. Brass was also used for attached moldings and pierced galleries. Another feature of the era was the use of fabric as a decorative panel element. Doors and panels were often fitted with silk curtains stretched within their frames, often behind pierced metal fretwork (see the photo at top on p. 108).

Other works that advanced the Regency designs included George Smith's *A Collection of Designs for Household Furniture and Interior Decoration* of 1808 and Rudolph Ackerman's all-encompassing periodical, *Repository of Arts, Literature, Commerce, Manufactures, Fashions and Politics*, which started in 1809 and continued for another 20 years. Thomas Chippendale Jr. also worked in the Regency style, and he is noted for his restrained use of ornament and elegant handling of the style, which some consider to be the best

practical interpretations of the ideals of the period.

English Regency furniture never possessed the same sense of unity or level of artistic achievement as French Empire designs. Much of the Regency style was borrowed from the Directoire and Empire designs but with the addition of more diverse ancient elements. Regency designs did not come from a central source as did the designs of Percier and Fontaine. Neither did they serve a unifying purpose as did the Empire designs in providing a stage set for Napoleon. The Regency was created in the trade rather than in the court, and designers and builders were free to add their own influences, for better or worse. Finally, the English craftsmen did not have the experience or skill in this kind of design to make the designers' ideas work as well as their French counterparts.

American Greco-Roman Revival

The American embrace of the second phase of the Neoclassical era permeated American society and extended well beyond the realm of furniture and interior design. The interest in the new European styles began to surge after the War of 1812 and was seen in all manner of popular tastes. Architecture underwent a strong Greco-Roman revival, and white-columned houses and public

buildings came to stand among the earlier Georgian buildings of every American town and city. Paintings of the period depict idyllic Neoclassical pastoral scenes and women in Greek-inspired clothing reposing on Grecian furniture forms. In the American expansion, many new towns took the names of ancient cities. There was a civility and sophistication in the late Neoclassical ideals that to Americans was the proper image to symbolize the continued success of their new nation.

The American Greco-Roman revival drew upon both the French and English designs. The publications of Sheraton, Fontaine and Percier, Hope, Smith and Ackerman were all circulated in America, and cabinetmakers took up the aspects of the style that suited their tastes and appealed to their clients. Their chosen pieces were bold but certainly more restrained than the imperial French designs. The American craftsmen captured the essence of the style without being carried away by its excesses.

EARLY EMPIRE
The Empire style in America tends to be divided into three parts, which very loosely describe its evolution during this period. The early Empire is sometimes called the late Neoclassical or American Directoire,

SCROLL-BACK SIDE CHAIR, NEW YORK, 1807.
One of a set of ten from the shop of Duncan Phyfe, this scroll-back chair shows the light and delicate nature of Phyfe's designs.
(COURTESY WINTERTHUR MUSEUM)

SCROLL-BACK SIDE CHAIR, NEW YORK, 1810–1820.
The influence of the Greco-Roman revival is evident in this chair in the *klismos* or saber-leg form with a lyre banister.
(COURTESY WINTERTHUR MUSEUM)

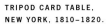

TRIPOD CARD TABLE, NEW YORK, 1810–1820.
This card table has waterleaf carving on the leg in the style of Duncan Phyfe, which was adopted by many New York makers. In this family of tables, a mechanism turns the side legs backward as the supports under the top are extended to hold the top when it is opened.
(COURTESY YALE UNIVERSITY ART GALLERY)

and, as in France, it was the transition period from the first to the second phase of the Neoclassical, or the transition from Sheraton to Empire as the dominant style. These designs predate the War of 1812 and first gained popularity in about 1805. Furniture of this era continued in the delicate spirit of the Federal period but included more of the Greek and Roman forms, most notably the *klismos* chair and other pieces, like pedestal tables, that shared the use of the saber leg. This era saw a gradual increase in carving as a decorative element. On American pieces, waterleaf carving was a favorite treatment for the tops of sweeping saber legs. The English Regency designs had limited impact on American styles.

Duncan Phyfe

Some of the finest examples of the early Empire style were executed by Duncan Phyfe (1768–1854). Phyfe was a Scottish immigrant with American training who opened a shop in New York City in 1792. He was a talented designer and craftsman, and his acumen extended to the business side of the trade as well. At its peak, his manufactory was considered one of the premier cabinetmaking and upholstery shops in the country, employing over 100 craftspeople working in every facet of the trade. Phyfe was at the forefront of the developing styles, and was always able to offer the most refined interpretation of the latest Neoclassical trend.

Phyfe is best remembered for his work in the first two decades of the 19th century. During this time, before the full weight of the Empire style had come to bear on the market, he produced elegant and delicate furniture that made use of the new Greco-Roman forms. His designs had the inspiration of the Sheraton style, but unlike Sheraton's they remained graceful after the later inclusion of French tastes. Phyfe's designs had a decidedly anglicized flavor that often finds parallels in the more restrained examples of the English Regency. To say that he worked in one style or another would be incorrect, since he drew on many influences to create his own Neoclassical style. The use of the saber leg

in chairs and pedestal tables, with its ornament of either waterleaf carving or reeding, is so closely associated with him that furniture of that design is popularly said to be in the Duncan Phyfe style. The firm continued in business until his retirement in 1847.

AMERICAN EMPIRE

American Empire refers to the furniture that has a more direct French Empire influence. These designs were made after the War of 1812 until about 1830. During this phase, American pieces assumed the solid austerity that marked the French designs. American makers took up the use of bronze mounts and included gilded carvings to contrast with glossy expanses of dark wood. The ancient forms of Grecian sofas and klismos and curule chairs were at their peak of American development. The height of the Empire period in furniture coincided with the peak of the American obsession with the aesthetic styles of the ancient civilizations.

A leading figure of the period was Charles-Honoré Lannuier, a French immigrant cabinetmaker and ébéniste who brought the best of the French Empire style to his practice in New York. His presence established a high standard for the Empire style and helped make New York the

leading center for its dissemination in America. Coming from France, Lannuier had a style that was very different from that of Phyfe. The true French Empire style depended heavily on carved and gilded acanthus leaves, wreaths and winged figures in supporting roles. His designs were rich, opulent, crisply detailed, deeply carved and bold. One of the notable features of his work is the calculated balance between bright gilding and ormolu, and the deep richness of the mahogany or rosewood. By

using both in the proper way, the qualities of each were enhanced.

American Empire designs from the peak years of the period are bold and exciting. The formality of the style, with its cold rectilinear features, prevented it from enjoying a popular usage across all levels of American society. The pieces executed by the leading cabinetmakers of the day were for the upper strata, and the vast majority of Americans furnished their homes with furniture that was a continuation of an earlier style with Empire-like details, or a simplified version of the Empire designs. Painted or "fancy" furniture was an American interpretation of the design ideals of the period, and grew to be a subset of vernacular furniture that enjoyed widespread popularity. These pieces were usually painted black or with a very dark brown graining and decorated with gold paint, emulating the decorative scheme of ormolu mounts on dark wood. Late Sheraton and early Empire forms were continued, with painted decoration being substituted for the earlier use of inlay and veneer.

LATE EMPIRE

Late Empire describes the period of 1830 to 1840, a decade that saw a degradation of the Empire style into a coarser, mass-produced version. The Late Empire pieces bear little resemblance to the original

French designs. Many concessions were made to manufacturing at this time, and the style assumed a heavy, ponderous and uninspired appearance. Production methods made furniture in this style available to a large number of people, and it became the mainstream Empire furniture that most Americans could own. In its final form, Empire furniture was characterized by large expanses of mahogany or rosewood veneered surfaces, the use of thick side columns, thick lyre or scrolled elements, and frequent use of wide ogee or gently rounded, pulvinated molding profiles. Ormolu mounts were phased out and inexpensive glass knobs were introduced. The vernacular style of the Empire had few endearing qualities and gave the style a bad connotation in later years.

The 1830s marked the end of cabinetmaking as it had been known since the end of the 17th century. The Industrial Revolution that had brought labor-saving machinery to the craft required a large capital investment. To cover the cost of that investment, furniture had to be made in quantity, and quantity required simplicity and homogeneity. As a result, furniture designs were largely stripped of their labor-intensive decoration and detail, and reduced to a manufacturable form. In order to mass-market these mass-produced pieces, manufacturers had to design them to have a universal appeal, necessitating the lowest common denominator of styling. Individually made pieces of custom furniture were still available to the more wealthy or discriminating buyer, but the vast majority of Americans purchased factory-made furniture. Workshops had become manufactories, and with the exclusion of hand work those became factories. While furniture of good quality became more affordable to the average person, it had lost its individuality and spirit in the process. Other interesting styles came and went, but the remarkable chain of events and web of circumstances that sparked the American masterpieces of the 18th century were not to be repeated.

A HISTORICAL SUMMARY

One hundred years is a relatively short period of time in the history of human events, but changes of great significance and monumental proportion occurred during the 18th century. The world was a very different place at the end of the century than it had been at the beginning, and furniture design, cabinetmaking and the wide spectrum of the decorative arts reflected these changes.

At the time of the Restoration of Charles II, designs developed among courtiers and royalty. As the nobility turned its attention to cultural pursuits and a prosperous middle class grew, court designs filtered down, eventually extending to the far reaches of the Empire as the 18th century dawned. Furniture design, now having been decentralized, became increasingly driven by the market and was shaped by the needs and tastes of customers. This trend culminated with the explosion of illustrated design books that appeared after the mid-century, making furniture designs marketable commodities in themselves.

The design books led to a much faster dissemination of styles. Only the time required for engraving, printing and shipping separated outlying colonists from the newest trends in London. These books also led to a more rapid succession of styles as designers competed with one another and improved upon earlier designs. Twice as many styles appeared in the second half of the century as in the first. The design publications also led to a more uniform interpretation of the styles. William and Mary pieces were diverse, imaginative and regionally distinct, but Sheraton pieces are so similar that their place of origin is often difficult to pinpoint.

For each style, the form and decorative elements were a reaction to the style that had preceded it. In contrast to the Jacobean designs, William and Mary pieces featured a deliberate vertical thrust and an emphasis on a rich and detailed surface. The Queen Anne designs increased the vertical emphasis but made it appear effortless, and shifted visual interest from the surface to the shape. The Chippendale era transformed this loftiness into a stately presence, and refocused interest toward a rich and opulently detailed surface. The Federal period called for an elegance of form with a simplicity of surface ornament. Even within the Neoclassical, the pendulum of style swung. Adam used applied surface ornament, Hepplewhite called for smooth surfaces with inlaid ornament, Sheraton augmented inlay with simple shallow carved detail, while the Empire designs called for all new forms.

From this series of opposites, similarities appear in every other iteration of style. William and Mary, Chippendale and Empire designs share similarities in their bold presence and importance of surface detail. Queen Anne and Federal pieces share an emphasis on a graceful form and the restraint of ornament. The writer Lewis Mumford was correct in asserting, "Every generation revolts against its fathers and makes friends with its grandfathers."

The styles are nearly perfect analogies for the lifestyles and outlooks of the times in which they existed. They reflect the increasing prosperity over the century and the value given to the decorative arts. The William and Mary period reflected the global influences and cultural interests of the Enlightenment that were unleashed in post-Restoration England. The Queen Anne style typified the standards of gentility and refined elegance pursued by the emerging upper class. The Chippendale-era designs reflected the need for richness and opulence born of increasing power and wealth. The Federal style embodied the structure, order, harmony and optimism of a Republic inspired by ancient civilizations.

Throughout the century, some aspects held constant. American designs came from English styles, and English styles came from

IMPORTANT DESIGN POINTS
OF FURNITURE STYLES

JACOBEAN
- Horizontal format
- Low center of mass
- Rectilinear forms
- Ornament applied to structure
- Contrasting surface ornament and/or shallow carving

WILLIAM & MARY
- Vertical format
- Evidence of raised mass
- Symmetry and orderly division of space
- Deep profiles to turnings and carvings
- Rich and visually interesting surfaces

QUEEN ANNE
- Extended vertical format
- Weightless appearance to disguise mass
- Extensive use of graceful, cyma-curved shapes
- Balance of solid and void
- Smooth glossy surface with occasional ornamentation

CHIPPENDALE
- Continuation of Queen Anne format
- Mass is made more evident
- Continuation of curved shapes with increase in rectilinear form
- Extensively carved surfaces and added ornamental elements
- Deep, rich and opulent surfaces

FEDERAL
- Delicate appearance with light, high, stable stance
- Amount of mass is minimized
- Rectilinear in elevation, gently curved fronts in plan
- Classical or geometrical elements used for ornament
- Lightly carved or decoratively veneered smooth surfaces

French and European trends. The manner in which the successive styles came to be adopted in a given country is remarkably similar over the century. The English undertook an Anglicized version of each style that differed in interpretation from the Continental version. On each occasion there is mention in the literature of the English taking up a style without a full appreciation of its development, mixing in other influences and arriving at their own version. This new style usually superseded a previous style that had evolved to a point of ornamental excess, and had been totally exhausted of new design possibilities. The Americans were consistently selective in what they chose to take up from England, their tastes filtering out the occasional excesses of English design. The Americans infused the designs with their own sense of proportion and detail, which yielded a spirited and distinctly American version.

By examining the events and circumstances that surrounded furniture making in the 18th century, it becomes clear why American furniture has a distinctly different character from English furniture. The attributes of American pieces were shaped by the prevailing tastes of the colonies, the small size of colonial cities and the nature of the cabinetmaking business at the time.

Conservative values of thrift and diligence were deeply rooted in the culture of American cities. The early Quaker Philadelphians and Puritan New Englanders were opposed to frivolous ornament and ostentatious display. Unlike in England, there was no aristocracy to support flamboyant furniture of unlimited cost. The tastes of the colonies had an underpinning of practicality and functional design, but the beauty of a piece was equally important. Good aesthetic qualities were a reflection of the owner's status and refinement and the cabinetmaker's skill as a designer and craftsman.

The American cities were very different both from one another and from London. They were scattered along the coast, each under a different regional government and each with its own relationship with England. These were very small cities: At mid-century, when Boston and Philadelphia were of nearly equal population, each was less than 2.5% the size of London. The relative isolation of American cities allowed regional preferences and variations to flourish.

Because of the small size of the cities, American cabinetmakers and their customers were on a more equal and personal basis than in England. The successful American cabinetmaker was a respected member of the community, and his clients were likely to be among the leading members of the same community. Each was known to one another and known about the city. They had a personal and often long-running relationship that did not end with the delivery of the finished piece. In London, a journeyman cabinet-maker could have worked in the employ of a shop master making furniture in a back street for the distant manor house of an aristocrat he would never meet.

The size of American cities was reflected in their cabinetmaking shops. At mid-century, even the leading American shops employed only a handful of workmen, and most of them were likely to be family members or live-in apprentices. Christopher Townsend's Newport shop measured only 12 ft. by 24 ft. At the same time, Thomas Chippendale's business occupied three houses, several outbuildings, and employed at least 22 specialized workmen. (Both businesses were dwarfed by the London firm of George Seddon, which employed 400 journeyman in the 1780s.) With such a small operation, the American cabinetmaker was personally responsible for every aspect of the work. He had none of the anonymity of being a small part of a large firm. In addition, small family-owned shops had a consistent and repetitive method of work that led to the continued development and refinement of a design over time. As independent craftsmen, American furniture makers were proud of their work and their individual style. Their good reputation and future commissions rested on the quality of every piece they made.

Although wealthy Americans could and did import English pieces, American pieces continued to be a favorite. To a successful American, furnishings of local origin, if they were equal in design and workmanship to those available from London, were a testament to the refinement and civility of their own city. Prominent citizens would naturally want to extol the virtues of a place they had helped develop. Their patronage of local craftsmen reinforced the regional style, furthered its development and set a standard of good taste for other members of the community to follow.

The period was remarkable for its evolution of design and noteworthy for its embodiment of lifestyles and prevailing tastes in its decorative arts. American furniture, sparked by a rare combination of opportunities and motives, and guided by an inherent sense of design and personal responsibility for the final product, transcends being mere artifact. Eighteenth-century American pieces stand without equal as milestones of achievement in applied art and design.

Part Two

THE METHODS AND MATERIALS
OF THE 18*th*-CENTURY
CABINETMAKER

The styles and designs of 18th-century American furniture were influenced greatly by the methods and techniques of its makers and the materials that were available to them. A familiarity with the construction of period pieces is essential to a thorough appreciation and understanding of 18th-century designs.

Throughout the 18th century, refinements in techniques allowed advancements in design, while trends in style and taste required updated methods of cabinetmaking. This pattern of alternating furtherance of style and technique is evident in every major phase of 18th-century design. During the William and Mary period, the technique of dovetailing allowed furniture to be built in a vertical format. The Queen Anne–era ideal of lofty grace required structural changes to accomplish that end. During the Chippendale period, opulently carved ornament was added to the established structure. By the Federal period, the technique of inlay and veneering and the joinery required for thin structures had advanced to satisfy the prevailing taste in Neoclassical designs. Technique and design progressed together, each spurring advancements in the other.

Looking at how furniture was made in the 18th century offers a revealing glimpse into American lives during the period. The cabinetmakers, many of whom worked in small, family-run shops, were designers and businessmen as well as extraordinary craftsmen. Their productivity, industriousness, inventiveness and quality of workmanship become apparent when their individual and collective works are examined in detail for both design and technique.

An examination of methods and materials can also offer insight into the economics of the cabinetmaker's trade. Urban examples often exhibit labor-intensive practices designed to maximize the yield from wood. These details indicate an abundance of available labor and a relatively high cost of materials, which were often imported. In contrast, rural examples show less of an investment in time and a willingness to use native materials freely. All cabinetmakers sought to optimize their methods of construction because they would be responsible for any future repairs that would be required. Since 18th-century cabinetmakers were in the business of making furniture, their products were shaped by economic forces as well as by stylistic influences.

The first part of this book concentrated on the evolution of furniture styles during the 18th century. This section focuses on the other half of the subject; it is a close look at the materials and techniques used by the 18th-century cabinetmaker. In the sections on materials, the purpose is to discuss what was available to the period makers, what the characteristics of the materials were, how the period makers used them, and what our current knowledge can add to the understanding of the material. The sections on technique explore the traditional methods of work, how they evolved over the century, how they were affected by the availability of materials and changing tastes, and how modern techniques compare and contrast with 18th-century methods.

7

PERIOD SURFACES

AND THEIR MAKING

The working methods of 18th-century cabinetmakers were dictated by their tools, their materials and the very designs they set out to make. Every period original shows the unmistakable signs of the maker's hand, whether it is in the undulating surface of a hand-planed board or in the marks made to lay out and cut the joinery. The evidence of hand craftsmanship is an integral part of the nature of period originals, though it often goes unnoticed to the untrained eye. The marks of original tools, and the methods of work they represent, are so important to the character of original pieces that they warrant their own detailed discussion. They speak to the fact that, in centuries past, a deliberate human effort was made to create an original object of beauty and utility from raw materials, basic tools and a practical education in design and the ways of wood.

The Importance of Period Surfaces

We have all seen replicas of important originals that are dimensionally accurate and academically perfect but lack the look and feel of the period piece. This shortcoming is most often the result of

applying modern methods of work to 250-year-old designs. A wide belt sander will yield a smooth table top of even thickness, but it will not have the unmistakable character of a hand-planed top. A duplicating carving machine will produce a close approximation of a ball and claw foot, but it will never capture the spirit of the hand-sculpted original.

Even handmade replicas are sometimes made in a manner that fails to capture the true character of the originals. One cannot apply the modern standards of absolutely flat surfaces, machine-like uniformity and perfection to objects that were originally made by hand with relatively simple tools. Period furniture should look like period furniture, and an 18th-century design with a 20th-century surface finish is not an accurate re-creation of the original. Understanding the original tools, methods and standards is essential to faithful replications.

Those who build furniture in the period manner need to achieve an authentic surface as a foundation for an authentic-looking finish. Apart from the obvious differences in color, finish and patina, the surface of the wood in a period piece is fundamentally different from a surface achieved by modern means. This

observation is not surprising, given the difference in available tools and the lack of power equipment in the 18th century. The importance in pinpointing the underlying basis for the look of a period surface is twofold: for the collector, it yields more information about how the piece was built; and for today's maker, it offers the key to replicating that look successfully.

THE CUT SURFACE

The most fundamental feature of original surfaces is the evidence that period makers cut, rather than sanded, wood. One reason for this was that they did not have the readily available, long-lasting abrasives that we have today. The first definitive reference to sandpaper appears in an 1827 edition of *The Cabinet-Maker's Guide*, published by Jacob B. Moore in Concord, Massachusetts. This practical guide describes how to make "glass-paper" by crushing glass in an iron mortar, sifting it through a sieve and sprinkling it onto glue-coated paper. Pumice stone, in solid-block form, is known to have been used as an abrasive, but, as with sandpaper, it was more for smoothing the surface for finishing rather than for shaping the wood. It is important to remember that the original makers were cutting, shaping and smoothing with sharp hand tools that left smooth surfaces, so there was very little need for sandpaper in the actual shaping of wood.

In any discussion of period surfaces it's important to distinguish between the levels of attention afforded different areas in a given piece. Primary surfaces are those that are visible and finished; naturally they are given the greatest care in preparation, smoothing and flattening. Secondary surfaces are those that are not readily visible, including the undersides of tops, the insides of cases and frames, and the backs of drawer fronts. They are planed flat and true but not dressed beyond that preparatory stage. Tertiary surfaces, such as the undersides of drawer bottoms and the backs of cases, don't warrant much planing at all. In most instances they are planed only to reduce their thickness, and they often show the saw marks of rough-sawn lumber (see the photos on p. 116).

On period pieces, the subtle marks of hand tools are everywhere, if they are fortunate enough to have survived. They are not always readily apparent, and it helps to know what to look for. Knowing what to expect requires being familiar with the methods of the original craftsmen, and knowing where a certain tool was likely to have been used. The parallel waves of the plane on secondary surfaces are the most obvious, but the traces of cabinet scrapers on primary surfaces and the inimitable marks of chisels and marking tools require closer scrutiny. To historians and scholars, these marks indicate the available tools and prevailing methods of the period; to collectors and antiquarians, they are a clue to originality and authenticity.

The Advent of Sawn Stock

The earliest American furniture was of Jacobean frame-and-panel design. Its components were either nearly square frame members or thin flat panels, both of which were relatively short. These were easily split, or riven, from short lengths of oak or ash using a froe and mallet and

Pitsawing is illustrated in *The Book of Trades,* an English publication reprinted in America in 1807. While water-powered sawmills were operating in the colonies as early as 1634, pitsawing was required to cut logs into boards in areas away from mills. Since the coastal furniture-making centers had an abundance of workers but few sawmills, pitsawing continued to be practiced into the 19th century. *(COURTESY DOVER PUBLICATIONS)*

dressed to their final dimension with drawknives and hand planes.

As the 17th century drew to a close and the William and Mary style came into vogue, frame-and-panel joinery gave way to the dovetailed joinery of thin boards (see Chapter 8). Dovetailing was a radical departure from the previous way of building furniture, and with it came different methods of work. Instead of thick frame members and thin panels, the new styles required thin boards that could only be produced by sawing them from a log.

As early as 1634 a sawmill was operating on the Piscataqua River, on what is now the border between New Hampshire and

Maine. By 1706 there were 70 sawmills in operation in the colonies. In more rural areas, mills did not arrive until the middle of the century. Most of these water-powered mills could develop only 2 hp to 3 hp—enough to operate only one reciprocating blade. Those that could develop more power had multiple blades cutting several boards simultaneously. The average mill was doing well if it cut 1,000 board-feet of softwood a day. Where there were no water-powered mills, sawing was done by hand with a pitsaw. Two men were required to work the saw, one standing atop the log and the other in the pit below.

The uneven marks of pit sawing are evident on the pine drawer bottom of a Hepplewhite sideboard.

Water-powered reciprocating saws left parallel blade marks, as seen on this underside of a maple tabletop.

Sawn lumber was used to sheathe houses, and by the end of the 17th century it was coming into use increasingly in the making of furniture. While the use of sawn lumber in cabinetmaking offered new challenges, it also created some new possibilities. Cabinetmakers were no longer restricted to using easily riven, straight-grained woods. Other native hardwoods with more attractive color and figure, such as maple, walnut and brittle fruit woods, all of which were not easily split but were readily sawn, came into widespread use. This change coincided with the emerging tastes in furniture aesthetics, wherein the surface features of the wood itself became an important part of the design, as evidenced by the extensive use of matched figured veneers on William and Mary pieces.

The saw marks of rough stock are rarely seen on finished furniture except on unseen surfaces such as drawer bottoms and case backs. The nature of the saw marks tells how the piece was sawn. Pit-sawn wood is distinctive in that the saw marks left on the board extend across its width, but show the variations that are inherent in hand work (top photo at left). The marks are not perfectly parallel or straight, since one sawyer could get ahead of the other, and there was nothing to hold the saw perfectly vertical. The advent of water-powered mills, which were basically mechanized pitsaws, produced saw marks that are straight and parallel (bottom photo at left). The spacing of these marks is often uneven, however, since the reciprocating blade cut at its own pace. Circular saw marks, with their distinctive curved shape, are not seen on 18th-century American furniture. The circular saw for cutting wood was invented in England by Samuel Miller in 1777, but circular saws did not come into widespread use in America until the middle of the 19th century, when there were steam engines powerful enough to run them. The bandsaw, also an English invention, was patented in 1808 by William Newberry, but it did not see popular use in the United States until after the Civil War.

Hand Planing

Once the roughsawn wood was properly dried, it was cut and planed by hand to its final dimensions. A number of different planes were used in preparing and finishing stock, each with a specific purpose.

FORE PLANES
The first task was to flatten the stock, remove the saw marks and plane it to an even thickness. This would have been done with what was then called a fore plane, a plane 12 in. to 18 in. long with a blade, or iron, about 2 in. wide (see the top photo on the facing page). Since the stock was wider than the plane, the cutting edge was ground and sharpened with a slightly convex edge, with not much more than 1/16 in. of crown, so the corners of the blade would not leave tracks. This convex shape is responsible for the distinctive waved surface of hand-planed wood, which is especially noticeable on secondary surfaces. Fore planes are more

commonly known as jack planes today, but a 1677 text mentions that while carpenters called them jack planes, joiners referred to them as fore planes because they were used to prepare the stock before using other planes. (Some sources state that fore planes were the longer of the two, but furniture makers were likely to have used smaller planes then carpenters.)

By using a fore plane and planing the surface alternately with the grain and then across it, a fairly flat and true surface can be achieved. This planing technique is especially important on wide boards or panels that have been assembled of boards glued edge to edge, where there may be some cupping across the grain. In the case of edge-glued panels, the boards were planed, glued together and then planed again to achieve a flat surface and uniform thickness. Some highly figured wood, such as tiger maple, flame cherry or birch, cannot be planed easily in the direction of the grain, since the figured grain tends to tear out. To dress their surface flat and true, they can be planed in alternating diagonal directions across the grain. Given the system of shop hierarchy at the time, this kind of preparatory planing would have been one of the first jobs for apprentices.

SMOOTHING PLANES

With the stock planed flat and to its near final thickness, a smoothing plane was used to dress the surface. Smoothing planes of the period were 7 in. to 9 in. long with a blade about 2 in. wide and a coffin-shaped wooden body (photo at right). As with fore planes, the blade was ground with a slightly convex cutting edge, though with less of a crown. Since the purpose of this plane was to smooth the surface rather than remove material quickly, it would be kept exceptionally sharp and set for a very fine cut. Smoothing planes were used on primary surfaces that were to be eventually finished, and probably would not have been used to smooth secondary surfaces. The cutting of the fore plane was usually adequate for those surfaces.

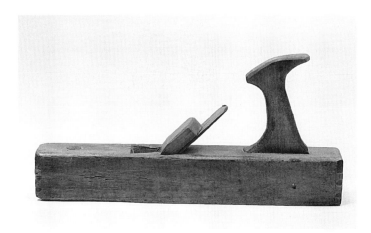

Measuring from 12 in. to 18 in. long, the fore or jack plane was used to flatten and true rough-sawn lumber and to plane it to the appropriate thickness. *(COURTESY BUD STEERE)*

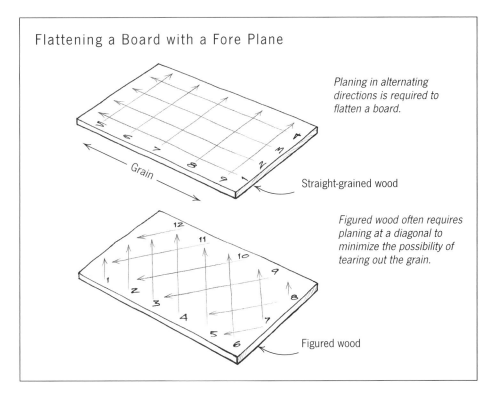

Flattening a Board with a Fore Plane

Planing in alternating directions is required to flatten a board.

Straight-grained wood

Figured wood often requires planing at a diagonal to minimize the possibility of tearing out the grain.

Figured wood

Smoothing planes, which measure from 7 in. to 9 in. long, were used for smoothing primary surfaces. This smoothing plane was made by Cesar Chelor, slave of Wrentham, Massachusetts, plane maker Francis Nicholson, some time between 1753 (when Chelor was given his freedom) and 1784 (when he died).

(COURTESY BUD STEERE)

The jointer plane measures from 20 in. to 30 in. long and was used to straighten the edge of boards before they were joined. The length of the jointer plane enabled it to flatten slight curves in edges that shorter planes would only follow.
(COURTESY BUD STEERE)

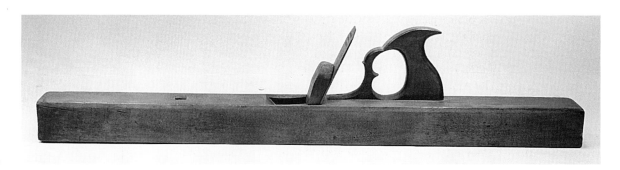

Cutting-Edge Geometry of Planes

SMOOTHING, FORE, TRYING
AND JOINTER PLANES

Iron

Wedge

Body

45°

25°

BLOCK PLANE

Wedge

Iron

Body

12° to 20°

JOINTER PLANES

To achieve the very straight edge required to join two or more boards together, a longer jointer (or joyner) plane would have been used. Jointer planes range from 20 in. to 30 in. long with blades about 2½ in. wide (photo above). Their long length enabled them to straighten curved profiles that smaller planes would only ride over. Since the jointer was required to make a flat cut, and since most edges were narrower than the blade, the cutting edge was ground and sharpened straight and flat. Shorter jointer planes were later referred to as trying or truing planes, since they would be used to make minor adjustments to the jointed edge, and obtaining that perfect edge-to-edge fit was a process of trial and error.

STRIKE BLOCK PLANES

Special planes for trimming across the end grain were called strike block planes in 17th-century references, and later were called straight block planes or miter planes. They were designed to hold the blade at a very low angle of 12° to 20°, so low that the beveled side of the blade is up. This low angle is required to cut cleanly across the grain, slicing the fibers directly across their length. Miter or strike block planes of the period are known to have been about 12 in. long. They were essential for smoothing the surfaces of cross-grain cuts made with a handsaw.

Most hand tools were imported, but over the course of the 18th century, American toolmaking grew, especially in the area of wooden planes. The body of American planes was made of a hardwood like yellow birch; English plane makers preferred to use

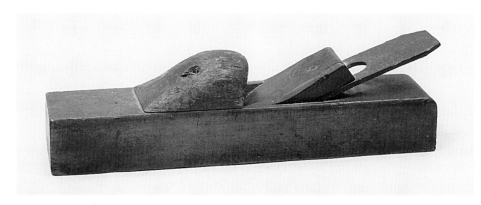

The low-angle strike block plane, sometimes called a miter plane, was designed to cut across end grain.
(COURTESY BUD STEERE)

beech. Cast-iron, brass or bronze planes did not appear until the end of the 18th century, and they did not see widespread use until the middle of the 19th century. Most plane irons, even for American-made planes, were imported from England. The irons were positioned at about 45° (except for low-angle planes) and held in place with a wooden wedge. The amount that the blade extended was adjusted by tapping the top of the blade gently. Irons are sharpened in the same manner as a chisel. The bevel is ground at about a 25° angle with a grinding wheel, and the beveled edge is sharpened with progressively finer oil- or water-lubricated stones. The final cutting edge

is honed with a leather strop that removes any wire edge that has formed and polishes the bevel.

The cutting action of a plane slices a thin layer from the surface of the wood. The quality of the cut surface is affected by the sharpness of the blade and whether the cut is with or against the grain. Cutting with the grain implies cutting in the same direction in which the wood fibers are rising. Cutting against the grain is cutting in the direction that the fibers are falling. When going against the grain, the shaving tends to split off ahead of the blade, and below the level of the cut. The result is a jagged surface of broken wood fibers. By cutting with the grain, in the direction of its rise, the shaving will split off above the level of the blade, leaving a smooth cut surface. The double-iron blade that is in general use today is intended to break the chips off before they can split ahead of the cut. Double irons first appeared in 1767 as imported irons for American-made planes.

When planing across the grain, the sharpness of the blade is especially important. Wood fibers are weak in their adherence to one another, and they tend to tear away from the surface before they are cut from it. Planing across the grain is often easier than planing with it, and material is quickly removed. While the final surface is not as smooth as a cut with the grain, cross-grain planing is often the only way to plane figured wood.

Scraping

After planing, primary surfaces were taken to a higher level of smoothness with cabinet scrapers. Scrapers were especially important to early cabinetmakers, and much of what is now accomplished by sanding was done by scraping in the 18th century.

Scrapers differ from planes in the geometry of their cutting edge and in the characteristics of their cut. A scraper (it is nothing like a paint scraper) is a sharp blade that is shaped to produce a microscopic hooked edge. This sharp hooked edge is

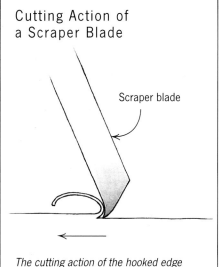

Cutting Action of a Scraper Blade

Scraper blade

The cutting action of the hooked edge of a scraper blade limits its depth of cut. The fine cut does not tear out the grain, making the scraper ideal for figured wood surfaces.

then drawn across the surface of the wood, in the direction of the grain, removing an exceptionally thin shaving, far thinner than shavings produced by most planes. Since the cut is so gentle and shallow, the scraper does not tear out chunks where the grain dips, as planes can do, and the orientation of the grain is not as important.

Scrapers fall into two categories: bevel-edge blades and square-edge blades. Bevel-edge blades are sharpened like plane blades, and then the cutting edge is rolled into a hook shape by drawing a hardened burnishing tool along its length (see the drawing on p. 120). Square-edge blades are sharpened with stones to have sharp square edges, which are then worked into hook shapes with a burnisher. Either blade is drawn across the surface so that the hook does the cutting. By burnishing the blade with a large or small hook, you can vary the cutting characteristics of the scraper. The blades can be hand-held, or fixed in any number of blade holders available for the purpose. Eighteenth-century blade holders were little more than blocks of wood with a slot to hold the scraper blade.

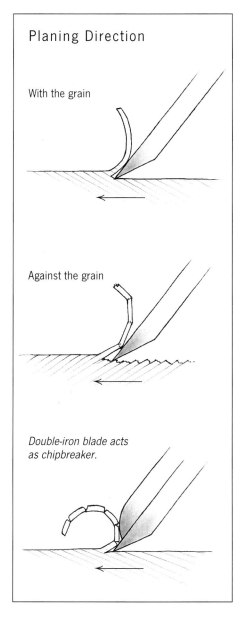

Planing Direction

With the grain

Against the grain

Double-iron blade acts as chipbreaker.

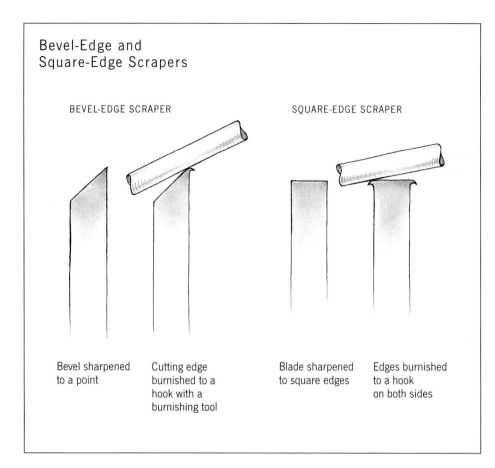

Bevel-Edge and Square-Edge Scrapers

BEVEL-EDGE SCRAPER

Bevel sharpened
to a point

Cutting edge
burnished to a
hook with a
burnishing tool

SQUARE-EDGE SCRAPER

Blade sharpened
to square edges

Edges burnished
to a hook
on both sides

Scrapers have been made in a variety of forms for use on surfaces of different shapes. Flat surfaces are smoothed with a straight-edged blade held by hand or in a simple wooden holder. Curved molding profiles that cannot be made with straight molding planes can be shaped with profiled scrapers.

The fact that the scraper cuts with its unique hooked edge prevents it from cutting deep below the surface. The shaving from a scraper can be less than one thousandth of an inch thick. By comparison, plane shavings are rarely less than two thousandths of an inch thick, and paper is about four thousandths of an inch thick. A shaving this thin is so flexible that it doesn't tend to splinter off material ahead of the blade, and the inside radius of the hook edge, which acts like a microscopic chipbreaker, further reduces that possibility. As a result, the scraper works nearly as well against the grain as it does with it, making it about the only tool that can cut and leave a good surface on highly figured wood. Since the scraper cuts the surface rather than abrades it, it leaves no scratches and does not clog the wood pores with dust.

While the scraper produces an authentic primary surface, its use does not end there. Almost any job that would be done by sanding today was originally done with a scraper. For example, to make two surfaces flush, such as where a drawer divider meets a case or a case joins to a leg, modern practice would call for block sanding. Using period methods, a hand plane or spokeshave would be used to even the surfaces, and the final leveling would be done by scraping. It is quicker, cleaner, easier and far less prone to error. A sharp scraper can remove a lot of material quickly, and it produces a smooth surface without scratching the adjoining areas. The user does have to pay attention to how the tools are cutting and change direction if the wood shows any signs of tearing out. Scrapers do not cut well across the grain, and that can be a problem where a level surface joins another at right angles. Using the scraper diagonally across the joint can minimize any ill effects. A craftsperson who is proficient with a scraper can build a piece that is virtually ready to finish without the use of sandpaper.

Spokeshaves

Spokeshaves are in essence little hand planes with handles on either side. They are used to shape and smooth complex shapes and sweeping curves like those of cabriole legs. Their cutting blades average about 1 1/2 in.

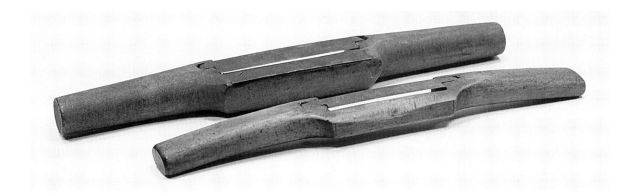

wide and are usually ground straight across. They are able to follow curved surfaces because the length of their sole is less than 1 in. For smaller-radius curved surfaces, there are curved-sole spokeshaves that can cut where flat-sole models cannot. For the more specialized tasks of hollowing and rounding, spokeshaves are available with convex and concave blade profiles.

A spokeshave is one of the most useful tools for making period pieces, and it is also a joy to use. It can quickly shape curved components that would have originally been rough-cut to shape with a bowsaw or framed saw. These pieces include cabriole legs, chair stiles, crest rails, back splats, apron profiles, and serpentine and bombé forms. A spokeshave can be used to round or chamfer any corner or edge, especially a curved edge, and can also cut a round or half-round section on square stock. The spokeshave lets the user make complex sculpted shapes with the safety and control of a tool that removes a consistent and adjustable amount of material with each pass. Like the plane, it is a sharp cutting tool and leaves a surface that is clean and smooth.

Rasps and Files

While spokeshaves are versatile, they do have their limitations, and anything they cannot do can probably be accomplished with a rasp or file. Rasps and files were an important part of the period furniture maker's inventory of tools. They were used for both shaping and smoothing, tasks that are usually done with abrasives today. Rasps have raised metal points that remove material aggressively, and are primarily used for rough shaping that can't readily be done with other cutting tools. Files have fine parallel cutting ridges, which leave a smoother surface, and are used for final shaping and smoothing. Some of the complex shapes of the period, such as cabriole legs, snake feet and sweeping aprons, were brought to their final shape with progressively finer rasps and files.

There are a few areas of period pieces that can be shaped only with rasps and files. Rasping is about the only way to shape the top of a pad or Dutch foot (see pp. 152-153) and blend it into the round section of an ankle. Similarly, rasping and filing can cut a smooth transition from the back side of cabriole leg into its knee block, as well as dress the top of a knee where it joins the apron. Rasping is a quick way of rounding a square corner or easing a sharp edge. In addition, a very fine rasp or wood file can do anything that a sanding block can do, and is especially useful in smoothing away any flat cuts from a curved surface that has been chiseled or spokeshaved to shape.

A careful examination of period pieces reveals the marks of rasps or files used in their making. They are most often seen in the inconspicuous places and undersides of curved aprons and rails. Many cabriole legs show their marks on the underside of the knee where it meets the knee block. File marks are frequently evident on the sharp inside corners of shaped arms and crest rails. On very well-preserved originals, the marks from individual teeth of the file used to break sharp edges or round a profile are often still visible. Files were used in places that other tools couldn't reach and in places that today would be sanded.

Rasps, with aggressive freestanding teeth, and files, with a series of raised cutting edges, were used to shape and smooth wood in areas that other tools were not able to reach. Both files and rasps were used in lieu of abrasives.

(COURTESY BUD STEERE)

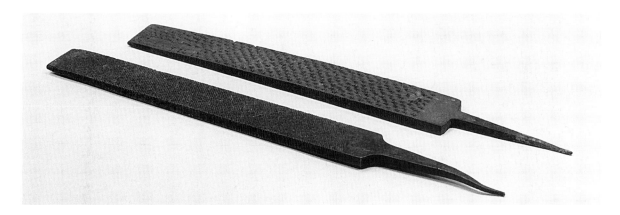

Shaping an Apron

Front of apron

Saw kerf

A saw was used to cut away most of the material. The final shape was cut with chisels.

Chisel and gouge marks

Chamfered edge

Inside of apron

Chiseling the final shape left the inside edge ragged and splintered, so it was usually chamfered.

Eighteenth-century cabinetmakers used a combination of sawing, chiseling and rasping to make shaped aprons and rails. The marks of these tools are usually evident on the underside of the components. (This photo shows the underside of the front leg and apron of the Queen Anne side chair pictured on p. 245.)

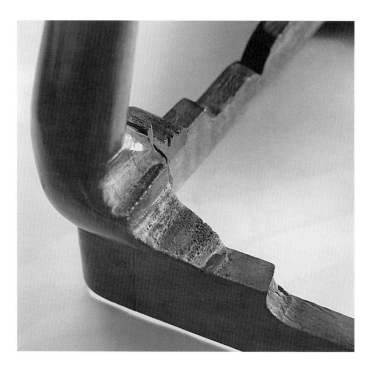

Cutting Shaped Elements

During most of the 18th century, American furniture was built with shaped aprons or rails as integral parts of the design. These shapes were intended to be seen in profile or as silhouettes and played an important part in creating the graceful shapes, the balance of solid and void, and the sense of constrained energy that were among the aesthetics of the period. These shapes include the curved aprons of high chests and dressing tables, the scalloped aprons of rectangular tea tables and the shaped seat rails of chairs.

Cutting these shaped parts was not always easy. Eighteenth-century cabinetmakers had handsaws used for cutting lumber and joinery, but these cut in straight lines. Cutting along a curved line required the narrow blade of a framed saw. Framed saws include those with a blade held in tension in the center of a wooden frame, which could cut gentle curves, and bowsaws, which have the blade mounted on the outside of a frame and are better able to cut more complex shapes. Even the most versatile bowsaw was limited by the width of its blade, which was not less than 3/8 in. and prevented the saw from cutting very tight curves.

Because of the limitations of their saws, 18th-century cabinetmakers used a combination of sawing, chiseling and rasping to achieve the final shapes of aprons. The gentle curves that could be cut to shape with a bowsaw were trimmed and adjusted with chisels and spokeshaves. Shapes that were more intricate were sawn where possible and chiseled the rest of the way (see the drawing at left). How much was sawn and how much was chiseled depended on the intricacy of the shape and the capability of the cabinetmaker's saw. The combination of sawing and chiseling from the outside edge toward the inside left a ragged and splintered inside edge. This edge was then cleaned up by chamfering.

The undersides of these shaped aprons are some of the most interesting parts of period furniture. The tool marks of the original maker usually remain clearly visible. They offer great insight into the tools and methods of the 18th century and are the cabinetmaking fingerprints of the craftsman who made the piece more than two centuries ago.

Making Moldings

Eighteenth-century moldings were either cut with molding planes or scraped with scratch stocks. Plane makers made molding planes in a number of standard shapes that could be used singly or in combination to produce more complex shapes. Scratch stocks were shaped scraper blades used to make shallow molding details.

MOLDING PLANES

Molding planes were made to cut only one shape. Many cabinetmakers used favorite molding planes so often that those molded profiles became indicative of their work. Planes could also be used in combinations to make a wide variety of shapes for cornice moldings. Thomas Sheraton's *Cabinet Dictionary* (London, 1803) illustrates how a rabbet plane is used to cut molding stock into a series of steps, and each step is then shaped with a different molding plane as if it was the edge of an individual board (see the drawing at right). Similarly, complex moldings could be assembled from single moldings, each made with a different molding plane.

SCRATCH STOCKS

Scratch stocks are shopmade tools that can be shaped to any shallow design. They are made by filing the desired profile in the edge of a scraper blade, sharpening the edge like a scraper blade, and affixing a fence of some sort. The blade is drawn along the surface of the wood repeatedly, guided by the fence, and the wood is cut by a scraping action. Since they were easily made, scratch stocks were a favorite tool of joiners for cutting shallow shadow moldings on the stiles and rails of joined chests. The use of scratch stocks continued through the century whenever a small molded shape, especially on a curved shape, needed to be cut. The beaded edges of curved chair stiles and the cockbeaded cases and drawer

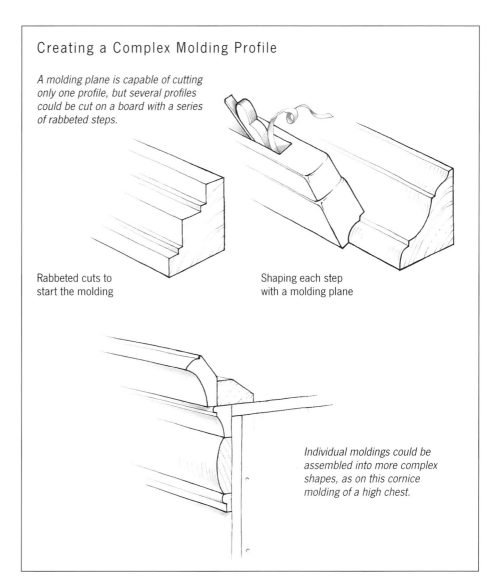

Creating a Complex Molding Profile

A molding plane is capable of cutting only one profile, but several profiles could be cut on a board with a series of rabbeted steps.

Rabbeted cuts to start the molding

Shaping each step with a molding plane

Individual moldings could be assembled into more complex shapes, as on this cornice molding of a high chest.

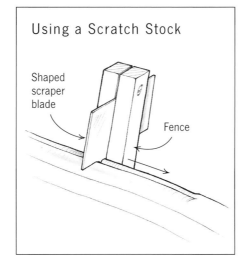

Using a Scratch Stock

Shaped scraper blade

Fence

dividers of curved-front case pieces are just two of the many uses of scratch stocks later in the 18th century.

Scratch stocks were also used to mold or flute tapered legs. Because molding or fluting tapered with the leg, the scratch stock could not be used with a simple fence. For this purpose, the molding box was devised. This box was designed to hold a component, like a tapered leg, in a fixed position while a scraper cutter in a sliding holder was guided along its length. By adjusting the position of the component, the cutter could be made to cut straight tapered flutes anywhere on the leg.

8

CONSTRUCTION

JOINERY

While American furniture of the 18th century is cherished for its aesthetic qualities, the pieces also set a standard for structural integrity and ingenuity. The trade of the cabinetmaker, which included more varied disciplines than that of the joiner, had not blossomed in America until toward the end of the 17th century, so the techniques were still quite new and under development during the 18th century. Nevertheless, the joinery and construction methods used during that period were sophisticated and elegant solutions to the task at hand. They reflect a familiarity and understanding of wood and its properties and were chosen with the functional requirements of the joint in mind. Over the century, American cabinetmakers optimized their joinery. One rarely finds joints that are more complicated than they need to be or examples that have failed because the joinery is not adequate. The requirement of having to make furniture of lasting integrity, balanced by the need to produce it by hand and for an affordable but profitable price, were driving forces behind the optimization of the joinery and structure of furniture.

The primary methods of joinery of 18th-century furniture were the mortise-and-tenon joint and the dovetail joint. The

mortise and tenon is a joint as old as woodworking itself, and was the primary joint of frame-and-panel furniture construction. Dovetails had been known for millennia but saw a resurgence in use near the end of the 17th century. The interlocking triangular elements of dovetail joints allowed thin pieces of wood to be joined without the need for a thicker joined frame. As exemplified by furniture of the William and Mary period, the new method of joinery revolutionized the way furniture was built. In addition to the important methods of joinery, there are a variety of methods of attaching tops, moldings and feet, all of which show an ingenuity, inventiveness and innate knowledge of the nature of wood.

Mortise-and-Tenon Joinery

The mortise and tenon is the most universal of joints. It is used to join framed pieces, like tables and chairs, that are composed of narrow members, as opposed to case pieces that are made up of flat panels. The mortise, or slot, is cut into the side of one member, and a snug-fitting tenon, made to fit into the mortise, is cut on the end

of the other member. When the tenon is assembled into the mortise, the two pieces are held securely at right angles to one another.

The joint is easily made with simple hand tools, including a saw, drill and chisels. Cabinetmakers lay out the joint with a mortising gauge, an adjustable marking gauge that can scribe two parallel lines simultaneously. The gauge is used to mark the size and position of both the mortise and the tenon. To cut the mortise, a series of holes are drilled between the scribed lines to remove most of the wood, and the remaining material is cut to the lines with chisels. Mortising chisels with thick blades were made expressly for this purpose. The tenon is cut with a tenon saw, a small backsaw made for just such cuts. The tenon is then trimmed to the scribed lines with chisels. The resulting joint fits together snugly and with a flush joint surface. Most mortise-and-tenon joints in period pieces were drilled and pegged through to lock the joint together.

Mortises and tenons that are $3/8$ in. wide are found on many 18th-century pieces, corresponding to the width of a standard chisel. The mortises are located $1/4$ in. to $1/2$ in. from the flush surface of the joint and are laid out to leave a shoulder on both

Laying Out and Cutting a Mortise-and-Tenon Joint

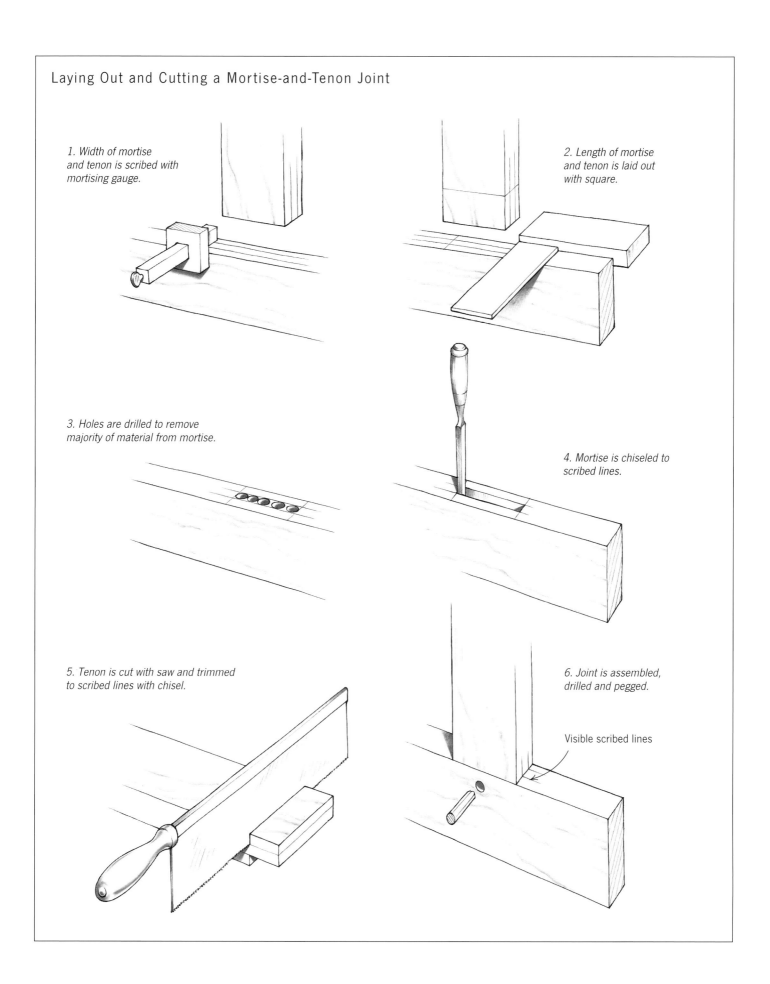

1. Width of mortise and tenon is scribed with mortising gauge.

2. Length of mortise and tenon is laid out with square.

3. Holes are drilled to remove majority of material from mortise.

4. Mortise is chiseled to scribed lines.

5. Tenon is cut with saw and trimmed to scribed lines with chisel.

6. Joint is assembled, drilled and pegged.

Visible scribed lines

sides of the tenoned piece. It is usually possible to see the original mortising gauge marks on the wood just outside the joint.

Mortise-and-tenon joints were made in a wide number of variations. Some were angled; some were housed to have shoulders on three or four sides; others extended clear through the mortised member; and some were doubled or appear in a series. They were designed and cut to suit the purpose of the joint without weakening the joined pieces.

Time-honored methods of joinery have achieved that distinction for their ability to accommodate the dynamic nature of wood. To join two pieces of wood securely is simple enough, but for the joint to endure it must maintain its structural integrity while the two components are continually expanding and contracting with changes in humidity. (For more on wood and wood movement, see Appendix I on p. 293.)

The key to maintaining a secure joint is to retain a compressive force between the shoulder of the tenoned member and the mating surface of the mortised part. A peg driven through a cross-drilled hole accomplishes this perfectly (see the drawing below). The compressive force that gives the joint its integrity can be achieved in one of two ways. The joint can be clamped tightly, and then drilled and pegged before the clamp is removed, or the joint may be draw-bored. In draw boring, the hole is drilled through the mortised part first. Then the joint is assembled and the exact position of the hole is marked on the tenon. The tenoned part is then removed and the hole is drilled slightly closer to the shoulder than the marking. When the joint is reassembled, the holes are slightly out of alignment; driving a peg through the joint draws the two parts tightly together.

Draw boring, while clever and effective, was probably not a common practice in the making of fine furniture during the 18th century. Most structural tenons in period pieces are $3/8$ in. thick and rarely longer than 1 in. With such a delicate tenon, a misalignment of more than about $1/32$ in. in the holes would result in breaking out the back of the tenon when the peg is forced through. The risk of breakage would be of particular concern when working with well-dried and somewhat brittle hardwoods. Period cabinetmakers frequently used spoon or shell bits that did not have an accurate center point to drill small-diameter holes, so they would have had difficulty in positioning a hole with the kind of precision required to make a draw-bored joint. Furthermore, any cabinetmaker of note would have had clamps among his inventory of tools, and would not have needed to draw-bore a joint.

In the pegged mortise-and-tenon joint, the tenoned piece is free to expand and contract without affecting the strength of the joint (see the drawing on the facing page). The mortised piece is also free to expand and contract, with the exception of the narrow width between the peg and the shoulder. That area is under constant compressive force in a tight joint, and is so small that expansion and contraction there would be negligible. Thus the pegged joint

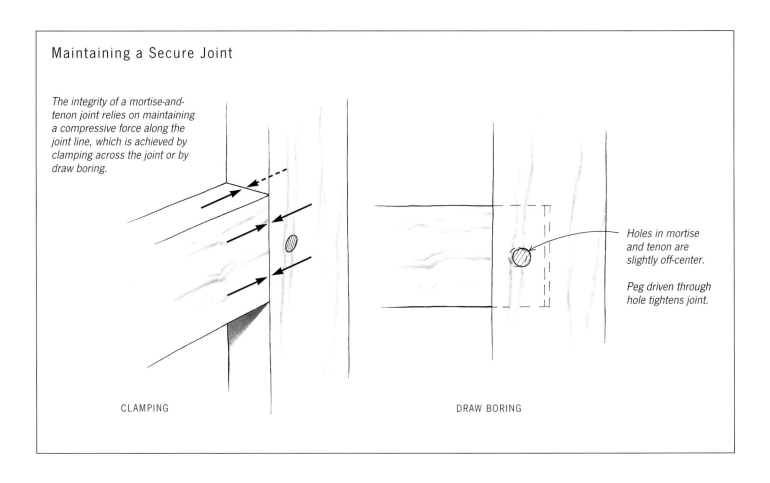

Maintaining a Secure Joint

The integrity of a mortise-and-tenon joint relies on maintaining a compressive force along the joint line, which is achieved by clamping across the joint or by draw boring.

Holes in mortise and tenon are slightly off-center.

Peg driven through hole tightens joint.

CLAMPING

DRAW BORING

is virtually immune to the effects of changes in humidity.

There are some other variations of the mortise-and-tenon joint that are occasionally seen in furniture, but most lack the durability of the simple pegged joint. One of these is the wedged mortise and tenon, where a through tenon is split with one or more wedges to tighten the joint. This joint relies on the outward pressure of the tenon at the outside edge to maintain enough friction to keep the joint together. Unfortunately, the tenon will shrink in width and the mortised member is free to shrink away from the tenon shoulder. Once that happens, the integrity of the joint is lost. The cross-wedged mortise and tenon is another variation of the joint that is often seen in early trestle tables. The tenon is long enough to pass through the mortised piece and extend out the other side. The wedge passes through the outside of the extended tenon, drawing the joint together. This arrangement allows for easy tightening or disassembly of the joint when needed. Although this is a great idea for furniture that will be assembled or disassembled frequently, it is not appropriate or practical for more refined pieces.

Dovetail Joinery

Dovetails are the interlocking triangular-shaped joints that enable wide, thin pieces of wood to be joined end-to-end, usually at right angles to one another. Because the grain in both pieces is oriented in the same direction, the pieces are able to expand and contract simultaneously with no adverse effect on the integrity of the joint. The joint evolved over the course of the 18th century as it was continually refined and optimized. The extensive use of dovetailing began in America with the William and Mary period at the end of the 17th century and signaled a fundamental change in the way furniture was made. The use of the dovetail and the more complex furniture designs that it enabled marked the divergence of the highly skilled trade of the cabinetmaker from that of the joiner. The new method of construction formed the structural basis for the many styles of furniture that evolved during the 18th century and after. Dovetail

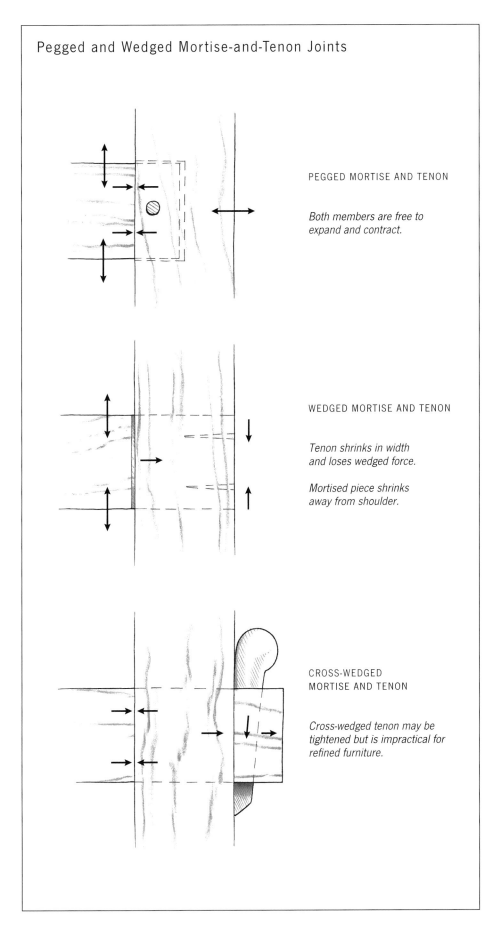

Pegged and Wedged Mortise-and-Tenon Joints

PEGGED MORTISE AND TENON

Both members are free to expand and contract.

WEDGED MORTISE AND TENON

Tenon shrinks in width and loses wedged force.

Mortised piece shrinks away from shoulder.

CROSS-WEDGED MORTISE AND TENON

Cross-wedged tenon may be tightened but is impractical for refined furniture.

Dovetail Joints

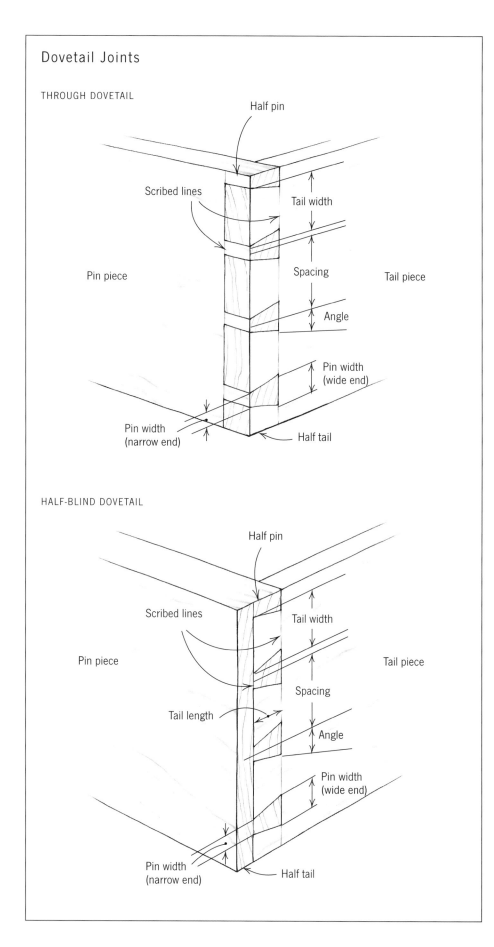

THROUGH DOVETAIL

Half pin

Scribed lines

Pin piece

Tail width

Spacing

Tail piece

Angle

Pin width
(wide end)

Pin width
(narrow end)

Half tail

HALF-BLIND DOVETAIL

Half pin

Scribed lines

Pin piece

Tail width

Tail length

Spacing

Tail piece

Angle

Pin width
(wide end)

Pin width
(narrow end)

Half tail

joinery is virtually synonymous with
18th-century drawer and case construction,
and for that reason it is best to explore the
use of dovetails in that context.

DOVETAIL ANATOMY

Dovetail joints are comprised of two pieces:
the tail piece, which has one or more angled
tails extending from it, and the pin piece,
which interlocks with the tail piece. The
shape of the tails on the tail piece is cut at
right angles to the flat surface of the wood.
The tail piece can then be used as a pattern
to trace the joint onto the wood from which
the pins are cut. The pins are cut at right
angles to the end of the pin piece, but are at
an angle to the surface of that piece. Among
the defining characteristics of a dovetail
joint are the angle, width and length of the
tails. The spacing of the tails determines the
width of the pin.

Dovetail joints fall into two main
categories: through dovetails and half-blind
dovetails (see the drawing at left). Through
dovetails extend through the thickness of
the pin piece and are flush with the outside
surface. In instances where the end of the
tail piece would be better unseen, half-
blind dovetails are used and the tails do
not extend through the pin piece. Half-
blind dovetails are preferred to join drawer
fronts to their sides and on certain areas of
case construction, such as the top edges of
slant-front desks where the joinery is not
covered by a molding (see the bottom
drawing on p. 139).

DOVETAIL LAYOUT AND CONSTRUCTION

The traditional method of making a
dovetail joint is to lay out and cut the tail
piece and use that as a pattern to mark and
cut the pin piece (see the drawing on the
facing page). A marking gauge is used to
scribe a line across the end of the tail piece
equal to the thickness of the pin piece or
the desired length of the tails. The locations
of the tails are laid out on the tail piece
using a bevel gauge set at the proper angle.
The triangular spaces between the tails are
sawn and chiseled away. The marking gauge
is then used to scribe the thickness of the
tail piece across the end of the pin piece,
and, in the case of a half-blind dovetail, the

Laying Out and Cutting Dovetail Joints

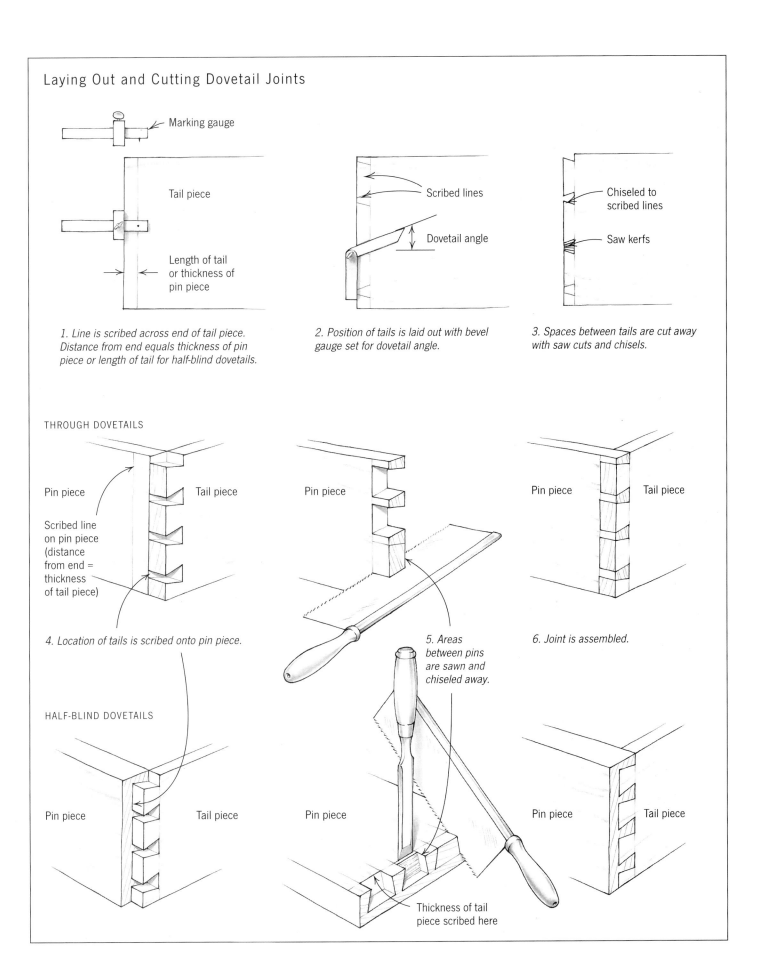

Marking gauge

Tail piece

Length of tail or thickness of pin piece

1. Line is scribed across end of tail piece. Distance from end equals thickness of pin piece or length of tail for half-blind dovetails.

Scribed lines

Dovetail angle

2. Position of tails is laid out with bevel gauge set for dovetail angle.

Chiseled to scribed lines

Saw kerfs

3. Spaces between tails are cut away with saw cuts and chisels.

THROUGH DOVETAILS

Pin piece

Scribed line on pin piece (distance from end = thickness of tail piece)

Tail piece

4. Location of tails is scribed onto pin piece.

Pin piece

5. Areas between pins are sawn and chiseled away.

Pin piece

Tail piece

6. Joint is assembled.

HALF-BLIND DOVETAILS

Pin piece

Tail piece

Pin piece

Thickness of tail piece scribed here

Pin piece

Tail piece

lengths of the tails are scribed across the end grain. The tail piece is positioned over the pin piece and the pattern of the dovetails is scribed onto the end grain of the pin piece. A saw cut is made on either side of the pins and the material between them is sawn and/or chiseled away to the scribed lines. The two parts of the joint may then be assembled.

DRAWER CONSTRUCTION

Drawers are an integral part of case furniture, and their method of construction is a primary method of dating a period piece. The details of drawer construction can be as revealing as the overall style of a piece.

The typical 17th-century drawer was side hung and built with nailed half-lap joints.
(COURTESY WETHERSFIELD HISTORICAL SOCIETY)

Over the course of the 18th century, dovetails (and pins) became smaller and more closely spaced.

Furniture in the Jacobean style, made in the American colonies as late as the 1680s, had drawers that were nailed together. In the English tradition, all the drawer parts were thick and usually made of oak. These drawers were side hung; that is, they were suspended and slid on runners nailed to the inside of the case that fit into corresponding grooves in the drawer sides (see the top photo below). The front of the drawer was joined to the side by a nailed half-lap joint, so the groove in the drawer side ended at the drawer front and was not visible when the drawer was closed.

This kind of construction had several advantages and disadvantages. The biggest disadvantage was the weight of the drawer.

Thick drawer sides were required to accommodate the side groove and to withstand being nailed together. The drawer bottoms were also nailed to the drawer sides, and in keeping with the rest of the drawer structure were substantial. The assembly, while strong and rugged, was also very massive. This weight limited the size and height of the case, and as a result Jacobean pieces remained low, horizontal and correspondingly strong and solid enough to support the drawers (see Chapter 1). In addition, side-hung drawers were not easily repairable if the groove wore out, which was inevitable given the weight they bore.

The greatest advantage of this system of drawer suspension was that the grooves running on the two rails fully constrained the movement of the drawer. Later drawers would need runners to slide on, kickers above the drawer to keep it from tipping down when pulled out, and guides on either side of the drawer to keep it moving straight. The grooves and runners of side-hung drawers did all these things. In addition, since the groove stopped at the drawer front, the front end of the runner acted as a very accurate drawer stop. Best of all, these drawers were easy to build, and, with the exception of their mass, worked quite well.

Toward the end of the 17th century, when dovetails came into more common use, they were large and few in number. Where drawer sides met the fronts, half-blind dovetails were used so the tails would not extend through to the drawer fronts (photo, far left). Through dovetails joined the sides to the backs. The drawer sides were the tail pieces and the fronts and backs were the pin pieces, thus orienting the joint to the stresses of being pulled in and out of a case. Since the joinery eliminated the need for nails, the drawer parts could be made thinner, lighter and from more fragile wood, such as pine. This trend precluded the use of grooves for side-hung drawers, and cases were designed with runners along the bottom of the drawer openings for the drawers to slide on (see the drawing on p. 26). The lighter, dovetailed drawers made possible the trend toward the vertical proportions of the William and Mary and later periods.

From the end of the 17th century through the beginning of the 19th, dovetailed drawer joinery evolved from what seemed to be an arduous but effective joint that tested the skill of the maker to a refined and sophisticated method of joinery that attested to the skill of the maker. The early dovetailed drawers had as few as one or two large dovetails at each corner. They were not delicate, but they did the job and were an improvement over the use of nails. By the start of the 18th century, cabinet-makers found that more dovetails made for a stronger and more durable joint, and this trend continued for most of the century. As the number of dovetails used in a joint increased, their size became smaller and their proportions more delicate (see the bottom right photo on the facing page). By the close of the century, as the Hepplewhite style was supplanted by Sheraton designs, drawer-front dovetails had become stylized enough almost to be considered decorative as well as functional.

Drawer fronts

Over the course of the century, some aspects of drawer-front dovetails remained the same while others evolved. In a casual survey of 18th-century pieces, the length and angle of the dovetail did not vary over time. Drawer-front dovetails were consistently about ½ in. long. The angle of the dovetail varied by a few degrees in a single piece and varied from 10° to 20°, averaging 15°, among pieces. The angle of the dovetail seems to have had more to do with regional or personal preference than with evolution over time. The most noticeable change during the century was the decrease in pin width and spacing. The narrower side of pin widths often exceeded ½ in. before mid-century but was frequently less then ⅛ in. by century's end. Similarly, the century began with dovetails spaced as far as 2 in. apart and finished with them closer to half that.

Drawer bottoms

The earliest (late-17th-century) dovetailed drawers had bottoms that were still nailed onto the drawer sides. Over the course of the next few decades, the drawer bottoms followed the trend of the rest of the drawer structure and became thinner and lighter.

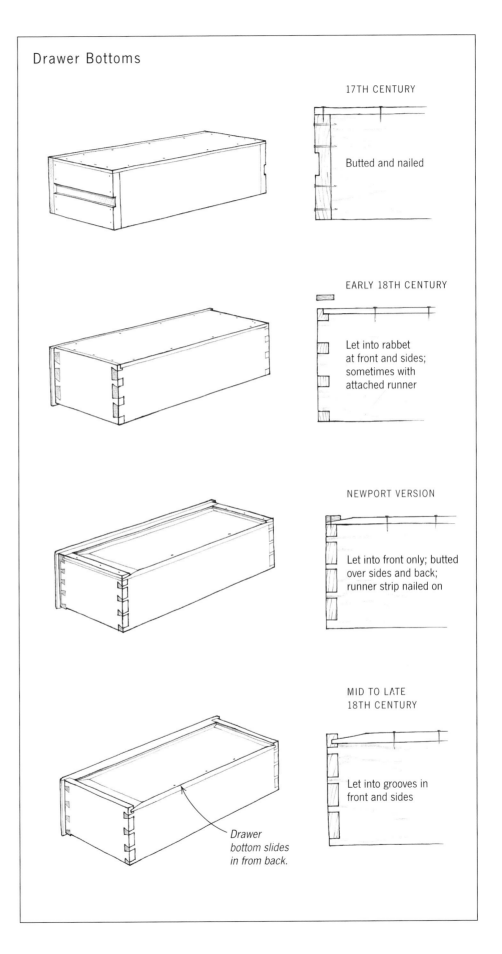

Drawer Bottoms

17TH CENTURY

Butted and nailed

EARLY 18TH CENTURY

Let into rabbet at front and sides; sometimes with attached runner

NEWPORT VERSION

Let into front only; butted over sides and back; runner strip nailed on

MID TO LATE 18TH CENTURY

Let into grooves in front and sides

Drawer bottom slides in from back.

Cabinetmakers with more refined methods rabbeted the bottom of the drawer components and let the bottom into them. Hide glue and progressively finer nails were used to secure the bottom into the rabbet. Newport cabinetmakers had a distinctive method of attaching drawer bottoms that persisted for the rest of the century. The drawer bottom, usually about 1/4 in. to 3/8 in. thick and tapered to 1/8 in. thick at the front and sides, fit into a groove in the drawer front and was nailed to the bottom of the sides and back. Two thin strips were nailed over the drawer bottom along each side. The drawer slid in and out of the case on these strips, which could easily be replaced if they ever wore out.

A superior method of drawer-bottom installation was to slide the bottom into grooves cut into the inside of the drawer sides and front. The bottom was then secured with small nails to the drawer back. The construction allowed for the seasonal expansion and contraction of the drawer bottom without splitting, and was a much more secure and elegant method of construction. This method had been adopted by many makers by the second quarter of the 18th century and was the preferred method of construction for the rest of the century.

Dovetail layout

The way that drawer dovetails are designed is essential to producing an attractive and functional joint. At the front of the drawer, the dovetails are laid out so that the grooves or rabbets for the drawer bottom are concealed under a full or half tail, as shown in the drawing below. The top of the drawer side is laid out with a full dovetail so that, from above, the side appears to butt rather than overlap the drawer front. This leaves the top surface of the drawer front unbroken and allows a molded or rounded top on the drawer side to terminate against the drawer front. The layout with a full tail at the bottom of the drawer front to conceal the groove leaves a very thin half pin (left, in the drawing below). An alternative method used during the period was to conceal the groove with a half tail (center, drawing below). Both layouts are historically accurate but the version with all full tails seems to have been more prevalent, despite its shortcomings. Newport-style drawers with nailed-on bottoms used full tails as well, with the bottom of the drawer sides higher than the front to allow for the thickness of the bottom (right, drawing below).

The rear joint where the sides meet the back also has a common recurring layout and variations that are equally effective.

The most prevalent layout (left, in the drawing on the facing page) places a full tail at the top and a half tail at the bottom. An alternative design (center, drawing facing page) uses half tails top and bottom. In both cases, the lowest pin is placed above the groove for the drawer bottom. The pins are evenly spaced and are usually close in size to the front tails, though there may be fewer of them. Some drawers with backs rabbeted for the drawer bottom (right, drawing facing page) have a layout that incorporates the rabbet with the dovetail. The first layout is well-suited to drawers where the top of the sides and back are flat and level. The second layout works well where the top of the drawer side is rounded or molded and the back can be made to abut it just below the shaped edge. The third layout is rare and used only for small, interior desk drawers.

With the regional and individual variations in dovetailed drawer construction, it is impossible to call any one method the best. While the size and spacing of the joints changed over time, a solid, reliable joint that concealed the grooves or rabbets was always the goal. Some methods, like sliding drawer bottoms, proved to be more successful than others, but many variations in drawer construction are historically correct. The joinery methods of a single

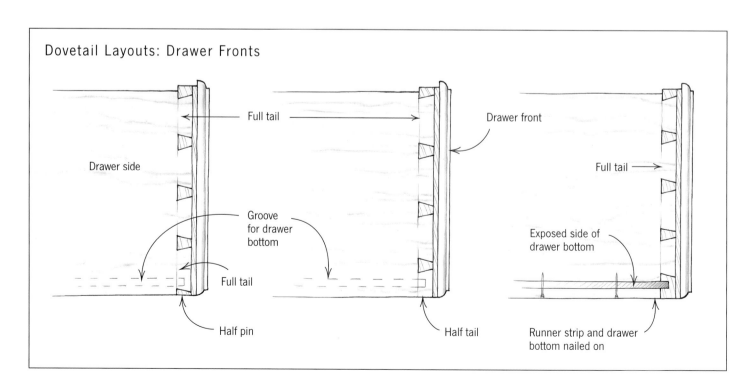

Dovetail Layouts: Drawer Fronts

Full tail

Drawer front

Drawer side

Full tail

Groove for drawer bottom

Full tail

Half pin

Half tail

Exposed side of drawer bottom

Runner strip and drawer bottom nailed on

cabinetmaker evolved and were perfected over time, so even the work of a single craftsman shows variations. Then, as now, the goal was to optimize the joinery to achieve an elegant and structurally sound drawer. The result is often so successful that it belies the forethought and planning that preceded the work.

BUILDING DRAWERS

The first step in building a drawer is to measure the opening in the case and plan the size of the drawer parts accordingly. Every drawer requires clearance room, which needs to be accounted for at the outset. A total of $1/16$ in. in width and height is usually enough clearance; more than that can cause a drawer to feel too loose in its opening. In addition, the builder should always anticipate the effects of expansion and contraction due to changes in humidity on drawer clearance. Because of the width of their components, taller drawers are affected more than shorter drawers.

Drawer fronts

Drawer fronts are made first, usually from stock planed to between $3/4$ in. and $7/8$ in. in thickness. Flush-fitting drawers should be cut $1/16$ in. less in height and $1/16$ in. less in width than the opening, and lipped drawers

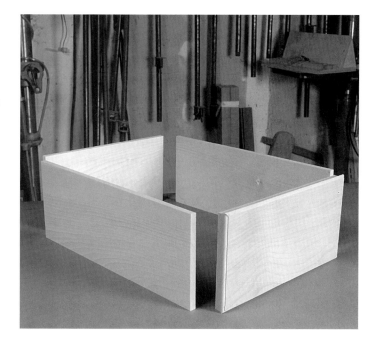

The front, back and sides of a drawer are prepared for dovetailing. The components should be squarely cut and planed to a uniform thickness.

should be cut about $1/4$ in. longer and $1/8$ in. taller than the opening to allow for the overlap.

Eighteenth-century lipped drawers have a $3/16$-in. or $1/4$-in. bead cut around their outside edge first. After the bead is cut, the top and side rabbet are cut to raise the lip. This rabbet is about $3/16$ in. deep and $1/4$ in. narrower than the thickness of the drawer front to leave the bead undisturbed. In order to make an even overlap, some makers like to cut the top rabbet first, adjust the clearance of the drawer front in the case by trimming the drawer bottom (which may necessitate recutting the bottom bead) and then cut the side rabbets. There is no overlapping lip at the bottom of the drawer. Once the drawer front has been cut, it can be tested in the drawer opening for fit and the appropriate amount of clearance.

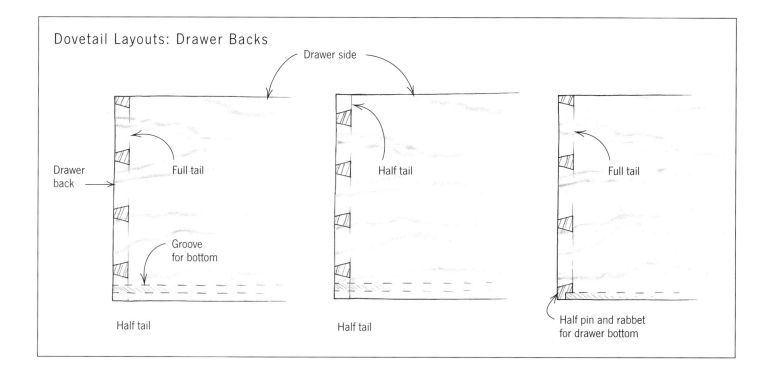

Dovetail Layouts: Drawer Backs

Drawer side

Drawer back

Full tail

Half tail

Groove for bottom

Half tail

Half tail

Half tail

Full tail

Half pin and rabbet for drawer bottom

Lines are scribed across the ends of each component indicating the thickness of the adjoining piece or, in the case of half-blind dovetails, the length of the tails.

The material between the tails is sawn and chiseled precisely to the scribed lines.

Lines are then scribed across the ends of the components with a marking gauge. It is helpful to have two marking gauges or one that is double sided. One gauge is set for the thickness of the sides and back, and the other for the length of the front dovetails, which is not related to the thickness of any of the components and is usually about 1/2 in. The gauge set for the thickness of the sides and back is used to scribe lines on the drawer back, the back end of the drawer sides and the back of the drawer front. The gauge set for the length of the front dovetails is used to scribe the front of the sides and the end grain of the drawer fronts. With the exception of the drawer front, the components are scribed on both sides.

Laying out the dovetails

Now the dovetails can be laid out and scribed on the drawer sides. In doing so, bear in mind the position of the groove for the drawer bottom. It is important to make sure that part of a tail covers and conceals the groove. As a general rule, the groove is usually 1/4 in. wide and 1/4 in. from the bottom edge. It is easiest to lay out the top and bottom features first and add the dovetails, evenly spaced, between them. Laying out the dovetails can be confusing, but thinking of the layout in terms of positioning the pins makes it less so. Taking the pin width at its narrowest part, this width is marked on the very end of the piece at regularly spaced intervals. The rest of the pin is marked back to the scribed line with the use of a bevel gauge set for the appropriate angle. The area within the pin position can be marked to be cut away to leave the tails (top photo at left).

Cutting the tails

Once the layout is complete, the marked areas between the tails can be removed. To save some time, both drawer sides can be clamped or taped together and cut simultaneously. The material between the tails is removed by cutting along the angled scribe lines with a saw, and then making a series of saw kerfs between the first two. The two sides are separated, and each is trimmed to the scribed lines with a sharp chisel (bottom photo at left). To ensure a straight joint, this trimming should be done

Remember that drawers built under humid conditions need very little vertical clearance and those built under dry conditions need the most. Side-to-side clearance is not affected by humidity.

Drawer sides and backs

After the drawer fronts are made and fit to the case, the sides and backs are made from thinner secondary wood. Thicknesses of 3/8 in. to 1/2 in. are common on period pieces, but thickness varies with the size of the drawer and the particular piece. The width of the sides and back is equal to or up to 1/16 in. less than the height of the front, excluding the overlapping lip. The length of the sides is dictated by the depth of the case, and the width of the back should be made to equal the width of the drawer front, excluding the lips at either end. It is important that the sides and back be planed to a uniform thickness and the ends of each piece be cut squarely. It is easiest to cut the sides and back as one long piece and then cross-cut them into the individual components.

Marking the Drawer Components

Each drawer piece is laid out with the inside facing up, and the top corners of adjacent pieces are numbered. The inside, outside, top, bottom and position of each piece are then identifiable.

from both sides of the piece. It is important to have the edges of the cuts straight and square, since these pieces will be used as patterns from which the rest of the joint is made.

The drawer parts may now be marked to indicate how they will go together. It is helpful to lay the sides, back and front in a long row as if the drawer assembly had been "unrolled" flat with all the inside surfaces facing up (see the drawing above). This arrangement positions all but one of the mating edges next to each other. The upper corner of each adjacent piece may be marked with a number. This way, when all the pieces are in a jumble, the inside, top and position of each component will be clear.

Laying out and cutting the pins

Next, the pins are cut in the back to accept the drawer sides. This is best done by clamping the drawer back vertically in the vise and laying the corresponding drawer side over the end. After careful alignment of the two pieces, the dovetails are scribed onto the end of the drawer back with a fine knife (top photo at right). If the drawer side is positioned so that it extends slightly over the back (only about 1/32 in. or so) while the joint is being scribed, the pins will be marked just a little larger and will ensure a very snug joint. Once the pins have been marked, saw kerfs are cut straight down on either side of them, just outside of the marked line, to the scribed line. The material between the pins is removed by cutting along the scribed line with a coping saw. The remainder of the material is trimmed on the bench with a chisel (bottom photo at right).

The drawer side is used as a template to transfer the tail layout onto the end of the drawer back.

The material between the pins is sawn and chiseled to the scribed lines.

The front pins are scribed from the tail piece onto the end of the drawer front in the same manner that the pins were scribed onto the back.

A saw is used to cut on either side of the pins. The saw kerf may extend across the back of the drawer front but cannot extend past the scribed line on the end grain.

The front dovetails are cut in a similar fashion, with the drawer front held vertically in the vise and the drawer side positioned over its end to mark the dovetails (photo at left above). Some makers shift the drawer bottom to one side so that it overhangs the bottom of the drawer front by about $1/32$ in. This positions the pieces so that the assembled drawer slides on the sides and the bottom edge of the drawer front does not drag over the case opening. As on the rear dovetails, the side can be shifted slightly to overhang the back to make the marked pins slightly larger and to ensure a tight joint. Once the dovetails are scribed, it is helpful to press the edge of a chisel into the marked lines to make them straight and more visible.

Cutting half-blind dovetails

In a half-blind dovetail, cutting the material away from between the pins of the drawer front is the most labor-intensive part of the work. In other parts of the work, most of the material can be sawn away, but in this phase it must be cut with a chisel. The drawer front is clamped face down with one end at the edge of the bench. The pin markings are extended along the inside of the drawer front for an inch or two with a

square. A cut is made with the dovetail saw on either side of the pins following this line and the scribed pin line on the end (photo at right above). In doing this, the saw cut is made across the edge of the piece and continues into the wood at an angle. This cut cannot extend past the scribed line on the end grain, but it can extend an inch or two across the back. Now the material

between the pins can be chiseled away by layers. A chisel cut is made just inside the scribed line across the areas that will be removed. Then horizontal chisel cuts are made from the end, splitting off a layer about $1/8$ in. thick (photo below). This is done repeatedly until the material between the pins has been cut to all the scribed lines. Narrow or bevel-edge chisels are needed to

Since the front dovetails are half-blind, the material between the pins must be chiseled away in layers and trimmed to the scribed lines.

remove material from the inside corners of those areas that the sawblade could not reach. All the cut surfaces should be flat, square and to the line.

Assembling the drawer

With all the dovetails cut, it's time for a trial fit. The joints should be snug enough to go together with some resistance. Any part of the joint that interferes with another should be found and trimmed. Several light taps with a mallet on a protective piece of wood will usually be required to close the joint completely. Once the drawer is together, a line is drawn around the inside to mark where the grooves for the drawer bottom will be.

The drawer is taken apart and the grooves are cut on all the pieces with a plane or dado blade. The groove should be about ¼ in. deep, but in no case should its depth extend more than halfway through the thickness of the sides, because that would weaken them considerably. The back, which stops flush with the top of the groove, should be marked at the top of the groove and cut to the correct width. At this point, the top of the sides should be chamfered or rounded as desired and any other sharp edges should be broken with a single pass of a plane. The bottom of the drawer front should be rounded slightly or chamfered on the inside edge to ease it over the drawer opening should it ever start to drag. With all the final details taken care of, the drawer may be glued and assembled. The joints are clamped across the width of the drawer to be sure the joints are fully closed. The squareness of the assembled drawer should be checked before the glue dries. Once the glue has dried, any part of the joints can be trimmed flush if necessary.

Finally, the drawer bottom is fit and secured. It is usually the same thickness as the drawer sides and tapered at the front and sides to the width of the groove. Because of their width, drawer bottoms expand and contract more than any other part of the drawer, and one should anticipate and plan for this movement as with any other wide piece of wood. The grain of the drawer bottom should be oriented along its longest dimension to minimize the effects of expansion and contraction. Drawer bottoms that are assembled under conditions of high humidity can be expected to contract, and those assembled during low humidity must be given room to expand. It is advisable to leave a little extra width on the drawer bottom extending from the back of the drawer so that future adjustments can be made if the wood shrinks considerably. The bottom is secured by a few cut brads nailed into the drawer back.

The drawer is now complete and may be fit to the opening. Flush drawers require drawer stops to limit their travel and may need some minor trimming to achieve an even space around their perimeter. Lipped drawers may require some minor trimming of the back of the lip in order to close tightly to the case all around.

CASE CONSTRUCTION

Just as the dovetail joint revolutionized the assembly of drawers, so did it change the basic construction of case pieces. The frame-and-panel system of the 17th century was supplanted by dovetailed case

A groove is cut on the inside of the components to receive the drawer bottom. The drawer back is cut away at the top of the groove for installing the bottom. Once in position, it is held in place by a few small brads driven through the bottom into the drawer back.

The completed drawer is ready for installation in the case.

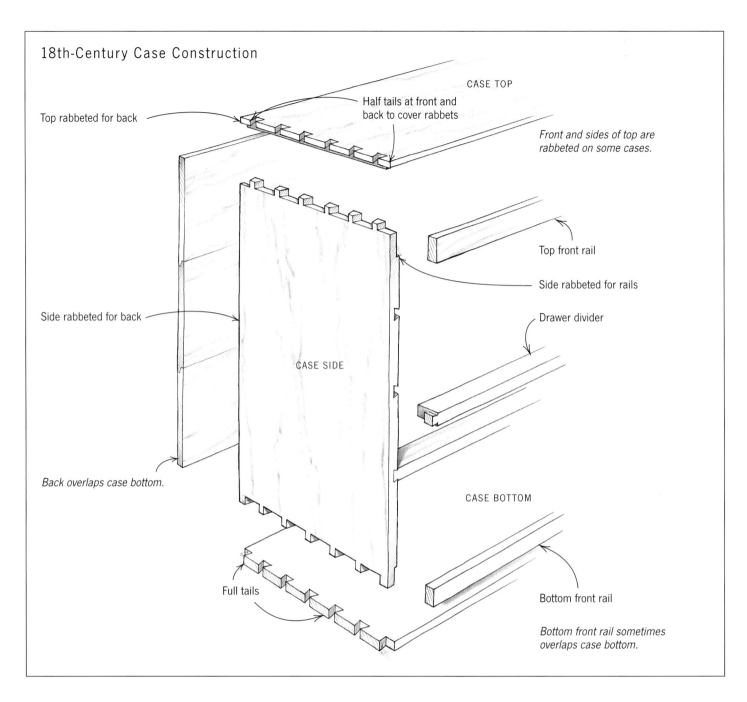

18th-Century Case Construction

Top rabbeted for back

Half tails at front and
back to cover rabbets

CASE TOP

*Front and sides of top are
rabbeted on some cases.*

Top front rail

Side rabbeted for rails

Drawer divider

Side rabbeted for back

CASE SIDE

Back overlaps case bottom.

CASE BOTTOM

Full tails

Bottom front rail

*Bottom front rail sometimes
overlaps case bottom.*

construction, reducing bulk and weight and facilitating the trend to vertically oriented designs. Whereas 17th-century construction required joined rails, stiles and panels for a component like a chest side, the newer construction reduced that to one wide board joined to the rest of the case by dovetails.

One nice feature of the frame-and-panel system was that its floating panels made the piece relatively immune to the effects of variations in humidity. However, the

limitations of this system outweighed whatever advantages it had, and by the beginning of the 18th century dovetailed case construction was ubiquitous. There were new concerns that arose from building cases from nothing but wide boards, such as how to deal with their movement, but these were nothing that could not be anticipated and planned for.

Like drawer construction, dovetailed case construction evolved in style over time. Early dovetails were large and widely spaced; over the course of the century they

came to be narrower and closer together. The dovetails usually do not show on primary surfaces, since they are planned to be either covered by a molding or oriented to be exposed on secondary surfaces. One of the few places where dovetails are seen on the primary surface of a case piece is on the top edges of slant-front desks, where they had to be aesthetically pleasing as well as functional (see the bottom drawing on the facing page). The cases of slant-front desks and chests, whether they are chests of drawers, chests-on-frame, chests-on-chests or the top case of high chests, are structurally similar. High-chest bases and dressing tables are also similar, having been of dovetailed construction early in the century and mortise-and-tenon construction later.

Chests and desks

Chests and desks begin as empty vertical boxes with only a top, a bottom and two sides joined by through dovetails. In most instances, the top and bottom of the case are laid out as the tail pieces and are used to transfer the dovetail pattern onto the upper and lower ends of the case sides. In laying out the details of the joinery, special consideration should be given to the rabbets for attaching the back of the case and the top and bottom front rails. The back meets the top in a rabbet and does not extend through to the top surface. The front rail abuts the underside of the top or meets it in a rabbet. An elegant way to provide rabbets at the front and back without having them extend through to the sides is to rabbet the front, back and sides to the same depth. This makes the dovetails somewhat less thick, but they become easier to cut and fit and are just as effective a joint.

By planning half tails at the front and back of the case to cover the end of the rabbets in the side, the result is a clean and uncomplicated-looking joint. The side of the joint, the pin side, is covered with a molding so only the tail side is ever seen. The bottom of the case is also a tail piece, but it is narrower than the top or sides. At the bottom of the case, the case back overlaps the bottom. The bottom front rail either abuts or overlaps the bottom. The case bottom can be laid out with full tails; no half tails are required. The lower-case molding covers the pin side of the joint that is visible on the case side.

In cases where the top dovetails need to be hidden, as on a low chest of drawers, half-blind dovetails are used. In these cases, the top of the sides become the tail pieces and are dovetailed to the top. They are laid out with a half tail at the back to cover the rabbet for the back in the case top and either a half or full tail at the front. The

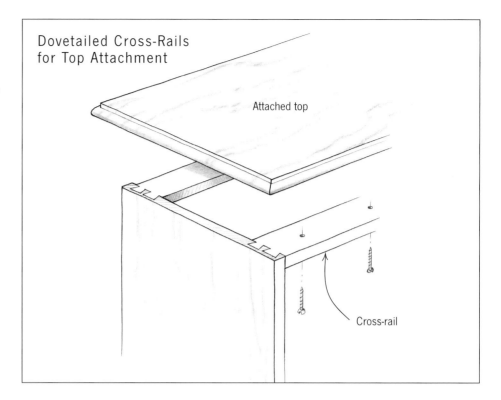

Dovetailed Cross-Rails for Top Attachment

Attached top

Cross-rail

joint is not visible from the top and is totally covered by a molding applied to the case side.

Cases that will have an attached overhanging top are often built with front and rear cross-pieces that are joined with half-blind dovetails to the case sides (drawing above). These cross-rails secure the case sides and provide a structure to which the top is later fastened. In these instances, the cross-rails are the tail pieces and the dovetails do not extend to the outsides of the case. The cross-rails and the joinery are hidden once the top is attached.

Slant-front desks also employ half-blind dovetails on the top joint (drawing at right). This joint is quite visible, and through dovetails would be too intrusive. By orienting the dovetails so that the desk top is the tail piece, the assembled joint is on the top of the case and the sides are left untouched. As with other cases, a half tail at the back of the case conceals the rabbet for the back board. The front of the joint uses a full tail so that the front of the top abuts the side and makes a nice, uncluttered joint.

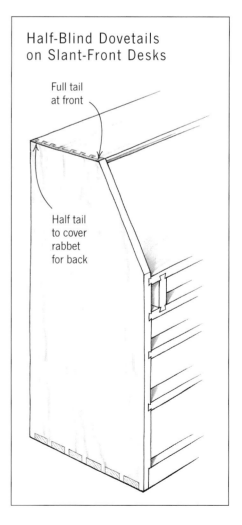

Half-Blind Dovetails on Slant-Front Desks

Full tail at front

Half tail to cover rabbet for back

Case Construction with Turned Legs

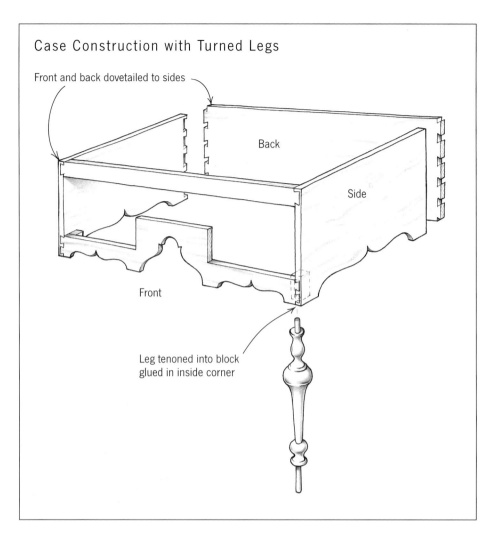

Front and back dovetailed to sides

Back

Side

Front

Leg tenoned into block glued in inside corner

Case Construction with Cabriole Legs

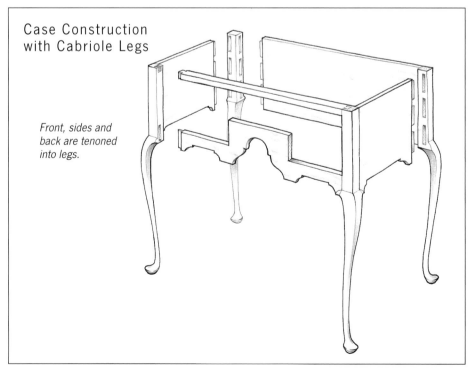

Front, sides and back are tenoned into legs.

Dressing tables and high-chest bases

Dressing tables and the bottoms of high chests share a structure that is different from that of chests. These pieces began the century as horizontal boxes comprising a front, back and sides joined at the four corners with dovetails. The back joints were half-blind dovetails with the back as the tail piece, so the joint was only visible from the back. The front rails and aprons were dovetailed to the sides in a similar manner. The joints on the front were either veneered over or hidden under thin strips of wood placed vertically along the front edges of the case.

The turned William and Mary legs of the period were joined to the case by means of glue blocks. These blocks were glued into the four lower inside corners of the case and were drilled to receive the turned tenon of the leg (see the top drawing at left). The turned legs were also joined to one another by stretchers just above the feet, which strengthened the assembly and distributed any side load among all the legs. When the William and Mary style passed out of fashion in favor of the Queen Anne style with its cabriole legs, this method of joining legs to the case was found to be in need of improvement. Without stretchers, each cabriole leg had to be attached independently and be able to withstand the sideways force of being dragged. The solution changed the essential structure of the piece.

Glue blocks were eliminated, and the square top section of the cabriole leg was extended up to the top of the case. All the components of the case, the front, sides and back, were tenoned into the legs, making the leg an integral part of the structure rather than an addition. The one drawback to this method of construction was that the horizontally oriented case components were not free to expand and contract with changes in humidity since they were constrained by being tenoned into vertically oriented leg blocks. Cracking of case sides and backs was frequently the result (see the sidebar on the facing page).

This new method of construction for dressing tables and high-chest bases became the norm everywhere but in Newport.

Most of the methods of joinery used by period furniture makers allowed for changes in humidity, but there are a few components that do not. The most notable are the sides of case pieces such as dressing tables and the bases of high chests. In both of these pieces, the grain of the sides runs horizontally and often exceeds 12 in. in width. Pieces this wide can show appreciable movement with even moderate changes in humidity, but since the sides are tenoned and pegged into the vertical legs, the normal expansion and contraction is constrained. Since the sides cannot move freely, and since wood is quite weak in tension across the grain, the sides will inevitably crack.

An effective way to prevent the cracking of these constrained pieces is to make sure they never go into tension across the grain. When the piece is being assembled, the sides can be clamped tightly across the grain to put the entire side into compression. The clamps are left in place until the glue in the joints has cured. Once the clamps have been removed and the joints have been pegged, the sides will continue to be in compression. When the piece is exposed to lower humidity, the compressive force will decrease. The precompression will prevent or at least drastically reduce the possibility that the side will experience enough tension to crack as its moisture content drops.

There is a limit to the amount of precompression that should be attempted. To compress a piece of wood more than 1% in its width will exceed the elastic limit of the wood. Beyond that point the wood will take on a permanent compressive set and will not return fully to its original dimension when the force is released. Within that 1% however, enough precompression is possible to offset a change in moisture content averaging about 3.5%, well within the range of normal variations in moisture content for well-sealed wood. This allows a precompressed side that was assembled at 60% relative humidity to experience a drop to 35% relative humidity before going into tension. (See also Appendix I on p. 293.)

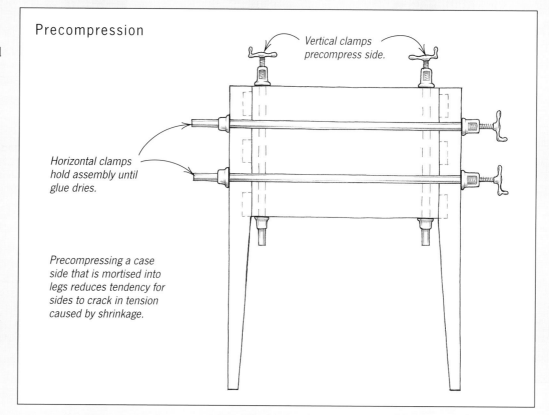

Precompression

Vertical clamps precompress side.

Horizontal clamps hold assembly until glue dries.

Precompressing a case side that is mortised into legs reduces tendency for sides to crack in tension caused by shrinkage.

Newport cabinetmakers continued to use the William and Mary case construction into the Queen Anne and Chippendale periods. They apparently were pleased with the way the case parts were free to expand and contract, and they found a good method by which to attach the legs. Newport makers dovetailed the case and affixed the cabriole legs with the leg block held in place on the inside corner of the case with glue blocks. The leg was shouldered just above the knee, so the weight of the case was borne by the leg itself and not a glued block. Glued and nailed blocks held the block of the leg into the inside case corner and resisted side loads on the leg, but they did not carry any weight. Judicious use of glue on these glue blocks left the legs free to be slid out of the case for transport.

Drawer dividers

Drawer dividers not only separate one drawer opening from another, but they also play a structural role in keeping the case sides straight and parallel. The dividers are dovetailed into the case with sliding dovetails, which are slightly different from the dovetails used to join case and drawer sides. Sliding dovetails join a tail cut across the end of a piece to a correspondingly

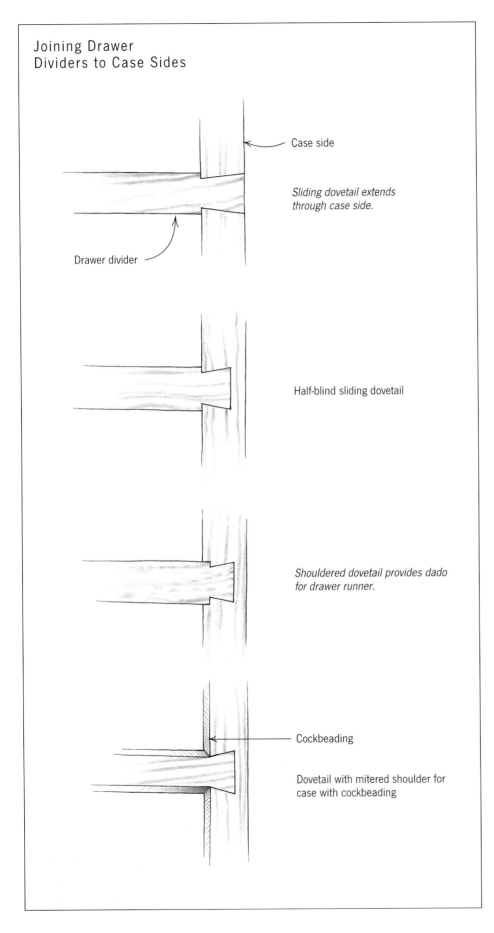

Joining Drawer Dividers to Case Sides

Case side

Sliding dovetail extends through case side.

Drawer divider

Half-blind sliding dovetail

Shouldered dovetail provides dado for drawer runner.

Cockbeading

Dovetail with mitered shoulder for case with cockbeading

shaped groove or cutout in another piece. A sliding dovetail can join a piece at right angles anywhere along the length of another. The joint is not limited to end-to-end joining as are standard dovetails.

Drawer dividers of 18th-century pieces are dovetailed into the case by a variety of means. Many pieces from early in the century have dovetailed dividers that extend through the full width of the case and are flush with the outside surface. The actual depth of the dovetail is less than 1 in., and the rest of the divider is a full 2 in. or 3 in. in width. While joints of this type were easily made and entirely functional, their aesthetic shortcoming was that the end grain of the divider showed on the case side. Interestingly, that was often the only part of the joint that was visible, since the front surface was often covered with a single- or double-arch molding surrounding the drawer openings.

The more elegant method, which came into widespread use, employed a shorter dovetail that did not extend through the case side. As with the earlier version, the divider was 2 in. or 3 in. wide, but the dovetail was less than 1 in. deep. This kind of blind sliding dovetail required more skill and time to make, but was required as refinements in cabinetmaking increasingly called for unbroken surfaces and a minimization of exposed construction.

Often the installation of drawer dividers was combined with a method for installing drawer runners. A good way to position runners was to let them into shallow ($\frac{1}{8}$ in.) dadoes and affix them with a couple of nails. This way, the dadoes carry the weight of the drawers and the nails serve to keep the runners in the dadoes. In cutting these dadoes, especially by hand with a saw and plane as the original makers did, it is easiest to let them extend to the front and back edges of the case. Rather than stopping short of the dovetail for the drawer divider, the two were simply superimposed and combined to make a shouldered dovetail. This arrangement ensured the proper alignment of the runner and divider at the outset and over time. The $\frac{1}{8}$-in. shoulder also positioned the dovetail so that it was not partially hidden under an overlapping drawer lip.

The bombé and serpentine case pieces of the second half of the century had cockbeading surrounding the drawer opening. Though straight-fronted pieces had beading on either the case or drawer, the complexity of the curved fronts required the beading to be cut from the solid of the case and drawer dividers. The bead had to be mitered where the dividers met the case. To do this, the dovetail on the end of the divider was given an angled shoulder, but this precluded the use of a runner dado that extends to the front of the case.

Drawer runners

In order to move smoothly in a case, drawers must be constrained in their up-and-down and sideways movement. The drawers slide on runners, are prevented from tipping downward when they are pulled out by kickers above the drawer, and are kept straight in their openings by guides along the drawer sides. In most dovetailed chest cases, the inside surfaces of the case act as guides and the runners for the drawer above serve as kickers. Top drawers need their own kickers nailed to the inside of the case.

As previously mentioned, the best way to attach runners is to nail them into shallow dadoes in the case sides. In attaching the runners, some thought should be given to their relationship with the expansion and contraction of the case side. The runners should be a fraction of an inch shorter then the depth of the case so that as the case shrinks the runners will not push off the back boards. A little gap of not much more than $1/16$ in. should be left between the back of the divider and the front of the runner so the divider is not pushed out in the same way. In nailing the runner in place, one nail should be close to the front end, and the other no more than halfway back. If there were to be one nail at either end of the runner, the case side would likely crack in the middle upon shrinking or loosen a nail upon expanding. Placing the nails in the front half of the divider allows most of the side to expand and contract freely and subjects the nails to only half as much wood movement. Similarly, if glue is used in addition to the nails, it should be applied only at the front section of the runner.

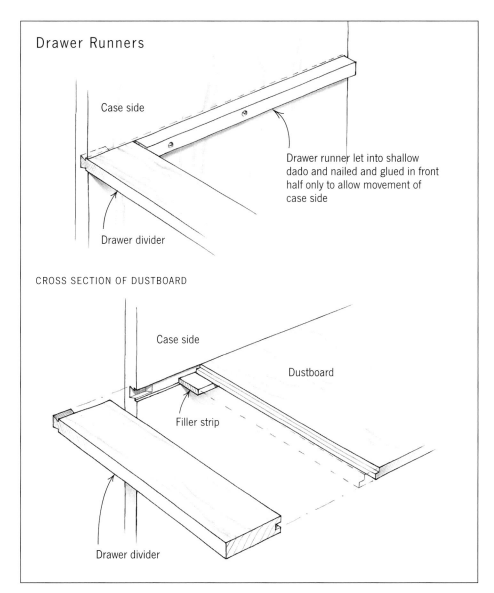

Drawer Runners

Drawer runner let into shallow dado and nailed and glued in front half only to allow movement of case side

Case side

Drawer divider

CROSS SECTION OF DUSTBOARD

Case side

Dustboard

Filler strip

Drawer divider

It is important to remember that with a let-in runner, the dado carries the weight of the drawer through the runner, not the nails themselves. The nails serve only to keep the runner in the dado. Often the runner will pop out of the dado at the rear of the case if it is nailed only at the front and the case side will cup inward. To counter this problem, the attached side of the runner may be planed with a slight concave shape along its length before it is nailed in place.

Some 18th-century pieces are known to have drawer runners that were affixed with shallow sliding dovetails that extended over their full length. These runners stay in place without the use of nails and allow the sides to expand and contract freely.

This is an elegant method of attaching drawer runners for which the original makers should be commended, but it is a labor-intensive method that never saw widespread use.

Dustboards

Many 18th-century cabinetmakers installed dustboards between drawers to keep the contents of the drawers as clean as possible. These dustboards extended the full width and depth of the case and doubled as drawer runners. The boards were let into the dadoes on either side of the case and were often dadoed into the back of the drawer divider. They were free to expand and contract within the side dadoes.

Dustboards were often made from the same thin-sawn secondary stock as the drawer components and are therefore often thinner than the width of the side dadoes. To make up the difference, a filler strip was added, thus filling the space and serving as a kicker for the drawer below (see the bottom drawing on p. 143).

Other kinds of cases require a more complicated system of runners and guides. Chest cases with front quarter columns have inner case sides that are not in line with the sides of the drawer openings. These cases require added drawer guides attached to the inner case sides, and a system of freestanding runners that are joined to the drawer dividers at the front and a rail at the back. Dressing tables and high-chest bases require runners let into the front and rear of the case, and guides and kickers that are either let into the inside of the leg blocks or nailed to the inner case sides.

Case Attachments

Many parts of 18th-century furniture—including tops, moldings and feet—are added to the basic structure of the case after it is assembled. Because these parts are not integral to the case, they are joined by a variety of means, each designed to attach the part securely while allowing both the case and attached parts to expand and contract independently.

TOPS

Pieces with attached tops present a unique problem for furniture makers. Tops are usually the widest component of a piece, and as such they are subject to the greatest amount of expansion and contraction. The top is also the one component that needs to remain flat and intact more than any other. We have already discussed chest tops that are integral to the case itself; we will now

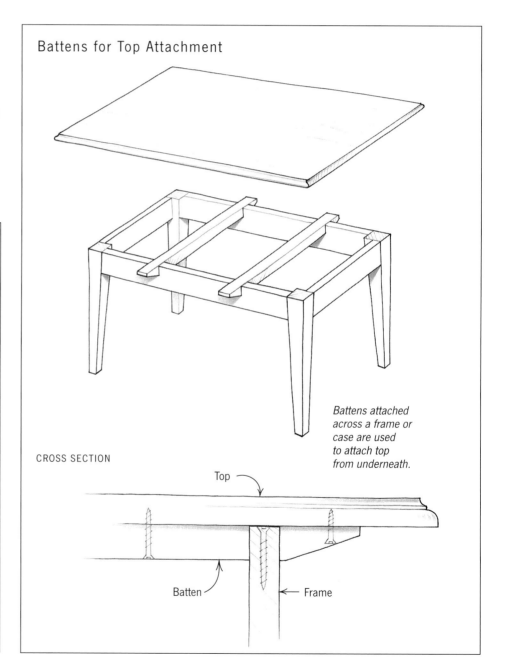

Battens for Top Attachment

Battens attached across a frame or case are used to attach top from underneath.

CROSS SECTION

Top

Batten

Frame

Sliding Dovetail for Top Attachment

Case top slides onto dovetail on case side.

Top

Side

Rabbet for back

A sliding dovetail joins a top to a side while allowing the top to expand and contract with changes in humidity.

look at other tops that are added to a case or, as with tables, a frame.

One way that a top can be added to a frame is with sliding dovetails. The geometry of the sliding dovetail allows the top to expand and contract along the dovetail while remaining securely attached. This method is sometimes used to join a top to a dressing table of mortise-and-tenon construction by cutting full-length tails on the top of the case sides so they extend up past the top of the leg blocks at the corners (see the drawing at left on the facing page). The dovetail cut into the under side of the top stops short of the front edge, so the top can be slid on from the front. The only visible signs of the joint are on the back edge of the top.

A similar method was used for attaching overhanging case tops, where the top joints of the case were sliding dovetails and the bottom joints were conventional through dovetails. Sometimes these sliding dovetails were tapered over their length so they would tighten as they were pressed into their final position. A variation on the sliding dovetail is a wedged sliding dovetail, where the dovetail is on only one side of the joint and small wedges are driven into the straight side of the joint to lock it in place. This method eliminates the extraordinary precision and trial-and-error fitting of straight or tapered sliding dovetails. It appears to have only half the holding power of two-sided sliding dovetails, but, with the use of the wedges, the joint can be made very tight over its entire length.

Cross-pieces were mentioned in the discussion of case construction (see p. 139). These members are dovetailed across the front and back of the top of the case and create a false case top to which the over-hanging case top is attached. Sometimes the front of the top is screwed in place and the rear is affixed with small sliding dovetails to allow the top to expand and contract freely.

Tops can also be attached with battens (see the drawing at right on the facing page). A batten is a narrow strip of wood that extends across the width of the top. It is first attached to the case or frame and then

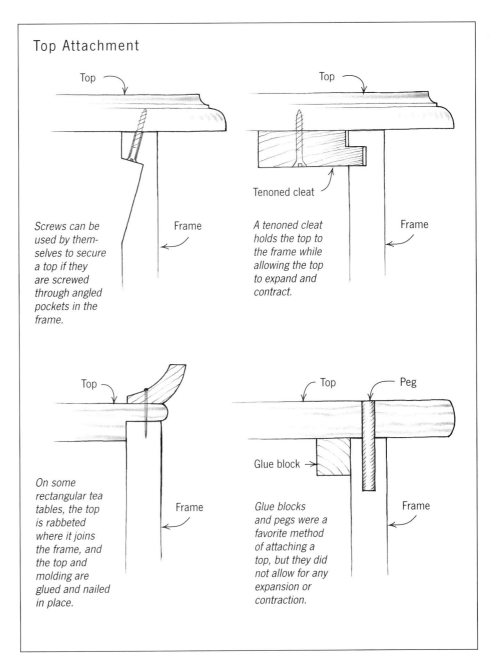

Top Attachment

Screws can be used by themselves to secure a top if they are screwed through angled pockets in the frame.

A tenoned cleat holds the top to the frame while allowing the top to expand and contract.

On some rectangular tea tables, the top is rabbeted where it joins the frame, and the top and molding are glued and nailed in place.

Glue blocks and pegs were a favorite method of attaching a top, but they did not allow for any expansion or contraction.

the top is attached to the batten, usually with screws. Battens were favored among Newport cabinetmakers, who used them to attach the tops of dressing tables, tea tables and dining tables.

Screws were also used to screw directly through frames into the underside of table-tops (see the drawing above). An angled pocket was chiseled into the inside of the frame, and the screw entered the top at an angle. By providing an oversized hole in the

frame, the top was able to expand and contract. A more elegant method involved the use of short cleats, which were tenoned into mortises in the frame and screwed or nailed to the underside of the top. The advantages of tenoned cleats were that they allowed the top to expand and contract freely while still holding the top securely in place.

A common method of construction for rectangular tea tables was to rabbet the underside of the top, thereby allowing it to drop onto the frame. The thin edge was given a rounded profile and allowed to overhang the frame. The top molding was applied directly over the top and nailed through the top into the frame. Because the top was not free to expand and contract across its width, many of these tables have cracked tops. A better method would have been to let the top into a rabbet in the frame and apply a molding to the frame, thereby securing the top in place while allowing it to expand and contract freely.

A less refined method of attaching tops was simply to glue them to the frame and add some glue blocks around the inside; often this method of attachment was augmented by driving wooden pegs through the tabletop into the frame. Made to fit tightly, the pegs helped to hold the top in place. Neither the pegs nor the glue blocks allowed the top to expand and contract, and the tops inevitably cracked and some of the glue blocks came loose. Nevertheless, there was still enough of a bond to keep the tops attached. Those that eventually came loose were frequently put back in place with pocketed screws through the frame.

MOLDINGS

The historically accurate method of attaching most case moldings is to glue and nail them in place. Original pieces were nailed with thin brads that were tapered over their entire length and held quite securely. Across the front of cases, the application of a molding is straightforward, but on the sides, perpendicular to the grain, the expansion and contraction of the case must be considered.

Moldings that are securely glued and nailed in place restrict the movement of the side and will lead to a cracked side or an unattached molding, depending on whether the side shrinks or swells. When the side expands, it usually pulls apart the mitered joint where the front and side moldings meet.

The best way to attach moldings to the case side is to affix the molding at the mitered joint securely and let the rest of the molding be less firmly attached. This means applying a concentration of glue at the miter joint and the area within a few inches of it, and much less glue along the length of the molding. The molding is best cross-nailed through the miter joint itself and at regular intervals of 4 in. or 5 in. along the length of the molding. The nails toward the back of the case will flex to accommodate the movement of the case side. When the case side expands or contracts as a result of changes in humidity, the front of the molding will remain secure and the miter joint will remain intact while the back part of the attachment yields.

Boston cabinetmakers were fond of gluing and nailing a strip of wood on the bottom of the case extending from front to back on either side. This strip provided a subframe of sorts, to which the molding and feet could be attached. The sides of the case were able to move on the subframe without seriously compromising the attachment of the molding or feet.

Applied-Molding Attachment

As case expands and contracts, front joint remains intact.

Cut brads

Side molding

Top of case

Very little glue is used toward back of case.

Front and miter are glued well.

Cross-nail miter joint.

Front molding

FEET

Finding a structurally sound method of attaching feet to a case is a challenge. The case side and bottom expand and contract across the grain, and the molding applied to the outside edge does not. The feet are attached to both of these dynamically dissimilar pieces and will have to bear the weight of the finished piece and the side forces of being dragged across the floor. In addition, the feet have to exhibit the ethereal or powerful qualities of the era in which they were made.

Attached feet depend on glue for their primary means of adherence. William and Mary ball feet were turned with a round tenon that was fit into a drilled hole in the underside of the case and secured with glue. Bracket feet and ogee bracket feet were also glued in place. Front feet are joined by 45° miter joints at the edges; rear feet usually have an abutting support on the back side. They are glued together and glued to the molding on the case bottom. A vertical glue block in their inside corner reinforces the miter joint and carries most of the weight of the case. Horizontal glue blocks between the feet, molding and case help to adhere the feet to the case bottom. Bandy legs, or short cabriole legs, were joined in much the same way. Their wide knee blocks served as large glue blocks both to support and adhere the feet to the case

The liberal use of glue and glue blocks did not leave much allowance for the expansion and contraction of the sides, and most cabinetmakers probably figured that enough big glue blocks would compensate for the effects of wood movement. In reality, the feet were adhered well enough to the case to move with it, and the glue joint with the stationary molding yielded. In retrospect, the Boston method of attaching the feet and molding to a strip of wood on the underside of the case was more structurally sound and offered better joint integrity.

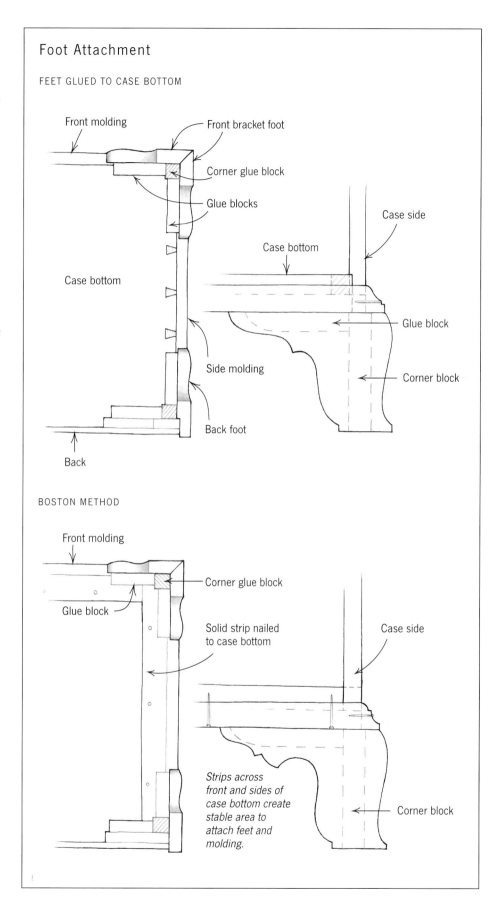

Foot Attachment

FEET GLUED TO CASE BOTTOM

Front molding

Front bracket foot

Corner glue block

Glue blocks

Case bottom

Case side

Case bottom

Glue block

Corner block

Side molding

Back foot

Back

BOSTON METHOD

Front molding

Corner glue block

Glue block

Solid strip nailed to case bottom

Case side

Corner block

Strips across front and sides of case bottom create stable area to attach feet and molding.

9

CABRIOLE LEGS

BALL AND CLAW FEET

The cabriole leg is one of the distinguishing features of Queen Anne furniture, and its use held over into the Chippendale period. Good cabriole legs are not difficult to make, but a discerning eye and careful planning are needed to achieve the subtle grace of the best original examples. Since the basis for Queen Anne design lies in sculpted shape, and the cabriole legs are often the most sculptural components on a piece, the success of the piece can lie in the refinement of the legs.

Ball and claw feet were one of several types of animal feet used to terminate cabriole legs. They are closely associated with the American Chippendale period—an association that is more by coincidence than design.

With the cabriole shape used for both legs and arm supports, and a strong presence afforded by bold ball and claw feet, the Newport roundabout chair is a tightly composed symphony of sculptural elements. This example was made by the author for a private collection after an original by John Goddard of Newport, 1760–1780.

Cabriole Legs

On original pieces, the characteristics of the cabriole legs can help identify the origin and skill level of the maker, and they are also indicative of the overall level of sophistication of the piece. High-style pieces from the shops of leading urban cabinetmakers have legs that flow smoothly and are well integrated with the entire design. More rural examples may appear out of proportion to the whole, or lack smoothly flowing contours. As with other aspects of 18th-century furniture, the cabriole legs of less-refined examples often show the idiosyncrasies that give the pieces their character, while formal pieces exhibit the skill in design and execution associated with the craftsmen who were leading the development of the style.

Because the curved shape of cabriole legs is fundamental to their form, even minor irregularities can be glaringly apparent. Irregularities become even more obvious after the piece has been finished to a nice luster, at which point it is too late to reshape the leg. These irregularities are not so much the result of variations in dimensions, but rather of awkward transitions from one part of a curve to another, or minor bumps or dips in an otherwise smooth curve. After a leg has been handcrafted, it makes very little difference if one leg is, for example, $1/16$ in. thinner at the knee than another, but it is glaringly apparent if the curves of the leg do not flow smoothly. A smooth shape is more important than an actual dimension. When it is well executed, the curve of the leg should carry the eye from the top of the knee to the tip of the foot in a seamless transition without interruption or distraction.

MAKING CABRIOLE LEGS

There are four steps in making a cabriole leg. First, a pattern is made to define the profile. Second, the profile is traced onto the prepared blank, which is then sawn to rough shape. Third, the bottom of the Dutch or pad foot is turned on the lathe. Finally, the contours are smoothed, and the leg is shaped to its final form. At each step of the process, careful attention to the profile will help ensure well-shaped and consistent results.

Making the pattern

Successful cabriole legs begin with a carefully made pattern. One pattern of the profile is all that is needed to define and create the leg. It is in this pattern that the dimensions of the leg are set and the curves are worked out before any wood is cut. If one is working from an original piece, the pattern making is reduced to the relatively simple task of copying the leg profile, either by tracing or measuring. If working from a photograph, it is helpful to have one that shows the leg profile from straight ahead. Because the legs are curved on all four sides, looking at the leg from an angle shows a shape that is an exaggeration of the pattern profile. Similarly, any part of the leg that is not round in cross section, and that can include all but the foot and ankle, will appear to be thicker than the pattern profile when viewed at an angle.

Defining Dimensions of Cabriole Legs

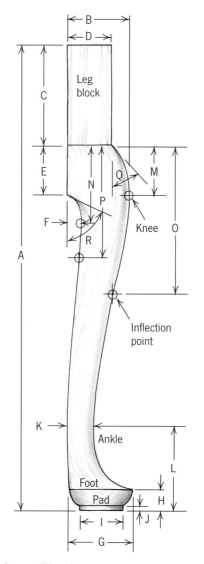

A. overall length
B. maximum width at knee
C. length of leg block
D. width of leg block
E. height of adjoining knee block
F. depth of back curve
G. foot diameter
H. foot height
I. pad diameter
J. pad height
K. ankle diameter
L. ankle height
M. distance to peak of knee
N. distance to peak of back curve
O. distance to front inflection point
P. distance to rear inflection point
Q. knee angle
R. transition angle to knee block

In making the pattern, there are many key features that can be measured to aid in faithfully replicating the originals. The drawing at left shows the dimensions that define a cabriole leg. Besides the obvious measurements, there are several points that are important in defining the curve. These points denote the width and location of the peak of the knee, the back of the knee, the thinnest part of the ankle and the inflection points. Inflection points are those points where the profile changes from concave to convex. It is rare to find period originals that have any discernible straight sections along the length of the leg. There are usually very slight curves throughout the length, and locating the inflection points aids tremendously in capturing their most subtle nuances.

There are a few general rules of thumb that apply to cabriole legs. Then, as now, the makers used rough stock in dimensions of inch multiples. Most large cabriole legs were cut from 3-in. stock, which after drying and planing could be more like $2^3/4$ in. or $2^7/8$ in. This dimension is a common thickness at the knee and foot for tall-chest, dressing-table and dining-table legs. Smaller legs, such as those on chairs and tea tables, usually measure $2^1/2$ in. to $2^5/8$ in. at the knee. Very slender legs, such as those on tuckaway tables, may have been squeezed from 2-in. stock. Because the leg is cut from a straight and square piece of stock, just wide enough to accommodate the pattern, the width at the knee is nearly always that at the foot. Proportionally, this works out very well: The foot usually looks to be of proper size when its diameter is close to the width of the knee.

Experience in measuring many cabriole legs has yielded a few more empirical maxims: Even on very robust legs, the knee rarely protrudes more than $3/4$ in. beyond the leg block. The block tends to be no less than two-thirds the width of the knee on well-proportioned legs, and the ankles are frequently about 40% of the knee width.

The location of the peak of the knee is critical to the appearance of the leg. A good first approximation is to locate it down from the block a distance about $1/4$ in. greater than the width of the leg block. The angle at which the top of the knee meets the block is about 45°. The height of the adjoining knee block is roughly equal to the width of the leg block. The height of the foot is about one-quarter to one-third its diameter, and the pad, which is usually worn down on originals, probably started at ¼ in. tall. Once again, the actual measurements of original legs are the best source for their replication, but these relationships in their geometry appear repeatedly. They may be of use where only a few actual measurements may be determined and the rest must be estimated.

Once the important dimensions of the leg have been determined, the pattern may be drawn and cut from posterboard or thin wood. It may take a few attempts before the profile pattern truly captures the feel of the original. Measurements can go only so far in quantifying the curves of a well-shaped cabriole, and a discerning eye is always essential. Even a direct tracing from an original will require some smoothing, as small variations in the shape can alter the look of the finished leg. It is very important to have smoothly flowing curves in the pattern, and sighting along the length of the pattern can help show any irregularities more clearly. The pattern will look like the drawing of the leg on p. 149, but it is not necessary to include the shape of the foot, because this will be turned later. The extra

Growth-Ring Orientation

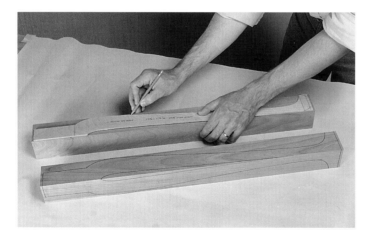

By orienting the growth rings on the end grain to point toward the knee, the grain patterns follow the contours of the leg. Orienting them in the opposite direction yields a less attractive pattern.

The pattern is used to draw the leg profile onto the wood. The extra ¼ in. at each end will be cut off when the leg is complete.

effort required to perfect the pattern more than pays for itself by making the rest of the work easier and yielding a well-shaped leg.

Preparing and cutting the stock

The stock from which the legs are to be cut should be dressed straight and square. It should be about ½ in. longer then the pattern or finished legs, and at least as wide. The extra length allows ¼ in. on each end of the leg that will be marred by clamping and lathe centers; it will be trimmed off when the leg is complete. A little extra width allows for a continuous cut over the knee without the blade running off the stock.

Before the pattern is traced on the stock, the orientation of the growth rings on the end grain should be noted. The leg should be cut so that those rings are oriented to point in the direction of the knee. As shown in the drawing at left, aligning the rings this way ensures that the visible features of the wood (the grain pattern) follow the shape of the leg. Aligning the end-grain growth rings across the leg, from side to side, orients the grain pattern in a way that is in opposition to the contours of the leg. While the grain orientation is not noticeable on darkly finished pieces, it is quite apparent on light pieces made of grainy wood like mahogany. On some pieces, like those in which the legs are the major element of the form, this orientation of the grain adds to the qualities of the finished piece. It is one of the small features that separates truly inspired furniture from the ordinary.

The best way to mark the stock for the optimal grain orientation is to draw a diagonal line on the end grain in the direction of the growth rings. One end of that line will be the corner of the knee, and the other will be the inside corner of the leg. In choosing which will be which, it's important to remember that the leg block and the ankle will be at the inside corner, and that corner should be free of any imperfections in the stock. It is helpful to mark the inside corner to aid in locating the pattern.

Once the best orientation of the grain is determined, the pattern can at last be traced onto the wood. With ¼ in. left at either end of the pattern, the profile is drawn on two adjacent sides of the blank so that the ankle and block are positioned in their marked corner (photo, facing page). For the sake of accuracy, a marking gauge should be used to scribe the straight line of the block. If the leg is to have a turned Dutch foot, the centers of both ends are marked by drawing crossed diagonal lines. The leg may then be sawn to shape.

To create a sharp corner where the block meets the knee, a cut is made along the scribed line of the block first (using a frame saw or bandsaw). Then, starting from the tip of the foot, the cut is continued up the leg, over the knee, to meet the first cut. By using a piece of stock slightly larger than the width of the leg, the cut over the knee can be made continuous and smooth. Very careful sawing will make the rest of the leg shaping that much easier. For the utmost in accuracy, half the line on the leg should be left.

After the profile on one side has been cut out, the scraps can be reattached with a spot of hot glue or double-sided tape and the second side can be cut out. Once all the sawing is done, the scraps can be pulled off to reveal the rough cut shape of the leg.

Turning the foot

Before the leg is shaped, the foot and pad are turned on the lathe (see p. 183). At this point, the foot is still square stock, defined by the sawn shape on the top and the pencil line from the pattern on the bottom. The leg is set up in the lathe using the center marks on either end, with the foot nearest the tailstock. The eccentricity of the piece will require starting the lathe at its slowest speed.

The square foot may now be turned to near round. Before the pencil lines are turned off, a parting tool is used to cut straight in below the bottom line, leaving a stub less than 1 in. in diameter. This stub is cut off when the leg is complete.

With the foot turned near round, the profile of the bottom of the foot and the pad may be turned. Using calipers ensures a consistent diameter of the foot and pad from leg to leg. The shape of the bottom of the foot is best determined by eye. Before the leg is completed, the lathe should be stopped to make sure there are no flats from the square stock remaining on the largest diameter of the foot.

Sawing the Profile Line

Sawing from both ends of the profile line to the intersection of the block and knee results in a sharp inside corner at that point.

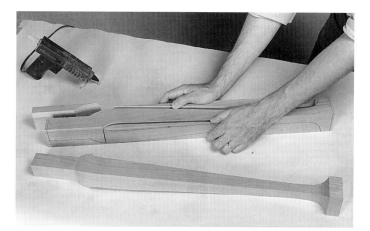

After one side of the leg has been cut, the scraps are reattached (with hot glue or tape) to aid in cutting the second side. With the scraps removed, the leg shows its rough-cut shape.

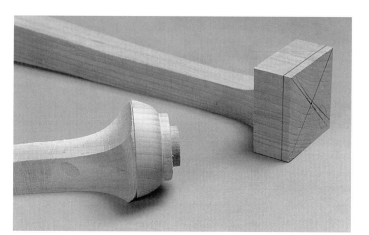

The foot is turned from the square using the lines on the wood and the sawn shape as references. A skew chisel is used to cut the line that will define the top edge of the foot.

With the leg securely clamped, a spokeshave is used to smooth the sawn contours of the leg.

The top of the foot is shaped round with rasps and files. The contour of the foot from the round ankle to its largest diameter should be smooth and continuous and show no trace of the flat sawn surfaces.

A line is cut with the point of the skew chisel to define the top of the foot. This cut is usually a good $1/16$ in. deep. The line should go all the way around the top of the foot, and not disappear at the bandsawn sections. A scribe line should be cut first; then, with the lathe stopped, the position of the line should be checked before the final cut is made. This line will be used as a guide in shaping the top of the foot and will remain a visible characteristic of the back of the foot. If any sanding is necessary, it can be done while the leg is still in the lathe.

Shaping the leg

Now that the bottom of the foot and the pad have been turned to their finished shape, the shaping of the rest of the leg may begin. At this point, the leg is cut to its rough shape and is probably difficult to hold while working on. One good way of securing it is to clamp it lengthwise in a pipe or bar clamp. The clamp may then be held vertically or horizontally in a bench vise (top photo at left).

With the leg held horizontally, a spokeshave is used to smooth as much of the curved, sawn surface of the leg as possible. The extremities of the leg, the top of the foot, the entire leg block and the top of the knee where it meets the block may be left rough for now. At this point, the goal is to shape the curved surfaces to their final contour. Most of this curve smoothing can be done with a flat-sole spokeshave. A flat-sole spokeshave will do a better job of flattening bumps, whereas a curved-sole spokeshave will tend to follow them. For best results, the spokeshave should be held at a skewed angle while cutting down the leg, in effect increasing its length. The spokeshave should be in peak sharpness, and set for a very thin cut.

If the pattern was smooth and the sawing was done carefully, this smoothing should amount to little more than cleaning off the saw marks. Sighting along the length of the corners and looking for irregularities is a good way to check the smoothness of the shape. With a well-sharpened and familiar spokeshave, irregularities can usually be felt better than they can be seen.

A smooth cut and a continuous shaving are indicative of a smooth shape.

By moving the leg to a near vertical position, the shaping of the top of the foot may be started (bottom photo, facing page). Shaping is done with a half-round rasp and finished with a fine file. Working from the ankle down, the sharp corners are removed so that the ankle is round in cross section and the round shape flows downward to the turned cut that defines the top of the foot. The sawn surfaces serve as guides to achieving the final shape, especially on the front of the leg. It can be helpful to make these sections octagonal first, and then round. This shaping is more art than science, so the most valuable tool is a keen eye. When properly shaped, there should be no bandsawn flats on the top of the foot, and the shape should be symmetrical when viewed from the front or back. When using the rasp near the outer edge of the foot, the cut should be made inward to avoid chipping off the outer edge.

The corners of the leg are shaped with a spokeshave so that they remain nearly square at the knee and blend into the round cross section at the ankle (top photo at right). Legs vary greatly in shape, with some being fully round from the knee down, and others being square through the ankle. Whatever the final shape, it is cut at this time. It's important to keep an eye on the symmetry and the side view of the leg as it is being shaped. As was the case with the top of the foot, it may be helpful to cut these corners at a 45° angle first, and then go back and round them. By doing that, the width of the cut is indicative of its depth, which helps make a smooth transition from a square knee to a round ankle. Chamfering the corners first also helps make the shaping from corner to corner and leg to leg more consistent. A fine file should be used to finish the shaping and blend the curves into the ankle and foot.

The leg is now in its final form, and the surface may be scraped or sanded smooth (bottom photo at right). Care must be taken not to round the corners of the leg block or the sides of the knee where the knee blocks attach. (Using a small sanding block on the flat surfaces of the leg helps detect and

The corners of the leg from the knee to the ankle are shaped with a spokeshave. The legs of original pieces vary from square to fully round at the knee. Over the length of the leg, that shape must show a smooth transition to the cross-sectional shape at the ankle.

A final scraping smooths the surface, and the cabriole leg is complete. A small sanding block may be used to flatten any minor irregularities, though careful work with the spokeshave usually makes that unnecessary.

flatten any irregularities.) The leg need only be smoothed from the knee down; the top of the knee and the transition to the knee blocks will be trimmed and smoothed later. Similarly, the outside of the leg block will be scraped to be flush with the rest of the piece after it is assembled. The extra $1/4$ in. on either end of the leg is cut off, and the leg is ready for mortising and assembly.

REGIONAL AND STYLISTIC VARIATIONS

This look at how cabriole legs are made used the case of a fairly generic leg that was square at the knee and round at the ankle with a Dutch or pad foot, not unlike what one would expect to find on a Queen Anne piece of New England origin. As mentioned previously, the profile and final shaping of a cabriole leg are indicative of its time and place of origin, and often its maker and his level of expertise. New England legs tend to be thin and straight, whereas Philadelphia legs tend to be stouter and with a more pronounced S shape to their profile. Newport cabinetmakers made the square cross section of their legs one of the signature elements of some of their designs,

while Boston makers produced examples that were more completely round from the knee to the foot.

The foot and pad are also distinctive features. Between individual makers, even in the same city, variations in feet and pads can be extreme. Some examples have wafer-thin feet on unusually tall pads, while others have feet of full thickness on nearly unnoticeable pads. Some feet have flat tops that look like discs, while other tops are conical and meet the foot at a more vertical angle. While individual makers had their characteristic shapes, these shapes were subject to change over time, and in fact could change from piece to piece. In replicating a leg, all of the subtle characteristics are as important to a successful leg as the major dimensions and shape of the cabriole. In designing a piece in the manner of the originals, these minor characteristics should be considered.

The shaping and detailing of cabriole legs give a good indication of the degree of sophistication of original makers. There are numerous examples of legs that are too straight, as well as examples where the legs are so curved as to be comical. Apart from

the continuity and fluidity of the curves and the balance of the knee with the foot, there are other details that point to the maker's level of skill. For example, you occasionally see tops of Dutch feet that are not quite round and still bear the vestiges of the sawn flat surfaces. This feature seems to point to a timid and weak effort on the part of the original maker. More sophisticated furniture makers would have had the confidence to make the shape of the leg conform to their wishes.

Knee Blocks

Knee blocks are one of the smallest components on any piece of furniture, but they are important enough to merit their own discussion. Knee blocks make the transition from the vertical form of the leg to the horizontal aspect of an apron, frame or seat rail. They also have the visually important job of finishing the sweeping curve of a leg and connecting it to either a robust cyma-curved apron, as on a Queen Anne high chest or chest-on-frame, or a rectilinear form, as on a Chippendale chair. On a piece like a chest with ball and claw

C-SCROLLS

C-scrolls are carved details that help blend the shape of the cabriole leg into the apron on more sophisticated Queen Anne pieces. The scrolls terminate in little volutes that protrude from the profile shape of the leg and apron, and they need to be planned for in the leg pattern from the very beginning. The bumps that will eventually be volutes have to be cut out and worked around until they are ready to be carved, which is usually about the last step in making the leg.

The C-scroll is not any higher then the surrounding surface, but it has that appearance because the adjacent material is carved in a gentle slope to the scroll. The depth of this carving is usually about $1/8$ in., and the width of the scroll itself is between $3/16$ in. and $1/4$ in. On well-executed examples, the carved relief that brings out the C-scroll continues un-interrupted from the apron, down the leg, and flows into the shape of the corner below the volute.

The C-scrolls at the top of cabriole legs are raised by carving away the surrounding area after the leg has been assembled to the apron.

feet or a bandy-legged desk, the blocks are wider, more elaborately shaped and visually important. Here they are structural as well, serving as large glue blocks to secure the short legs.

In most cases, the knee blocks are added after the piece has been assembled. Knee blocks fall into two groups, those that go over an apron, and those that attach under the apron or rail. In both cases, they make the transition from the leg to the apron, and make a logical terminus for the cabriole shape. The over-the-apron knee block is seen in the Queen Anne period on examples from Boston and the North Shore, and the Connecticut River Valley, most notably, the Deerfield area. The under-the-apron knee block is far more common, and makes up the bulk of knee blocks on Queen Anne and Chippendale pieces.

In either case, the blocks are made to fit their position, cut to rough shape, attached, and then trimmed to final form. Except in the case of a very wide knee block, the grain is oriented vertically to match that of the leg. A square blank of sufficient size is first held in place, and then the profile of the top curve of the knee is drawn onto it (drawing at right). That shape is then cut, forming the front curve of the block. Then the profile of the block is drawn onto that face, using a cardboard pattern, and that shape is cut. The block is now cut to shape and may be glued in place. Once the glue has set up a little, a couple of small cut nails should be added and set for good measure. The original makers did use both glue and nails to secure the knee blocks. (Glue alone should be sufficient for the over-the-apron blocks.)

After the glue has dried, the top of the knee and the knee block may be cut to final shape. A skewed, horizontal cut with a sharp chisel across the knee and block works well. The top of the knee and the block are then scraped, filed or sanded smooth. The side profile of the block should be cleaned up with a fine rasp or chisels. As with shaped aprons, the inside corner of the block should be chamfered to remove the rough edge (see p. 122).

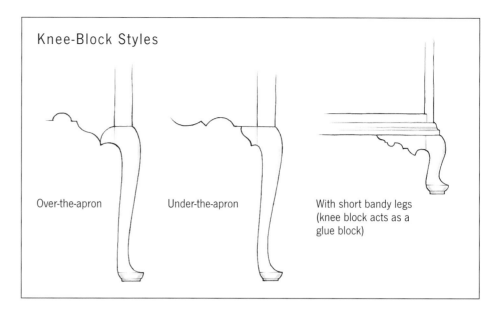

Knee-Block Styles

Over-the-apron

Under-the-apron

With short bandy legs (knee block acts as a glue block)

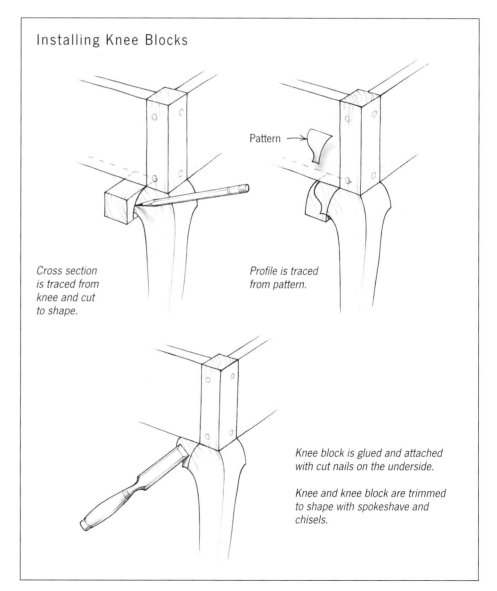

Installing Knee Blocks

Pattern

Cross section is traced from knee and cut to shape.

Profile is traced from pattern.

Knee block is glued and attached with cut nails on the underside.

Knee and knee block are trimmed to shape with spokeshave and chisels.

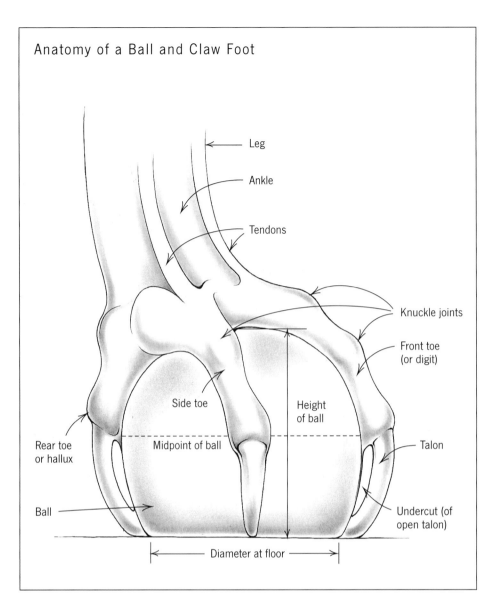

Anatomy of a Ball and Claw Foot

Leg

Ankle

Tendons

Knuckle joints

Front toe
(or digit)

Side toe

Height
of ball

Rear toe
or hallux

Midpoint of ball

Talon

Ball

Undercut (of
open talon)

Diameter at floor

Ball and Claw Feet

While Dutch or pad feet were the most common type of foot for a cabriole leg, especially during the Queen Anne period, ball and claw feet were also a popular terminus. Ball and claw feet were seen in English furniture during the first quarter of the 18th century but did not come into use in America before about 1740. They came into fashion during the Queen Anne period, but peaked in popularity with the Chippendale style, and therefore, quite by coincidence, are associated with American Chippendale furniture.

The association is appropriate, since the foot portrays the power and presence

that was a design goal of the period. The ball and claw was based upon the Chinese symbolism of strength as the guardian of purity from evil, as exemplified by a dragon clutching a pearl, but it was modeled closely after the claws of English and American birds of prey. Like so many aspects of the furniture, American ball and claw feet often have a spirited presence that exceeds their function as mere decorative elements and makes them remarkable in their own right.

The carving of ball and claw feet is one of many signatory features of American furniture of the period. As in many other aspects of the furniture, regional preferences and styles emerged (see the drawing on the facing page). Massachusetts ball and claw feet have the distinctive characteristic of

side toes and talons that are swept back at an appreciable angle. Newport feet are exceptionally life-like, with strong knuckle joints and often an open space between the ball and talon. Philadelphia feet tend to be stout and powerful. They often have a slightly flattened ball with a web stretched over it between the toes, and show very little of the talon. New York feet are similar but have a distinctive square and sharp-knuckled quality. Neglecting all the other details of design and construction, ball and claw feet alone can indicate the place of origin of a piece.

Ball and claw feet can identify the maker as well as the place of origin. No two makers carved feet exactly the same way, so an individual carver's work was as unique as a signature. The works of John Goddard and John Townsend, two Newport furniture makers whose work was often lumped together in the past under the heading of the Goddard/Townsend school, are immediately recognizable and distinguishable from one another by the characteristics of their ball and claw feet alone. Goddard feet feature a bulbous hallux and ankles that are set well back on the ball. Townsend feet show a more vertical aspect, with a smooth, continuous hallux extending from an ankle that is positioned closer to the top of the ball. The stylized ball and claw feet of the Hartford area's Eliphalet Chapin are clearly recognizable. Many of the larger urban shops employed carving specialists for their work, so the shop may not have had a distinct individual style. While the work of individual hired carvers is identifiable, most worked in obscurity and carved for a number of shops during their careers.

With practice, carvers of ball and claw feet arrive at their own individual styles over time. A carver who is not trying to emulate another carver's style will develop a unique method of work, a set of details and a preferred style. Once one has established an individual style, it is more difficult to replicate someone else's style, but that is necessary for an accurate and authentic replication of a piece. The analogy of a signature holds that it is more difficult to forge a signature convincingly than to sign your own effortlessly.

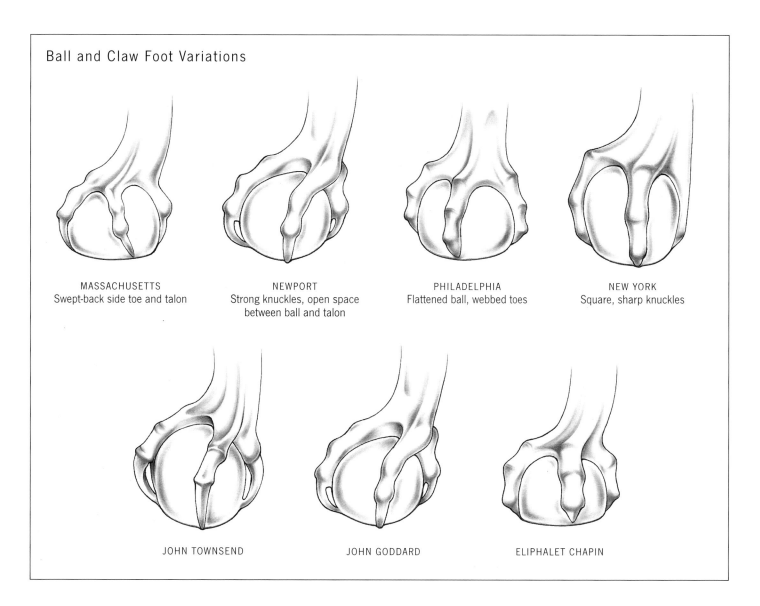

Ball and Claw Foot Variations

MASSACHUSETTS
Swept-back side toe and talon

NEWPORT
Strong knuckles, open space
between ball and talon

PHILADELPHIA
Flattened ball, webbed toes

NEW YORK
Square, sharp knuckles

JOHN TOWNSEND

JOHN GODDARD

ELIPHALET CHAPIN

CARVING BALL AND CLAW FEET

Ball and claw feet can be carved methodically, one step at a time—they are not just chiseled from the solid in an off-hand manner. This method ensures a well-formed foot with a continuous spherical ball, straight and symmetrical claws, and a consistency and uniformity among other feet in the set. As a general overview, the emphasis is first given to forming a well-shaped ball, and then the toes and talons are carved to conform to it.

Making the pattern

Like the cabriole legs to which they are attached, good ball and claw feet begin with a good pattern. The pattern defines the block from which the feet will be carved.

The block from which the foot is carved is part of the pattern of the cabriole leg.

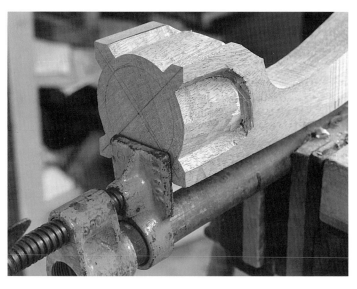

The layout of the foot is drawn on the rough-cut leg and includes a center, the approximate position of the toes, and circles that define the shape of the ball.

Material is cut.from around the talons and the ball is cut to a cylindrical shape using the large circle on the bottom as a reference.

The shape of the block locates the position of knuckle joints and defines the transition of the foot to the leg. Working from an original, a drawing or a photo, the shape of the pattern is an extension of the shape of the leg and can be taken from a profile view. When in doubt as to the exact profile shape of the foot, it is best to err on the side of caution by leaving a block that is at least as tall as it is wide. The width of the block is equal to the diameter of the ball, which is usually equal to the width of the leg at the knee. The foot block is cut while cutting the shape of the cabriole leg.

Laying out the ball and claw

The first step in the layout is to mark the center of the bottom of the foot with crossed diagonal lines (photo at left above). The lines also serve as reference lines for the position of the claws. From the center, one circle is drawn tangent to the outside edges of the block and another circle about 1/4 in. in from it. The larger circle is the diameter at the midpoint of the ball, and the smaller one is the diameter at the floor. Lines are drawn about 1/4 in. to 3/8 in. from the edges of the shaped block to mark the position of the toes. As the lines converge at the top of the ball, they must be drawn to conform with the shape of an original foot. There is no formula or method for this, but the point where they converge can be estimated

relative to the height of the ball and the position of the ankle. Determining where the digits meet is not critical at this point; they can be adjusted later in the carving.

Carving the ball and claw

The leg needs to be held securely while it is carved—a pipe or bar clamp held by the bench vise is ideal for the purpose and allows the leg to be fixed in almost any position (photo at right above). Most of the carving is done while the leg is clamped

horizontally. The position of the toes is defined by cutting along the inside of the claw lines to a depth of about 1/4 in. with a V-shaped tool, veiner or gouge. The ball is then shaped to a cylindrical form with a flat chisel, using the larger diameter circle on the bottom as a guide. A line is drawn around the cylinder to mark the midpoint or "equator" of the ball. The cylinder will be cut to a sphere above and below this line.

The top of the ball should be shaped first, using a flat chisel to work the cylinder

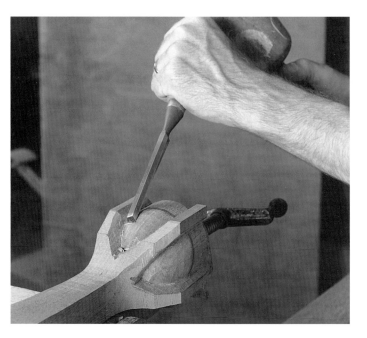

The midpoint of the ball is drawn on the cylinder and the top of the ball is cut to a hemispherical shape. The claws are left uncarved until the ball has been fully shaped.

to a hemisphere. It is important to note that the top of the ball, the "north pole," is under the front digit, not at the ankle. As the top of the ball is shaped, a veiner is used alternately to redefine and deepen the cuts on either side of the toes. The ball should be carved on all four sides of the foot until it has the appearance of being round and continuous. It should be inspected from all angles to ensure that it is the same height on either side of the toes.

Next the bottom half of the ball is shaped, using the smaller circle on the bottom of the foot as a reference (photo at right). Depending on the geometry of the foot, the smaller circle may have to be redrawn. Feet that show more of a fully spherical ball will have a smaller diameter at the floor. At this point, the ball should be roughly shaped and the position of the toes should be clear. If the ball appears too flat or too tall, it should be adjusted. The width of the claws may also be adjusted to clean up the line where they meet the ball.

The toes themselves are carved next. Their position is defined and their width is already approximated, but the layout of the joints remains to be marked. A mark is made at each joint and at the top of each

The bottom half of the ball is shaped using the circle on the bottom as a reference. The shape of the ball is then adjusted and refined to a fully spherical form.

talon where it meets the toe. The talons must be of equal length and the layout of the joints must be consistent from foot to foot. The position of these features is gauged relative to the top of the ball, the midpoint of the ball and their relative distance from one another. The digits are carved flat between the joints, and then the

joints are raised by carving those sections thinner and concave. The slimness or knobiness of the toes is determined by how the joints are carved at this point.

The stance and "grip" of the claw are determined by the strength of the toes and the way they blend into the ankle. Powerfully gripping claws conform tightly to the

Once the ball has been carved, the position of the knuckle joints is marked and the toes are carved to shape.

The toes are carved to blend into the ankle. These Goddard feet have thin tendons that emphasize the grip of the claw. The tendons are raised by removing the adjacent material.

The width of the talon is carved to a taper from the toe to the floor. These talons are left thick enough to be undercut.

Open talons are made
by undercutting the talon
with a small knife or
skew chisel.

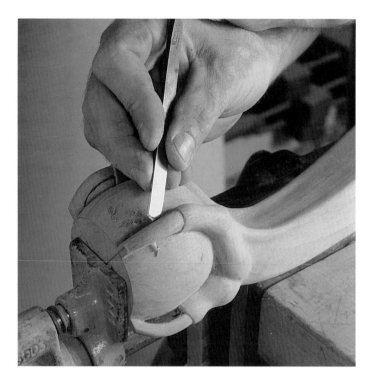

removed by cutting its outline and then cutting away the material within that. Material is cut away from both sides of the claw until the undercut meets in the middle (photo at left). The underside of the talon is trimmed to shape, and the ball is trimmed to flow smoothly from one side to the other. A small skew chisel or sharp pointed knife is recommended for undercutting claws.

The ball and claw foot is now completely carved to shape, but many refinements and adjustments are inevitable. To finish with a crisp and well-detailed foot, as much of it as possible should be shaped with chisels or cutting tools. Some very fine sanding will be required to blend the remaining tool marks and to achieve a surface smooth enough for finishing. There is some question whether original carvings were sanded or not, but close inspection of some very well-preserved originals shows an absence of tool marks and a surface consistent with having been smoothed with something like shark-skin or a sand leather. The foot will have some luster when it is finished with a top coat, and any irregularities in its shape will then be more apparent. Wetting the foot thoroughly with water and examining it while it is still wet and shiny offers a preview of what the finished foot will look like.

ball, show the tension of raised tendons at the ankle, and hold the ball from behind. Less-powerful grips hold the ball from above and show a more relaxed grasp. There are no formulae for making the transition from the foot to the ankle, other than to make it look natural and continuous. Like joints, tendons are raised by removing the material on either side of them. It is best to have a model or good photo on hand from which to work. This is the aspect of the carved foot that requires the greatest amount of artistry.

Finally, the talons themselves are carved. Philadelphia and some New York feet show little more than a suggestion of the talons; often the end of the toes is simply carved to a blunt point. Boston talons are more apparent and are frequently delicate and thin. The talons of the Newport ball and claw feet, however, are a significant part of their design. They are long, often starting at or near the midpoint of the ball, and are so pronounced as to stand away from the ball, leaving an open space and meeting the ball again just above the floor.

These distinctive Newport open talons are carved by first shaping their outside contour high enough to allow for the undercut. The area under the talon is

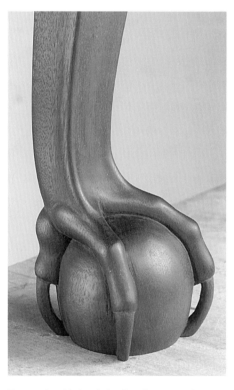

The completed ball and claw foot. Wetting the foot with water offers a preview of what the foot will look like with a more lustrous finish.

CARVING A SET OF BALL AND CLAW FEET

To make a set of ball and claw feet that are uniform and consistent from foot to foot, it is best to work on all four of them simultaneously. By performing the same step on all four feet before going on to the next, they progress simultaneously and, it is hoped, equally. With any ball and claw feet, and especially the more sophisticated ones, many refinements and iterations are required to achieve just the right look. That look has to include a continuous and well-rounded ball, symmetrical and authentically detailed claws, and a consistency among the feet of the set. In addition, if the piece is a replica of an original, the work requires capturing the spirit of the original feet. Making a good set of four legs with Newport open-talon feet can take as long as four days. Exemplary feet cannot be hurried.

The spirit and presence of the feet are one of the most important yet least definable attributes of the ball and claw. They exude a presence, and, as an important part of the American Chippendale aesthetic, they were intended to do so. That presence can range from the graceful and delicate perch of a light piece to the powerful and muscular grip of the flattened ball of a case piece. Between is a range of ball and claw feet from thoroughly life-like to charmingly stylized. Replicating an original design achieves its goal if it imparts the same startling impression that the original does.

Other Feet

In addition to ball and claw feet and Dutch or pad feet, several other kinds of feet were in use during the 18th century. Newport cabinetmakers found stylistic success with slender, pointed, slipper feet. Philadelphia furniture makers sometimes used three-toed trifid feet and occasionally scrolled feet, both of which were closely linked with prevalent English styles. Makers in both Massachusetts and Pennsylvania are known to have used square feet, which are very much like Dutch feet before they have been turned.

SLIPPER FEET

Slipper feet are a trademark feature of Newport cabinetmakers. The foot enhances well-shaped cabriole legs and furthers the aim of the Queen Anne style by giving the finished piece a delicacy, lightness and small footprint. Cabriole legs that end in slipper feet are made in the same manner as those that end in Dutch feet. The layout and cutting of the leg are identical, but the foot is cut to shape rather than turned. The footprint is the shape of a teardrop, and the foot tapers slightly toward the floor. Some examples of original Newport legs with slipper feet are square in cross section at the ankle, with a gentle ridge extending along the top of the foot to the tip of the toe. Other examples are round at the ankle, which extends along the foot as a softly rounded top.

Slipper feet are made by drawing the pointed pattern of the footprint on the

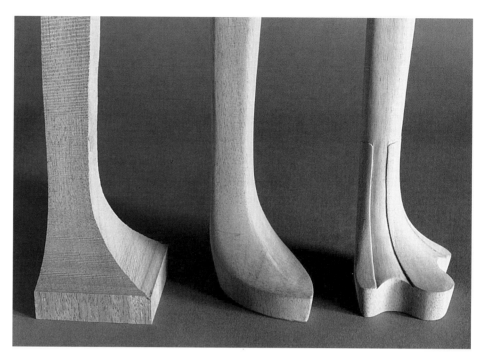

Cabriole legs with slipper feet or trifid feet begin in the same manner as those with pad feet (left). With slipper feet (center), the foot is shaped to a tapered teardrop shape rather than turned. Trifid feet are similar but are cut to a three-toed pattern with chisels and gouges (right).

bottom of the leg, and cutting the foot to shape. Since the foot actually tapers from top to bottom, the footprint pattern should be sized to fit on the stock with about $1/8$-in. space all around it. That way, the top of the foot will be as large as the stock permits. Slipper feet do not have a pad, and there is no need for the extra $1/4$ in. left on legs with Dutch feet. Therefore, the foot on the leg-profile pattern may be aligned with the bottom of the stock when the leg is laid out. Except for the foot, the leg is cut out and shaped as usual. In shaping the foot, the bulk of the material may be sawn off, and the rest is best shaped with a spokeshave. The shape of the leg flows right into the shape of the foot, so some of the shaping of the foot and leg can be done concurrently.

Whereas Dutch feet have a turned line to mark the top of the foot, the tops of slipper feet are not so well defined. A pencil line $5/8$ in. or $3/4$ in. from the bottom and extending all around the foot helps in shaping the front outside corners of the foot to a crisp line and uniform height. When the leg is cut carefully according to the pattern, and the shape of the foot has

been cut, there is surprisingly little more shaping to do. These two operations define most of the shape of the foot, and all that is left is some smoothing and fine shaping. There is not nearly as much stock to rasp off as when shaping the top of a Dutch foot. As with Dutch feet, the symmetry of the foot should be checked from the front and back. Once the foot is in its final shape, a spoke-shave is used to chamfer the bottom edge about $1/8$ in. wide to avoid chipping of the bottom edge.

TRIFID FEET

Trifid feet (sometimes called "drake" feet) differ from slipper feet in little other than shape. The layout, cutting and shaping of the leg are identical, but rather than cutting the foot to the teardrop shape, a three-toed pattern is used instead. As with the slipper foot, the trifid shape is cut at a taper. To avoid chipping off edges, it is best to shape the top of the foot in the same manner as a Dutch foot before the trifid shape is cut. The more intricate shape requires the use of flat chisels and gouges, after which the shape is cleaned up with rasps and files.

10

SURFACE

ORNAMENTATION

The decorative treatments given to furniture surfaces during the 18th century are among the elements that distinguish the important style periods. Along with form and proportion, the surface aided in making the piece achieve the design ideals of the period. During the William and Mary period, the focus on the surface was intense, with symmetrically arranged, burled veneers providing most of the interest. During the Queen Anne period, the emphasis shifted to the grace of the form, and the smooth surfaces were punctuated by the restrained use of carved ornament. The Chippendale era was witness to an increased use of carving, as elaborately carved details were used to create a sumptuous surface. The Federal era brought the surface treatment full circle, returning once again to smooth but elaborately veneered and inlaid furniture surfaces, and confirming the idea that true revolutions in art restore more than they destroy.

Fan and Shell Carvings

The use of centrally located fan and shell carvings is a Baroque style of ornamentation that came to England with the influx of foreign influences following the Restoration of Charles II. There are many parallels between early English shell carvings and those of Germany and the Low Countries. These carved ornaments came to the fore at the beginning of the 18th century, when the aesthetics of the English Queen Anne period called for smooth surfaces and graceful lines interrupted only by well-placed and carefully proportioned carvings. Over the next few decades this restraint was abandoned, culminating in

the ornament-encrusted designs of William Kent in the 1740s. The Chippendale-era tastes called for rich and florid carving, and many of the Baroque carved ornaments were updated to include more of the fluid Rococo influence. The Neoclassical trends that followed relied on inlaid ornament, so carved shells and fans fell out of fashion in furniture.

American furniture followed English trends in regard to carved ornament, but American tastes and practical considerations

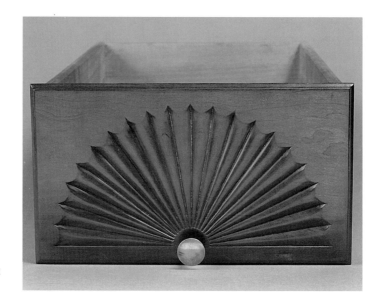

A flat, straight-ray fan is typical of rural New England central carved ornament.

filtered out most of the English excesses. The relative simplicity of American designs made the restrained use and proper placement of central carvings that much more important. As with most aspects of American furniture, there were distinct differences in the sophistication of carving between urban and rural areas. Urban cabinetmakers carved designs that were as deep and bold as English work, while rural makers tended toward shallower, geometric designs. Given the individualistic nature of American cabinetmaking, shells and fans ran the gamut from simple to ornate, with each region and maker having a preferred method and style of carving. Like so many other aspects of furniture of the period, the designs and characteristics of carvings are usually indicative of the place of origin and sometimes identify the individual maker or carver.

Given the wide range of American carving styles and designs, the best way to demonstrate the technique of fan and shell carving is to illustrate examples from both ends of the spectrum. The steps in carving both simple and complex designs follow.

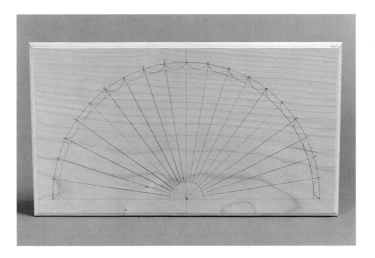

The pattern of the fan is drawn on the drawer front.

CARVING A STRAIGHT-RAY FAN

Among the simplest of central carvings is the flat, straight-ray fan (photo facing page). This design is shallow and geometric, and can be carved with just a few tools. Fan carving is typical of a rural northern New England carving used to ornament a central drawer on a case piece.

The first step in making the carving is to draw the design of the fan on the drawer front (photo above). This is a very simple design made with a compass and straightedge directly on the wood surface. A V-shaped carving tool or a skew chisel is used to carve a V-shaped channel between the rays of the fan (photo at left below). These channels are cut in proportion to the width of the ray: At the outside of the fan, the cuts are deep and wide; at the center, they are shallow and narrow. A small vertical cut at the small end of the channel acts as a stop line and prevents the wood from breaking off past the inside circle.

A V-shaped carving tool is used to cut a channel between the rays of the fan.

Each ray is rounded with a flat chisel.

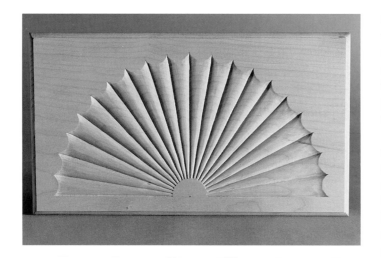

The fan carving is complete, sanded and ready for further assembly or finishing.

several decades on Newport furniture, with only minor variations. Newport shells are three-dimensional, fluid and exactingly detailed. They have a sophisticated grace that exemplifies the Newport craftsman's philosophy of rendering elegant designs with detailed precision.

The carving of a Newport shell begins with drawing the outline of the carving on the workpiece. The outline is two concentric arcs with the wavy edge of the lobes drawn between (see the photo at right below). When a shell is carved on an apron, as shown in the accompanying photos, the shell is fully integrated into the design of the apron, and it is important that the shell be sized accordingly. Since this is a dished shell, the shape of the surface of the carving is established first. Using gouges, the area to be carved is scooped away to the appropriate depth (top left photo, facing page). This dishing defines the depth of the finished shell, so it is important that the shape be uniform, symmetrical and to the proper depth. Drawing the profile of the dish on the bottom edge of the apron helps in achieving the proper shape. When the preliminary shaping is finished, the surface should be smooth enough to draw on the pattern of the carving in some detail.

Once the channels between the rays have been carved, each ray is carved to a rounded shape with flat chisels (bottom right photo, p. 163). A fine line is often drawn down the center of the ray to aid in rounding both sides evenly. To avoid cutting against the grain, most rays have to be cut toward the center on the top of the ray, and away from the center on the bottom. It may be necessary to deepen the channel between rays as the carving progresses.

The finished carving may be further smoothed or sanded to remove any flat cuts from the chisels that remain visible. On such a geometric design, any areas that require adjustment will be evident and may be reshaped easily.

CARVING A CURVED-RAY SHELL

Contrasting with simple fan carvings are the deep and detailed carvings of urban cabinetmaking centers. One of the more distinctive of these is the Newport curved-ray shell, developed and used extensively by the Goddard and Townsend families of cabinetmakers (see the photo at left below). These shells were used over the course of

The Newport curved-ray shell is the focal point of this Goddard dressing table.

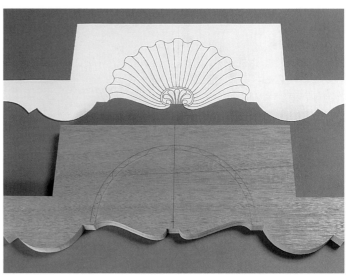

An outline of the shell is first drawn on the apron.

The carving begins by dishing out an area to establish the depth of the shell.

Using a gouge, the concave lobes of the shell are carved according to the drawn pattern.

A flat chisel is used to round the convex lobes of the shell.

The details of the center medallion or rosette are carved last.

The pattern of the carving is drawn onto the dished surface freehand. It is helpful to draw a vertical centerline for use as a reference. Since the carving is cut to follow the drawn design, it is important to draw the pattern carefully and precisely. Once the pattern has been drawn, the concave lobes of the shell may be cut with gouges to a depth proportional to their width (top right photo).

A flat chisel is used to round the convex lobes of the shell (bottom left photo). Because the lobes are three-dimensional, one side of a lobe may change directions relative to the grain over its length. The direction of the carving may have to be changed if the cut begins to go against the grain. Here again, drawing a line to mark the top center of the convex lobes aids in rounding them and keeping them shaped to the correct curve.

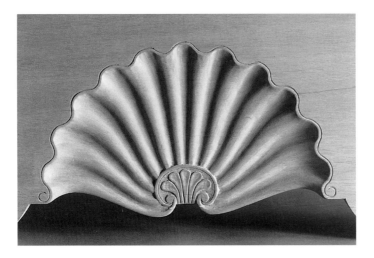

The carving of the Newport shell is complete and ready for assembly to the case.

Once the lobes of the shell are carved to shape, the center ornament or rosette is carved. Because of its fine detail, the carving of this area leaves little room for error: The design should be drawn very carefully and carved with great patience. The details of the sheaf are in very low relief and require sharp definition to be clear. The shell shown in the photos is for a relatively small dressing table, but larger shells for desks and other case pieces have larger and more highly detailed rosettes.

The shell is now carved to its finished shape, and adjustments can be made as needed. Wetting the carving with water will give a rough idea of how the shell will look with the low luster of a finish. With the shell carved and smoothed, the apron may be assembled to the case.

Veneering and Inlay

The use of veneers and inlaid decoration was an important decorative element of 18th-century American furniture. The decorative use of veneer was at its peak in the opening and closing quarters of the century. During the William and Mary period, which dominated the first quarter, burled and bookmatched veneers were used as a lively surface treatment. Inlaid banding or stringing served as borders for those veneers on drawer fronts and panels. This practice diminished in the Queen Anne and Early Georgian era, as shape supplanted surface detail in visual importance. By mid-century, the use of veneer and inlay had all

but ceased, as carved detail and pierced fretwork became the dominant decorative treatment in Chippendale-style furniture. With the popularity of Neoclassical designs after the American Revolution, veneered surfaces and inlaid details re-emerged as the preeminent surface for this new furniture. The Neoclassical period was the pinnacle of the use of veneer and inlay in the history of American furniture.

Like most other aspects of American furniture design, the use of veneer came directly from English inspiration. English court furniture after the Restoration was extensively veneered in keeping with the

latest Continental trends. Where cost was seemingly no object, nearly every surface was covered with decorative veneer. European cabinetmakers had taken up the practice of building panels from pieces of glued-together secondary wood and veneering their entire surface. Especially popular were "oyster" and "roundel" veneers, medallion-like patches of veneer cut directly across or at an angle across small diameter logs. The court furniture also included a number of other labor-intensive details such as moldings cut across the grain of the wood to match cross-grain banding and edges.

The American interpretation of this work was much more restrained. Tempered by practical considerations and given an abundant supply of attractive cabinet-grade wood, the American use of veneer was generally limited to the facades of case pieces, including desks, chests and dressing tables. American makers used veneers of burled walnut and maple to enliven the surface. Veneer was bookmatched to achieve the symmetry and order important to the aesthetics of the period. Most veneered panels and drawer fronts were also bordered with a mitered veneer banding. Cross banding was cut perpendicular to the grain, and feather or herringbone banding consisted of two strips cut at a 45° angle to

Throughout the 18th century, veneers were cut by hand with a framed saw. This illustration is from Roubo's *L'art du menuisier ébéniste* (Paris, 1774).

the grain and arranged in a chevron-like fashion. Cross-grain moldings were generally too labor-intensive for American makers.

During the Neoclassical era, the similarities between the English and American use of veneers were greater. The design books of Hepplewhite, Sheraton and others were very specific about the use of veneer and the details of inlaid ornament so its use was less open to interpretation. American makers were also known to have used imported English inlays. The use of figured veneer was so pervasive that a lively trade had emerged in satinwood, crotch mahogany and figured birch, and similar materials were readily available on both sides of the Atlantic. The term *marquetry* is generally applied to European and English inlaid decoration, but similar work on American pieces is said to be *inlay*.

VENEERING SURFACES

Throughout the 18th century, veneer was cut by hand from blocks of figured wood using framed saws (see the illustration on the facing page). The sawn veneer was then scraped flat. During the first quarter of the 18th century, corresponding to the William and Mary period, the coarseness of the saws and the fragile nature of the burled wood preferred for veneer resulted in relatively thick sheets of veneer. This early veneer was sometimes as much as ⅛ in. thick—more like thin boards. Since the William and Mary furniture designs did not have curved surfaces, there was no requirement for the veneer to be thin and flexible. Surfaces that were to be veneered (the ground surfaces) were first scored with a toothed plane to improve the adhesion of glue. The veneers were trimmed roughly to shape and attached with liberal amounts of hide glue. Period references mention that the veneer was held in place under boards that were either clamped or weighted. The usual method of veneering with inlay or borders was to apply the veneer to the ground surface first, and then add the banding or stringing once the glue had dried.

By the Federal period, and with the passing of more than half a century, the

A veneer hammer is the traditional tool used to press thin veneer into place and force out excess glue.

methods of cutting and applying veneer had become more sophisticated. The requirements of veneer in this period were different from those of the William and Mary period. Veneer needed to be flexible enough to conform to the curved surfaces of Neoclassical forms and capable of being inlaid in minutely detailed designs. The use of figured woods instead of fragile burled wood, and a general refinement of saws, allowed veneers to be sawn thinner than they had been previously, averaging about ⅟₁₆ in. thick. They were still cut by hand; no use of machinery to cut veneer is known until the early 19th century.

If the figured wood from which the veneer was cut had an elevated moisture content, the veneer would continue to dry and shrink after it had been cut. Because of the irregular grain, the veneers would often dry too wavy or lumpy to be used, and they would have to be flattened. Flattening veneer is accomplished by sprinkling or sponging the wood with water to soften it. It is then stacked with a sheet of absorbent blotter paper between each sheet of veneer, and clamped or weighted between two boards. The paper is changed daily for dry sheets until the veneers are fully flat and dry.

Hammer veneering

Like the veneer itself, the methods of applying veneer had also evolved by the Federal period. Primary among the methods was hammer veneering, wherein the veneer is pressed into place with a hand-held tool. The veneer hammer has a 3-in. or 4-in. wide wooden and brass head and a hammer-like handle, and it is used like a rolling pin or squeegee to press down the veneer and force out excess glue. As with the veneering method of the William and Mary period, the ground surface is first scored with a toothed plane or scraper blade. The ground surface and the veneer are coated with hot hide glue, and the two are joined.

The veneer hammer is held with one hand on the head to exert downward pressure, and the other on the handle to guide its travel (photo above). The head is moved across the veneer in such a way as to force the glue and any trapped air pockets toward the outside edges of the veneer. On the ideal flat surface, this usually means moving the hammer in parallel strokes starting across the center and progressing toward the outside, on one side and then

Hammer Veneering

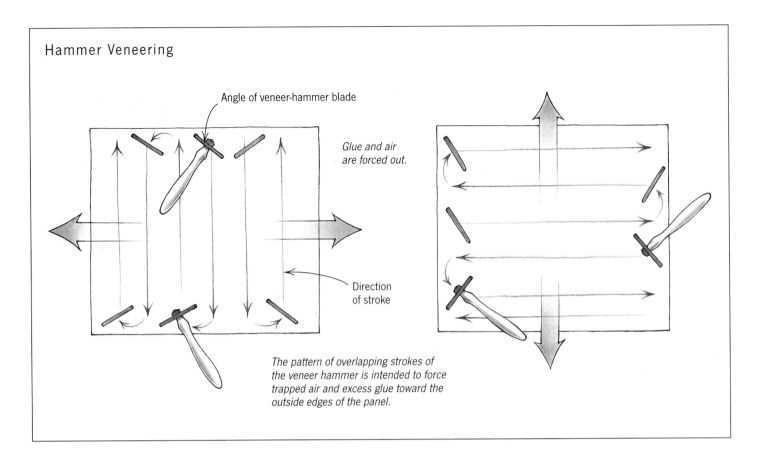

Angle of veneer-hammer blade

Glue and air are forced out.

Direction of stroke

The pattern of overlapping strokes of the veneer hammer is intended to force trapped air and excess glue toward the outside edges of the panel.

the other, holding the head at an angle so the excess glue is always squeezed outwards. This process is then repeated in the perpendicular direction, until the glue has cooled and set. The same general method is used on curved surfaces, though it is not always possible to use the hammer in as many directions. Glue applied to the outer surface of the veneer serves to lubricate the motion of the hammer throughout the procedure. It is later washed or scraped off.

The method of hammer veneering cannot be fully appreciated or understood without a familiarity with genuine hide glue. Hide glue is available in a dry granular form, which is mixed with roughly an equal volume of water and then heated in a double boiler or hot glue pot. It has to be kept hot (140°F–150°F) for use. Once dissolved, the hot glue has a syrupy consistency and feels slippery between the fingers. As it cools it becomes stickier and more viscous. It has a firm, gelatin-like quality at room temperature. Overnight, the moisture evaporates, leaving it hard and

somewhat brittle. Because of the hide glue, the process of hammer veneering is very dependent upon temperature. Both the ground surface, the veneer and the hammer are best warmed to keep the glue from cooling too soon. As the veneer is worked with the hammer, the glue cools and sets. Areas that have not adhered properly may be reheated with an iron and pressed down again. Once the veneer is properly attached and the glue has cooled to near room temperature, the glue is strong enough to hold the veneer in place overnight until the glue dries.

Caul clamping

The other traditional method for gluing down veneer is to use cauls. Cauls are solid-wood molds used to clamp the veneer in place on a flat or curved surface. For curved surfaces that have been sawn from the solid, the scrap that was cut away is worth saving as a perfectly shaped caul (see the photo on the facing page). As with hammer veneering, the ground surface is prepared by scoring it with a toothed plane. It is

recommended that the caul be heated along with the ground and veneer to help the glue flow and penetrate. The veneer is then positioned, covered with the caul, and clamped down until the glue has set or dried. For repetitive work, cauls of the period were oiled and greased to make them resistant to glue, and used repeatedly like any other shop fixture. Experience has shown that it is helpful to place a layer of soft and resilient material (like felt, corrugated cardboard or thin plastic foam) between the veneer and caul to protect the surface and distribute the pressure evenly.

Veneering methods compared

The methods of using a veneer hammer or cauls each have their advantages. Because the method is a bit arcane and not in general practice, hammer veneering has a certain allure. Like many other aspects of the craft, hammer veneering is best perfected through practice, but once you have become familiar with the method, it is a quick and reliable way to adhere veneer without clamps, especially edgings and bandings. Best of all, it offers the crafts-person control of the work; you do not have to wait until clamps are removed to see the results. The position of the veneer may be adjusted and areas that are difficult to adhere may be reheated and pressed down. On the other hand, hammer veneering does require some specialized material and equipment, it can be messy, the glue on the top of the veneer has to be cleaned off thoroughly, and it doesn't always adhere some stubborn areas of the veneer.

The use of cauls, or the similar flat veneer press, is less of a lost art, but it is a direct and effective method. A caul will hold slightly wrinkled veneer flat until the glue has set, and the clamping pressure can be left on until it is thoroughly dry. Cauls can also hold veneers against irregular shapes and small-radius curves. Panels comprised of different veneers can be pre-assembled with paper and glue and clamped in place with a caul. With a caul, the choice of glue is not limited to hot hide glue and there is little or no glue to clean off the surface. On the downside, the results cannot be seen until the caul is unclamped. Areas that have not adhered, though they

are rare with a well-shaped caul, are more difficult to re-attach. In that case, glue has to be injected under the veneer and the area must be clamped again. Both hammer veneering and the use of cauls are histori-cally accurate methods. The choice of method depends largely on the nature of the veneer and the surface to which it is to be applied.

Modern advances in veneering

In addition to the period methods there are some modern ways of attaching veneer that are worth noting. Vacuum-bag clamping is the latest method of veneering or laminating. The veneer is glued in place on the ground surface and placed inside a thick, clear plastic bag. A vacuum pump evacuates most of the air, bringing the pressure of the atmosphere to bear on the veneer. The great advantage of this method is the ability to distribute even pressure across irregular surfaces. No caul is required, and almost any kind of modern glue can be used. With vacuum pumps able to reduce the pressure inside the bag to 2 psi, the net pressure from the 14.7 psi atmosphere is 12.7 psi. That is roughly

equivalent to one wooden hand clamp capable of exerting 1,000 lb. pressure for every 9-in. square area or 81 sq. in.

Other modern advances concern the glue itself. Contact cement has been used successfully for a few decades to hold veneer, but its longevity over centuries is not certain. It is applied to both surfaces and allowed to dry, and the parts are assembled and pressed with a roller. Contact cement is tenacious but not readily sandable, and it is difficult to cut through and remove to add inlays. Hot-melt glues are available in sheets of soft thermoplastics that allow the veneer to be ironed in place. The sheet of glue comes on a coated paper backing and is ironed on. When it cools, the paper may be peeled off, leaving only a thin layer of glue. The veneer is positioned and heated with the iron to remelt the glue. The veneer is then rolled with a roller until the glue has cooled and set. Contact cement and hot-melt glues are very strong and, unlike hide glue, are resistant to dampness and water.

Trimming veneer

Whatever method is used to attach the veneer, once it is in place any overlap is trimmed away with a veneer saw or sharp knife. If there are to be any borders of cross bandings or feather bandings, their application is the next step. The main veneer is trimmed at the line where the border is to start, and the excess glue and veneer are sliced away. Because they are small, borders can usually be attached with hide glue and the veneer hammer, though there are instances where they need to be held in place with a clamp or caul. If there is to be any inlay work, it is let in by cutting through the applied veneer with a sharp knife, and cutting away the veneer to the depth of the ground with chisels.

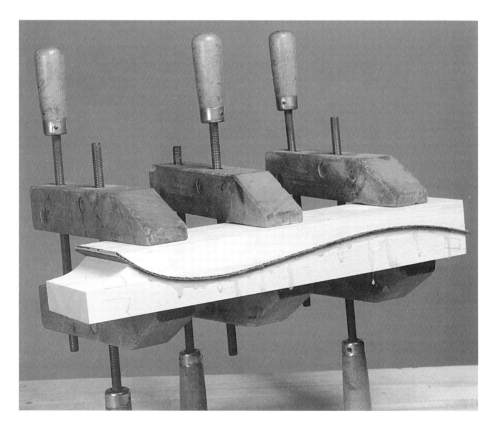

A caul is used to clamp veneer to a curved surface. The caul for this curved rail is the scrap that was sawn from it. A thin layer of resilient material (corrugated cardboard) has been placed between the veneer and caul to protect the surface and distribute the pressure.

INLAY

In their broadest sense, inlays are veneers let into either veneered or solid-wood surfaces. Stringing and banding are inlays of linear strips of veneer. Some are a single line of wood, some have two or more contrasting strips running parallel, and others have more intricate patterns of alternating woods along their length. *Paterae* include all kinds of medallion-like circular and oval inlays, including fans and shells. In addition, there are a number of other designs and styles of inlaid decoration on American furniture that are not categorized so easily.

With its fine detail, inlay making is a very interesting facet of the cabinetmaker's craft. The 18th-century inlay maker cut and assembled his inlays from holly, ebony, satinwood and boxwood veneers. Light-colored woods, such as holly, were often dyed any number of colors, but most often black to simulate ebony. The field was specialized enough to support craftsmen who made and supplied paterae, stringing, banding and other inlays to cabinetmakers. Most busy urban shops would have bought their inlays ready-made or had them made to order from these local inlay makers or "ebenists," as they sometimes called themselves. As a result, shops of a given region or city used inlays from the same few makers, and the patterns and styles of the inlay became indicative of a piece's place of origin.

Stringing and banding

The simplest of all inlaid banding is stringing, the narrow strips of veneer used to outline drawers, panels or legs. To make stringing, veneer is cut into thin strips about $1/16$ in. wide. A more interesting kind of banding features a dark string between two light strings, or vice versa. Rather than actually assembling precut stringing, the inlay maker would laminate a dark sheet of veneer between two light ones and slice it lengthwise into $1/16$-in. strips (see the drawing on the facing page). The resulting slices were an assembled stringing of veneer thickness. This method produced a great quantity of very uniform string inlay.

More complex patterns could be made in a similar manner. By laminating alternating colors of veneers and recutting them on the diagonal, a rope-like band could be made. This core of diagonal stripes used to make rope stringing could also be used to made a herringbone design. By cutting the laminated veneers directly across the grain, alternating colors and checkered designs were possible. The patterns have the appearance of having been assembled from tiny pieces of veneer, but are in reality slices from inventively prepared laminations. The terms stringing and banding are used somewhat interchangeably, though stringing implies the more narrow linear inlays and banding is more appropriate for wider, more intricate designs.

Stringing and banding are inlaid into the veneered or solid surface by making two knife cuts the width of the inlay and then removing the material between them with a narrow chisel to a depth no greater than the inlay's thickness. On veneered surfaces, this depth is reached when the ground is visible, but on solid wood a careful estimate of the depth is required. Once the inlay is in place it should be just higher then the surrounding surface. The inlay will shrink as the moisture from the glue evaporates. The cut should be just wide enough that the stringing or banding is held snugly in place. After a thin layer of glue is spread in the cut channel, the banding is installed. It is often helpful to press it in with a roller to ensure that it is seated and to squeeze out the excess glue. A roller, such as a wallpaper seam roller, also helps wider bandings remain seated until the glue has started to set. Once the glue has dried thoroughly, the inlay is scraped or sanded flat to the surrounding surface.

Paterae

The formal definition of *patera* is a raised or embossed oval or circular surface ornament, such as the applied composition ornaments used on the furniture of Robert Adam (see pp. 81-82). The Neoclassical furniture that followed the Adamesque designs substituted inlaid ornament for the composition. Circular and oval inlays in the patterns of fans or shells are generally considered paterae, and were commonly

called that (or something similar) in the 18th century.

Inlay in decorative patterns like fans or shells was not as easily produced in quantity as stringing and banding, and that fact is reflected in its price. The 1800 inventory for Baltimore inlay maker Thomas Barrett shows his most expensive "shell," at 25 cents, to be twice as expensive as a yard of his best banding. At the prevailing wage of $1 a day, the productivity of an inlay maker like Mr. Barrett is evident. The idea that inlay makers made "lengths" of rosettes or fans and sliced off individual inlays has been suggested, but it is unlikely that any paterae were ever made this way. The orientation of the grain in period inlays is such that the maker would have had to cut the segments across the grain, since inlay does not have end grain on its surface. The fineness of detail, such as where the points of a fan meet, are so precise that they could not have been made to match unless they were assembled individually. Furthermore, segments that are made of dyed wood could only have been dyed as a veneer, not as a solid segment. Finally, these specialists were equipped to work with veneer and probably would not have had the tools required to make solid lengths of inlay.

From the inspection of individual inlays and accounts of the day, these inlays had to be cut and assembled individually from veneer. The process of making them could be expedited by standardizing the designs and by making component parts in quantity. The maker could then assemble a number of inlays at one time. For irregular shapes, several could be cut out simultaneously by stacking veneers, rather than cutting one at a time. In spite of efforts to make the work easier, inlay making remained a precisely detailed and labor-intensive field. Inlay was the focal point of a piece of Federal furniture, and there was really no way to make outstanding inlay without a substantial investment of time.

For an inlay like the commonly used quarter fan (see the photo on p. 172), the pie-shaped segments would be cut at a $22\frac{1}{2}°$ angle with a simple template or angular guide of some kind. These same

String Inlays

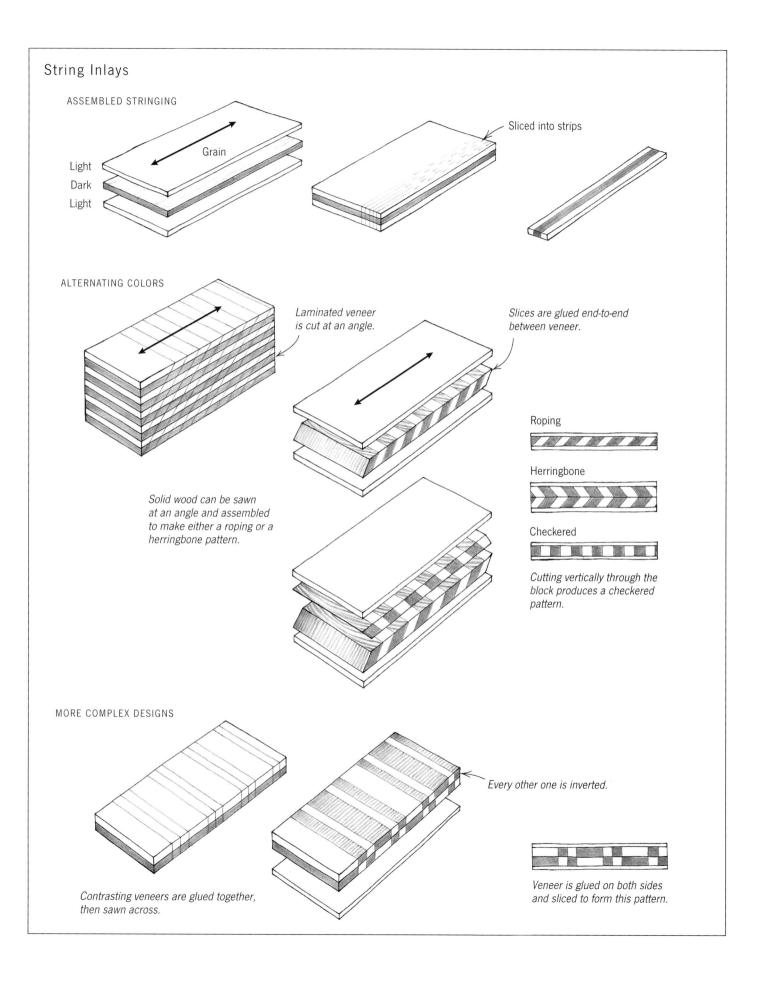

ASSEMBLED STRINGING

Grain

Light
Dark
Light

Sliced into strips

ALTERNATING COLORS

Laminated veneer is cut at an angle.

Slices are glued end-to-end between veneer.

Roping

Herringbone

Checkered

Solid wood can be sawn at an angle and assembled to make either a roping or a herringbone pattern.

Cutting vertically through the block produces a checkered pattern.

MORE COMPLEX DESIGNS

Every other one is inverted.

Contrasting veneers are glued together, then sawn across.

Veneer is glued on both sides and sliced to form this pattern.

This quarter-fan inlay is on the drawer front of a Massachusetts or New Hampshire Hepplewhite sideboard of the 1790s. Inlays such as these were assembled from segments of veneer.

segments could be used to make a circular inlay of 16 segments, also a commonly used decoration. The segments were assembled with glue to thin paper or fabric. Once assembled, they could be trimmed to their circular shape. If the ends of the segments were to be "filled at the end," the ends were cut away with a curved gouge and filled with a curved segment of contrasting wood. With the ends filled, the shape of the whole inlay was trimmed round and circled with a string inlay. Modern inlays are instantly recognizable because the circle of string inlay is die-cut from a solid sheet of veneer, meaning that the grain runs in one direction rather than around the circumference. Given the way these circular inlays were made, it was probably just easier to make quarter fans by cutting a fully circular inlay into four parts.

Oval fan inlays are made in the same manner, but their pie-shaped segments are not all of the same angle. Oval inlays are designed so that the ends of each segment are of roughly equal width. Shorter segments have a larger angle than long segments. Within each oval there are segments of four or five different angles, each used four times (one in each quarter— see the drawing at left). Given that the inlay maker had some standard-size oval fans, he likely had some angular templates and could cut out many segments ahead of time. As on round inlays, filled ends of segments and a surrounding string inlay were common. *The Journeyman Cabinet and Chair Makers' New York Book of Prices* of 1796 lists the price for an "oval patrie, two and a half inches long, with twelve straight points, fill'd up at the end with different wood, and a single string round ditto" as one shilling three pence, and "letting in" each as three pence. Given the daily wage of seven shillings six pence, a journeyman should have been able to make and inlay five of these in an 11-hour day. (Twelve pence equals one shilling; twenty shillings equal one pound. Both pounds and dollars were used during this time. The daily wage of seven shillings six pence equals one dollar.)

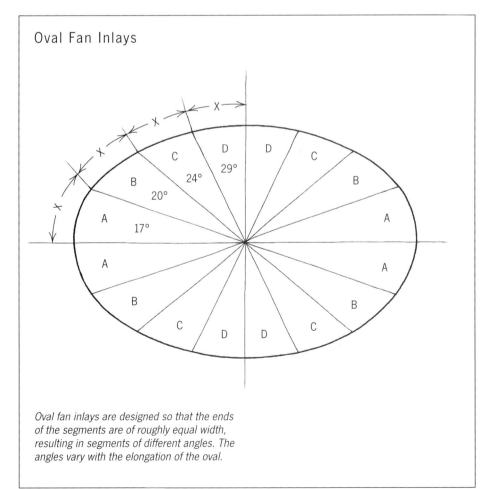

Oval Fan Inlays

Oval fan inlays are designed so that the ends of the segments are of roughly equal width, resulting in segments of different angles. The angles vary with the elongation of the oval.

Some inlay patterns of round and oval fans have shaded edges on their segments rather than alternating light and dark wood (see the top photo at right). This shading gives the inlay a very fine appearance and the fan a sophisticated, three-dimensional effect. It is achieved by heating the edge of the individual segments to darken them. To do this, an iron pot is filled with fine sand and heated on a fire or stove until it is hot enough to darken, but not ignite, the edge of a piece of paper dipped into it for about a minute. When all the segments of the inlay have been cut to shape, the edge of each is dipped into the hot sand until it starts to turn brown.

This shading is best done a little at a time until the proper color is obtained. It is better to have the sand too cool rather than too hot, so the veneer is darkened all the way through rather than just on the outside of the wood. The wood should have a deep brown shading with no hint of being burned. Shading can be added to the center of a segment by heaping a little of the hot sand in the desired area. The key to achieving an attractive inlay of this type is to make the shading uniform among the segments. It is best to have many extra shaded segments so the most similar ones can be assembled into an inlay.

Other circular or oval inlays used curved-ray segments and were made in a fundamentally different way. Rather than being assembled from pie-shaped wedges of veneer, these inlays were cut from solid sheets. Close examination of the inlays shows that the grain runs in the same direction rather than radiating from the center. To make circular or oval inlays, light and dark veneers were stacked and the pattern of the inlay was drawn on them. Both sheets would be cut simultaneously with a fine framed saw akin to a jeweler's saw. The inlay would be assembled and glued to paper alternating the dark and light segments. When trimmed to final shape, the result was two inlays, one the negative of the other.

This same method of cutting the segments from a continuous sheet was also used with inlays of one color, where the

The edges of inlay segments are shaded by darkening the individual pieces in hot sand before they are assembled.

Curved-ray inlays were sawn from stacked veneer with a small framed saw.

Pictorial inlays of one color, such as the shell shown here, were sawn from a continuous sheet, shaded with hot sand and reassembled.

This icicle inlay is from a Hepplewhite Pembroke table made in the Connecticut River Valley of Massachusetts in about 1795.

Icicle Inlays

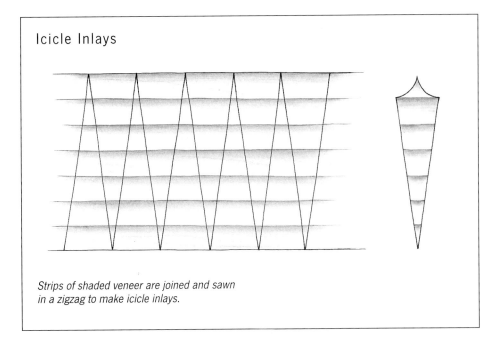

Strips of shaded veneer are joined and sawn in a zigzag to make icicle inlays.

segments were shaded in hot sand and reassembled. A similar approach was used in making pictorial inlays, like eagles, floral designs and sea shells (see the bottom photo on p. 173). Different veneers were stacked and sawn simultaneously, and contrasting colors of veneer were assembled to make the finished inlay. The shapes of individual parts and what appear to be fine kerfs suggest that inlay was sawn rather than cut with a knife.

To make these sawn inlays in quantity, the inlay maker used some clever, time-saving techniques. To make a pattern that could be transferred quickly to the veneer, the maker drew the design on paper patterns and pricked the lines at close intervals with a pin. The pattern was then placed on the veneer and dusted with fine bitumen (asphalt) powder to transfer the design. Heating the surface of the veneer melted the bitumen and affixed it to the wood. To make many pieces at once, as many as six sheets of veneer of various woods were cut simultaneously. A sheet of low-grade veneer was placed at the bottom of the stack to reduce the tearout caused by the saw. The thickness of many sheets actually made the stack stiffer and easier to handle than one or two sheets. To cut several sheets at once and have the sawn parts be interchangeable, it was important that the sawblade be held perpendicular to the work. To aid in this, a bench called an inlay maker's donkey was devised to clamp the veneers and hold the framed saw at right angles to the surface of the veneer.

Paterae are inlaid into the surface by first tracing their outline with a fine knife. The knife cut is deepened, and the area inside it is cut away with chisels to the depth of the inlay. The inlay is then glued in place, with the paper side facing out. Once the glue has dried thoroughly, the paper may be removed by moistening it and scraping it off. The inlay is then scraped or sanded flush with the surrounding surface. It is important to allow the glue under the inlay to dry thoroughly; if the inlay is leveled while the glue and wood are still moist, the area will continue to dry and shrink, and its surface will dip noticeably below the level of the surrounding area.

Other inlay

The inlays discussed to this point have been either string inlays or round, quarter-round or oval paterae. Other inlays include icicles, inlaid flutes and husk and drop or pendent bellflower designs. Icicle inlays, for use on legs, were a favorite of makers along the Connecticut River Valley. They were made by shading one edge of strips of veneer, 3/8 in. to 1/2 in. wide, and assembling them on a paper backing. The tapered icicles were then cut across the strips. Some icicles have the shading on the top of each segment, while others are shaded on the bottom, suggesting that the assembled strips of veneer were cut in a zigzag pattern with very little waste (see the drawing on the facing page).

Inlaid flutes, also called book inlays, were used at the tops of legs and on plinths throughout the Middle Atlantic and New England coastal regions. They consist of three or four strips of light veneer, shaded on one edge and cut with a convex top and concave bottom. A variation of this has the outer strips turned upside-down to become an inlaid linen fold, a decorative detail seen in earlier carvings.

Husk and drop, or pendent bellflower, inlays descended the length of most tapered Hepplewhite legs. The motif derives from the classical *anthemion*, the string of honeysuckle buds used by Robert Adam as an applied ornament. Rather then being a pre-assembled inlay, these consist of single buds cut from veneer. Each was individually inlaid along the length of the leg, usually with some stringing to connect them. A wide variety of bud shapes was used, each with regional characteristics. Three-petal, tightly closed buds were seen all along the coast. Some makers preferred a more flared, bell-shaped bud, the Newport cabinet-makers among them. A descending series of shaded and overlapping ovals is associated with New York makers. The 1796 *Book of Prices* puts the price of each inlaid bud at four pence, making a string of four or five equivalent to a small oval fan paterae. The 20th-century counterpart of this inlay is a reassembled sheet of die-cut veneer made to cover the entire face of the leg, which is quite different from the period method.

Inlaid flutes or book inlays were a commonly used decorative motif. These inlays are from the same Pembroke table as the icicle inlay on the facing page.

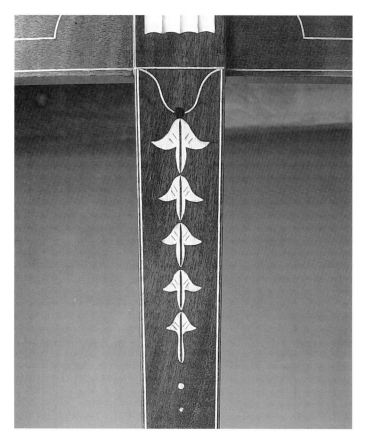

Husk and drop, or pendent bellflower, inlays derive from *anthemion*, the ornamental string of honeysuckle buds used by Robert Adam. This example is the design used by Newport cabinetmaker John Townsend.

11
TURNING

The work of turning wood on a lathe was a branch of the furniture-making trade that paralleled and coincided with cabinetmaking over the course of the 18th century. There was a distinction between the turner and the cabinetmaker, just as there had been with the cabinetmaker's predecessor, the joiner. In the 17th century, the frame-and-panel method was the predominant type of construction and it was the domain of the joiner. Joiners built their furniture using straight pieces of wood, joined mostly at right angles, with mortise-and-tenon joints. Turnings were not necessarily an integral part of their work.

Turners had their own purview. Equipped with little more than a lathe, turners made handles, wooden plates, bowls, goblets, candleholders, balusters and wagon and mechanical parts. They also made chairs. Turners' chairs are comprised of nearly all turned parts and are joined with turned tenons inserted into drilled

mortises. Joiners' and later cabinetmakers' chairs were made from flat or shaped stock joined by mortise-and-tenon joinery. Naturally, there were many accomplished joiners who owned lathes and could make turnings, but those who did not, including many of the very early craftsmen of America, could call upon skilled lathe owners for their turned parts.

The Use of Turnings in 18th-Century Furniture

During the Jacobean period in American furniture, turnings in the forms of bosses and split spindles were used as applied ornament on case pieces. Throughout the first quarter of the 18th century, turnings remained an important element of William

Joseph Moxon's *Mechanick Exercises* (London, 1703 edition) illustrates a lathe driven by a hand-cranked great wheel that turned the workpiece directly by a cord.

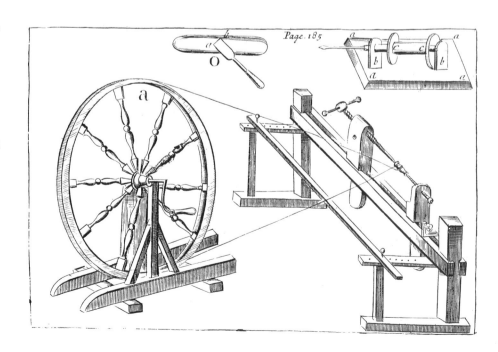

and Mary designs, and turners continued to be used as specialists and subcontractors. Urban shops of the day were busy with joinery, veneering and finishing. Turning, which did not have to be done on the premises, could be given to an independent turner. In a 1733 bill, Boston turner John Underwood describes selling cabinetmaker Nathaniel Holmes the turned legs, ball feet and drop finials for a William and Mary dressing table. In more rural areas, where furniture makers had to master all aspects of their craft and there was not the volume to support full-time turners, the cabinet-maker was more likely to make his own turnings.

Beginning with the Queen Anne period, turnings became less important as decorative elements. When they were used, they were more integral to the piece rather than separate components or added embellishments. Because of this development, it made more sense for shops to do what little turning work was called for in the course of building furniture. The field of cabinetmaking had grown from the joiner's trade as a range of varied skills including dovetailing, veneering, carving, finishing and then turning became part of the repertoire of skills required to build the 18th-century designs. The turnings required for furniture likely remained an in-shop operation for the remainder of the century as shops grew in size.

While cabinetmakers went about making their own turnings, turners were still busy making the things they always had, including affordable banister-back and ladder-back turned chairs. As the society became busier and more mechanized with horse, water and wind power, there was an increased demand for turned parts. It was not until the Neoclassical period, specifically with the Sheraton designs, that turnings became a major element in furniture design again. By that time, the larger shops employed many different in-house specialists, such as upholsterers and finishers, and full-time turners would have been among them.

This English lathe of 1804 uses a foot-powered treadle to drive a flywheel, which turns a drive center in the headstock. It also has an adjustable tool rest and can be used to cut threads on wood.
(COURTESY COLONIAL WILLIAMSBURG)

EARLY LATHES

There is a dearth of information on English and American tools for most of the 18th century. Between Joseph Moxon's *Mechanick Exercises, or the Doctrine of Handy-Works* (published in London beginning in 1677) and the tool catalogs that appeared at the end of the 18th century, there are no illustrated publications with which to trace the development of tools. From what is known, we can infer that a tool such as a lathe was simple, basic and either locally made or built by its owner. In this regard it is more similar to a workbench than to hand tools, many of which were imported. Moxon's illustrations, which are based on French tools of the day, show a lathe powered by a "great wheel," a large, hand-cranked wheel located behind the lathe that turned the workpiece by a belt or cord (see the illustration on the facing page). By the end of the 18th century, foot-powered lathes were in use. These used a foot treadle to drive a flywheel that was belted to the headstock (photo above).

The centers on which the wood turned on early lathes were little more than pointed rods, threaded to be adjustable. The wood rode directly on these centers, so they could not be overtightened and were often greased to reduce friction and prevent the wood from being burned. The Moxon lathe shows two centers, with the drive belt from the great wheel driving the workpiece directly. Improvements during the century brought the headstock with a drive center, a shaft driven by the power source, which in turn rotated the workpiece. Early tool rests were little more than a wooden rail parallel to the lathe bed with few provisions for adjustment. By the century's end, better lathes had adjustable iron tool rests. By comparison, modern lathes are luxurious with variable-speed electric drives, ball-bearing headstocks and centers, fully adjustable tool rests, and stiff, heavy lathe beds. It is the poor workman who blames his or her modern lathe.

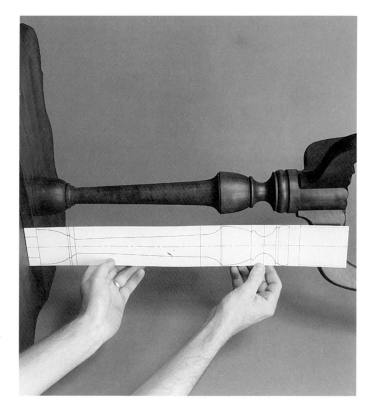

workpiece, and the tail center, which supports the far end of the workpiece and keeps the wood in contact with the drive center. The tool rest is an adjustable bar parallel to the surface of the turning stock on which the cutting tools are supported as they cut the wood.

There are three main types of turning tools: the parting tool, the gouge and the skew (see the drawing on the facing page). Each is a long-handled chisel with a very stiff steel blade made specifically for use on the lathe. The parting tool has a tall, narrow blade that is sharpened to a point as viewed from the side. It is intended to make a narrow, flat-bottomed cut straight into the workpiece, and is used to establish the major diameters of features, as well as for all sorts of straight plunging cuts. Gouges are made in a variety of sizes and are used for rough cutting, quick removal of stock and making concave shapes. Skews are flat chisels, beveled on both sides, and have a cutting edge angled at about 30° across the end. Skews are used for the fine shaping of straight and gently curved sections of a turning, as well as for cutting in sharp details and scribed lines. Other types of turning tools for specific purposes are seen occasionally, but these three types of tools can do nearly everything.

In the physics of turning, the bevel on the cutting tool plays an important and often overlooked role. The bevel rides on the surface of the wood (see the drawing on p. 178), serving three functions. First, the bevel provides a point of support for the front of the tool. Along with the tool rest, the tool is then supported at two points, making it more stable and controllable and preventing it from tipping into the spinning workpiece. Holding the tool is so effortless that cuts can be made with one hand (but two should always be used for safety's sake). Second, by positioning the tool so the bevel rides on the wood, the depth of cut of the tool is limited and a fine, continuous shaving, the mark of a good cut, is the result. The surface is cut cleanly and is burnished by the bevel. Third, the pressure of the bevel on the wood prevents the workpiece from vibrating or whipping. To find the ideal position of the tool on the wood, the bevel is held against the round

TURNING PATTERNS

Like other artisans of the period, turners looked for ways to make their work faster and their time more productive. This meant using patterns and time-saving devices whenever possible, as well as making turnings in quantity. (The Connecticut Windsor chairmaker Ebenezer Tracy, 1744–1803, left 6,400 turnings in his shop at the time of his death.) A pattern for a turned shape could be either an actual turning or a flat profile of it on thin wood. Both are good guides from which to replicate a shape, but a flat pattern is easier to use and store. The pattern not only shows the profile, but also is used in the turning process to mark the features of the shape directly onto the workpiece (see the top left photo on p. 181).

The pattern for any turning is a full-scale drawing of the profile. It is best to have the pattern on cardboard or thin wood so it is stiff enough to use at the lathe. A typical pattern is shown in the photo above. The pattern is the size of the blank from which the turning is made and has all the features of the profile on it. The profile is drawn symmetrically about a centerline, and cross lines are drawn to mark the location of each

turned feature. A pattern is easily made from an existing turning or scaled from a photo by measuring the diameter of features and their distance from either end. There are only two variables in turned parts—diameter and location—but as with other shaped parts the faithfulness of the duplicate lies in the role of small details. The profile in the pattern should capture the angle at which one feature meets another, the sharpness or rounding of edges, and other subtle features of the turning that are worth noting. There's no need to cut out the pattern; in fact, it's easier to transfer the pattern to the turning blank if it is left uncut.

Turning on the Lathe

The skill of turning wood on the lathe is perfected only through experience and practice, and by acquiring a feel for the work. Apart from practical experience, there is something to be gained by looking at some of the principles and forces involved in turning.

The stock or workpiece in a lathe is held in place by two centers: the rotating drive center, which is spurred to spin the

Turning Tools

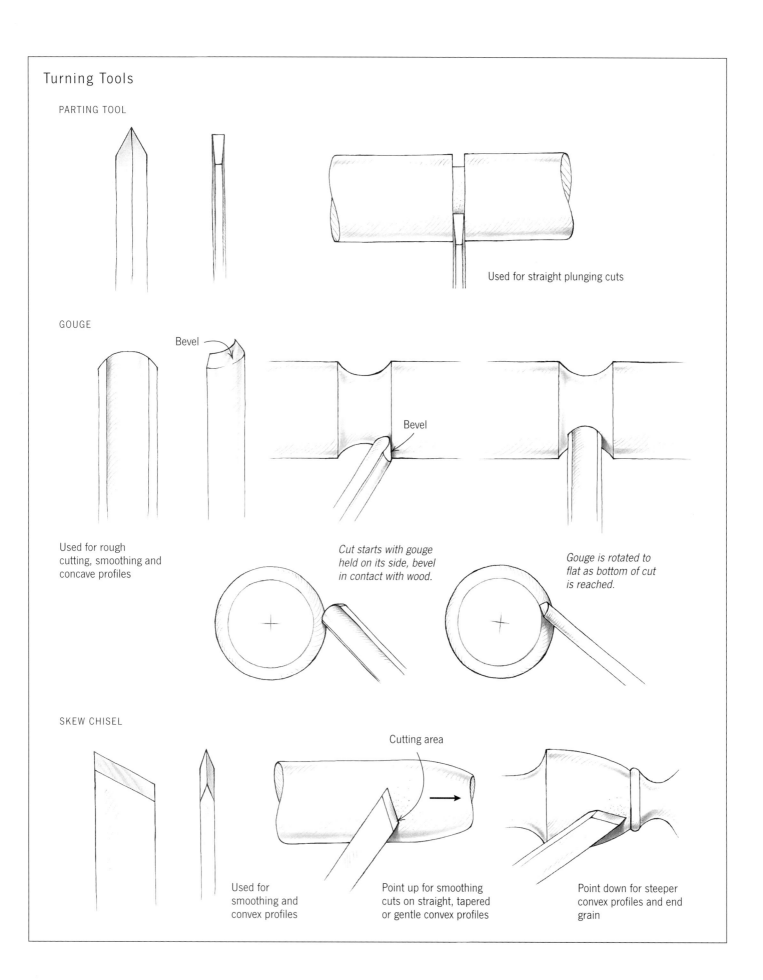

PARTING TOOL

Used for straight plunging cuts

GOUGE

Bevel

Used for rough cutting, smoothing and concave profiles

Bevel

Cut starts with gouge held on its side, bevel in contact with wood.

Gouge is rotated to flat as bottom of cut is reached.

SKEW CHISEL

Cutting area

Used for smoothing and convex profiles

Point up for smoothing cuts on straight, tapered or gentle convex profiles

Point down for steeper convex profiles and end grain

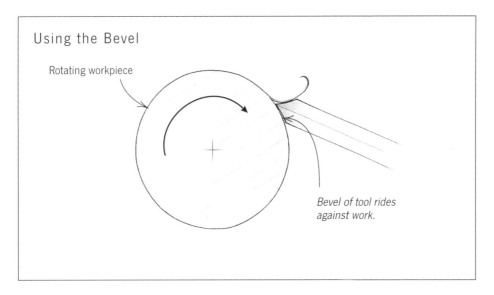

Using the Bevel

Rotating workpiece

Bevel of tool rides against work.

workpiece and slid back until the cutting edge starts to shave off material.

The problem of slender stock whipping about off-center, rather than remaining straight and true while being cut, is one of the more persistent and frustrating problems in hand turning. There are a few things that can be done to minimize this whipping. Backing off the pressure of the tail center on the workpiece to the bare minimum will reduce the tendency of the stock to buckle in compression. Reducing the speed of the lathe will diminish the tendency of centrifugal force to pull the stock off-center. Increasing the pressure on the tool bevel will restrain the stock from whipping freely. If the whipping persists, it is necessary to restrain the workpiece in other ways. Wearing a leather glove, you can wrap the palm and fingers of the left hand around the workpiece to steady it while using the thumb to guide the turning tool. The final resort is to use a steady rest, a fixture with adjustable blocks or rollers that's mounted to the lathe bed to steady the center of the workpiece as it is being cut. Sometimes the characteristics of the wood have a strong bearing on its tendency to whip. Some pieces of wood, especially those with crooked grain or internal stresses, will start to whip at the first touch of a tool, whereas a more select piece of stock of the same wood will be thoroughly cooperative.

SPINDLE TURNING

Making the turning from the pattern begins with cutting the appropriate size stock for the workpiece. Enough extra length, at least ½ in., should be left so the center marks on the ends can be cut off later. The center points are marked on the ends with crossed diagonal lines. If there are sections of the turning that will remain square, those sections should be marked on at least one side of the workpiece. If the workpiece will be turned over its entire length, a time-saving idea is to cut the stock to an octagonal shape before turning it. This can be done

quickly with a table saw but is not worth doing by handsaw. Once the workpiece is mounted in the lathe, the sections that are to be rounded can be turned to a straight cylindrical shape, just removing the flat sides (photo below). A large gouge is the best turning tool for this heavy stock removal. If the turning includes sections of square, unturned stock, those sections (which should already be marked) must be cut around and have their corners rounded before turning the adjacent sections to a cylindrical shape.

With the workpiece turned round, the locations of the features are drawn directly onto the stock. While the wood is turning, the pattern is laid on the tool rest alongside the stock. At the cross line of every feature in the pattern, a pencil may be touched to the stock (top left photo, facing page). A clear, visible line will result. Early turners who turned many of the same pattern used a length of wood with sharpened nails along its length to scribe the lines simultaneously.

At each line, the diameter of the feature can be cut into the workpiece, usually with the parting tool (top right photo, facing page). The diameter is checked with calipers that have been set to the diameter on the pattern (bottom left photo, facing page). Any wood that is clearly waste can be turned off with a gouge. The final profile shape is

The square or octagonal workpiece is first turned to a cylindrical shape with a large gouge.

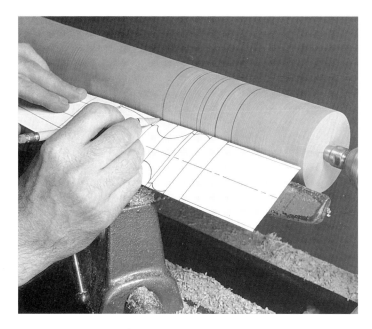

The pattern is used to transfer the locations of the turned features on the spinning workpiece.

The diameters of the features are cut with the parting tool.

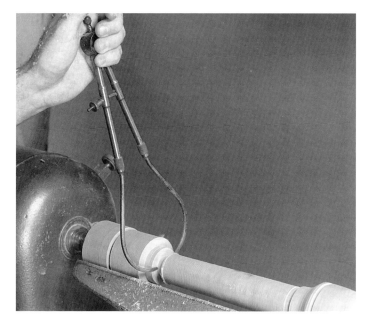

The diameter of each feature is checked with calipers.

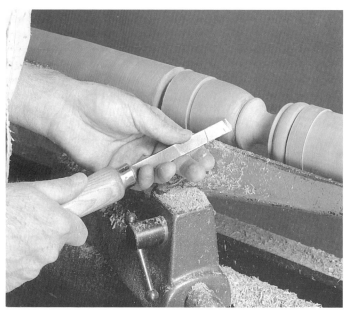

The shape between the diameters is turned with skews and gouges.

turned between the feature diameters using a gouge or skew chisel, depending upon the shape (bottom right photo, above). The usual procedure is to turn a few feature diameters at a time and then turn them to their final shapes. This is done in a progression rather than turning all the feature diameters at once. To maintain a stiff workpiece and prevent whipping and vibration, it is advisable to leave as much of the workpiece with as large a diameter as possible until it is turned to shape. For this reason, areas that are to be turned to a small diameter are often left until last to prevent weakening the stock at the outset.

The cuts that bring the profile to its final dimension must be light and smooth to achieve a smooth surface. Because spindle turning is always cutting across the grain, there is a limit to how smooth the final surface will be. It will never match the surface finish of wood that is hand-planed with the grain. The quality of the final surface is greatly dependent on the sharpness of the turning tools, since in cross-grain cutting the wood fibers have a tendency to pull off the surface rather than be cut cleanly. It is a good idea to give the tools a quick honing before the final cut to get the best possible surface. Attention

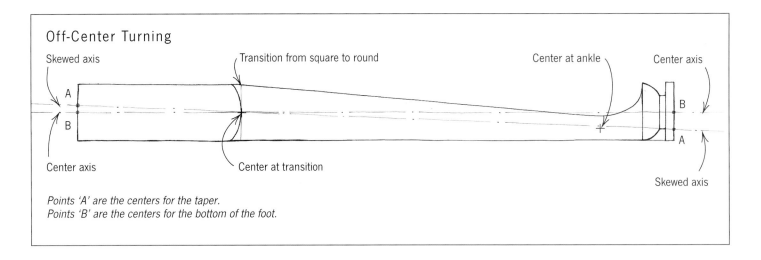

Off-Center Turning

Skewed axis

Transition from square to round

Center at ankle

Center axis

A

B

B

A

Center axis

Center at transition

Skewed axis

Points 'A' are the centers for the taper.
Points 'B' are the centers for the bottom of the foot.

should be paid to the turned surfaces of original pieces. Rural and early pieces usually have the marks of the turning tools in evidence. More formal and later pieces usually have a more refined surface. In working in the period style, you should not overlook the fact that the appropriate surface on a turning helps define the character of the piece.

Turning in real life is never as idyllic as in the textbook representations. The importance of producing a properly shaped turning always takes precedence over displaying flawless technique. Besides, cantankerous turning stock and unexpected whipping can bring an embarrassing end to even the most impeccable exhibition of turning technique. It may seem crude to say that the ends justify the means, but there are many instances where the turning tools have to be used "improperly" to scrape rather than cut cleanly in order to achieve the proper shape of the profile and its details. It is not always possible to have the bevel in contact with the work and produce fine shavings. Cutting can leave a rough surface that has to be smoothed on the lathe with a file or abrasives. Given the limitations of 18th-century lathes, the period makers had to do whatever they could to produce good turnings. There is no reason to think they would not have used a file, sharkskin or a sand leather whenever necessary. Their interest was in the result, not the technique. While it is a great accomplishment to turn a piece that is cut to perfection, some sanding should be expected.

OFF-CENTER TURNING

Straight tapered legs with pad feet, like those used on a number of informal chairs and tables of Queen Anne design, must be turned on two different axes. One axis (the one used to turn the bottom of the foot) is the center axis of the workpiece as established by crossed diagonal lines. The other axis (the one used to turn the taper of the leg) is skewed.

To determine the shape of the leg and the location of the skewed center points, a full-size pattern of the leg's profile is made (photo below). The profile shows that these legs are straight along one side and cut away on the other side to make the taper and foot. As with cabriole legs, the pattern is traced onto two adjacent sides of the stock, so the finished leg is straight on the back two sides and tapered on the front two

In making turned and tapered legs with pad feet, the pattern is traced onto two sides of the stock and the turning centers are marked. Once marked, the profile of the leg is cut.

The taper of the leg is turned first, using the center points for the skewed axis.

The leg is remounted on its true centers to turn the bottom of the foot.

sides. From the pattern profile, the center of the leg is marked at the top and bottom of its taper. From these two points, a line is drawn to both ends of the pattern, and where it crosses the ends represents the center points for the tapered part of the leg. Since the pattern is laid out on two sides of the stock, these center lines must be extended across the ends of the stock to the points where they intersect. In laying out the leg, the pattern is used as a guide to mark the position of the foot, the top, the transition line from round to square and the profile of the taper. The taper of the leg is then cut away from two sides, leaving a square taper.

The taper is turned first by mounting the leg in the lathe on the two skewed center points. Once the leg is rotating, the stock should appear to be turning on center at the transition line, but it will appear off-center elsewhere. On this axis, the transition from square to round, the taper and the top of the foot are turned. They should be brought to their final surface finish before proceeding because the skewed center point on the foot will be cut off while turning the bottom of the foot.

The top of the foot is shaped with rasps and files, as on the pad feet of cabriole legs.

Next, the leg is remounted on the lathe on its true center points and the bottom of the foot is turned. This is done just as on a cabriole leg, with a bottom pad and a line to define the top of the foot. As on the cabriole leg, the top of the foot is shaped with rasps and files to its final shape. The extra material at the top and bottom of the foot is trimmed off, and the leg is complete.

FACEPLATE TURNING

In furniture making, faceplate turning is used to make dished circular tabletops. This kind of turning differs from spindle turning in that the workpiece is not rotating between two centers. Instead, the round tabletop is affixed to a rotating plate on the headstock of the lathe and spins about its center. Turning tools are used to cut a

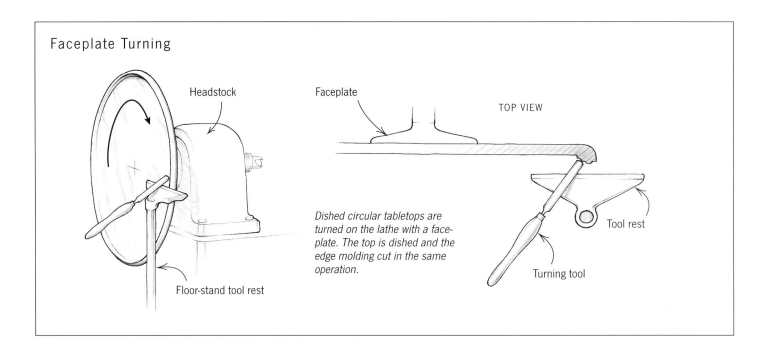

Faceplate Turning

Headstock

Faceplate

TOP VIEW

Dished circular tabletops are turned on the lathe with a face-plate. The top is dished and the edge molding cut in the same operation.

Tool rest

Turning tool

Floor-stand tool rest

molding around the edge and dish the surface of the tabletop. Rather than always cutting across the grain, as in spindle turning, faceplate turning of a tabletop is cutting alternately with and against the grain as the workpiece rotates. To avoid tearing out the grain on the molded edge, the turner must be sure to make very fine cuts and hold the cutting tool more perpendicular to the surface of the work. This position causes the tool to scrape more than cut and minimizes the chances of tearout.

An alternative method is to use a modern electric router. The router can be used to cut a circular molding by substituting a steel rod for its fence. The rod turns about a pin or bolt protruding from an anchor plate attached with glue or short screws to the center of the top. Once the outer molding is cut, a flat cutter can be used to dish most of the top by cutting smaller and smaller circles. The remaining center section is removed with chisels and a spokeshave and the surface is scraped flat.

Kiln-dried wood usually has internal stresses that can make any dished top deform badly as soon as it is cut by either method. In drying the wood, the outside layer dries and hardens first. The inside dries and shrinks afterwards, leaving the inside in tension and pulling the outside

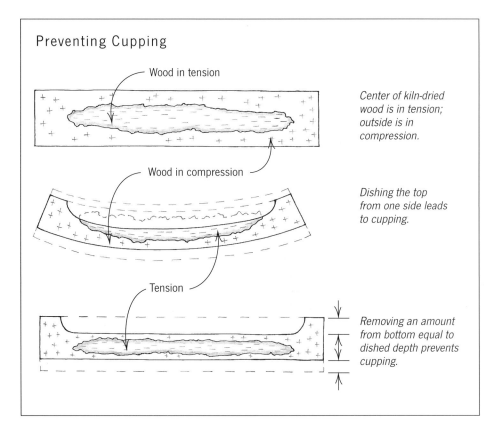

Preventing Cupping

Wood in tension

Center of kiln-dried wood is in tension; outside is in compression.

Wood in compression

Dishing the top from one side leads to cupping.

Tension

Removing an amount from bottom equal to dished depth prevents cupping.

skin into compression. When the compressed layer is removed by dishing the top, the remaining unbalanced forces cause the wood to cup. To balance the forces through the thickness of the top, the final thickness must be taken from the center of

the rough stock. To do this, a layer of wood equal to the depth of the dishing is removed from the bottom of the stock first. When the top of the stock is dished the resulting piece will have less of a tendency to cup.

12

FINISHING MATERIALS

AND TECHNIQUES

There's an old rule of thumb that states that it takes as long to finish fine furniture as it does to build it. That may be an exaggeration (unless you include drying time), but the point is that the finishing process should not be hurried. Of all the aspects of furniture making, there is none other that can spell success or failure as quickly as the quality of the final finish. Everyone has seen examples of well-designed and well-built pieces of furniture that have been seriously compromised in their final stage of completion by a hideous finish. A poor finish can instantly undo many months of even the most skillful cabinetmaking. But, conversely, even the most stunning finish cannot make up for poor workmanship. It is important not to let the imminent completion of a piece cloud one's judgment in finishing it, or to expect the finish to compensate for other shortcomings. Finishing has to be considered the final step in building a piece, and the process and the preparation for it call for as much care in execution as the initial steps.

When working in the period styles, the final appearance and feel of the piece are as important as the integrity of the joinery. The color, depth, surface and luster separate an immediately noticeable, run-of-the-mill reproduction from a serious replica that rivals the appearance of a well-preserved original. The presence of a fine original piece is as much the result of its patina as its form. Capturing the essence of that patina is the goal of finishing. Modern standards and methods of finishing are not applicable to period replications.

An important element in the patina of original pieces is the acquired marks of use. Some originals show little or no sign of having been used, and indeed many were covered and stored for many years before being displayed in a protective museum environment. Still others show incredible amounts of use; so much that the wear has changed the shape of component pieces and become a discernible modification to the form. Such wear is part of the history of the piece, and attests to its heritage. In replicating a piece, the amount of wear that is chosen to be included depends on the personal preferences of the cabinetmaker and client. Some makers want their work to appear as the originals did when they were finished so they can start their own legacy of use. Others want their pieces to be indistinguishable from originals, with signs of age and use included as part of the patina. Neither approach is inherently right or wrong, but either can vary in degrees of historical accuracy.

In the 18th century there were a plethora of finishing techniques, colorants and top coats. Some are well documented, and others are more folkloric. Without the convenience of commercially prepared finishes, each shop was likely to have its own preferred, and no doubt secret, formulae and procedures (see Appendix V on pp. 298-299 for some period finishing formulae). In spite of the limited number of available ingredients, no one finish was universally employed during the period. Finishes varied widely in ingredients, complexity of preparation and ease of application. Naturally some were far better than others. The better formulae were passed down and at some point published, and what was available for ingredients during the period is documented. Like the furniture itself, period finishes and methods varied among individual makers, but all had the same end in mind.

Some mention should be made of the vagaries of 18th-century terminology and some words that have acquired different meanings two or three centuries later. *Dyeing* and *staining* now have slightly different meanings from those in early references. During the 18th century the terms had more to do with the intended purpose of each rather than their physical qualities. Early references use the words *gum* and *resin* interchangeably, though almost all the components of period varnishes were true hard resins. The term *varnish* was applied to all clear top coats, though today the term is generally reserved for oil-based finishes.

Polishing encompassed a wide variety of operations, including burnishing the wood surface, rubbing in oils, applying finish by the French method, leveling and rubbing out the surface with pumice, and, as agreed upon today, the application and buffing of a final polish to achieve gloss. The simulation of Oriental lacquer was called *japanning,* though the origin of the original lacquer pieces included China and other countries. The distance between East and West and a general misunderstanding of the cultures (they were all equally exotic) eroded the distinctions among the various Asian cultures. Period documentation is thoroughly enlightening, but a casual use of terms should be expected.

Surface Preparation

A prerequisite for achieving a historically accurate finish is the creation of a wood surface that would have been left by the smoothing tools of the 18th century. The pieces of the period would have been planed flat and usually scraped smooth, though the smoothness of the surface varied with the sophistication of the piece and when it was built. The surface produced by a smoothing plane was sufficiently smooth at the early part of the century, but the Queen Anne aesthetic called for smoother scraped surfaces. As the century progressed, the aesthetics called for flatter and more lustrous surfaces. By the end of the century, hand-tool marks on the primary surfaces were not to be evident, because the tastes of the day required a highly refined surface.

The level of sophistication varied with region and purpose. Smoother and flatter surfaces required skill and time to achieve, which translated into increased cost. Utilitarian or rural pieces would naturally have a less refined surface than those of urban pieces. Whatever the character of the surface, it is the foundation for the appropriate and authentic appearance of the finish.

To achieve the final surface, 18th-century cabinetmakers relied more on cutting the wood with sharp tools than with abrasives (see pp. 114-115). There is little room for improvement on the smooth surface cut by a well-honed blade. The few abrasives in use were employed to prepare the surface for a finish, or between coats of finish, rather than actually to shape the wood. Glass paper and sandpaper were known to have been available early in the 19th century, and no doubt came into use during the preceding one, but the smooth surface left by a cabinet scraper needed little or no sanding. Sharkskin, sand leathers (leather impregnated with fine abrasive particles) and dried rushes were abrasive enough to smooth raised wood fibers in preparation for finishing. Solid blocks of fine pumice stone are also known to have been used as an abrasive when needed. From a purely economical point of view, all of these abrasives would have been consumed in use, while sharp cutting tools could be resharpened and used for years. If there was little to be gained by using abrasives, there was little reason to use them up. Files also played an important role in shaping and smoothing wood. A close examination of well-preserved pieces shows that files were used to ease sharp corners, a job that usually would be done with abrasives today.

Using waterproof silicon-carbide sandpaper and powdered pumice to fill the pores of an open-grained wood simulates the original method, which called for rubbing the surface with a solid block of pumice.

Most 18th-century dyes or stains were dissolved in water and raised the grain of the wood. An experienced cabinetmaker knew that this could be avoided by wetting the surface first, allowing it to dry, and then lightly sanding or abrading the wood surface to remove the raised fibers. The effectiveness of this procedure is increased if the wood is sized, that is, wet with a very dilute mixture of animal hide glue in water. The dried sizing holds and stiffens the raised fibers, allowing them to be cut off more effectively. André Jacques Roubo's *L'art du menuisier* ("The art of the joiner," 3 vol., Paris, 1769–1774) and subsequent publications describe another procedure wherein a block of pumice is rubbed in the direction of the grain on still-wet wood. The wood is allowed to dry and the process is repeated. This technique actually works very well, though a modern substitute for the pumice block would be waterproof silicon-carbide sandpaper.

FILLING THE GRAIN

The open grain of woods like mahogany and walnut presents a special problem for finishers. Rather than filling with finish and becoming level with the surface, the open pores of the surface remain apparent through a top coat. These pores need to be filled before the finish is applied. The

method described by Roubo and others calls for filling the pores with a mixture of pumice, wood fibers and glue. Thomas Sheraton's *Cabinet Dictionary* (London, 1803) describes rubbing powdered brick dust and linseed oil into the surface of the wood with a cork block. Other references mention rubbing clay, whiting and cornstarch into the surface, with a drying oil like linseed to serve as a vehicle and dryer. Whatever the method, the purpose was to fill the pores with solid particles that were either transparent or the same color as the wood. The filler needed to harden in place, be unlikely to shrink and provide a level base for top coats.

Modern, commercially prepared fillers are thick liquids composed of ground silica in oil with dryers, thinners and pigments. The silica is called silex, a ground flint that breaks into tiny, sharp, geometric particles that interlock and pack together in the pores. In oil, the silex is nearly transparent, but it sometimes appears white after the oil has dried, so a pigment is added to match the filler to the color of the wood. These fillers are brushed onto the surface of the wood, first with the grain and then across it to work it into the pores. After some of the solvents have evaporated and the filler becomes quite stiff, the excess is wiped off the surface with a pliable scraper, like a

credit card, and a coarse cloth such as burlap. The wiping is done across the grain so as not to pull the soft filler from the pores. Because of the oil binder, modern fillers take up to 72 hours to dry. The filler must be allowed to dry thoroughly; otherwise, it will shrink in the pores under the top coat, giving the pores a white cast.

Coloring the Wood

The use of stains or dyes for coloring wood was a frequent practice for most of the 18th century. Dyestuffs and pigments were commonly traded commodities and were used for textile dyeing and in the preparation of paints, so there is no reason to believe that they were not available to cabinetmakers. Original pieces that seem to have a light natural color frequently have been stripped and show traces of deeper original colors under moldings and behind drawer lips. Often, stains were applied to lighter woods to simulate the appearance of walnut or mahogany, both of which were considered desirable woods for most of the century. Applying a stain or dye to the wood not only deepens the color and enriches the appearance, but also evens the tone of dissimilar parts and enhances the figure of the wood. One exception to the use of overall staining occurred during the Federal period, when the use of inlaid veneer of contrasting shades prevented the practice. At the same time, the practice of dyeing veneer before it was cut and assembled into paterae or stringing became common.

Period pieces were stained with colors derived from a variety of plant and mineral products, both domestic and imported (see Appendix IV on p. 297 for a listing of period colorants). As with most finishing details, each cabinetmaking shop or region had its preferred formulae. The majority of these colorants were made by boiling or steeping the dyestuffs in water, though some were dissolved in alcohol. Occasional references were made to adding nitric acid or other chemicals to prevent the colors from fading. Oils were not in general use as vehicles for stains, but there are many references to linseed oil, tinted red with alkanet root, being used to deepen the color and enhance the grain of mahogany.

Modern prepared fillers contain ground silica in oil with pigmented color. They are brushed onto the surface, and the excess is removed by wiping across the grain.

Because they have no solid pigments in suspension, dye stains (left) have a greater clarity and their colorants are able to penetrate the wood surface. Pigmented stains (right) are more opaque, and the pigments remain on the wood surface. Both of these samples are of equal film thickness and produce similar colors.

DYE STAINS AND PIGMENTED STAINS

A distinction should be made between dye stains and pigmented stains. By modern standards, dyes are solutions of colorants in water, alcohol or oil. Since they are dissolved in solution, there are no particles in suspension to settle out. The colorant penetrates the wood, changing its color. Pigmented stains contain ground pigment suspended in a solvent with binders and are formulated to help the color disperse and make it adhere to the wood. The pigments are not in solution and must be stirred up from the bottom of the container before use. Once applied, and after the solvents have evaporated, the pigments remain mostly on the surface of the wood.

Eighteenth-century colorants were mostly dye stains. The early methods of boiling or steeping the dyestuffs put the colorant into solution, and the stain was then strained to filter out the solids. Literature from late in the period makes a distinction between dyeing and staining that has more to do with the process of coloring the wood than the actual characteristics of the stain. In period terms, staining meant to apply a colorant to the completed piece of furniture as part of the finishing process. Dyeing referred to the

coloring of veneers so the color thoroughly penetrated the wood before the veneers were cut for use. This practice was most common in the last quarter of the century and involved submersing the veneer in troughs of dye, which were periodically heated to boiling, for days at a time.

Modern dye stains, called aniline dyes, are coal-tar derivatives available in powder form. They are available in a wide range of colors and are soluble in water, alcohol or oil. Water-soluble aniline dye stains closely replicate the effect of period water-based stains. They penetrate the wood surface, and since they contain no solids, they color the wood with remarkable depth and clarity. The deep penetration of the dye enhances the figuring and brings out the best qualities of the wood. In a dilute solution, dye stains augment the natural warm color of the wood without overpowering it, and allow it to darken and age gracefully. Much of the rich surface of fine period originals is due to the depth and clarity of the coloring, and the use of water-based aniline dye stains is essential to capturing that aspect of the finish.

Oil-soluble anilines also add a transparent color. Like alkanet root, they can be used to tint linseed oil, and they are well suited for imparting color to replications of very early pieces that would have

originally been finished with an oil and beeswax finish. Alcohol-soluble anilines are not light-fast and are used mainly as a touch-up colorant.

Pigmented oil stains are not recommended for the authentic replication of period finishes. Because these stains are suspensions of ground pigments in oil and solvents, much of the colorant is left on the surface of the wood as the carriers penetrate the wood or evaporate. The result is a layer of opaque color on the surface. While the pigments impart color to the surface, they also mask the grain and figure, and obscure the natural tone of the wood. Some manufacturers produce penetrating oil stains that have more of their color in solution, which improves the clarity and depth of the finish like an oil-soluble aniline. Another drawback of oil-based stain is the tendency to seal the wood with the first application, preventing subsequent coats from being effective.

Varnishes

The search for the ideal clear and durable top coat was one of the more elusive goals of the 18th-century cabinetmaker. The search had all the mystery and intrigue of alchemy, and the potential rewards must have seemed as promising. A good film finish not only had to be clear and durable, but also relatively easy to prepare and apply. The period makers knew little or nothing about the chemistry involved, so much of the development was done on a trial-and-error basis. In addition, the purity, origin and even identity of the ingredients, many of which were imported from distant lands, were uncertain at best. Even after having arrived at a very successful varnish formula, the chances of being able to repeat it were not guaranteed.

In 18th-century parlance any clear-film top coat was called a varnish. Varnishes fall into two categories: spirit varnishes and fixed-oil varnishes. Spirit varnishes consist of resins dissolved in an evaporating solvent, usually alcohol. Once applied to the surface, the solvent evaporates, leaving a hard film of resin. Modern shellac is one such spirit varnish. Fixed-oil varnishes are similar to modern oil-based varnishes and consist of resins dissolved in a drying oil. These varnishes dry by the more complex process of oxidation of resin and oils and the molecular linking of the constituents.

Before exploring the variety of varnishes, we should consider what was used in their absence. All references point to oil and wax, alone or in combination, as the long-standing alternatives to varnish. Linseed oil, heated and with a lead-oxide drier added, made a fast-drying oil that left a protective film. The addition of a resin made a simple soft varnish. Beeswax was shaved and mixed with spirits of turpentine to make a wax paste that could be rubbed into the surface and buffed. Neither left a hard, protective film finish, but they sealed the wood and imparted a little protection and luster.

Because of its hardness, clarity and solubility, sandarac was the resin of choice for 18th-century spirit varnishes. For a comparison of clarity, modern orange shellac is shown at right.

SPIRIT VARNISHES

Among the spirit varnishes of the 18th century were every kind of resin that could be dissolved in an evaporating solvent (see Appendix III on p. 296). Thanks to the industries of colonial America, solvents were easily obtained. One of the leading industries in coastal New England was the distillation of West Indian molasses to make rum, so there was no shortage of alcohol. Sometimes referred to as spirits of wine (spirits generally meaning distillates at the time), alcohol was often rectified, or re-distilled, to reduce its water content.

Sandarac

A number of tree resins are soluble in alcohol, but during the 18th century sandarac was the spirit-varnish resin of choice. Sandarac is a brittle, pale yellow resin from a cypress- or juniper-like tree of northwest Africa. It is the hardest of the spirit-soluble resins, so softer resins, like

FRENCH POLISHING

French polishing, or friction varnishing, is a method of applying shellac that results in a rich and lustrous surface. The shellac is applied with a rubbing pad rather than a brush, so the application constitutes many thin layers instead of a few thick ones. By applying the shellac this way, there is no need to level or rub out the finish once it has hardened, and the pores are filled simultaneously.

A small ball of muslin or flannel is wrapped in fine linen, and dampened with a thinned shellac consisting of about 1 lb. of resin in 1 gal. of alcohol, with some raw linseed oil added as a lubricant. The pad is rubbed in a circular motion on the wood, covering about 1 sq. ft. at a time working from the center toward the outside. More shellac and a drop or two of linseed oil are added to the pad as needed.

By various accounts, the process is repeated from three to eight times, allowing the finish to dry between applications. Powdered pumice or brick dust is sprinkled on the surface prior to the second application and worked into the pores with the shellac by the rubbing pad. The final layer of shellac is brought to a high gloss by "spiriting off" the oil residue and amalgamating the surface with a cloth just slightly damp with alcohol. A thin polish of the soft resin benzoin in alcohol is sometimes used in this last process to impart a high gloss.

Like any other aspect of finishing, French polishing requires skill and patience to achieve good results. Those who work in the 18th-century styles but choose not to become master French polishers can take solace in the fact that neither shellac nor the French method of applying it were in general use during the period. The first definitive mention of the procedure is in an 1825 edition of *The Cabinet-Maker's Guide*, published in London and America under different authors' names. It is not mentioned in the earlier 1809 or c.1818 editions. While the practice of French polishing no doubt predated this guide and could well have been used late in the 18th century, it was not the prevailing method of finish application.

mastic or soft copal, were usually added to sandarac to make it more elastic and less brittle. Sandarac spirit varnishes were valued for their clarity and luster above all others. Spirit varnishes with sandarac resin are mentioned by Stalker and Parker in the 1688 *Treatise of Japanning and Varnishing* and by Roubo in *L'art du menuisier* of the 1770s. Soft copals, resins from a wide variety of tropical trees and one type of American sumac, were generally soluble in alcohol and were also used as spirit-varnish resins.

Shellac

Shellac is spirit varnish of lac resin dissolved in alcohol. The resin itself is exuded through the pores of the Southeast Asian insect *Laccifer lacca* and forms encrustations on the twigs and branches of the trees on which the insect feeds; up to 90,000 insects are required to make 1 lb. of shellac resin. The resin is collected by gathering and scraping the branches. In its natural state, this stick-lac contains about 66% lac resin, 6% shellac wax, 6% gluten and 11% lac dye; the balance is impurities. The lac dye, a strong red color, was an important commodity before the advent of aniline dyes, and was at one time more valuable than the lac resin. The dye is water soluble and most of it can be washed from the resin. The remaining brown resin is heated and squeezed through fabric bags to filter out impurities. Various grades of shellac have undergone different levels of refining to remove the impurities. The warm resin is stretched into sheets, allowed to cool and harden, and broken into flakes. The quality of shellac is judged by its clarity and purity.

Contrary to many long-held opinions, shellac was not the most popular spirit varnish during the 18th century (see the sidebar on French polishing on p. 189). Even in its most refined state, the resin had a cloudy brown cast that made it inferior to other common resins like sandarac. "Shell-lac" varnish is mentioned in an uncomplimentary way by Stalker and Parker in 1688. Not until the end of the century were the filtering and bleaching processes perfected by which the lac could be made more transparent.

Spirits of turpentine

Another type of spirit varnish includes those based on spirits of turpentine, the liquid distillate of conifer sap. As with alcohol, American industry produced this solvent in abundance. Sap from a variety of coniferous trees, especially the Southern yellow pine (*Pinus palustris),* was an important natural resource in the 18th century. The sap was boiled down to produce pitch, which was used to caulk ships or could be distilled to produce spirits of turpentine. Rosin or colophony, the resin left behind after the distillation, was an inexpensive varnish resin. A number of resins, like mastic, dammar and rosin, are soluble in spirits of turpentine, and produced soft spirit varnishes that were generally inferior to sandarac varnish. Varnishes using spirits of turpentine as a solvent are sometimes called volatile-oil or essential-oil varnishes, but since they dry solely by evaporation they are spirit varnishes.

The shortcoming of spirit varnishes is that constituent resins are limited to those that are soft and easily soluble. These soft resins have low melting points, which make the finish intolerant of heat. Since they are deposited by evaporation, they remain susceptible to damage from solvents like alcohol and water, though a protective layer of wax helps them resist liquids.

FIXED-OIL VARNISHES

The practice of using oil to protect and seal wood seems as old as the use of wood itself. The application of oil to any wooden object sealed and protected the surface and gave it a nice appearance as well. Oils of various extraction have been mentioned from the beginning of recorded history, but those that dry offered the best protection.

Unlike petroleum distillates, most oils extracted from vegetable and plant material will dry slowly by oxidation. The best-known among these is linseed oil, which is extracted from flax seeds, the plant of which is grown to make linen. Linseed oil is a heavily bodied oil that was in abundant supply during the 18th century. Other drying oils that were in use during the period include walnut oil, poppy-seed oil and almond oil. All of these dry rather

THE LONG HISTORY OF FIXED-OIL VARNISHES

Fixed-oil varnishes have been traced as far back as ancient Egypt. The interiors of mummy cases are coated with a pale yellow varnish. Given that many of the resins used in the 18th century originated from Africa and the Mediterranean, and knowing that the Egyptians produced flax and olive oil, it is thought that these coatings are likely a fixed-oil varnish. Interestingly, the varnish was spread on with a knife rather than brushed.

The Greeks are known to have valued varnish as well. In the third century B.C., Berenice, the wife of the king of the Greek North African colonies, sacrificed her amber hair to the goddess Venus for the safe return of her husband from an Asian war. The Greeks, who traded in Baltic amber, came to call the substance *berenice* or *pherenice*, with the "ph" pronounced as a "v." The Latin spelling became *verenice*, and later *vernix*, from which comes the English *varnish*.

Other references confirm the use of varnish to protect paintings as early as the fourth century B.C. In the tenth or eleventh century, the Swiss or German monk Theophilus Presbyter wrote of how powdered amber and linseed oil (in the proportions of 1:2 by weight) were mixed and heated to make varnish. The general principle remains unchanged to the present day.

slowly and tend to remain gummy. The heating and addition of a lead-oxide or similar dryer speeds up the oxidation and makes these oils dry faster and leave a harder film. Oils that are sold as boiled, as opposed to raw, have undergone this heating for the addition of dryers.

The addition of natural resins to drying oils combined the best of two finishes: the water-resistant and penetrating qualities of oil, and the toughness and luster of a resin film. The combination is called a fixed-oil varnish, connoting that the oil dries in place. The development of these varnishes is an intriguing facet of the cabinetmaker's trade (see the sidebar on the facing page).

Fixed-oil varnishes are decidedly more difficult to make than spirit varnishes, but they are far more durable and resistant to damage from water and alcohol. These varnishes have drying oils such as linseed, poppy or walnut oil (and more recently china-wood or tung oil) as their bases. The resins used for fixed-oil varnishes can include the harder fossil resins, like amber and hard copal, since oil is the only solvent that can be heated high enough to dissolve then. Even so, both resins have to be "run" or liquefied before they can be dissolved in hot oil, and this can entail heating them in excess of 500° F. The process, involving liquefied resins, boiling oils and hot spirits of turpentine, all done on an open fire in the 18th century, was exceptionally dangerous. This kind of work was left to varnish and paint makers in urban areas. Unfortunately, the heating required to dissolve fossil resins and chemical processes that accomplished the same thing both contributed to their decay, and these finishes soon deteriorated.

Many softer resins, like those used in spirit varnishes, could be used in fixed-oil varnishes. Because they liquefied at lower temperatures, the preparation of these varnishes was relatively safe. Almost all of the soft resins melt between 200° F and 300° F. A common oil varnish consisted of rosin dissolved in boiling linseed oil, with some spirits of turpentine added to thin it. English formulae used soft copal and shellac resins dissolved in hot oil. As with spirit varnishes, various resins were used to alter the properties of the finish.

Varnishes made with the favorite 18th-century resins are still available through artists' supply sources, but they tend to be expensive in the quantities required for finishing furniture. The modern equivalents of these varnishes contain natural and synthetic resins in linseed and/or tung oil. These varnishes are formulated with a variety of characteristics depending on their purpose. Long-oil varnishes have a large percentage of drying oil relative to the amount of resins, 40 to 55 gal. of oil for each 100 lb. of resin. They take a long time to dry, remain tough and elastic, and are highly water resistant. This kind of varnish includes marine spar varnishes and floor varnishes. Short-oil varnishes contain less than 12 gal. of drying oil for each 100 lb. of resin. Furniture and gloss-oil varnishes are of this type, drying hard quickly. Rubbing and polishing varnishes are short-oil varnishes, but formulated with hard resins that may be polished to a high gloss.

Rubbing Out

Eighteenth-century aesthetics called for smooth and well-polished furniture surfaces. Clear, durable and lustrous finishes were the goal of varnish makers, cabinetmakers and their customers. Given the shortcomings of period finishes and centuries of use, few original finishes remain. Those that do survive have degraded from their original appearance in terms of clarity and luster and don't represent the original appearance of the piece. The effort to achieve a high luster in original work is evidenced by period references to the glossy qualities of varnishes and by descriptions of methods to smooth and enhance their shine. Just how high a gloss the original makers were able to obtain is not certain given the variable nature of the materials at their disposal.

The process of rubbing out the applied finish includes smoothing its surface and polishing it. Smoothing the surface means leveling any bumps in the varnish caused by dust or raised wood fibers. To create a flat surface it must be rubbed with an abrasive backed by a flat block (see the photo below). Period references mention rubbing with a flannel or felt impregnated with tripoli or pumice and lubricated with water or linseed oil. These pads were backed up with a block of cork or rubber to aid in leveling the surface. The next step was to bring the surface to a high luster. This was done by rubbing the surface with a succession of increasingly fine abrasives

Period cabinetmakers leveled the surface of the finish by rubbing it with pumice and linseed oil using a pad backed by a cork block. The modern equivalent is to use steel wool or a waterproof silicon-carbide sandpaper.

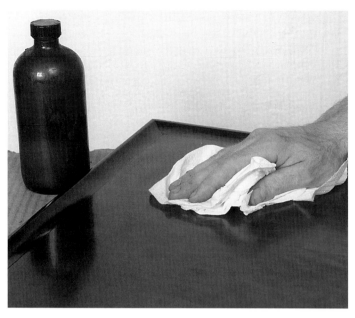

The luster of the finish is increased by rubbing it with finer pumice or rottenstone lubricated with oil. Here, mineral oil and mineral spirits, mixed in equal parts, serve as the lubricant.

The final step in finishing is to polish the surface. Here, a linseed-oil polish has been applied and buffed off.

until the desired luster was achieved. Period surfaces that were first leveled with pumice and oil were brought to a higher luster by rubbing with emery powder, rottenstone, whiting and even flour. Flannel, felt, linen and wool were all cited as good fabrics with which to rub the surface, as were sharkskin, sealskin and soft leather impregnated with abrasive powder.

This process has changed little to the present day, with the exception that different abrasive media are used. The finest grades of steel wool are generally used for leveling the surface. On soft finishes, like shellac, steel wool can usually level the surface without a backing block. On tougher finishes, like oil-based varnish, very fine waterproof silicon-carbide sandpaper (600 grit or finer), lubricated with water and used with a felt block, may be needed to flatten bumps before steel wool is used. By modern methods, once the surface has been leveled with steel wool it can be rubbed with pumice and oil, followed by rottenstone and oil. It should be noted that there are different grades of pumice available commercially; the most common grades are 2F and 4F, 4F being the finest. To

achieve the highest gloss, a surface would be rubbed with 2F pumice, 4F pumice and finally rottenstone, with thorough cleaning of the surface in between, stopping at the desired level of luster. Mineral oil and mineral spirits (paint thinner) mixed in a 1:1 proportion make a very good lubricant for rubbing out. Linseed oil is too viscous and difficult to clean off, and water can only be used on oil varnishes.

The final step in finishing the surface is the application of a polish. On a microscopic level, this step uses a wax, oil or resin to fill the last remaining abrasions from rubbing out. The many period polishes consisted of beeswax softened with a solvent like turpentine, or those based on boiled linseed oil. They left either a wax or dried oil film on the surface that could be buffed out to impart a final gloss. Both provided a protective layer that resisted liquids, an important benefit for spirit varnishes. More aggressive polishes used soft resins, like benzoin or shellac, in alcohol. These polishes, usually used for rejuvenating old surfaces, laid down a new top layer of soft resin or softened and amalgamated the top layer of existing finishes.

Patina

The applied finish, whatever its makeup, is only a small part of the patina of an original piece. The finish that was applied as a last step by the maker was only the starting point for two or three centuries of use. During that time, the inevitable marks of use and the effects of age were added to the original finish. These additions were far longer in the making than the piece itself, and they contribute greatly to the appearance and character of the furniture. They are part of the history of the piece and point to a legacy of care and use that new furniture does not possess. The qualities of the acquired patina fall into three categories: luster, wear and grime. For anyone interested in preserving or replicating the character of the aged surface they are worth examining in closer detail.

LUSTER

Through accounts of procedures and formulae for finishing, period pieces are known to have had lustrous finishes when they were new. Time and the environment eventually took their toll on the finish, and, if it escaped being refinished or recoated, it has survived in what is probably a degraded state from the original. As they appear today, early finishes retain very little of their original luster. While the surface is not matte, neither is it glossy enough to be described as satinlike. These surfaces defy easy description because they have become textural from cracking or beading of the finish or from the marks of use.

WEAR

Centuries of use cause a variety of effects, from the worn stretcher of a turned chair, to the well-rubbed smoothness of an often-polished surface. Recreating this wear requires considering how a piece was valued and used, and what kind of marks would have likely been left on its surface. Good furniture was expensive in its day, and it was treated with care. The furnishings of a house were among its owners' most prized possessions, so they would show subtle signs of use. More utilitarian pieces were meant to be used with less regard to damage.

Different parts of a piece of furniture are subject to different kinds of wear. The feet and legs of any piece are subject to dings and dents from shoes and boots, and, more recently, vacuum cleaners. The tops of ball and claw or pad feet are subject to being stepped on and having things dropped on them. Drawer lips and drawer dividers show both dents and scratches from things being taken in and out of them. The edges of tops see dents from objects falling against them, from having been moved and from having been bumped by passersby. Tops fare the worst, and are likely to have been scratched, dented and stained. Even the sides of cases are likely to show marks from handling and moving. Fingernails, rings, belt buckles, pets and falling objects all leave their distinctive marks in the surface.

GRIME

Wear marks, along with the crevices of original details, are usually accentuated by an accumulation of grime. This is understandable considering how homes were heated in previous centuries. During the 17th and 18th centuries, open fires for cooking and heating burned continually. During the 19th century, wood and coal-burning stoves served the same purposes. Furniture of the period was constantly exposed to black sooty grime in the air.

When pieces were polished, waxed or recoated with a new finish, the black grime became permanently sealed into pores, pits, scratches and crevices. As grime was rubbed into recessed details, the finish was rubbed off the raised details, and a contrast in color and texture began to emerge. Raised details became lighter, smoother and more polished, while crevices became increasingly black and crusty. The process enhanced the three-dimensional effect of details like moldings and carvings by adding differences in luster and tone. As with signs of wear, the extent of this effect varies among examples of furniture. Pieces that received frequent polishing show a more pronounced contrast in color, while pieces that were literally untouched do not.

The decision to add the effects of time, use and grime to a replica (or to a repair to an original) is up to the discretion of the maker and client. Some owners of replicated pieces want them to be indistinguishable from an aged original, with all the features of an old surface. Others want their pieces to appear as they

The patina of a candlestand from the third quarter of the 18th century shows the marks of use and an accumulation of grime in the marks and details.

A black-pigmented oil stain may be applied to a surface to enhance the marks of age and replicate the accumulation of grime.

did when they were delivered to their original owners so they can add their own family's signs of use over time. Because early originals are nearly always well worn, signs of use seem to be a necessary and integral part of pieces from the first part of the 18th century, and replicas look incomplete without them. Examples from later in the century show fewer signs of age, and replicating an aged patina is less important to the overall appearance of the piece.

If the marks of age and use are to be replicated, the key to doing so successfully is to put the appropriate wear in the correct places. The only guideline is to consider how a piece would have been lived with; that is, how it was used, moved and where it would have been handled. The marks of use are not distributed randomly across the surface of a piece; they are concentrated in the areas of use. Any black-pigmented oil-based stain can simulate the grime accumulated over the centuries. Since it was acquired after the original finish was applied, so should it be applied to the replica, or perhaps between successive coats of finish. To give a newly finished piece an authentic patina takes a long time; you are trying to replicate two or three hundred years of use in a few days. An authentic-looking treatment requires patience, experimentation and caution. The marks of age are more easily added than removed.

Ebonizing

Ebonizing is a treatment used to blacken wood and give it the appearance of ebony, a dense, hard tropical wood that is black with streaks of brown. While ebony was rarely used in 18th-century American furniture (except as decorative inlay), it was used in European court furniture of the 17th century. The contrast of light and dark wood in a single piece of furniture was an important part of the Jacobean aesthetic. In order to achieve the same contrast without actual ebony, American makers of the 17th century had to settle for a painted simulation. Ebonized parts, like bosses, split spindles and turnings, are an

important part of the design of American Jacobean furniture, and ebonizing continued to be used into the William and Mary period for chairs and turned legs. The process fell out of favor for the rest of the century as rich woods and lighter colors came into vogue. Veneer was dyed black to simulate ebony for stringing and inlay in the Federal period, but that process differed from earlier ebonizing.

In ebonizing, the quality of the surface was as important as the color. Ebonized parts were intended to be smooth and lustrous, with the appearance of having been well polished. To achieve this effect, a dense close-grained wood like maple was preferred. The process is no more involved than applying a heavily pigmented black stain or paint. There are a few known ancient methods, and all call for black pigments, like lamp black or bone black, to be suspended in a carrier and binder and applied to the part. The most common method of ebonizing would include the most readily available materials such as black pigment added to linseed oil with dryers. This mixture makes a thick, black

paint/stain that penetrates the surface of bare wood. The excess may be wiped off, leaving pigment in the wood and a nice luster from the oil. Two or more applications, with drying time between, build a nice ebonized surface. This surface can be buffed, with or without wax, or top-coated with varnish with the rest of the piece for a higher gloss. Modern solid-color oil stains are nearly equivalent to the pigment and oil mixture.

A later method of ebonizing calls for one of the black pigments to be mixed with a spirit varnish (1 heaping tablespoon per 8 fl. oz. shellac varnish). Up to seven coats are applied with light sanding between, and the final surface is rubbed with pumice and oil.

Strong black dyes were used for the vat dyeing of veneer intended for stringing and inlay in the Federal period. These colorants were made from dyestuff rather than pigment to penetrate clear through the veneer. Of the several known formulae, most start with logwood chips or sawdust boiled in water to make a dark red stain (see Appendix V on pp. 298-299). That color is

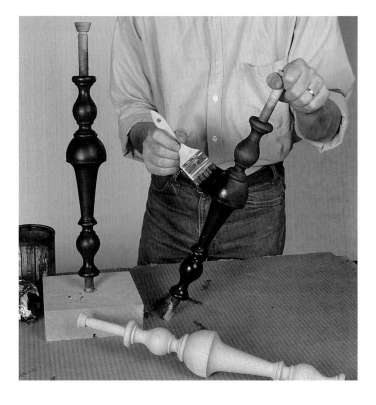

Ebonizing is the application of a heavily pigmented black oil paint/stain to simulate ebony. It is brushed on and the excess is rubbed off, leaving a soft luster on the wood. The process is repeated as needed to reach the desired opacity.

then turned black with the addition of tannic acid (from oak galls or bark) and copper compounds, or iron filings in vinegar. Because of the more complex nature of this formula, it is unlikely that it was ever used for the early Jacobean or William and Mary ebonizing.

Japanning

The exotic allure of things Oriental, or *chinoiserie*, has fascinated Europeans for centuries, but none so much as Oriental lacquer. Throughout the European history of finishing and varnish-making, the quality of Oriental lacquer has stood as the benchmark by which all other finishes are judged. The many formulae and arcane processes for making varnish were largely intended to rival the brilliance of authentic lacquer finishes. Trade brought decorated Chinese lacquer boxes to Europe where local cabinetmakers were often called upon to build stands for them. Before long, cabinetmakers began to replicate the boxes and the lacquer decoration themselves. The decoration featured figures and scenes in gold, displayed on a black or mottled background. The Oriental process was complex, time-consuming and required fairly exotic materials and resins, but the Europeans sought to replicate the lacquer with the materials and methods that were available and familiar to them. Stalker and Parker's *Treatise of Japanning and Varnishing* of 1688 helped disseminate both the method of and interest in japanning. (For more on the history of japanning in America, see p. 57.)

Real Oriental lacquers are made from the resin of the lac tree *Rhus vernicifera*. Lacquer is not related to the lac resin of insect origin used to make shellac, though many 19th-century "lacquers" were little more than shellac spirit varnish. Chinese and Japanese lacquers are made from the same resin but with different additives. Chinese lacquer contains additives to give it more body, while Japanese lacquer, which was considered harder and more durable, contains only camphor to thin it. Burmese black lacquer is similar, but comes from a different tree *(Melanorrhea usitata)*. Like oil

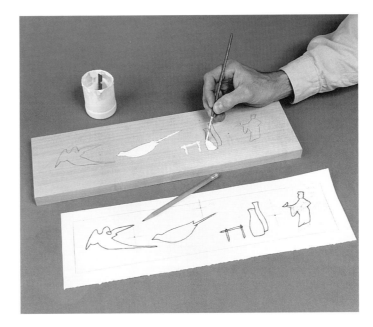

Japanning begins by drawing the design directly on the wood surface and building up the figures with gesso.

A red-pigmented oil paint/stain is applied over the gesso and allowed to dry. This is followed by black paint-stain. A mottled or streaked effect can be obtained by wiping through the layer of black.

varnishes, real lacquer cures by oxidation, not evaporation. It is clear when first applied, and then turns red, and finally black as it hardens. Proper hardening occurs only under humid conditions; the resin remains soft and gummy under warm and dry conditions. Modern lacquers are made with nitrocellulose and synthetic resins in complex solvents and dry by evaporation. Some of the credit for the durability and longevity of Oriental lacquer should be given to the wood to which it was applied. Many lacquer finishes were applied to teak, and teak's expansion and contraction with

humidity is among the lowest of all the cabinet woods—less than half that of most American or European hardwoods. As a result, Oriental lacquer was less apt to crack and deteriorate.

THE JAPANNING PROCESS

It was the goal of the Western japanner to try to equal the work of Eastern decorators with the materials that were readily available. Furniture was built specifically to be japanned, and could be built from something other than the most desirable

The raised figures and designs are painted or gilded and smaller details are added in black paint.

Several coats of a spirit varnish are applied to seal the work.

wood. Most japanned pieces were built from a variety of woods, including maple, pine and oak.

The designs for the figures and scenes were copied or traced from patterns. Evidence for these patterns includes not only their mention in inventories, but also the similarity of decorative designs on many different pieces of furniture. (Stalker and Parker's *Treatise of Japanning and Varnishing* included many engraved plates with suggested scenes for japanned decoration, as well as directions for tracing them onto the surface of the furniture.) Like the cabinet-makers' patterns, japanning patterns made the work go faster and left designs that are indicative of certain craftsmen. The designs for the figures and scenery were traced onto the surface and built up with gesso (see the top photo on p. 195). Gesso is a thick-bodied, paintlike substance made of whiting, hide glue and a plasticizing material like gum arabic.

Some references cite the drawing of the figures and the application of gesso as having been done on the bare wood, and others refer to its having been done following the coats of red and black paint. Since both references are based on actual

japanned pieces, the method must have been up to the discretion of the japanner. While it would have been easier to draw the figures on the prepared background (rather than painting over them and having to re-draw them), the gesso would adhere better to bare wood.

The base coat of color was a red-pigmented paint/stain that sealed the wood and prepared a ground. Over this, a black-pigmented oil paint/stain was applied (see the bottom photo on p. 195). The black coat was left thick on some pieces, and on others it was daubed through with a brush or cloth to reveal some of the red beneath. This caused the mottled effect that simulated the patterning of tortoiseshell. On other pieces the patterning is more of a deliberate streaking, showing a sharp contrast between the red and black.

The raised figures and other decorative elements were covered with silver or gold leaf, powder or paint (see the photo at left above). The leaf or powder was adhered to the figure with sizing, or powder could be mixed with a varnish to create paint. Many areas on japanned pieces, such as borders and small decorative details, were painted in gold without having been raised with gesso. Fine details of the figures and scenery

were added in black paint over the gold using a fine pointed brush. The entire piece was then given several coats of either a spirit or oil varnish to protect the japanning and impart a smooth and glossy luster (photo at right above).

From the trial-and-error nature of period formulae and the uncertain composition of raw materials, the durability of japanned pieces must have varied widely. The process of japanning builds up many layers of dissimilar materials, each with varying degrees of adherence to one another. Additionally, the process was applied to expanding and contracting wood subject to the extremes of humidity of the New England climate. Japanned decoration is subject to deterioration as gesso and paint layers either flake off or crumble. In spite of the japanners' obvious skill, the fact that some pieces have lasted for close to three centuries while others have deteriorated is largely the result of the right combination of materials, formulae, technique and care. Based on the number of known japanners and the duration of its popularity, the three dozen surviving Boston pieces must be only a tiny fraction of the number of pieces that were made originally.

13

MEASUREMENTS AND

DRAWINGS

When making any piece of furniture, it's important to establish clearly the design and details of the work. With the very first cuts, the possibility of altering the design begins to diminish. This is especially true in the making of 18th-century designs, where the cabinetmaker is further constrained by period designs and methods and is less able to exercise artistic license. With so much of the essence of 18th-century American furniture designed into the piece rather than added on, proper planning from the start is important. Whether the piece is inspired by one original or is an amalgamation of several examples, the aesthetic success of the finished piece depends on its proper design and planning. If you are undertaking an exacting replica of an original, accurate dimensional information is the cornerstone of its authenticity.

Reliable and accurate dimensions are best taken from original pieces, but they may also be determined from photographs. Unknown dimensions and peculiar construction details may be worked out by making full-scale drawings. All of these contribute to gathering a reliable set of dimensions and details from which to work and aid in making accurate and precise patterns and component parts.

Measuring Originals

Unless you are fortunate enough to have a fine original in your care or possession, it's most likely that you'll have only one chance to measure an important original piece in detail. Unfortunately, the opportunity to measure a piece in a museum or private collection does not extend to the luxury of being able to draft full-scale drawings on location at your leisure. You can only hope to come away with a complete set of notes, sketches and dimensions. As a cabinet-maker, you need to know what is important to measure and what you will need to know to build the piece. It is important to be thorough and complete without overstaying your welcome.

To ensure the safety of the original and the peace of mind of its owners, you should assemble a set of non-marring measuring tools, including a fabric tape measure, long and short wooden rulers, and a set of wooden or plastic calipers (see the photo on p. 198). Anyone who has been around fine furniture is naturally careful and respectful of it and could certainly measure a piece with everyday shop tools without inflicting damage, but a set of non-marring measuring tools instills confidence in the owners, shows consideration on your part and can prevent accidental marks from occurring.

An added courtesy is to wear white fabric gloves while examining the piece. Granted, originals have been handled and used daily for two or three hundred years, but out of respect for the original and its owners, gloves prevent your handling of the piece from adding to its patina. This precaution really is important on the bare and unfinished surfaces of drawer and case interiors and undersides. These areas are unsealed and unprotected and have the potential to absorb dirt and oil. We would all like future generations to be able to examine these pieces and find them in the same condition that we did.

TAKING MEASUREMENTS

The task of measuring a complicated piece may at first seem overwhelming, and knowing where to begin is part of the problem. Measuring it as it would be built offers a logical and systematic way to measure all the components and note how they are interconnected. Start with the fundamentals of its structure and then proceed to its attachments and adornments.

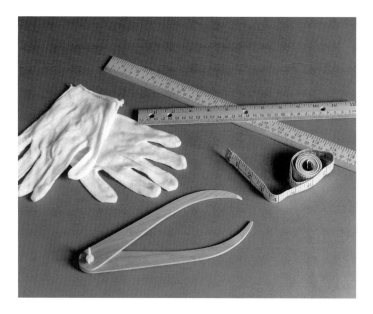

Non-marring tools for measuring original pieces include a fabric tape measure, long and short wooden rulers, wooden or plastic calipers, and gloves.

Using the example of a case piece such as a chest of drawers, consider first the bare case itself without drawers, feet or moldings. Note the dimensions of the top, bottom and sides of the case and the layout of the case joinery. From there, measure the location of the drawer dividers, their joinery and any internal construction details like drawer runners, guides or kickers. To this information on the empty case add details of the attachments like moldings and feet. With the measurement of the drawer components and their joinery the task is complete. The same methodology applies to all case pieces, no matter how complex they are. In the case of chairs, the structure of the back is one subset of the piece, the front, sides and stretchers are another, and the arms are last to be added.

When measuring a piece on location it is very helpful to have a sketch of the piece prepared ahead of time, or some photocopies of a photograph of the piece. Working this way allows you to mark the dimensions directly onto the copy or sketch as they are measured, and you can spend your time studying the piece and its details rather than trying to draw a reasonable likeness of the original.

There are some aspects of fine furniture that are difficult to measure, such as the sweeping curves of aprons or cabriole legs. Without tracing the curves, which would probably be frowned upon, the next best way to record them is to note the position and depth of their features. This is why two rulers are called for in the measuring kit. Use one to record the horizontal features of the curve and the other for the vertical features. For any curve, the relevant points that define it are where its features start and stop, their maximum and minimum points, and the position of inflection points (those points where the direction changes). The defining features of cabriole legs are enumerated in the section on their layout and making (see p. 149). In keeping with the idea of measuring the piece as you would build it, consider all the information you would need to make a pattern as you are measuring.

Some details like carving or elaborate fretwork cannot be adequately defined by measurement alone. These areas really need to be photographed. Some museums will allow photography, others will not. If the museum does not allow photography, there may be stock museum photographs available for purchase or you may have to resort to sketching. Some places object to flash photography only, in which case photos can be taken with high-speed film or using a tripod. If you are able to photograph details, take the photos from angles that will be the most beneficial to the replication. Get straight-on views of carvings and fretwork, and straight-on profile views of apron curves or cabriole legs. Ball and claw feet require profile views as well as 45° views from the front (center talon) and side to capture their detail fully. In each case, take some oblique photos to capture the three-dimensional nature of the detail, and supplement the photos with measurements of major features and the depth of the carving.

Scaling from Photographs

When it is not possible to gain access to an original, or in cases where its whereabouts are unknown, it is often necessary to work from photographs and what is known of the piece's major dimensions. Scaling from photos is quite simple if the photos are taken directly from the front and side of the piece (orthographic views) and there is little distortion evident in the photos. However, furniture photographs are rarely published in straight-on views, and photographs are full of both obvious and subtle distortions.

DISTORTION IN PHOTOGRAPHS

In viewing a scene, the mind naturally takes into account the effects of perspective, that is the characteristic of more distant objects to appear to be smaller. In an obvious example, we know that a road has a constant width even though it appears to narrow toward a point on a distant horizon. In a more subtle case, we can judge whether the legs of a table are parallel from an elevated point of view, even though perspective makes them appear to taper inward. Photographs, however, present a literal image of what the eye sees, without the corrective judgment of the mind, so differences in distance and the effects of perspective become part of the image. In addition, there is an inherent distortion in the photographic image based on the angle of view of the lens and the foreshortening of objects away from the center of the image.

Wide-angle lenses of short focal length yield the most distortion in photographs. This effect is seen clearly in photos taken with wide-angle "fisheye" lenses, which illustrate the effect of lens distortion in the

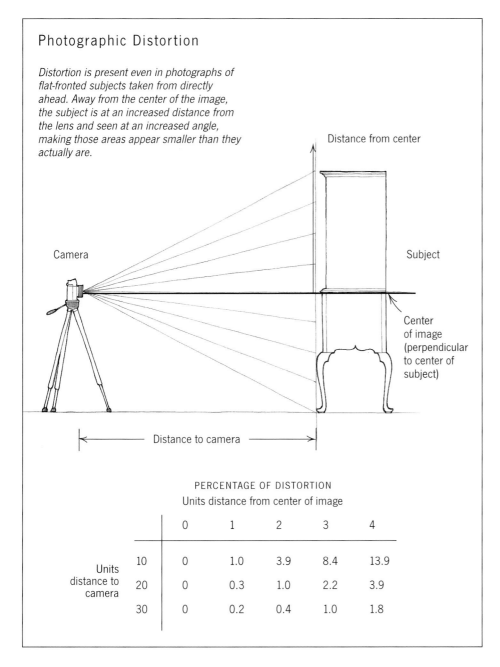

Photographic Distortion

Distortion is present even in photographs of flat-fronted subjects taken from directly ahead. Away from the center of the image, the subject is at an increased distance from the lens and seen at an increased angle, making those areas appear smaller than they actually are.

Distance from center

Camera

Subject

Center of image (perpendicular to center of subject)

Distance to camera

PERCENTAGE OF DISTORTION
Units distance from center of image

		0	1	2	3	4
	10	0	1.0	3.9	8.4	13.9
Units distance to camera	20	0	0.3	1.0	2.2	3.9
	30	0	0.2	0.4	1.0	1.8

extreme. The very wide angle of view (180°) of the lens results in an increasingly compressed image away from the center, giving the image its distinctive "bulging" quality. The opposite effect is given by lenses with extremely long focal lengths, or telephoto lenses. These lenses have a narrow angle of view (less than 8°) and minimize the effect of distance, and therefore perspective. Camera lenses for everyday use are somewhere between the two extremes, with angles of view of about 45°, which makes them wide enough to encompass a scene without noticeable distortion.

Two factors contribute to distortion in photographs, even in photos of flat subjects directly in front of the camera and perpendicular to the center of its line of sight. One of these factors is perspective: Away from the center of the image, the subject is at a greater distance from the lens, thus it appears slightly smaller. The other factor is foreshortening: Away from the center of the image, the subject is seen at a slight angle, and foreshortening causes it to appear even smaller. The farther the lens is from the subject, the smaller the angle from the top to the bottom of the subject, and

the less the angular distortion due to perspective and foreshortening. If the camera is kept 4 ft. from the subject for every 1 ft. of subject height, the total of these distortions is kept under 2%. If that ratio is increased to 5 ft. for every 1 ft. of subject height, distortion is held to 1%.

Given that all photographs exhibit some degree of distortion but its extent and compensation are unknown, the best advice is to be aware of it, anticipate it and never trust a photograph to be the final authority. When scaling up measurements from a photo, take them from as near the center as possible, since that is the most reliable part of the image. Sometimes there are enough clues in the photo to estimate from how far away the photo was taken, which offers an idea of the inherent distortion. The drawing on p. 200 shows how to use the location of feet, cornice moldings and other details to construct a scale drawing of the subject and determine its distance from the camera.

SCALING FROM AN ORTHOGRAPHIC VIEW

Scaling from photographs is simply taking very accurate measurements from a small photograph and multiplying them to full scale. A small inaccuracy in the initial measurement will be amplified greatly when it is multiplied to full scale. If you are scaling a 3-ft. wide dressing table from a 4-in. wide photo, the photo measurements are multiplied by nine, making an error of $^1/_{16}$ in. translate to an enlarged error of $^9/_{16}$ in. The smaller the photo and the larger the actual piece, the larger the magnification of errors will be. Thus it is necessary to measure the photo as precisely as possible, and to compare the scaled-up dimensions to those of other known pieces. A machinist's caliper is the most accurate tool for the precise measurement of photos. This tool is equipped with either dial or vernier scale, and measures inside and outside lengths to $^1/_{1000}$ in. This kind of precision in the photo measurements ensures the accuracy of scaled dimensions.

Accurately determining the dimensions of an original this way requires a clear, sharp photograph. It is best to have as large a photo as possible, but making an enlarged

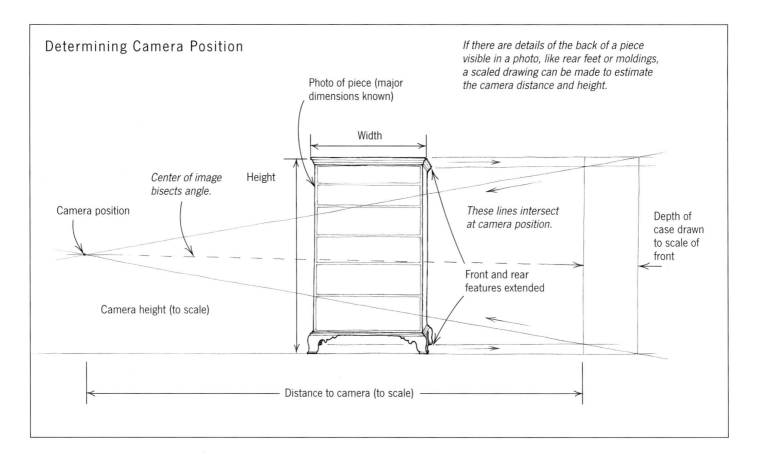

Determining Camera Position

If there are details of the back of a piece visible in a photo, like rear feet or moldings, a scaled drawing can be made to estimate the camera distance and height.

Photo of piece (major dimensions known)

Width

Height

Center of image bisects angle.

Camera position

These lines intersect at camera position.

Depth of case drawn to scale of front

Camera height (to scale)

Front and rear features extended

Distance to camera (to scale)

---

copy usually sacrifices sharpness for a larger size, so little is gained. A small original photograph can be used for scaling, but the measurement of it must be very precise and any lines that are constructed on it must be very fine. If the photo seems sharp enough to enlarge without losing detail, it is worth doing. This can be done in a number of ways, but an enlarged color copy, even of a black and white print, is the quickest and easiest way to get a high-quality, high-resolution enlargement. (Color copiers can make quick prints from 35 mm and 2¼-in. transparencies.) Copy photos can also be made by photographing the small photo (using a copy stand) and making larger prints of it, or by scanning the image and making an enlarged, high-resolution print.

When scaling dimensions from the photo, draw one horizontal and one vertical reference line along which to take the measurements (see the photo on the facing page). Chances are that the top and bottom and left and right of the piece in the photo are different sizes, and the vertical scale is probably different from the horizontal

scale. Along those lines, measurements are scaled up from known dimensions with a simple proportion:

$$\frac{\text{known major dimension}}{\text{measured major dimension}}$$
$$= \frac{\text{unknown detail dimension}}{\text{measured detail dimension}}$$

The left side of this equation is a constant along the line of measurement. The known major dimension, such as a known case width, is divided by the case width measured from the photo, and that number is a constant. The measured dimension of any detail along that line, multiplied by that constant, is the actual size of the detail. Most original pieces were measured off in ⅛-in. increments, so rounding to the nearest ⅛ in. is appropriate. In another part of the photo the scale may be different, and you need to determine a new constant from the measurement of a known major dimension. Similarly, a different constant must be determined for the vertical scale as well. It is best to measure the individual sizes of each detail and check that they all add up to the major dimension, since that forces you to make

minor corrections. Referencing all the dimensions from one point, such as the distance from the ground, takes the photograph literally without the benefit of making necessary adjustments.

In referring to published dimensions for pieces, be careful to determine what they include. Some references, especially older ones, give overall dimensions for pieces, which include moldings and feet. There are no strict conventions for presenting measurements, but most sources mention the guidelines they follow. Some publications give overall dimensions—except for case pieces, where case width and depth are specified—and note whether the height listed includes finials. In the case of chairs, note whether the depth is an overall depth, or the depth at the seat. Newer and more scholarly references are more specific and complete in presenting all the important dimensions.

To double-check all the scaled measurements along the reference line, add all the measurements to ensure they equal the known major dimension. Because of the small inaccuracies in measuring that are

Scaling Measurements from an Orthographic View

Height of chest is known to be 71½ in.; measures 4.730 in. on photo.

Height of drawer Y measures 0.320 in.

$Y/0.320 = 71.5/4.730$
$Y = 4.85 = 4⅞$ in.

Width of lower case is known to be 37⅝ in.; measures 2.475 in. on photo.

X measures 0.895
$X/0.895 = 37.625/2.475$
$X = 13.61 = 13⅝$ in.

If this process is repeated for all the vertical or horizontal elements, they should add up to the known major dimension.

magnified in scaling up, they are usually close but rarely equal on the first try. At this point, the dimensions of the details have to be adjusted somewhat to add up to the known major dimension. Some of the details that could have been rounded either up or down to the nearest ⅛ in. may be adjusted the other way to favor the total. Most original makers would have had a consistent method of graduating drawer sizes, with each one being a given amount taller than the one above it. Remember, too, that lipped drawers overlap the case sides and drawer dividers by a fraction of an inch. Considering the inherent distortion due to the camera's view of the subject, it is best to

add fractional dimensions in areas well above or below the camera's height, or subtract them at or near its level. After a few iterations the measurements of all the details should add up to the known major dimension.

SCALING FROM AN ANGULAR VIEW

It is rare to have a photograph with a good orthographic view to work from when scaling the dimensions for a piece of furniture. Most published photos show the piece at an angle so both the front and side may be seen and to give a better suggestion of the depth of the case and the details. While this

is a more natural way to view the piece, it presents a problem for anyone hoping to make scale measurements, especially horizontal measurements, from the photo. Both the front and side recede toward vanishing points on the horizon line, so a linear scaling of their details is impossible. As they recede into the distance, equal units of measurement appear to diminish in size. If one could "rotate" the piece toward the viewer, this effect would be eliminated and accurately scaled measurements could easily be taken. This can be done graphically by taking the steps used by draftsmen to create perspective drawings from orthographic views and applying them in reverse order. This process adheres to the basic rules of perspective and involves finding the vanishing points, establishing a horizon line, and then constructing a plan or elevation of the piece from which dimensions may be accurately scaled.

The first step in constructing the scalable view is to establish the two vanishing points on either side of the image. Start by affixing the photo to a large sheet of paper or a drawing board. Working carefully and accurately, extend the lines of the top and bottom of the piece, on both the front and side, to the points where they intersect (see the top drawing on p. 202). For more accuracy, extend as many clear horizontal details as possible toward the vanishing points to confirm their locations. In the event that they do not all intersect in exactly the same point on either side, choose a point where most do meet to be the vanishing point. The lines from the extreme top and bottom of the piece are going to be the most accurate determinants of the vanishing points. Those that are nearly horizontal converge at a smaller angle and are less accurate. Draw a line through the vanishing points (VP_1, VP_2) to establish the horizon line.

The center of vision (CV) line is the vertical reference line from which the plan and elevation views will be drawn. Their dimensions will be in the same proportion as measurements along this line. In an angular view of furniture, this line is chosen to be along the front corner of the piece, neglecting moldings and feet. Draw the CV line well beyond the top and bottom of the

Scaling Vertical Measurements from an Angular View

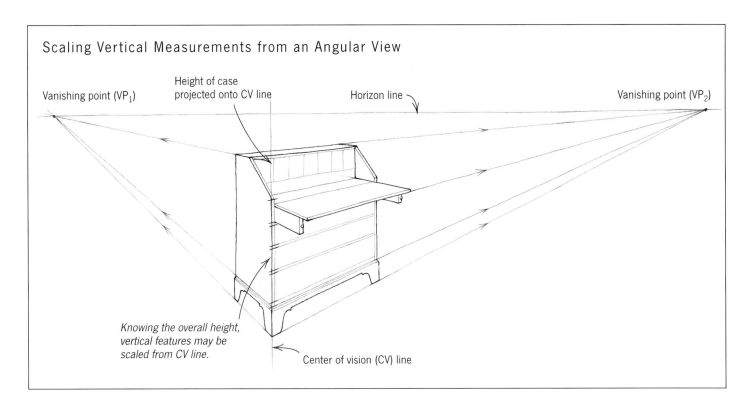

Vanishing point (VP$_1$)

Height of case projected onto CV line

Horizon line

Vanishing point (VP$_2$)

Knowing the overall height, vertical features may be scaled from CV line.

Center of vision (CV) line

Accounting for Protruding Feet and Moldings

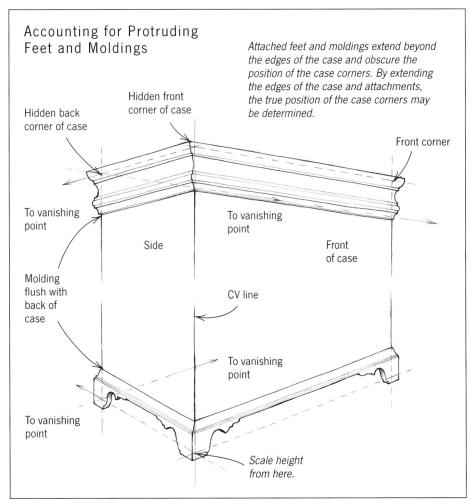

Attached feet and moldings extend beyond the edges of the case and obscure the position of the case corners. By extending the edges of the case and attachments, the true position of the case corners may be determined.

Hidden front corner of case

Hidden back corner of case

Front corner

To vanishing point

To vanishing point

Side

Front of case

Molding flush with back of case

CV line

To vanishing point

To vanishing point

To vanishing point

Scale height from here.

piece. This line should be perpendicular to the horizon line.

At this point in the process, there are three options depending on what information needs to be scaled: vertical dimensions may be taken directly from the CV line without much further construction; another method will produce a plan view to scale; the third will produce elevations of the front and side to scale.

If vertical dimensions are all that are needed, they can be scaled from the CV line. An example would be a piece like a chest of drawers or a chest on chest, where the case width is known, but the height of the feet and the drawer sizes have to scaled. Details that do not extend to the CV line may be extended from the vanishing points (see the drawing at left). Extending these points allows you to determine accurately the vertical dimensions of pieces like slant-front desks, desk bookcases or any piece that has a stepped front. By extending the lines of the case and its attached moldings and feet to the vanishing points, the true corners of the piece without attachments may be constructed.

To construct a plan view by the projection method, follow these steps (and the drawing on the facing page):

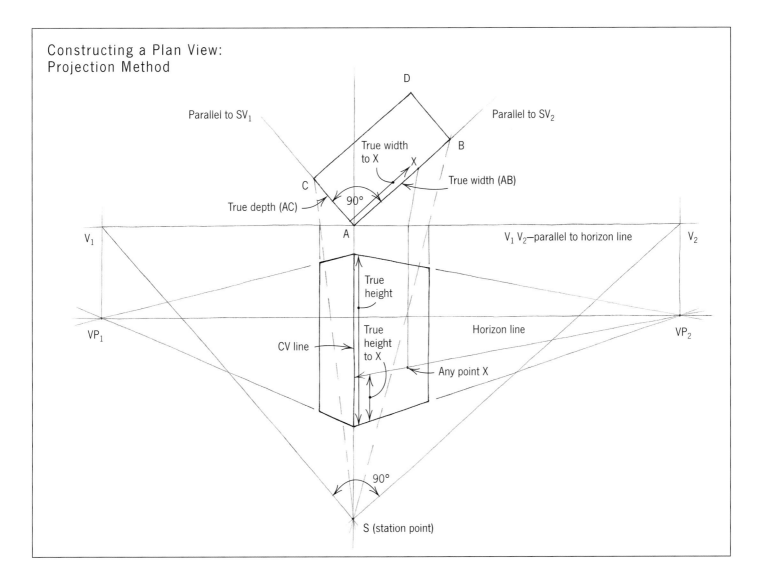

Constructing a Plan View: Projection Method

Labels in figure: D · Parallel to SV₁ · Parallel to SV₂ · True width to X · B · X · True width (AB) · C · 90° · True depth (AC) · A · V₁ · V₂ · V₁ V₂—parallel to horizon line · True height · VP₁ · VP₂ · CV line · True height to X · Horizon line · Any point X · 90° · S (station point)

1. Draw a line parallel to the horizon line just above the photo image. Extend vertical lines from the vanishing points to this new line. Their points of intersection will be called V₁ and V₂.

2. Using a square, draw lines from V₁ and V₂ that meet at right angles at the CV line. This point on CV is called the station point (S).

3. From the point where line V₁V₂ intersects CV (point A), extend two lines parallel to SV₁ and SV₂. These lines will meet at a right angle at point A.

4. From the left and right sides of the piece in the photo, extend vertical lines to line V₁V₂.

5. From point S, draw lines through the intersections of the verticals and V₁V₂ to the points where they intersect the lines from A. These points are labeled B and C.

Lines AB and AC are the true width and depth of the piece, proportional to height along the CV line.

6. The other two sides of the plan view may be drawn parallel to AB and AC to establish point D, the back corner.

Any point X on the front or side of the photo image may be extended vertically to line V₁V₂ and projected onto the plan view by a line drawn from S. If only the height of the piece is known, the width and depth may be scaled from the height along the CV line. If the width is known, use its known measurement to scale details projected onto the plan.

To construct elevations of the front and sides using the two-point, or measuring-point, method, follow these steps (and the drawing on p. 204):

1. Using a square, draw two lines from the vanishing points (VP₁, VP₂) that meet at right angles at line CV. That point is the station point S for this construction.

2. Strike an arc or measure to establish a point on the horizon line the same distance from each vanishing point as point S. These two points on the horizon are the measuring points M₁ and M₂.

3. Draw two horizontal lines that cross line CV at the top and bottom corners of the piece. These lines represent the true height.

4. From the measuring points M₁ and M₂, extend lines through the upper and lower corners of the piece (A, B, C, D) to their intersections with the upper and lower horizontals. These intersection points (A₁, B₁, C₁, D₁) mark the corners of the

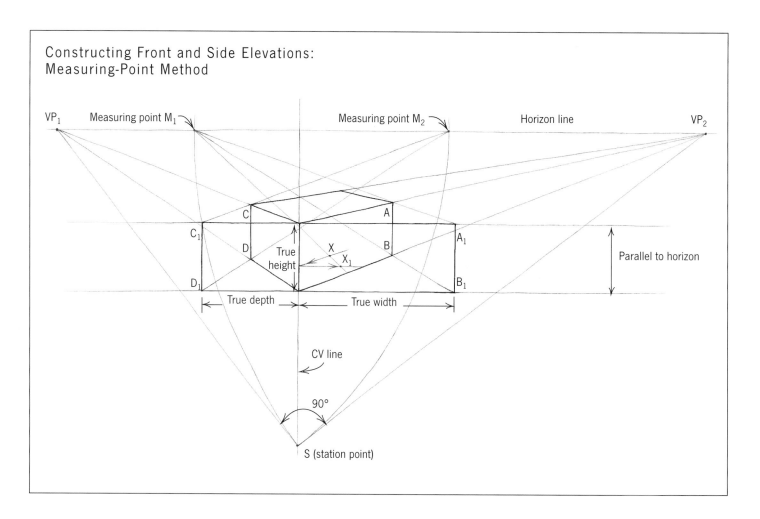

Constructing Front and Side Elevations:
Measuring-Point Method

VP₁ · Measuring point M₁ · Measuring point M₂ · Horizon line · VP₂

C · A

C₁ · A₁

D · X · B · Parallel to horizon

True height · X · X₁ · B₁

D₁ · B₁

True depth · True width

CV line

90°

S (station point)

true size elevations and are connected by vertical lines.

5. Horizontal details may be extended vertically to the top or bottom of the angular case and projected on the elevation by a line drawn from the appropriate measuring point M.

The position of any point X on the front of the piece may be projected onto the elevation as follows: Extend its vertical position to line CV from its vanishing point, and then extend a horizontal from the intersection with CV across the elevation. Project the position of X by a line drawn from the measuring point M₁ to its intersection with the horizontal line across the elevation. Using this method, the major details of pediment tops may be projected onto the orthogonal view of the elevation (as shown in the drawing on the facing page). Note that in angular perspective, pediment tops have their own vanishing points equidistant directly above and below their respective vanishing point on the horizon.

ONE-POINT PERSPECTIVE

Many shorter pieces of furniture are photographed from straight ahead but from an elevated camera angle, especially if the features of the top are noteworthy. The examples in these photographs illustrate single-point perspective, where a single vanishing point lies behind the subject. It is tempting to use the rules of one-point perspective to determine the depth of the piece and to construct a plan view of the top, but with too many unknowns, including the camera angle, it is impossible to determine both. If, however, the depth of the piece is known, the shape of the top may be constructed as follows:

1. Begin by extending the sides and front edge of the top to find the vanishing point and the outline of the top (A, B, C, D) (see the drawing on p. 206).

2. Draw a vertical line CV, perpendicular to the front edge of the top, through the vanishing point.

3. Construct a plan view of the outline of the top by drawing two vertical lines up from the front corners of the top. Connect these with a horizontal line to establish the scale depth of the piece based on the known width and depth.

4. Draw a line from the back corners of the plan view D₁ and C₁, through the back corners of the perspective view D and C, to the point where it intersects the CV line. The point where these lines intersect CV is the station point S.

5. From point S, any point on the edge of the perspective view (E) may be projected onto the plan view (E₁). Any other point X on the perspective view may be projected to the plan view by first extending its vertical position horizontally to the edge of the perspective view and projecting that onto the plan view, and then projecting its horizontal position to the front edge from the vanishing point. These two projected points on the edge of the plan view mark the projected position of the X.

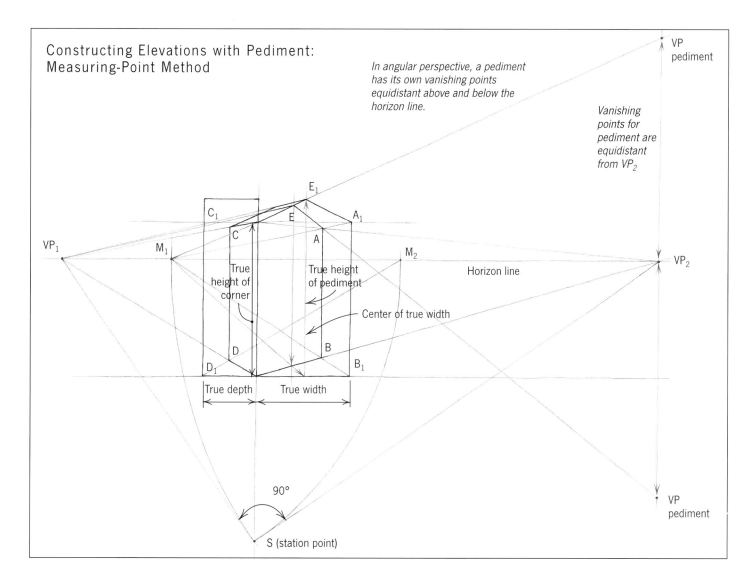

Constructing Elevations with Pediment: Measuring-Point Method

In angular perspective, a pediment has its own vanishing points equidistant above and below the horizon line.

VP pediment

Vanishing points for pediment are equidistant from VP$_2$

True height of corner

True height of pediment

Center of true width

Horizon line

VP$_1$ M$_1$ M$_2$ VP$_2$

C$_1$ E$_1$ A$_1$

C   E   A

D   B

D$_1$ B$_1$

True depth   True width

90°

S (station point)

VP pediment

HISTORICAL REFERENCES

The use of angular and one-point perspective is nothing new to the field of furniture design. Thomas Chippendale's *The Gentleman and Cabinet-Maker's Director* of 1754 presented drawings of pieces in orthographic projection, wherein the front face of the piece is shown orthographically and the third dimension recedes towards a vanishing point. Thomas Sheraton's *The Cabinet-Maker and Upholsterer's Drawing Book* of 1793 illustrated and explained in great detail two-point perspective using measuring points and one-point perspective. In both cases the authors were stressing the importance of being able to communicate designs to customers and the methods by which the cabinetmaker could produce handsome perspective

drawings. In this way, they were illustrating how to make perspective views from shop drawings, rather then the opposite approach taken here.

Working Drawings and Patterns

Once measurements have been taken from the original or derived from photographs, working drawings can be made. The extent of these drawings depends on the complexity of the design and the personal methods of the builder. They can range from quick sketches with which to establish dimensions to full-scale working drawings to show every aspect of detail.

Simple rectilinear pieces rarely require complete drawings. For something like a chest of drawers or a tea table, a sketch with important dimensions is usually enough to convey the design. For pieces that include some curved details, such as bracket feet, a curved apron or cabriole legs, a few full-size patterns are needed to supplement the sketch and dimensions.

Complex pieces do require more sophisticated drawings, and if the piece is especially sculptural, it is advisable to make full-size drawings. A full-size drawing is the only way to work out the interplay of components with confidence before building the piece. The drawing need not include every detail, only the particularly vexing areas of construction. Sometimes making a full-size drawing allows the

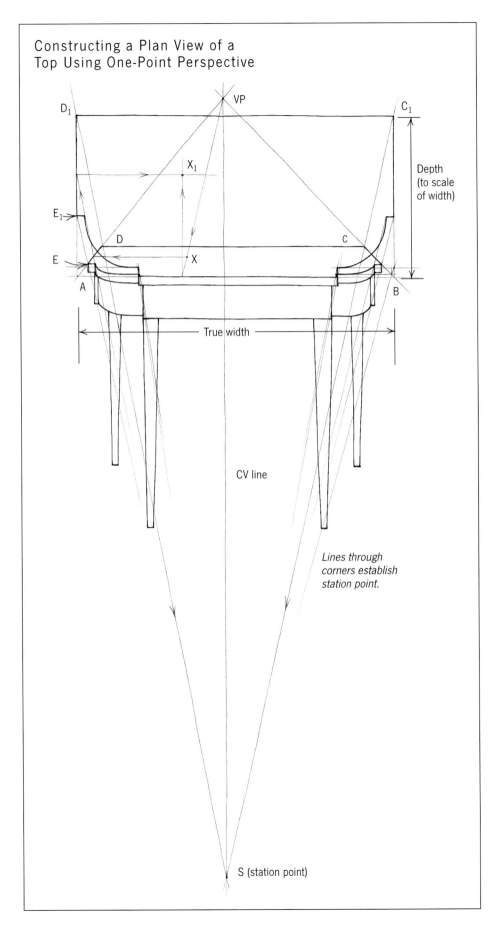

Constructing a Plan View of a
Top Using One-Point Perspective

VP

D_1 C_1

X_1 Depth
(to scale
of width)

E_1

D   C

E   X

A   B

True width

CV line

Lines through
corners establish
station point.

S (station point)

builder to work out some dimensions
graphically that could not be determined
when the piece was measured or scaled.

MAKING PATTERNS

The one shortcoming of full-size drawings
is that the profiles of curved parts must be
transferred onto something more rigid for
use as a pattern. Whether this is done with
carbon paper or a toothed pounce wheel,
the process is time-consuming and adds
potential inaccuracies. In building a piece of
furniture, the quality of the pattern is of
prime importance. An elegant solution to
this is to draw the full-scale drawing on
posterboard or similar heavy stock to begin
with. This drawing can then be cut to serve
as patterns. In this way, the drawing literally
comes apart to become separate patterns for
component parts and reassembles to show
the piece in its entirety. The shapes of
components are transferred directly to the
wood without losing subtle details of shape.
If you are willing to cut them apart, existing
paper drawings can be glued to heavy stock
(3M spray adhesive works well for this).

Rigid materials like posterboard or
matboard are more than sufficient for
patterns that will be used a few times, but
with extended use their edges become soft
and their crispness degrades. Patterns that
are to see a lot of use require a harder
material that will withstand the ravages of
time and use. Thin patterns of solid wood
are fine, but they can be fragile and
adversely affected by humidity. One of the
best permanent pattern-making materials is
$1/8$-in. birch plywood. It is indestructible
as a pattern, easily cut and shaped, and
dimensionally stabile. A standard sheet will
yield many patterns and pay for itself in
convenience and accuracy in the long run.

Original Methods

Most 18th-century cabinetmakers
approached drawing and pattern making in
much the same way as presented here. They
were not likely to waste time making full-
scale drawings when a descriptive sketch
and some wooden patterns would do. As
full-time professional cabinetmakers, they

A full-size drawing on posterboard can be cut apart to double as patterns.

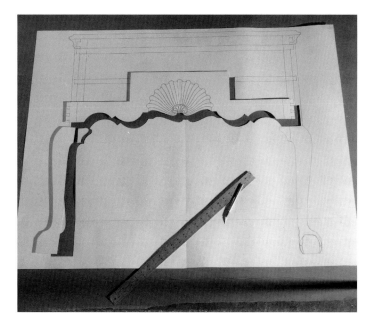

and more than one original has back boards that show these constructions.

Patterns and their shapes play an important role in tracing origins and evolutions of period pieces and their designs. Eighteenth-century makers relied primarily upon wooden patterns, many of which have survived to the present day and link existing pieces to a known maker's shop. These patterns were used repeatedly, and components for new pieces were likely adapted from the patterns of existing ones, so certain shapes became indicative of certain makers. As apprentices learned their trade in a shop, they would adopt the styling and make similar pattern shapes in their own practice. As with other aspects of cabinetmaking, regional styles and shapes developed, evolved and became more pronounced. The shapes of component parts became distinct features that give insight into the regional preferences, evolution of design, and travel and trade patterns of styles and makers.

did not need to know all the details of construction as presented in a formal working drawing; as cabinetmakers they had an innate sense for those. They did need to record important dimensions and shapes so they would not have to work them out from scratch again, and so they could repeat designs for other customers. As the manufacturers of their day, they were likely to repeat their designs more than a custom furniture maker of the present day, so their reliance on patterns for speed, consistency and quantity was great. With good patterns, even the less-skilled apprentices could produce furniture parts. There is clear evidence that patterns were also used for the finer details, like carved ornament. The distinctive knee carvings of John Goddard and John Townsend are consistent enough from knee to knee and piece to piece over a long period of time to have obviously been traced onto the knee from a pattern.

The only really formal drawings known from the period are those from the top designers and builders that were used to convey the designs to clients or other workmen. That is not to say that cabinet-makers did not use detailed drawings to develop their designs. A Newport block and shell desk-bureau is inscribed "Daniel Goddard—his draugh," implying that he had drawn and developed the design ahead of time. Often the details of an important

shape, like a pediment, would be designed in the building process and worked out on the piece of wood from which it would be cut. Sometimes these shapes would be developed on a piece of secondary wood,

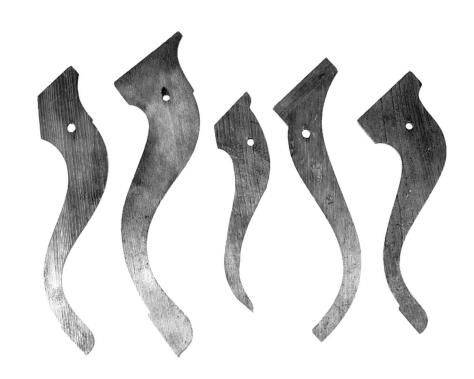

Cabinetmakers of the 18th century used wooden patterns to lay out the shapes of pieces quickly, accurately and repeatably. These patterns for the legs of tripod tables are from the workshop of the Dominy family of East Hampton, New York.
(COURTESY WINTERTHUR MUSEUM)

Part Three

EXAMPLES OF STYLE AND STRUCTURE

In studying American furniture of the 18th century, there's no substitute for a close examination of an original piece. The volume of literature on the subject is enormous and continually growing, but nothing is as direct as learning from the source. Those who handle original pieces agree that there are very few pieces from which they have not learned something, even if the piece only confirms what they already know. A firsthand familiarity with the original pieces makes design elements, construction details and regional similarities and variations clearly evident and recognizable. Furthermore, discovering the nature of 18th-century furniture from original examples seems to make the lessons learned more memorable and permanent.

The purpose of this section is to spotlight some examples of American furniture that are important to the study of the field. In American furniture history, the 18th century encompassed a wide variety of forms, methods of work and design philosophies. The nation, its people and their tastes were very different at the end of the century than they had been at the beginning. These pieces reflect those changes by tracing the evolution of furniture design through the era.

For each example, this survey begins with the objective information regarding a given piece: a description, the materials, date and place of origin, the identity of the maker (if known) and any other related historical information that may be available. Next follows a more subjective evaluation, in which the attributes of the design are discussed in the context of the prevailing design philosophies of the period. In other words, if the example is in the William and Mary style, what attributes make it so, and how effectively does it uphold the design principles that prevailed during the period when it was made? With a world of events, culture and commerce contributing to each of the major design trends of the century, examining how well a piece embodies those trends is a measure of the sophistication of its design.

By studying a very good example from a certain period, other examples may be compared and evaluated for their success in capturing the spirit of the era. There are many examples of Queen Anne tea tables in existence, but only a few capture the essence of the period and are everything a Queen Anne piece should be. In comparison, other pieces show a weakness in design or an aspect of incomplete development that makes them seem less impressive. This is not to imply that the others are not noteworthy, since every original has its story to impart, but on a relative scale of sophistication and execution, they may not represent as high a level of achievement.

It is also valuable to consider regional variations of the same type of piece; that is, how other makers who worked at the same time but in a different region were varying the style in accordance with local customs and tastes and their established methods of work. We shall also examine each piece in relation to others that came before and after. It is important to note where an example fits in relation to the development of the form. Knowing the prior and later development of the form places it in a more meaningful historical context.

Finally, and perhaps most importantly, the structure and construction details of each piece will be presented. This is not intended to be a section on how to build a specific piece of period furniture, but rather on how these pieces were built. The structural details and construction methods are important to the collector as a means of verifying the origin and authenticity of a piece. For the maker, the construction methods used in a particular piece can be applied to any similar design, and those same principles can be applied to almost any stylistic or regional variation. The fundamentals of the forms are primary, and how the forms were interpreted and executed by local craftsmen is secondary. One could even use these basics of structure to create purely original variations in the historically accurate manner of original makers. Regardless of the aim, the construction details of 18th-century American pieces are ingenious and intriguing and should be of interest to anyone interested in the furniture of the period.

WILLIAM & MARY

CHEST *with* DRAWERS

NEW ENGLAND, 1700–1750

Soft maple; white pine, chestnut

H 35¼ in.   W 38½ in.   D 18⅝ in.

case
W 36⅞ in.   D 17¾ in.

Courtesy
Yale University Art Gallery

Dressing table

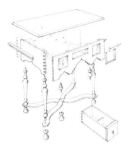

HISTORICAL NOTES

The Yale dressing table (see pp. 216-217) is similar in design to at least three other examples of Philadelphia origin. One of these is inlaid with the date 1724, and the other is thought to have been made shortly before the 1726 marriage of Catherine Johnson of Germantown, Pennsylvania. This table has a history of ownership in the Frankenfield family of Philadelphia, and it was part of the Reifsnyder Collection before being added to the Garvan Collection in 1929.

ANALYSIS

This dressing table exemplifies well the attributes of William and Mary–period designs. The case is held aloft by four well-developed, crisply detailed, turned legs. The legs are fountainlike in their flared shape. The pointed arches of the sides and arcaded front and the finial at the intersection of the cross stretchers add to the vertical emphasis of the design. The turned feet, flattened in their profile, are a reminder of the raised mass, and if four are not enough, a fifth center foot reinforces the idea. The legs, feet and drop and center finials have deep turned profiles and are the primary means of ornament.

The overall design is logical and orderly. The cyma-based pointed arches repeat in the profiles of the sides and front apron and are echoed in the shape of the cross-stretchers. The center foot and its finial provide a focal center for the symmetry of the design. The single, upward-pointing finial offers an interesting counter-point to the pair of drop finials extending from the case. The drawers, the openings of which are framed in double-arch moldings, are positioned directly above the three arches. The spaces between the drawers balance the spaces at the sides of the case, the latter being necessitated by the internal structure. The large cove molding under the top echoes the flare of the legs and eases the transition to the overhanging top, which, in turn, caps off the design.

RELATED FORMS

The basic structure of this piece is representative of most dressing tables of the William and Mary era. A similar type of construction was used throughout the colonies, and it continued to be used in Newport until near the end of the century. Besides regional variations in the shapes of turnings and aprons, New England examples typically do not have spaces between the drawers greater than the width of the applied double-arch molding, nor do they use a molding on the case below the top. Most New England examples have the case dovetails on the front of the case, where they are concealed under a thin vertical strip of wood or veneer.

STRUCTURAL NOTES

The case is of half-blind-dovetailed construction, with the exposed dovetails visible on the case back and the front of the case sides. Interior corner blocks extend the full height of the case and are pegged in place through the exterior (they are nailed from the case back). The front of the case is one board, with the three drawer openings cut from the solid. Two vertical blocks are glued to the inside of the case front between the drawer openings. They extend the full height of the case, with

Chest *with* Drawers

HISTORICAL NOTES

There is no known early history for this chest with drawers, but it is similar in design to many New England chests of the period. The use of chestnut in addition to soft maple and white pine suggests a western Rhode Island or eastern Connecticut origin. The high quality of the craftsmanship seems to rule out a more rural point of origin. The drawer construction is similar to methods used in, but not limited to, Rhode Island, and the case construction is not unlike that of Boston pieces.

This chest is one of many that simulate a case of drawers, though only the two bottom drawers actually slide out. The two upper drawers are the false fronts of a lift-top chest. This family of chests combined the traditional lift-top chest, with its large storage capacity, with the practicality of drawers in a single case.

ANALYSIS

One of the most notable aspects of this chest is its nearly square proportions. With these proportions it is similar to the upper cases of the high chests and chests-on-frame of the same era, and falls squarely between the horizontal format of the Jacobean-era designs and the more vertical aspects of Queen Anne–period ideals. In its imitation of the most fashionable four-drawer chests, the top false drawer front is larger than the second false front. This uneven graduation of drawers is reminiscent of earlier Boston chests with a similar layout. In this logic of design, the size of the top drawer is made to repeat that of the bottom drawer.

The figured maple is not intended to be ornamental, since this piece was probably painted originally. The ornament is limited to the applied double-arch moldings and the base and lid moldings. The mass of the case is raised by the ball feet on tapered discs, which through their oblate shape emphasize their weight-bearing role. The feet are inset from the corners, and the case was given a bold base molding to make the lift of the case, small as it is, evident.

RELATED FORMS

Chests of this type bridge a gap between rural and traditional methods of design and construction and the fashions and methods of more sophisticated urban centers. Cases of all drawers were common in urban areas by the turn of the century, and this design captures their appearance and some of their function without abandoning the traditional lift-top design. Less-refined examples feature ball feet in the front only, with extended case sides cut to form the rear feet. Among these chests, the drawers vary from uniform size on more rural examples to a careful and deliberate graduation of sizes on more refined versions. The placement of the brasses, which do not divide the drawer fronts evenly, reflects the relaxation of strict order in the second and third decades of the 18th century.

STRUCTURAL NOTES

The upper half of the front and the case back are nailed into rabbets in the case sides, while the case bottom is dovetailed to the case sides with relatively refined through dovetails. The bottom of the upper chest compartment is let into dadoes in the case sides. The drawer divider is dovetailed to the case sides, and the runners are nailed in place. The bottom drawer slides directly on the bottom of the case.

In the Boston manner, the base molding extends below the bottom of the case and glued base blocks are added to the bottom. The feet have turned tenons that fit into holes drilled through the base blocks and case bottom. The top is cut with an overhanging thumbnail molding on the front and sides. It is hinged with iron snipe-bill hinges. Two battens are nailed to the underside of the top.

The chestnut drawer sides and back are joined with fine dovetails. The drawer bottom is nailed to the sides and back and into a rabbet in the drawer front. Running strips are nailed to the bottom on either side of the drawer.

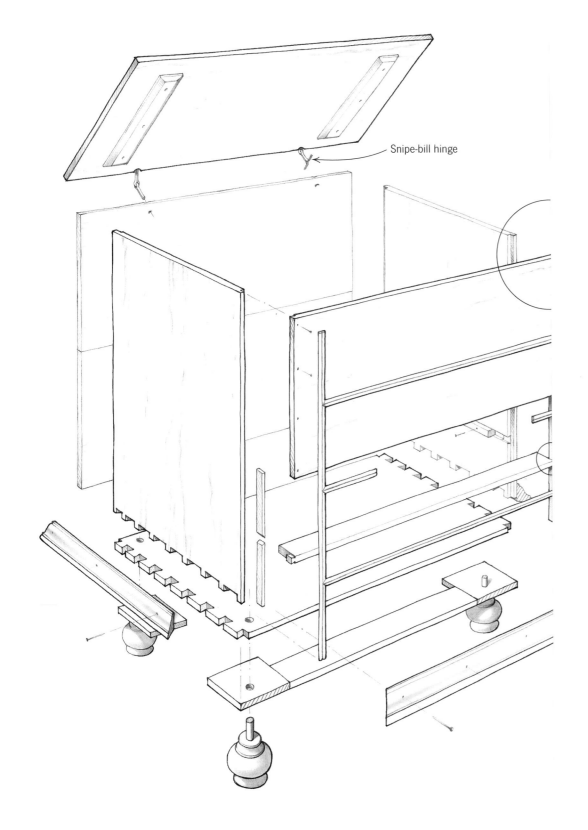

Snipe-bill hinge

PHILADELPHIA, 1700–1730

Black walnut; yellow pine

H 29 in.   W 33⅞ in.   D 20⅛ in.

case
W 28⅛ in.   D 18⅛ in.

Courtesy
Yale University Art Gallery

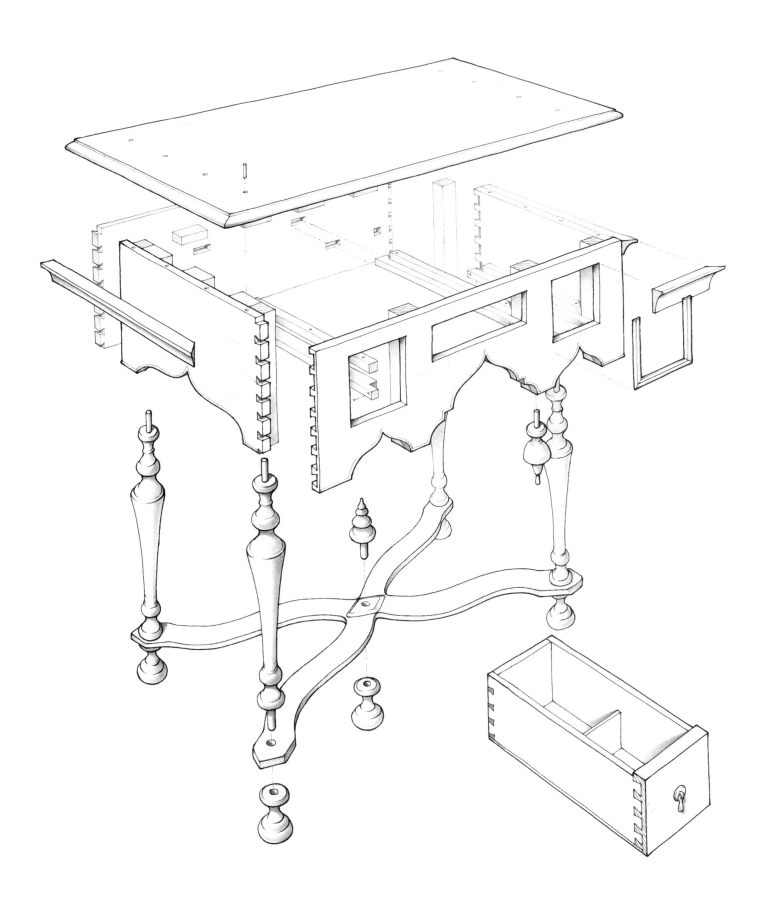

HIGH CHEST *of* DRAWERS

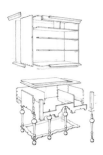

HISTORICAL NOTES AND ANALYSIS

This high chest of drawers exemplifies all the skills required of the cabinetmaker in the first quarter of the century, including turning, dovetail joinery of the case and drawers, veneering and finishing. In addition, the design is a complex combination of elements and shapes requiring a sophisticated sense of proportion to execute well. The design marks a radical shift from the earlier Jacobean aesthetics toward the loftier goals of 18th-century design.

High chests of this caliber are a marvel of organization and design. Its overall design exemplifies the vertical proportions and appearance of raised mass that were essential to the design goals of the period. The vertical thrust of the six powerful legs is capped by the strong horizontal moldings and drawer bandings. The design shows an orderly division of space in the careful graduation of drawer sizes. The shape of the lower case apron is reflected in the shape of the stretchers. All the drawer fronts are divided into equal sections by bookmatched veneer and an even spacing of the brass pulls and escutcheons.

The design and its component parts show a near obsession with symmetry and the logical division of space. The turned legs and feet are exceptionally bold, with a deep profile that emphasizes the raised mass of the case. The burled veneer provides a surface of intense visual interest. A complete analysis of the design of this piece is presented in Chapter 2.

RELATED FORMS

The level of development of furniture designs shows a close correlation with a region's prosperity as reflected by its growth rate. The population of Boston nearly doubled during the period when the William and Mary styles were in vogue, and this high chest is an example of the high development of the style during that period. The sophistication of design and quality of workmanship indicate that this piece originated in one of the better urban shops and was built for a client of means. Pieces of more rural origin were frequently made of indigenous woods and rarely achieve the level of veneering and fine sense of vertically formatted proportion of this example. A variation on the inverted cup turnings are flared trumpet turnings, which were seen later in the period. Many New York examples have three drawers across the top instead of the two seen here.

STRUCTURAL NOTES

The lower case shows a rare combination of construction methods. The front and sides are tenoned into front corner posts, a method that came into widespread use in the later Queen Anne era, but the sides and back are dovetailed together in the more prevalent William and Mary–period method. The legs are tenoned into the front corner posts and into glue blocks inside the rear of the case. The lower part of the legs is tenoned through the stretcher into the ball feet. The stretchers are half-lapped at the corners, and their inner profiles are glued onto the inside edge. (On some examples, the shape cut from the front of the stretcher was glued onto the inside.)

The vertical drawer dividers are nailed to the sides of the front apron on either side of the center drawer opening in a typically New England method and attached with a sliding dovetail to the back of the case. Drawer runners are nailed to either side of these dividers. The top of the lower case has feather-edged dustboards let into dadoes on the inside edge of the waist molding. That waist molding consists of a lower half attached to the base and an upper half attached to the upper case.

The upper case is dovetailed together with half-blind dovetails at the top and through dovetails at the bottom. The case sides are the tail pieces of the joints. The center drawer divider is dovetailed through the case, but the upper and lower dividers are let into dadoes. The upper divider is a dustboard of nearly full depth let into dadoes in the case side on which the top drawers slide.

The second- and third-level drawers ride on runners let into dadoes, and the lower drawer runs on the case bottom. Like the distinguishing feature of later Boston case pieces, the lower molding of the upper case extends below the case bottom and is reinforced by a series of glue blocks under the case. The drawers, with nailed-on bottoms, are through-dovetailed with wide tails at the front and back. The veneer on the drawer fronts conceals the exposed ends of the dovetail joinery.

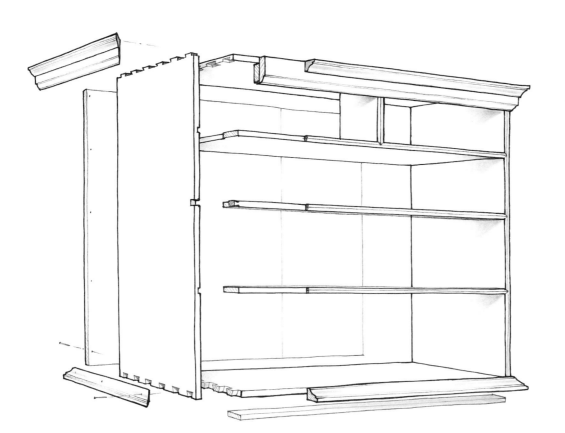

MASSACHUSETTS, 1700–1725

Maple; pine, burled maple and walnut veneer

H 65½ in.   W 40 in.   D 21⅜ in.

lower case
W 37½ in.   D 20 in.

upper case
W 35½ in.   D 19⅛ in.

Courtesy
Museum of Fine Arts, Boston

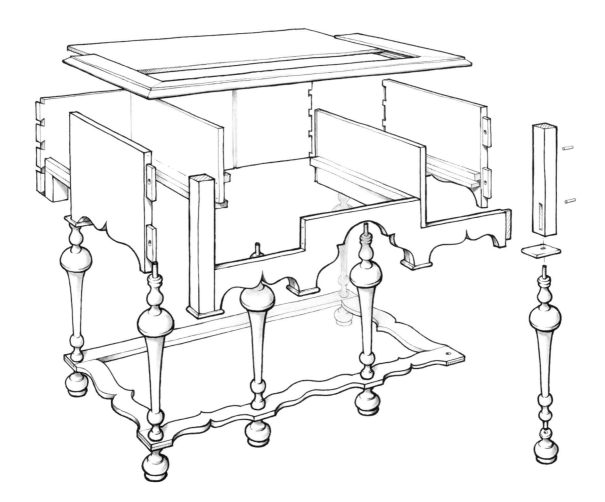

Drop-leaf gateleg table

HISTORICAL NOTES

Historic Deerfield's magnificent drop-leaf gateleg table was originally owned by Ruel Williams of Maine and has a history of ownership in the Bowdoin family. James Bowdoin III (1752–1811) founded Bowdoin College and was ambassador to Spain under President Thomas Jefferson. Drop-leaf tables had proven to be a practical solution to the need for a large dining surface that could be folded and stored when not needed. They had come into widespread use throughout the colonies by the end of the 17th century and were made in a wide range of sizes. While other New England gateleg tables may have been made of maple, the outstanding Boston examples were made of walnut. Like the turned chairs of the period, these tables were primarily the product of the turner's shop.

ANALYSIS

The bold turnings are certainly the major decorative element in this example, as they are in most gateleg tables of the era. The structure of William and Mary gateleg tables is limited to a framework of straight elements consisting of legs, rails and stretchers. Because they are turned, the legs and stretchers are straight and square in cross section. The design of this type of drop-leaf table shows the result of applying the decorative features of the day to purely utilitarian form: The structural parts are turned, but there are no purely decorative elements. In keeping with the period's emphasis on showing a raised mass, the legs and stretchers are emphasized by their turned detail, and the structure and complexity of the base become the focus of the design.

Like other turned elements in furniture of the period, the turnings are deep and bold, resulting in a rich and interestingly detailed overall appearance. The turned ring-and-baluster shape, a design from antiquity, is a common profile used in gateleg tables and chairs of the period. In New England tables, the profile is used in a symmetrical mirror image and repeated in each turned element, giving the base an orderly arrangement and logical division of space.

RELATED FORMS

The gateleg drop-leaf table was the predominant form of table for dining during the first quarter of the 18th century. Since these tables were numerous and in widespread use, a great many regional variations of the form evolved, most differing in turned detail. New York tables often employed urn-and-baluster shaped turnings, more of an English style, rather than the symmetrical baluster design shown here.

Throughout the colonies, the variations from stylish urban designs to less-refined rural interpretations were reflected in the shape of the turnings, which ranged from deep and robust to thin and timid. The same form was made in a range of sizes from 3 ft. to over 5 ft. in length. The frame often incorporated a drawer in one or both ends. This example features a drawer that is nearly as long as the frame. Turned ball feet are most common, but a few examples have Spanish feet. They are made with and without feet below the pivoting posts.

STRUCTURAL NOTES

This table is of pegged mortise-and-tenon construction throughout. The turned elements are from 2-in. square stock. The mortises and tenons are $\frac{3}{8}$ in. wide with a $\frac{3}{8}$-in. wide front shoulder. The joints are blind-pegged, with single pegs at the stretchers and double pegs at the rails. The gates swing on pivot posts with turned tenons let into drilled holes in the top rail and stretcher. The outer legs of the gates meet the rails and stretchers in half-lap joints.

The full-length drawer slides on a center runner that is let into the rail below the drawer and nailed to the underside of the back rail. To support the top, a cross brace is let into the top of the rails behind the drawer opening. The top and each leaf are made of two butted boards. The top is pinned to the frame, and the leaves are hinged with iron hinges. When they are raised, the leaves meet the top in a tongue-and-groove joint. (Rule joints with concealed hinges were not used until the advent of the Queen Anne style.) The long drawer has a pine back and sides, joined with two large but carefully made dovetails at each corner. The pine drawer bottom is nailed into a rabbet in the bottom of the drawer front and to the sides and back.

DROP-LEAF GATELEG TABLE

BOSTON, 1695–1720

Walnut; white pine

H 28¾ in.   W 50⅜ in.
D *(open)* 60¼ in.   D *(closed)* 20 in.

frame
W 39⅛ in.   D 17⅛ in.

Courtesy Historic Deerfield

ARMCHAIR

HISTORICAL NOTES

Banister-back chairs of this type illustrate the movement away from the severe rectilinear forms of Jacobean-era designs. The period term for a chair with arms was "elbow chair." Chairs of a similar design but with regional variations were made all along the New England and New York coast. The Gaines families of Essex County, Massachusetts, and nearby New Hampshire made exemplary chairs of this style, as well as related articles of furniture, and their name has come to be synonymous with this school of design. This chair was repainted black in 1963 since its original black paint had been removed sometime prior to 1928, when it was first lent to the museum. It has not been cut down or built up and retains its original dimensions.

ANALYSIS

The most striking feature of this chair is its tall, vertical format, especially in comparison to the joined frame-and-panel chairs of the previous century. Besides its proportions, a number of elements contribute to its

upward sweep, including tall Spanish feet, upwardly tapered turnings, upswept arms and a fountain-like crest-rail design. Unlike case pieces, there is no solid mass, and the design seems to revel in its absence, putting all its emphasis in unbounded vertical thrust.

The chair exhibits the symmetry and well-ordered division of space that is characteristic of the period. The stretchers are placed halfway between the seat and the floor and, in an unusual style, are all at nearly the same level. The five banisters extend upward from the mid-point of the back and are evenly spaced, so the distance between them is nearly equal to their own width. The shape of the banisters echoes that of the turned upper stiles that flank them, and the same tapered profile is used on the top of the front legs to support the arms.

The crowning element, the carved crest rail with C-scrolls and plumage, shows the influence of Flemish design and the Gibbons manner of deep and airy carving. This carving, along with the bold turnings and Spanish feet, creates a rich and

interesting surface. In case pieces of the period, this same intention of bringing focus to the surface was achieved through the use of burled veneers. The design, with its pierced carving and open spaces, foreshadows the more fully developed balance of solid and void employed in the subsequent phase of furniture design.

RELATED FORMS

Given that banister-back chairs were turned chairs, the turned decorative elements could be varied without altering the structure. But throughout the range of chairs the baluster shape and flared taper repeat as favorite turned designs, as does the ball-and-ring design of front stretchers. Similar chairs were made with turned ball feet, which were a less expensive alternative to carved Spanish feet. Flared Spanish feet require that the leg be sawn to shape from a larger piece of stock before it is turned. Ball feet may be turned from a straight piece of smaller stock. Regional variations are most pronounced in the design of the crest rail,

with most areas having preferred styles. Few, however, are as elaborate or sophisticated as this example.

STRUCTURAL NOTES

The armchair is of mortise-and-tenon construction throughout. The arm supports, seat rails and front stretcher have turned tenons fitting into drilled mortises. The side and medial stretchers end in square blocks and are tenoned into rectangular mortises $3/8$ in. wide. The medial stretcher is through-tenoned into horizontal mortises in the blocks of the side stretchers. The crest rail, lower banister rail and back of the arms are joined with conventional mortise-and-tenon joints, all of which are pegged.

ARMCHAIR

**COASTAL NEW ENGLAND
(PROBABLY MASSACHUSETTS), 1700–1720**

Maple and ash

H 47½ in.   W 23 in.   D 18 in.

*Courtesy
Museum of Fine Arts, Boston*

QUEEN ANNE

CHEST of DRAWERS

This five-drawer chest has many construction features that allow it to be attributed to John Townsend (1732–1809). Townsend served his seven-year apprenticeship in his father Christopher Townsend's shop starting at about age thirteen. The proportions of the drawers are similar to those of the upper case of a high chest made by Christopher Townsend in 1748. Later chests had a more even graduation of drawer sizes. The earliest piece signed and dated by John Townsend is a mahogany dining table dated 1756. From the design and execution of this chest, it is reasonable to assume it was made late in his apprenticeship or shortly after he became a journeyman. Traces of the original finish show that this was a deep red color, simulating mahogany. The feet and brasses have been replaced.

ANALYSIS

This Newport chest is a rare example of a Queen Anne chest built while the style was in fashion in a major coastal city. Apart from the brasses, applied case moldings and ogee bracket feet, there are no ornamental embellishments. The shape of the feet, like those of other Newport pieces of the period, offers a spring and lift to an otherwise boxlike case. The graduation of the drawers aids in giving the appearance of height. The graduation of their sizes is not even, but the two smaller drawers at the top balance the tall bottom drawer. The delicate case moldings finish off the top and bottom effectively without being strong horizontal elements that would otherwise make the case appear heavy or low. On a piece that is essentially a solid and square box, the graduation of the drawers, the moldings and the feet combine to give the design the subtle grace, lift and restrained ornament essential to the Queen Anne style.

RELATED FORMS

Chests of drawers of this simplicity were made throughout the middle to later part of the 18th century in the colonies. Such pieces were built to be functional, and, as a result, their simplicity often makes them difficult to date. It is only through the attribution given this chest that it may be dated to mid-century. Many examples of common chests were made with plain bracket feet, rather than the ogee bracket feet shown in this piece. While maple was commonly used as a primary wood in rural areas, its use in urban areas is largely overlooked. Price books of the period show that maple pieces were priced one-third less than identical mahogany pieces. Many of the finest houses were furnished with the best mahogany furniture on the first floor and in the largest bedrooms, but with maple furniture elsewhere.

The rarity of higher-style chests of drawers from this period is attributable to customers opting for chests-on-frame or high chests for greater visual impact. Blocked and other shaped fronts on chests did not come into use until the advent of the Chippendale-era's Rococo aesthetics.

STRUCTURAL NOTES

This chest is joined by through dovetails that are visible on the top and bottom of the case. The drawer dividers are joined to the case sides with shouldered dovetails. The drawer runners are nailed to the inside of the case but not let into dadoes as the shouldered dovetails suggest. The center drawer runner half-laps the top drawer divider and a similar horizontal support let into grooves at the back of the case. The back is nailed into rabbets provided in the top and sides. The case moldings are glued and nailed in place. The feet are joined to the case with mitered glue blocks.

The drawers are built in the Newport manner, with the bottoms extending through the drawer sides and running strips applied along the bottom sides. The top drawers were originally equipped with spring locks on their undersides, which are now missing. The drawer construction, proportions and moldings are indicative of Newport. The mitered glue blocks at the feet and the letters A through E in graphite on the back of the drawer fronts and backs indicate the hand of John Townsend.

CHEST *of* DRAWERS

NEWPORT, RHODE ISLAND, c.1750

Soft maple; white pine

H 41⅜ in.   W 37⅜ in.   D 20⅛ in.

case
W 35⅝ in.   D 19 in.

Private collection

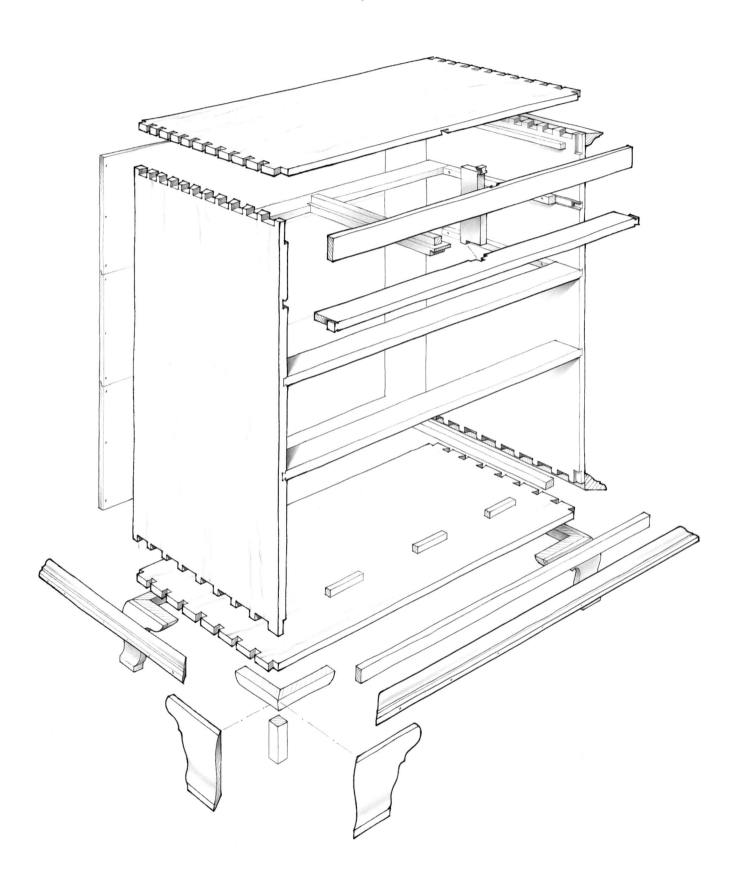

Flat-top high chest

HISTORICAL NOTES

Flat-top highboys, or high chests, in the Queen Anne style were the next evolution of the multi-legged William and Mary designs. The proportions and apron detail indicate that the high chest shown on p. 232 was made in the Hartford or Wethersfield area. Two existing high chests with arched-pediment tops are similar enough in detail and construction to have been made by the same maker. This indicates a busy, professional shop with consistent and repeated designs and well-established methods of work.

ANALYSIS

This remarkable high chest is a striking example of the Queen Anne style as it was practiced at a distance from the furniture-making centers of Boston and Newport. The arrangement and graduation of the drawers illustrates how their size and number were used to give the piece the appearance of height. Even without an arched pediment, the eye is drawn upward through a progression of increasingly smaller drawers.

The effect of the vertical format is augmented by the sense of lightness offered by the high, gently curved apron and slender legs. The legs themselves are exceptionally well shaped and support the case with grace. The length of the legs and the shape of the apron give the piece the spirited lift that is characteristic of the finest designs of the period. Given that lift, the space below the case becomes as much a part of the design as the case itself. The solid facade of the drawer fronts is punctuated by the upper and lower carvings, in keeping with the restrained use of ornament favored in the Queen Anne era.

RELATED FORMS

Flat-top high chests, while evolving from earlier designs, continued to be made concurrently with more elaborate (and expensive) bonnet-top designs. Early versions continued the wider proportions, apron designs and molding details of earlier examples. As the form developed, the ethereal goals of the Queen Anne style led to more delicate proportions, increased lift and the arched pediment or bonnet top.

This design, with four small drawers flanking a top center drawer and central upper and lower carved drawer fronts, was a favorite among Connecticut makers. Rhode Island highboys tend to have aprons with more dramatic scrolling, rarely have more than two drawers across the top, and are of slightly stouter proportions. The aprons of Rhode Island examples are more center-oriented, with reversing small-radius scrolls rising to a center drop finial. Boston and other Massachusetts makers opted for taller proportions, flat-topped apron arches and a pair of drop finials, the latter being vestigial remnants of William and Mary designs.

STRUCTURAL NOTES

The apron, sides and back of the base are tenoned into the posts of the four legs and secured with two or three pegs in each tenon. The sides and back are each joined to the legs with two large double-pegged tenons at each joint. The top front rail of the base is dovetailed to the top of the front legs. The drawer dividers throughout the piece are joined with shouldered dovetails, though the dovetails are only about $3/4$ in. deep. The drawer runners in the base are $3/4$ in. thick and taper to $3/8$ in. at either end. They are mortised into the case back and let into rabbets in the front apron.

In the upper case, the top, sides and bottom are through-dovetailed, with the top and bottom as the tail pieces. A rail is let into rabbets in the back of the case sides to support runners for the top bank of drawers. These runners are mortised into the top drawer divider and back rail. The boards that form the vertical dividers for the top drawers are let into grooves in the center drawer runners and dadoes in the case top. The drawer runners on the case sides and vertical dividers are nailed in place. The top molding is a composite of two molded shapes, glued and nailed to the case. The waist molding is glued and nailed to the base. The drawers have thick ($5/8$ in.) sides, backs and bottoms and are joined with large dovetails. The drawer bottoms are let into grooves in the drawer sides and front and nailed to the under-side of the back.

Flat-top high chest

CONNECTICUT, 1750–1780

Cherry; white pine

H 71½ in.

upper case
W 35 in.   D 18⅞ in.

lower case
W 37⅝ in.   D 20⅛ in.

Private collection
(Photo courtesy Israel Sack, Inc., N.Y.C.)

BONNET-TOP HIGH CHEST

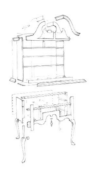

HISTORICAL NOTES

The high arching apron, slipper feet and arched pediment show this chest to be unmistakably of Newport origin. Pages from a 1765 Marblehead account book are pasted on the back of the upper case, covering gaps in the back boards. The three finials and plinths were added early in the history of the piece, since they are quite old. Their profile is not unlike that of other finials from the Boston and North Shore area. With Quaker communities in both Newport and northern Massachusetts, a history in the Marblehead area seems likely.

A very similar high chest with a flat top is inscribed "Christopher Townsend made 1748," and is one of the few Newport pieces that is signed and dated. The signed piece serves as a reference by which pieces of similar design and construction, like this one, may be compared. Based on those similarities and known Townsend methods, this high chest is attributable to Christopher Townsend (1701–1773) as well.

ANALYSIS

All the definitive elements of the Queen Anne style are embodied in this piece. The apron features reverse scrolls that give the base a high lift above the floor. This shape is identical to that of other early Newport high chests, and is seen on some dressing tables as well. The well-curved cabriole legs terminate in slipper feet. In combination, the feet, legs and apron give the piece a stable but light stance. They suggest a spring in its carriage and a great lift in its base. The upper case has evenly graduated drawer heights and is crowned with a pediment of academically perfect proportions. Originally, the central opening would have held one finial. Even without the added plinths and finials, the open pediment and arched moldings give the upper case a sophisticated loftiness.

This high chest is a virtual checklist of the Queen Anne–era ideals of furniture design. The lift of the base and the soaring pediment extend the vertical format of the design while belying the mass of such a piece. The balance of solid and void is used effectively in the top

as well as in the base, as both areas invite the viewer to examine the spaces left by the solid. Finally, the period's ideal of smooth, uninterrupted surfaces is evident in the solid facade of plain drawer fronts.

RELATED FORMS

The design of this high chest typifies the form and proportions of Newport high chests of the era, but regional variations abound in the design of major pieces such as this. The differences are most obvious in the shape of the apron, legs and pediment, and in the proportions of the case and its divisions of space. For example, Boston makers often used an apron design of flat-topped arches with a pair of drop finials. The Wethersfield area had an identifiable apron design distinguished by a double half-round shape in the center, as seen in the example of a flat-top Queen Anne high chest. The shape of the arched pediment and its openings is characteristic of the Newport school, and other areas used distinctly

different proportions. The use of slipper feet was largely confined to the Newport area, with Dutch or pad feet the norm elsewhere.

STRUCTURAL NOTES

In the Newport manner, the front and back of the lower case are dovetailed to the sides. Thin vertical strips on the front outside edges conceal the front dovetails from view, but the back dovetails are visible from the rear. The blocks of the legs extend about 6 in. into the inside corners of the case and are positioned there with glue blocks. These legs are glued in position, but those of similar high chests (and dressing tables) were frequently left unglued so they could be slipped out for ease of shipment.

Within the lower case, the drawer dividers are pine, fronted with 1/4-in. mahogany strips. The horizontal divider is dovetailed into the front of the case sides. The top rail is nailed into rabbets in the top of the case sides. The vertical dividers are nailed into a rabbet in the apron rail on either side of the center drawer, secured with glue blocks behind the apron, and let into

NEWPORT, 1745–1765

Mahogany; white pine, maple, chestnut

H 81½ in. *(not including finial)*
W 39¼ in.   D 21½ in.

upper case
W 36⅛ in.   D 18¾ in.

lower case
W 37⅝ in.   D 19¾ in.

Courtesy Historic Deerfield

dadoes in the horizontal divider. The three lower drawers ride on runners in the center of the drawer openings, which are let into rabbets in the front rail and mortises in the case back. Guides are nailed to the case sides and tenoned into the vertical dividers and case back. Runners for the upper drawer are half-lapped to the drawer divider and let into mortises in the back. Guides for the upper drawer are nailed to the runners. Kickers for the upper drawer are nailed to the underside of the upper case.

In the upper case, the top and bottom are dovetailed to the sides. The drawer dividers are pine, fronted with mahogany, and joined to the case sides with shouldered dovetails. To note their assembly position they are marked in graphite A, B and C, from top to bottom, in a recognizable Townsend family script. The drawer runners are nailed to the case sides. Behind the upper drawer divider, a rear rail is let into dadoes in the back sides of the case. A center runner for the top two drawers is half-lapped to the front divider and tenoned into the rear rail. The vertical divider is let into dadoes in the top divider and case top.

The front pediment board is nailed to the front of the case top. The bookmatched panels were applied after installation of the board, since they cover the nail holes. The rear pediment board is attached to the top of the case. Two stringers connect the pediment boards at the top and bottom of the curve on each side. The thin pine covering boards are nailed to the pediment boards and stringers. The pediment moldings are glued and nailed to the case sides, front pediment board and upper stringers. The waist molding is glued and nailed to the upper case, extending below the bottom by about ⅛ in. to cover any gap between the two halves.

The drawers are made in the typical Newport manner, with fine dovetails and the drawer bottom nailed to the sides and back and let into a dado in the front. Running strips are applied along the lower sides of the bottom. The lower three drawers, which ride on center runners, are flush-bottomed, with the bottom nailed into a rabbet in the drawer front and onto the sides and back. The two top drawers have spring locks that are ingeniously dovetailed into the drawer bottoms. The drawers in each case are lettered in graphite A through E and A through D. The script is upright on the inside of the drawer back, indicating that it was written before the bottom was attached. This is the same structure used on Newport dressing tables, and a continuation of the high chest structure of the William and Mary period.

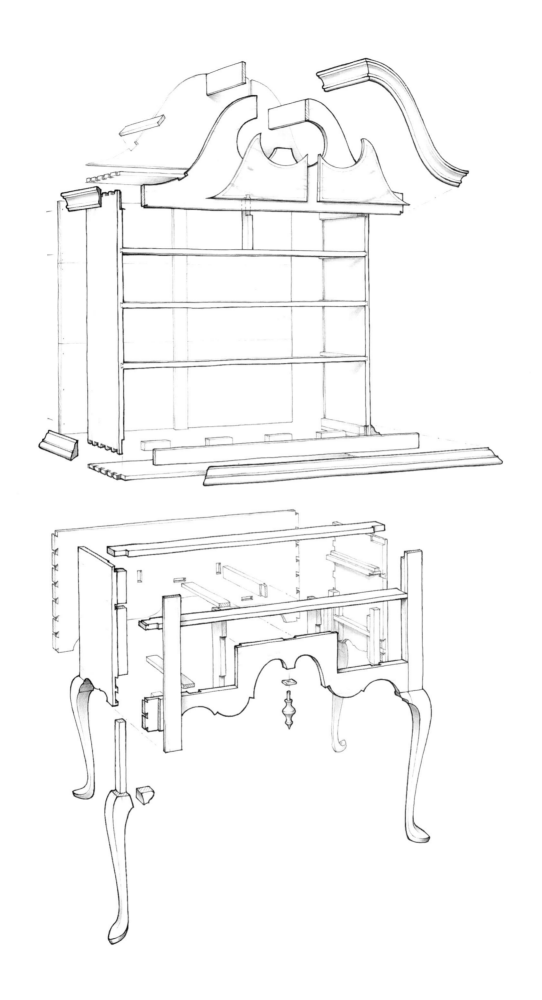

Dressing table

HISTORICAL NOTES

Little is known of the history of this dressing table but a great deal may be inferred from its style and structure. Its styling is that of a Boston piece, and it reveals the work of an urban shop in its details. String inlay, although usually associated with the Federal era, was used to outline the drawer fronts and other significant features of some Boston pieces. The inlaid fan is a detail more commonly seen on English case pieces, but it was a detail adopted by some Boston cabinetmakers.

ANALYSIS

Albert Sack has called this lowboy "a little thoroughbred" because of its perfect proportions, crisp detailing, academic cabriole legs and nut-brown walnut color. As an example of the American Queen Anne aesthetic in lowboys, this piece has few equals. As if in a reaction to the busy design of William and Mary lowboys, the Queen Anne design exudes a quiet calm. Replacing the frenzied assemblage of stretchers and elaborately turned feet and legs are four

smooth, graceful and refined cabriole legs. The legs end in the delicate wafers of thin pad feet. The flat-top arches span the stance of the piece with a calm repetition, punctuated by a pair of drop finials.

The ease with which the case is borne testifies to the period's aim of diminishing the apparent weight of the piece. The space below the case, as outlined by the apron shape and legs, becomes important in showing the lift of the design. The surface is smooth throughout, with a warm glow from the walnut. The lone surface ornament is the concave inlaid fan, which continues the smooth surface across what would otherwise be a carved fan or shell. The thin top caps off the design, and its large overhang makes the case appear smaller.

RELATED FORMS

Similar aesthetics are shown in other dressing tables of the era, though they are expressed by different means. Most examples have a carved fan or shell central to their design. Those that do not usually have a central focal point in their apron shape or drop finials. In each case, the

shape of the legs and the profile of the apron are important design elements and are key to achieving the grace and lift that characterize the period. Dressing tables were often made *en suite* with high chests so they share the same regional variations in structure, proportion, design and detailing, but at about 80% the size of the base of a high chest. Since they also share a kinship with tables, dressing tables can exhibit features associated with tabletops. The most striking top feature is the scalloped-top treatment of the Connecticut River Valley, which was applied to tables, chests and dressing tables.

STRUCTURAL NOTES

The sides, back and front apron rail are tenoned into the legs. This is an important structural change from earlier William and Mary designs, where the case was dovetailed together and the legs were tenoned into interior corner blocks. Here, the sides and back are joined to the legs with a series of three tenons at each joint. The front and back tenons are pegged, the sides are not. The fronts of the drawer

dividers are angled and rest in angled pockets in the front rail, which is a feature of urban Boston shops. The center drawer runners are tapered to $3/8$ in. and fit into mortises in the back of the case. The backs of the side runners are nailed to the rear legs. The drawer dividers are joined with shouldered dovetails. The top rail is dovetailed to the top of the front legs. The top is pinned to the case sides with four pins on each side. The knee blocks overlap the case sides and front and are glued in place.

The drawers have thin ($5/16$ in.) sides, backs and bottoms and are joined with delicate dovetails. The drawer bottom is nailed into a rabbet in the drawer front and nailed to the sides and back. Running strips are applied along the sides of the bottom in the Newport manner. Lest the details and ideals of Queen Anne–era furniture construction seem too serious, the drawer sides and backs have chalk drawings of geometric designs, chickens (or ducks or geese) and a lobster from early in the history of the piece.

Dressing Table

BOSTON, 1735–1750

Walnut; pine

H 29½ in.   W 34 in.   D 19⅛ in.

case
W 30 in.   D 17 in.

Private collection
(Photo courtesy Israel Sack, Inc., N.Y.C.)

TEA TABLE

HISTORICAL NOTES

Historic Deerfield's Queen Anne–style tea table is similar to a number of other rectangular New England tea tables, especially two illustrated in *The Magazine Antiques* (December 1970, inside front cover, and November 1930, p. 446), one of which was owned by Nathaniel Hawthorne. All of them have characteristics that point to an eastern Massachusetts origin. This table is in black paint, and the use of paint as an original finish is suggested by the use of two different hardwoods in the construction. The styling of the table is consistent with well-developed coastal pieces, but the ridges along the top of the feet indicate an origin in other than an urban shop.

ANALYSIS

It would be difficult to find an example of 18th-century American furniture that better embodies the Queen Anne–era ideals of design than this tea table. The slender cabriole legs, which are only ⅝ in. thick at the ankles, exude the utmost in grace, and flow smoothly from the feet into the apron of the table. These legs give the piece an unusually high degree of lift, yet their wide stance ensures exceptional stability. The cabriole legs themselves are remarkable in that their shape has enough of a cyma curve to give the piece a quality of buoyancy. That shape, exceptionally well rendered in figured maple, is a careful balance between straighter legs that appear stiff and lifeless and those which have an exaggerated curve.

The thin apron, with its scrolled skirt and delicately molded top, reinforces a sense of lightness in the piece. The surfaces are smooth and without embellishment. The uncluttered design allows the silhouette of the table to be as interesting as the table itself, which exemplifies the era's desire to balance the visual interest of solid forms with the voids they delineate.

RELATED FORMS

Rectangular tea table designs were favored in the New England colonies. Among them, Massachusetts examples showed some of the highest levels of sophistication in overall proportions and the integration of the design as a whole. The high degree of aesthetic refinement is one important factor in attributing this table to an eastern Massachusetts origin. Newport makers made similar tables, but usually with a straight apron rather than the scrolled design. They also used the distinctive Newport slipper foot in their tables, and continued the design with ball and claw feet into the third quarter of the century.

Connecticut tables in this form usually feature a more elaborate layering of moldings, which give the piece a decidedly different appearance. The Connecticut versions often lack the sleek, ethereal qualities of well-executed Massachusetts examples. More formal versions of New England tea tables include candle slides on either end.

STRUCTURAL NOTES

Just as this is an example of simple elegance in design, so it is in construction. The rails of the frame are tenoned into mortises in the legs. Each joint is double pegged with pegs that stop flush with the inside surface. The scrolled aprons are applied to the outside of the frame, and the scrolled shape is cut into both the apron and rail. The underside of this shaping is rough and shows the marks of chisels and rasps. The top is two butted boards, about ⅝ in. thick, which are nailed to the top of the frame sides. The surrounding molding is one piece, nailed to the outside edge of the top and mitered at the corners.

From the underside, the table looks quite spartan; there are no glue blocks, extended pegs or cross braces, only the secondary surfaces of the top, rails and legs. Like any virtuoso, the craftsman who built this table made it look easy. One interesting note is that the back of one side rail shows the marks of a water-powered reciprocating-saw blade, indicating a point of origin that was developed enough to support a hardwood-cutting sawmill.

TEA TABLE

EASTERN MASSACHUSETTS, 1730–1760

Maple and cherry

H 25¾ in. W 28½ in. D 21¼ in.

Courtesy Historic Deerfield

SIDE CHAIR

HISTORICAL NOTES

This side chair is attributed to a member of the Proud family. John Proud (1714–1794), Joseph Proud (1711–1769) and William Proud (1720–1779) were all chairmakers working in the Newport and Providence area. The chair was stained a light-brown color to simulate walnut, one of the more desirable woods of the period. Others are known to have been painted black to simulate the ebonized finish of English chairs made of beech. This chair is one of a pair from what was probably a larger set; it is identical to those in a set in the collection of the Society for the Preservation of New England Antiquities and one belonging to the Newport Historical Society.

ANALYSIS

This example embodies the elements of the Queen Anne style with a simple sophistication. While there are more elaborate examples with curved compass seats and carved shells on the crest rails or knees, this piece relies on form and line

without undue ornamentation. The solid shapes and voids are well balanced, avoiding either a chunky or spindly appearance. The carefully shaped profiles of the back and seat rails invite looking through as well as at the chair. The curves flow smoothly from one component into another. The front legs are shaped fully round from just below the knee to the foot, avoiding the angular appearance of square-section cabriole legs. The shape of the rounded knee is carried up through the leg block to the edge of the seat. The curve of the cabriole leg is restrained, in keeping with the quiet refinement of the overall design. The stretchers are delicate, crisply detailed and visually interesting without distracting from the composition. The Queen Anne–era ideals of lightness, grace and balance of solid and void are well met.

RELATED FORMS

Similar chairs made in Boston at the same time are nearly identical, but a closer examination shows that the Rhode Island chair is more delicate in

the splat, legs and turned stretchers. Higher-style chairs from both areas added compass seats, carved shells on the crest rail and knees, more elaborately shaped stiles and splats, voluptuous cabriole legs and sometimes ball and claw feet.

Philadelphia versions tended toward more elaborate backs with compass seats. Philadelphia compass seats consist of side rails tenoned into the front rail, with the front legs joined to the bottom of the seat assembly with a single turned tenon. New York, Newport and Boston chairs with compass seats were built with the seat rails tenoned into the leg blocks, which extended to the top of the seat and were shaped to follow the compass curve. Their structure was similar to this example in that regard.

STRUCTURAL NOTES

This chair is of pegged mortise-and-tenon construction throughout, with the exception of the medial and back stretchers, which have turned round tenons fitting into corresponding drilled holes. The drilled holes for the pegged

joints are blind, stopping short of extending through the rear of the joined pieces. The side stretchers are joined to the front legs by a tenon that is the full height of the stock from which it was turned, leaving the back of the tenon exposed in the mortise. This is a typical period method of joining the stretcher to the leg.

All the tenons are cut so as to extend straight from their components, and they fit into angled mortises. The seat-rail tenons are mortised into the front legs and shouldered at the top so as not to be exposed when the seat rabbet is cut into the top of the leg block. The small tenons that extend from the stiles into the crest rail are shouldered on the outside edge, making them hidden from the outside, but the joint is visible from under the crest rail. Those joints are pegged from the back. The sides of the splat have a simple bevel, and the back edges of the stiles and crest rail feature a continuous chamfer.

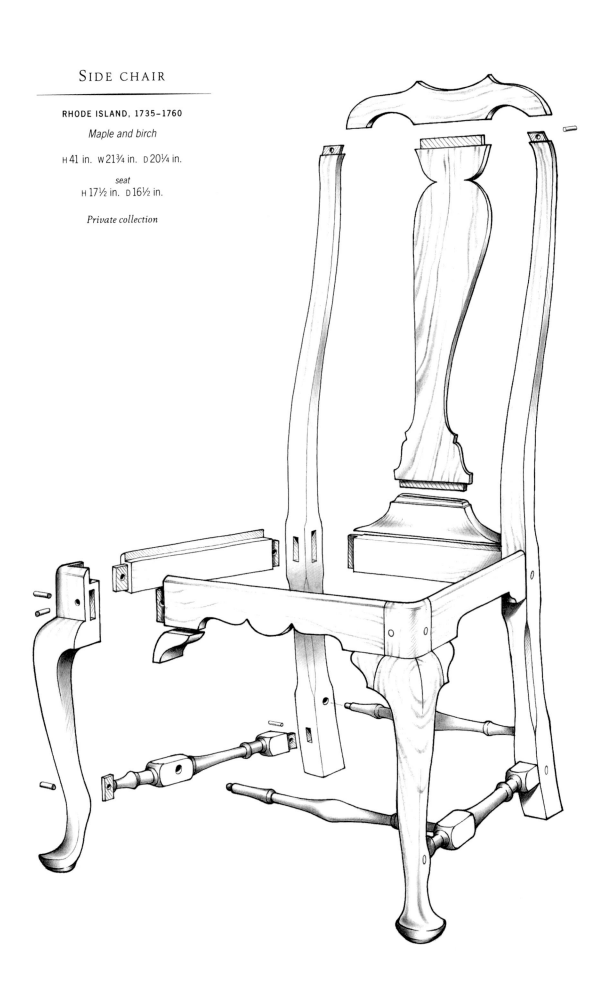

SIDE CHAIR

RHODE ISLAND, 1735–1760

Maple and birch

H 41 in.   W 21¾ in.   D 20¼ in.

seat
H 17½ in.   D 16½ in.

Private collection

CARD TABLE

HISTORICAL NOTES

Card tables are an intriguing blend of practicality and period design philosophy. Besides being a piece intended for a specific purpose, a card table, like a tea table, was furniture central to a social activity. As a result, the design was required to be functional while incorporating the attributes of the finest furniture of the day. The Boston card table shown on pp. 248-249 is important not only for its folding-top form, but also for retaining its original needlework top.

A similar example, in the Bayou Bend Collection, belonged to Peter Faneuil (1700–1743), one of Boston's most successful merchants. His ownership of such a table testifies to its age and the social status associated with a table of this caliber.

ANALYSIS

The turreted corners are based on English examples of the period and help the function as well as the aesthetics of this design. The turrets allow the front cabriole legs to be spaced farther apart, offering more knee room below the table (a persistent shortcoming of 18th-century tables), and give

the piece a wider and more stable appearance. The rounded turret shape is continued to the shape of the tabletop, and provides ideal places for shallow candlestick wells in each of the four corners. These wells, the scooped pockets for counters and the inset needlework top are outlined by a checkered string inlay of alternating black and white wood. The accordion-like action of the side rails in extending the rear legs gives the appearance of full-length sides when the top is open, a point important to the aesthetics of the piece and a feature missing from tables with swinging fly legs.

In total, this card table exhibits the high and lofty stance of Queen Anne–era design. The slender cabriole legs accentuate the vertical aspect of the form and support the table with ease. The thin table frame spans the legs and minimizes any appearance of weight that may be associated with the structure. The shape of the top, the turrets, the molded blocks abutting the turrets, and the rounded knees of the legs are the smooth curved surfaces that preclude the need for further ornamentation in Queen Anne–style furniture.

RELATED FORMS

This form of card table, with a folding top and a hinged or folded mechanism to support it, began a long tradition of similarly designed tables that continued well into the 19th century. There were clear advantages in a functional and useful table, the top of which was protected by its folding, that could double as an attractive side piece when not in use. The form was given Chippendale-era features in the second quarter of the 18th century, and was brought to a high level of development by New York cabinetmakers, who often added a fifth fly leg. The table reached a stylistic crescendo in the Federal period since its form was well suited to the design ideals of that period. This style of turreted corner, which was also used by Philadelphia cabinetmakers, influenced tea-table design, and a number of related turreted tea tables have Boston and Philadelphia origins. The shape of the tabletop is thought to have been the inspiration for the family of Rhode Island porringer-top tables.

STRUCTURAL NOTES

The front turrets are an integral part of the structure of this piece. The front and side rails are tenoned into the turned turrets, as are the cabriole legs. The knee blocks are glued to the underside of the turrets, and the molded blocks abutting the turrets are glued in place. A pine cross-brace is let into the rear underside of the side rails, where it is nailed in place and doubles as a back rail and a support for the drawer runners. The back rail is tenoned into the rear legs. The folding side rails are hinged to the front and back of the table with a pair of iron hinges at each joint.

The center joints, which fold inward, are hinged with brass card-table hinges let into the top and bottom of the rails. The top folds on the same type of hinge. A total of 14 hinges are used to deploy the rear legs and unfold the top. A rotating cleat on the inside of the back rail locks into a shallow mortise on the underside of the tabletop to lock the structure closed. The front half of the top is attached by two screws extending from pockets in the front rail. The dovetailed drawer uses chestnut as a secondary wood, and the drawer bottom is nailed in place.

CARD TABLE

BOSTON, 1730–1750

Mahogany; pine, chestnut

H 27 in. W 35⅝ in. D 35⅛ in.

Courtesy
Museum of Fine Arts, Boston

CARD TABLE

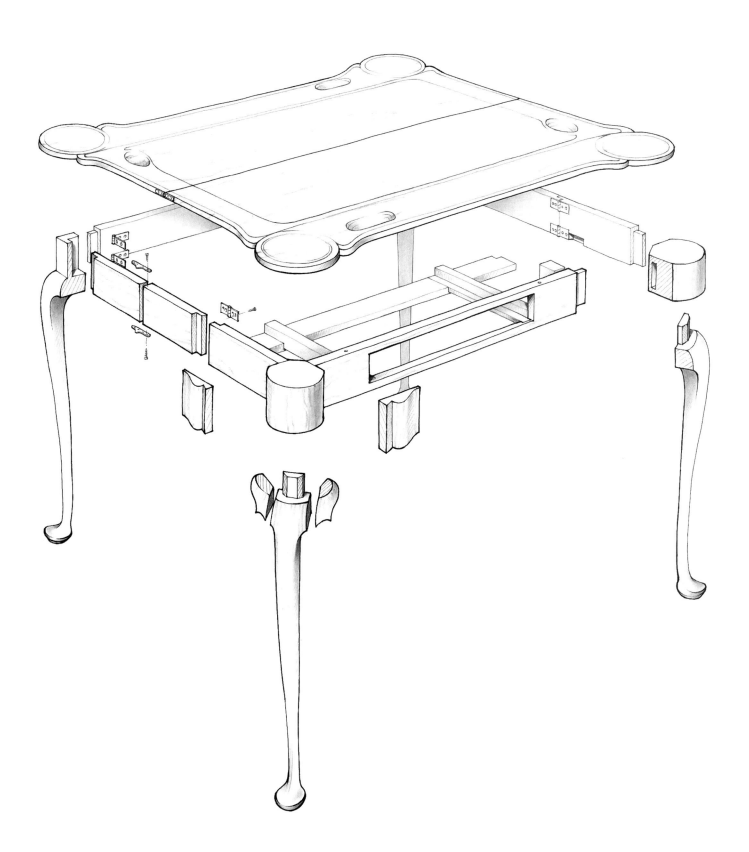

Easy chair

HISTORICAL NOTES

Easy chairs came into use early in the 18th century, and at first exhibited many qualities of William and Mary designs. By the second quarter of the century, they were improved for comfort and appearance and made to incorporate Queen Anne–era aesthetics. They continued to be made in the same manner with only stylistic changes through the Neoclassical period. Easy chairs were very expensive in their day; the frame of the chair represented only about 20% of the cost of such a piece. This example typifies southern New England easy-chair design and construction. A nearly identical chair that retains its original padding and wool worsted upholstery is in the Brooklyn Museum (see the photo on p. 252).

ANALYSIS

The functional requirements of an easy chair limit its aesthetics qualities, but the ideals of the era are evident nonetheless. The flowing curves that were fundamental to Queen Anne–period design are worked all through the shape of this chair. Every edge has a graceful shape, and the effect is sculptural. A well-designed Queen Anne easy chair is to be admired from every angle. This example includes a compass or balloon-shaped seat in addition to the contours of the arms, wings and crest rail. While it is difficult to incorporate the usual Queen Anne–period ideals of loft and lightness into such a piece, the cabriole legs and stretchers do emphasize a comfortable support of the frame. In its complexity, the base offers an interesting play of solid and void that is offset by the soft grace of the upholstered parts. Whereas Queen Anne case pieces exhibit a lofty grace, easy chairs exude a relaxed ease. In their own way, they show the same elegance, tempered by restraint, as other pieces of the era.

RELATED FORMS

Easy chairs share many structural and stylistic similarities with the side (and arm) chairs of the period, and are no less sophisticated. A similar type of joinery and detail was used on the legs and stretchers of both chairs, and, given the usual regional differences, they are an aid in determining a probable place of origin. This example has a front (medial) stretcher with block ends that is tenoned into the side stretchers, a method used in, but not limited to, Newport and Boston. Most easy chairs of the period have a stretcher with turned tenons that fit into drilled holes in the side stretchers. Such block ends on the stretcher are usually associated with later Chippendale-era chairs. Those later chairs, showing the subdued New England inter-pretation of the Rococo, are likely to have straight front and side seat rails tenoned into the front leg posts, a serpentine crest rail, ball and claw feet, and perhaps carvings on the knees. These features give the later designs a crisp, detailed quality that is a change from the relaxed ease and inviting shape of Queen Anne easy chairs.

STRUCTURAL NOTES

The frame of this chair is maple, with the exception of the highly visible front legs and front and side stretchers, which are walnut. The rear legs are continuous with the stiles, and are maple, as is the turned rear stretcher. The rear and side seat rails are tenoned into the rear legs. The side seat rails are tenoned into the front seat rail. Both the side and front seat rails are shaped on the inside and outside surfaces. The front legs are joined by a single large dovetail extending into the front seat rail. They are reinforced by large, glued knee blocks. The side stretchers are tenoned into the front and rear legs like those on Queen Anne side chairs. The front stretcher is joined with

NEW ENGLAND, 1730–1760

Walnut; maple, white pine

H 47 in.   W 37 in.   D 25¾ in.

seat
H 12⅞ in.   W 30⅝ in. *(front)*, 23¾ in. *(rear)*   D 23⅞ in.

Upholstered chair:
Courtesy The Brooklyn Museum
Frame only:
Courtesy The Metropolitan Museum of Art

horizontal tenons to the side rails. The crest and lower back rails are tenoned into the stiles. (On other chairs, the stiles are sometimes tenoned into the crest rail.)

The wing components and arm supports are tenoned into the stiles and seat rails. (On some other chairs, the top of the wing joins the stile in a half-lapped dovetail joint.) The horizontal arm rests are screwed to the vertical wing stiles and nailed to the top of the conical arm supports. The inner half of each conical arm support is maple, and the outer half, nailed to the inner, is white pine. All the mortise-and-tenon joints are pegged, with the exception of the front and rear seat rails, the crest and lower back rails and the front stretcher.

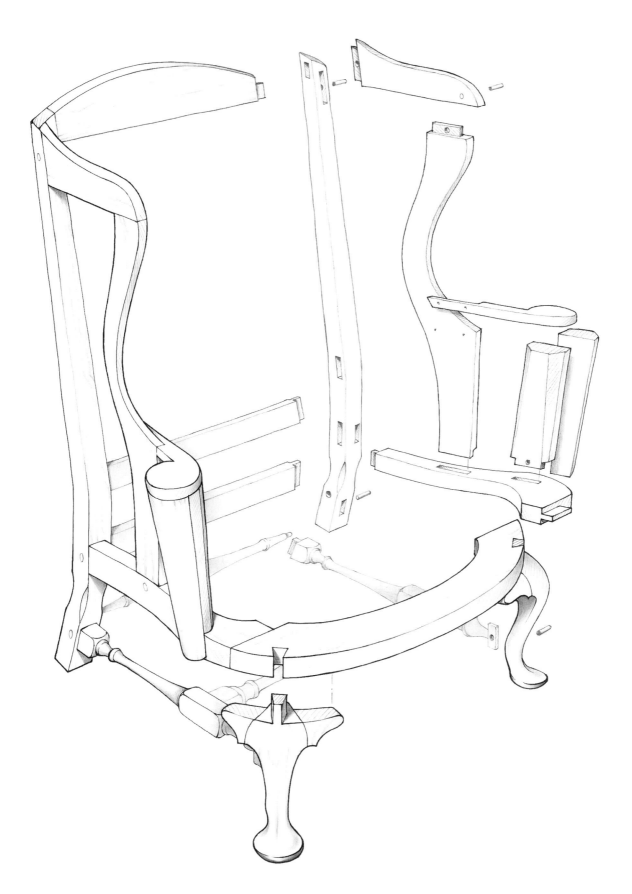

CHIPPENDALE

REVERSE-SERPENTINE
CHEST *of* DRAWERS

HISTORICAL NOTES

Historic Deerfield's stately reverse-serpentine-front chest of drawers has the attributes that suggest it was made in one of the better Boston cabinetmaking shops. Among the many chests made with shaped fronts as part of the Chippendale aesthetic, it ranks high in terms of development and sophistication, indicating an urban origin. It also shows several features of design and construction that are typical of Boston case pieces. The chest has old brasses and a pleasant, glowing patina. The underside of the case has mid-20th-century restoration work, which is not readily visible.

ANALYSIS

The serpentine front, like the bombé and block-front shapes, was a treatment by which cabinetmakers instilled Chippendale-era aesthetics into case pieces in the fourth quarter of the 18th century. Structurally, this chest varies little from those that preceded it, but aesthetically it is very different. By keeping the overhang of the top to a minimum, the maker maintained a solid, rectilinear form and maximized the appearance of the case width. Overhanging tops tend to reduce the apparent width and depth of the case and cap the height. To this solid mass of the case, the reverse-serpentine front adds an element of depth. Such curved-front treatments imply mass and increase the presence of the case. The curved front also yields patterning in the grain of the mahogany that would not be seen with a flat front. The result is a rich, deep and visually interesting surface.

Bold polished brasses, aligned along the highest and lowest points in the profile, highlight the shape of the front and contrast with the rich mahogany. The powerful Boston feet, with swept-back side talons and flattened balls, exude a commanding presence and radiate the strength required to support such a case. The combined effect is a powerful expression of opulence and dignity that does not need to be augmented with carving or embellishments to achieve its design goals.

RELATED FORMS

Similar chests with serpentine fronts are shaped with the concave curves at the drawer pulls and the convex curve at the center. There is little difference between the two, but the reverse-serpentine shape, with two convex curves across the front, offers a fuller appearance to the case and results in an obtuse rather than acute angle at the front corner. Some find this to be more aesthetically pleasing and more in keeping with the design goals of the period. Block-front cases bring the same focus to the front surface and add strong vertical lines and an intricacy of detail to the facade.

STRUCTURAL NOTES

The top is joined to the case sides with sliding dovetails that are barefaced on the outside of the case and angled on the inner side. The bottom is dovetailed to the sides with a series of through dovetails, the bottom being the tail piece of the joints. The mahogany-fronted drawer dividers, with cockbeads cut from the solid, are joined with shouldered dovetails to the case sides. A thin ($\frac{1}{4}$ in. thick) strip of wood, with the vertical cockbead cut from it, is applied to the front edges of the case sides to conceal the dovetails. The drawer runners are nailed to the case sides. The bottom drawer slides directly on the bottom of the case in the typical Boston manner, and the applied base molding extends below the case bottom.

Filler blocks, which have been replaced in this piece, are glued to the bottom of the case flush with the bottom of the molding. The feet, knee blocks, and backing glue blocks are glued to the base molding and underside of the filler blocks. The case back is nailed into rabbets in the case sides. The drawer fronts are shaped on the inside to follow the curve of the outside. The sides and back show typical Boston shop dovetailing, which is precise and functional without being overly delicate or ornamental. The drawer bottoms slide into grooves in the drawer sides and front and are nailed to the drawer back.

REVERSE-SERPENTINE
CHEST *of* DRAWERS

BOSTON, 1775–1800

Mahogany; white pine

H 32⅜ in. W 35½ in. D 21 in.

case
W 33½ in. D 19½ in.

Courtesy Historic Deerfield

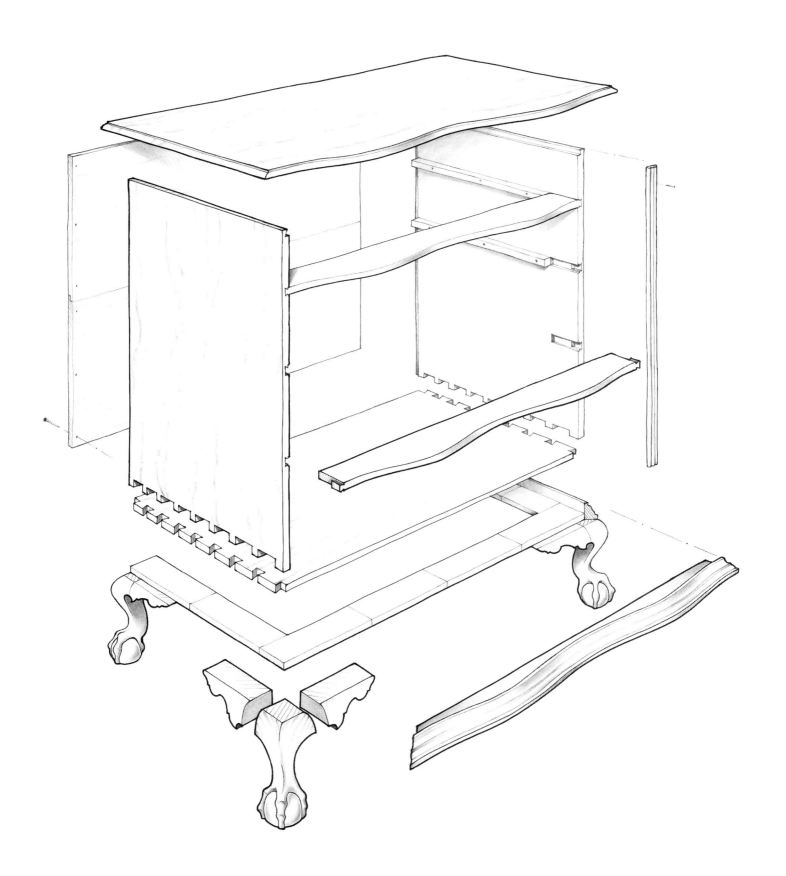

BOMBÉ CHEST *of* DRAWERS

HISTORICAL NOTES

The Rhode Island School of Design's bombé chest has a clear provenance, having descended in the Dexter family of Boston, Dedham, and later Providence until it was purchased for the Pendleton Collection at an auction in 1887. The bombé form is unique to the Boston and Salem area and was used for desk cases, the bases of desk-bookcases and chests-on-chests, and chests of drawers. The materials, level of skill and amount of labor required to build a bombé chest limited their ownership to only the wealthiest members of Boston society. Dated pieces span the years from 1753 to 1782, the earliest being a desk and bookcase by Benjamin Frothingham, Sr. (1708–1765) now in the Diplomatic Reception Rooms in the Department of State in Washington, D.C. The Frothingham piece predates Chippendale's *Director* by a year, and the inspiration for it is thought to be imported English or possibly Dutch pieces.

ANALYSIS

Though predating and differing from the designs in the *Director*, the Boston bombé forms express the aesthetics of the era and are an important facet of the American Chippendale style. To describe this piece as exhibiting a stately presence is an understatement. The attention commanded by the chest exceeds its modest dimensions. The shape of the bombé sides is exceptionally well formed, flowing smoothly but dramatically from the top to the base. The serpentine front, which is superimposed over the bombé shape, results in a rich and undulating surface of compound curves that is amplified by the patterning brought out from the grain of select, luminescent mahogany. The shape of the piece and the qualities it draws from the mahogany are so rich and opulent as not to require further ornamentation.

In opposition to the more ethereal Queen Anne–era aesthetics, the bombé form revels in its mass and the expanses of rich surface. The bulging shape seems to be formed by its own mass. The ball and claw feet and short cabriole legs are made to exhibit proudly the mass they bear. In the ultimate tribute to Chippendale-era aesthetics, the viewer's eye is drawn downward by this form—not upward as in loftier Queen Anne–era designs.

RELATED FORMS

A bombé case such as this piece with a serpentine front represents the highest development of the form. Other bombé pieces were made with the swelled shape to the front but without the serpentine curves. A few, including the early Frothingham piece, were made with the ends of the drawers aligned vertically, not following the shape of the sides. Like the block-front and serpentine-fronted pieces of the same era, the bombé form was a method by which to impart Chippendale-era ideals of a grand presence to the utilitarian form of a case of drawers.

STRUCTURAL NOTES

Like other American bombé pieces, the curved sides of this chest are shaped from solid 3-in. stock. The sides of the bombé chest are dovetailed to the base with a series of through dovetails, the sides being the pin pieces. The top is secured to the sides with sliding dovetails that are tapered on the outer side and barefaced on the inner side. The interior of the sides are flat-sided between the drawer dividers, with only the front inch or so shaped to follow the outer curve of the side. The drawer dividers are dovetailed to the case sides with mitered cockbeads, cut from the solid, surrounding each drawer opening. The drawer runners are nailed to the inside of the case. In typical Boston fashion, the bottom drawer rides on the case bottom, and the base molding, which is glued and nailed on, extends below the case. Pine blocks are glued to the case flush with the bottom of the molding.

The feet are tenoned with square tenons into mortises in these blocks and are reinforced with knee blocks and supplemental glue blocks. The case back is nailed into rabbets in the case sides. The drawers are dovetailed in a conventional manner with slanted, but not curved, drawer sides. Because of the straight drawer sides, the curved ends of the drawer fronts overhang the sides. The drawer bottom slides into grooves in the sides and front and is secured with glue blocks and nails.

BOSTON, 1760–1785

Mahogany; white pine

H 32 in. W 38 in. D 20 in.

Courtesy Museum of Art,
Rhode Island School of Design

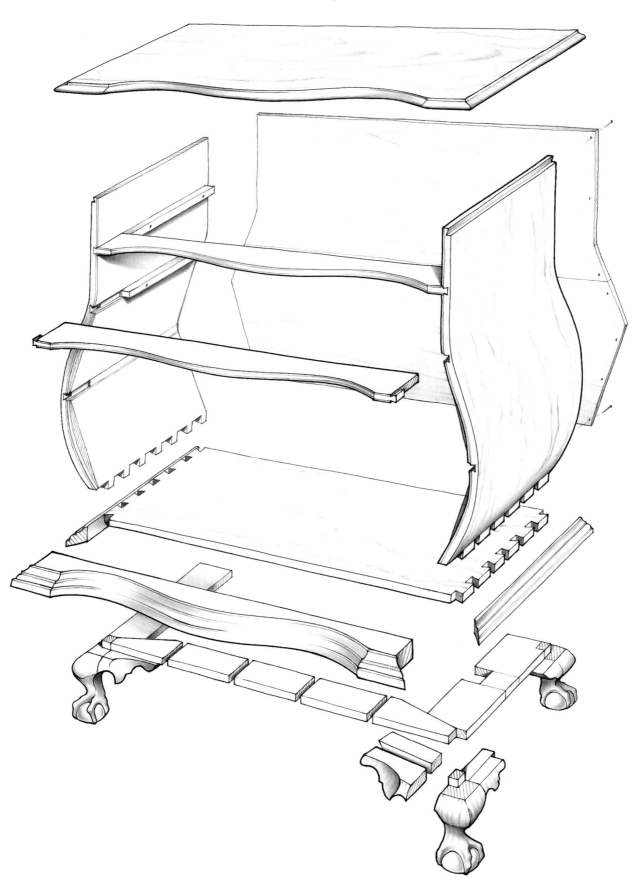

Slant-front desk

HISTORICAL NOTES

Yale's slant-front desk has a written record of its ownership on the sides of the document drawers, the earliest inscription reading "Wm. Butler / September ye 10, 1768." Included are inscriptions by owners in 1830, 1838, 1861 and 1874. Both the first and last recorded owners are known to have been residents of Nantucket. It is not thought to have been made on Nantucket, however, since the island is not known to have had cabinet-makers of this caliber. Differences from Boston case-construction methods may be indicative of a southeastern Massachusetts origin. The brasses and hinges have been replaced, and there are repairs to the bottom edge of the lid, top of the case and drawer fronts.

ANALYSIS

This desk represents a vernacular version of a Chippendale-style slant-front desk. The vast majority of desks built at this time did not have the more expensive blocked front and were more like this mainstream American Chippendale example. The form was continued from the Queen Anne period but the Chippendale-era aesthetics were achieved by ample case width, rich mahogany surfaces, bold brasses and ball and claw feet. The size of the case and its stance on well-curved cabriole legs denotes mass and weight. The richness of the exterior is limited to its size, the quality of the wood and its finish, and the use of large brasses.

The interior, however, is of stronger visual impact. Here, the viewer is treated to the opulence of expensive pieces on a small scale. The upper tier of drawers features blocked fronts with fan carvings on the upper left and right interior drawers and the center prospect door. The document drawers are fronted with applied half-turnings. The open center section provides quick storage for often-used papers or a ledger book. The interior includes all the intricate details essential to achieve the opulent appearance that was sought after at the time. In short, the overall design has a strong, but not overpowering presence that addresses the prevailing aesthetics of the era from the mainstream of American cabinetmaking.

RELATED FORMS

In the range of Chippendale slant-front desks, this Massachusetts example is a good measure of those in the center. It is not an unsophisticated desk, yet it does not exhibit the development of a contemporary example from an urban Boston shop. It does not have a block-front case that would be indicative of the next higher level in taste, skill and price. The ball and claw feet also lack the power and refinement of urban examples. It is, however, more advanced than rural examples, which would have eschewed ball and claw feet for straight or ogee bracket feet and may have been built with a smaller case size. Given these points, a suburban origin or an origin in a lesser urban shop seems likely.

STRUCTURAL NOTES

The case of the desk is dovetailed with half-blind dovetails visible on the case top and through dovetails on the case bottom. The drawer dividers, which are pine faced with mahogany, and writing surface are joined with shouldered dovetails to the case sides. As on Boston case pieces, a thin strip on the front edge of the case sides covers the dovetails. The base molding is a profile typical of Boston case furniture; it is glued and nailed to the case. As on Rhode Island examples, the bottom of the molding is flush with the bottom of the case and the bottom drawer rides on runners on the inside of the case. A full-width rail backs up the base molding within the case. The vertical backboards are nailed to the case bottom and into rabbets in the case top and sides. The feet are glued to the case bottom and reinforced by the knee blocks and backing glue blocks. No tenoning of the feet into the case bottom is apparent.

The four case drawers have $5/8$-in. thick sides and backs, which are finely dovetailed. The drawer bottoms slide into grooves in the sides and front and are nailed to the back. The partitions of the desk interior are let into dadoes in the inside of the case. The partitions are butted mahogany and pine (the mahogany extends the first 2 in. or 3 in. of their depth). The drawers in the interior are finely dovetailed. Their bottoms are let into rabbets in the fronts and sides and flush with the back.

SLANT-FRONT DESK

BOSTON AREA, C. 1768

Mahogany; white pine

H 44¼ in.   W 45 in.   D 22¼ in.

case
W 41⅞ in.   D 20¼ in.

Courtesy
Yale University Art Gallery

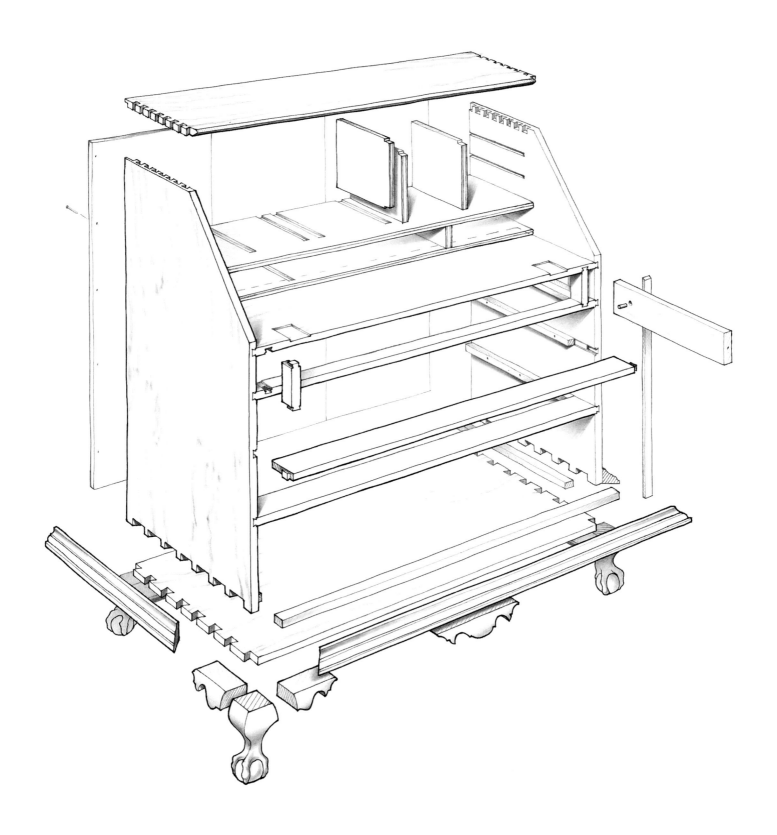

DESK *and* BOOKCASE

HISTORICAL NOTES

This desk and bookcase has a history of ownership in the Potter family of Kingston, Rhode Island. It was acquired by Arthur B. Lisle about 1915 and later bequeathed to the museum. Of the ten related Newport desk-bookcases, none are signed, but this one bears the inscription "Made by John Goddard 1761 and repaired by Thomas Goddard his son 1813." The inscription was likely written by Thomas Goddard (1765–1858) in 1813, and while it aids in the attribution of the desk to John Goddard (1723–1785), it alone cannot be considered to be authenticating. If the inscription is completely accurate, this is the earliest dated piece of Newport block-front furniture and it stands as an important reference by which to measure related pieces. It was conserved and refinished in 1986 at the Society for the Preservation of New England Antiquities Conservation Center in Waltham, Massachusetts.

ANALYSIS

To say that the Newport desk-bookcases embody the aesthetics of the Chippendale era would be

a severe understatement. They clearly exceed most expressions of grandeur of the period and are quite unlike anything envisioned by the Georgian cabinetmakers of England. The block front with integrated shells was inspired by Boston pieces but was developed to an unparalleled level of sophistication by the Goddard and Townsend cabinetmakers. The arched pediment, which is quite perfect in its Newport rendition, continues the Queen Anne period's trend for lofty height. The mass of the piece is evident in its sheer size, but at 97 in. this is among the smallest of the ten (the largest, now in a private collection, is a towering 113 in. tall). The case depth should be noted as well; at 26 in. it makes the base substantial.

The surface treatment of the blocked front with curved-ray shells is integral to the design of the facade. It unifies the three planes of the front and extends all the way to the scrolled volutes of the feet. Like other shaped-front treatments, it confers mass and substance on the cases. The six shells, each remarkable feats of carving in themselves, are the epitome of the rich, carved

surface. The treatment of the front is enhanced by the richness of select West Indian mahogany.

The period designers used mass, surface and form to achieve the aesthetic goals of the period and the Newport desk-bookcases meet and exceed each point. While achieving an impressive dignity and stately grandeur through their size, design and richness of material and detail, the true genius of the designers and builders of the Newport desk bookcases is in giving the pieces their regal bearing without them becoming ponderous.

RELATED FORMS

The Newport design should be noted as the apex of both good taste and the cabinetmaker's art in Rhode Island. Other regions used different designs to achieve the same goals. Comparably impressive Boston and Salem pieces featured block-front or bombé bases and upper cases with paneled doors and architectural elements. In Philadelphia, the desk bookcase followed more closely the examples illustrated in English

design books, especially Chippendale's *Director*. There, high chests seemed to be the object of choice in which to display the full effect of the cabinetmaker and carver's art.

STRUCTURAL NOTES

The base of the desk features standard Newport case-construction details. The top of the desk is dovetailed to the case sides with half-blind dovetails hidden by the mid-molding. The case bottom is dovetailed to the sides with through-dovetails. The mahogany-fronted drawer dividers and the writing surface are dovetailed to the case sides with shouldered dovetails. The drawer runners are nailed in place. The cockbead on the horizontal elements is cut from the solid, but it is inset into a rabbet in the case sides and mitered to the cockbead of the dividers. The side base moldings are glued and nailed flush to the bottom of the case. The front molding is mitered to the side moldings and joined to the bottom of the case in a half-lap joint. The cockbeaded rail below the bottom drawer is dovetailed to the case sides and nailed to the front base molding. The feet

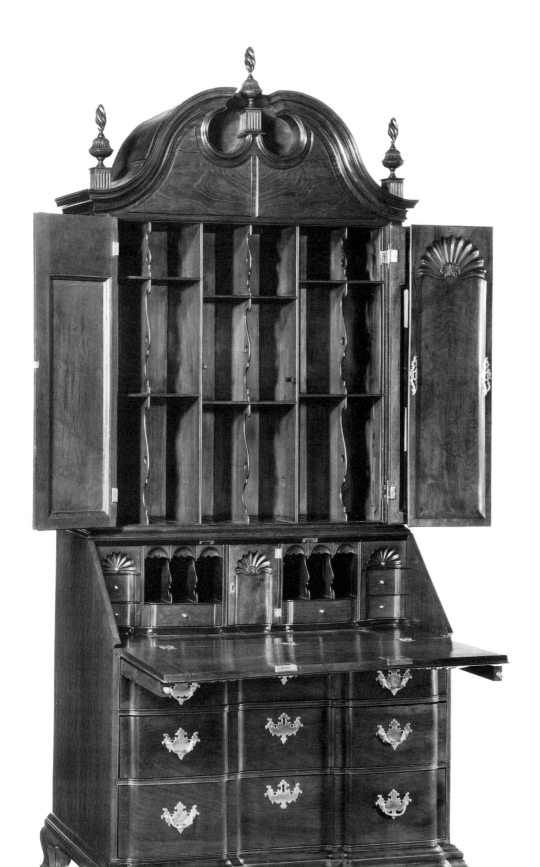

DESK and BOOKCASE

NEWPORT, 1761

Mahogany; white pine, red cedar, poplar

H 97 in.   W 45¼ in.   D 26 in.

lower case
H 37⅜ in.   W 41⅞ in.   D 23¾ in. *(side)*

upper case
H 39⅝ in. *(to top of side molding)*
W 40 in.   D 12¾ in.

Courtesy Museum of Art
Rhode Island School of Design

are mitered and glued to the case with glue blocks. The case back is nailed into rabbets in the desk top and sides and overlaps the case bottom.

The two lower drawer fronts are cut from solid 1½-in. stock. A ½-in. thick panel has been glued to the interior of the drawer front behind the center concave blocking to increase its thickness. The convex blocking of the top drawer is applied. The drawers are dovetailed throughout and the drawer bottom is nailed to the sides and back and let into a groove in the drawer front. Running strips are applied to the bottom edges. The sides of the top drawer are inset from edges of the drawer front to accommodate the sliding lopers. The drawer sides are let into dadoes or sliding dovetails in the back of the drawer front.

The shells of the lid are applied. The shell and its blocking are two separate pieces joined in a straight joint just below the shell. The interior is a standard Goddard/Townsend desk interior with blocked drawer fronts and three carved shells. The drawers are marked with chiseled Roman numerals on the top edge of the drawer fronts to mark their position. The partitions and drawer dividers of the interior are let into dadoes in the interior of the case. The well slides open for access to the top drawer, and a horizontal rail inside the case back supports the members that frame the well.

In the upper case, the top and bottom panels are half-blind-dovetailed to the sides. The pediment is built up from the top of the case with front and back pediment boards. Glue blocks support the side pediment moldings, which overlap the top of the case by only ¼ in., a substantial difference from Townsend family construction where the top of the molding is flush with the top of the case. The front pediment board is dovetailed to the case sides, and the rear pediment board is glued to the top of the case. The quarter columns are glued to the front of the case sides and to an inner frame from which are hung the doors.

The interior shelves are let into the case sides. Secret, removable panels are let into dadoes in the shelves flush with the inner door frame. The convex blocked doors are framed with mortise-and-tenon joinery. The block and shell of the door are two separate pieces, joined along the bottom profile of the shell and applied to the door frame. The center door is carved from the solid. The vertical backboards are nailed into rabbets in the top and sides of the upper case and to the back of the shelves. X-ray photography has revealed that the finials, long thought to have been assembled with the urn section upside-down, were intended to look the way they do.

UPPER CASE

LOWER CASE

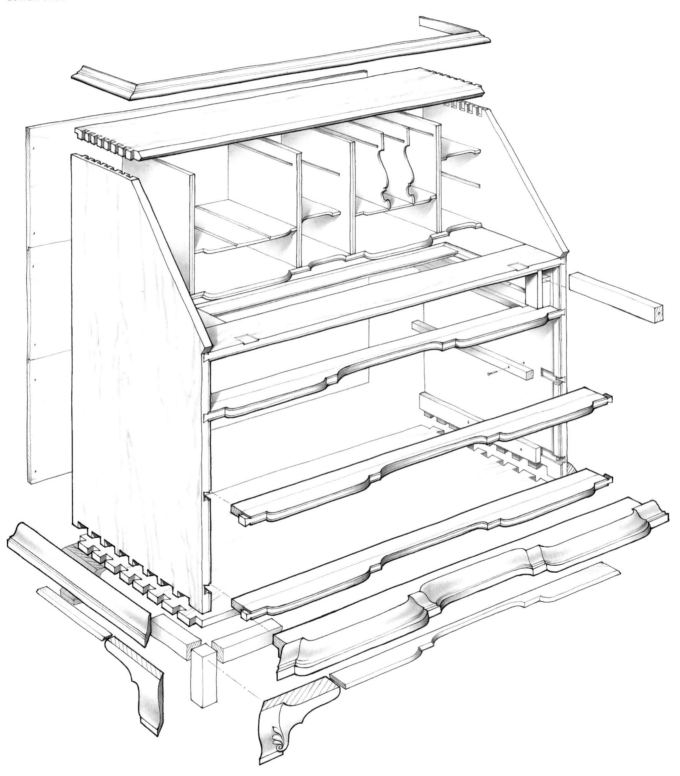

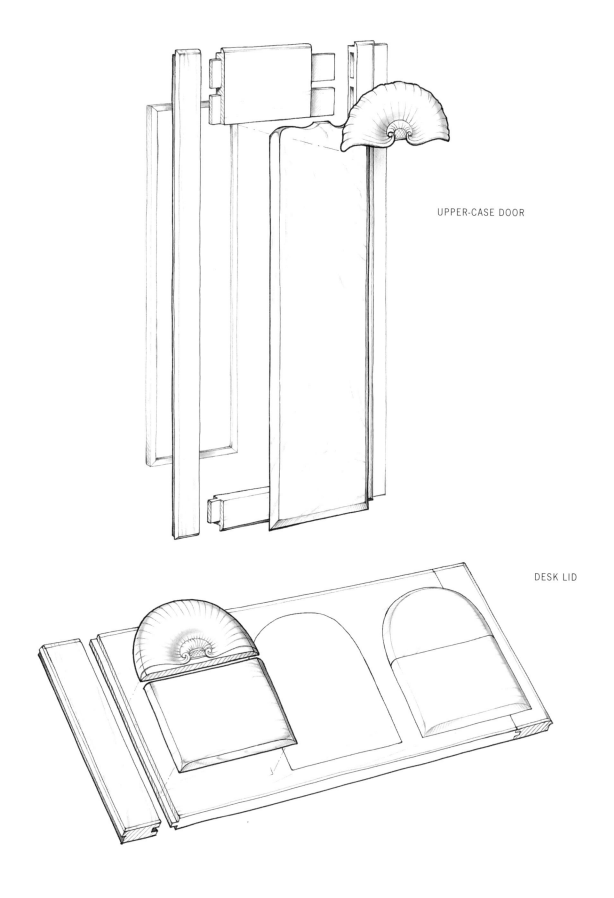

UPPER-CASE DOOR

DESK LID

RECTANGULAR TEA TABLE

HISTORICAL NOTES

There are seven known Newport tea tables of this style. Six, including this one, are in the style of John Goddard (at least four of these are authenticated to him). The seventh is in the manner of John Townsend. The same design was made with and without open talons on the ball and claw feet. Three of the Goddard tables and the one Townsend example have open talons.

ANALYSIS

Although this table is a very high-style piece, enough examples of this form exist to consider it in the mainstream of tea-table design in Newport during the third quarter of the 18th century. The form continues many of the overall proportions of the New England and Newport rectangular tea tables of the Queen Anne period, but the designs have been updated to include Chippendale-era aesthetics.

The mass of the table is made more evident by the cyma-shaped surface and profile of the aprons, a shape that is carried through the top and its molding. Similarly, the strong ball and claw feet appear to bear the weight of the piece. The carving of the feet and knees and the shaping of the aprons and top create a rich surface. The square corners and straight apron sides hint at the increase in rectilinear forms supplanting curved forms, giving this design an underlying strength and solidity. In total, the effect is an opulent and stately design with the powerful presence sought after in the era of the Chippendale style. In the characteristic New England manner epitomized by the Newport masters, this is achieved without undue or excessive ornamentation.

RELATED FORMS

This specific design is unique to the Goddard and Townsend craftsmen of Newport, who used similar features in the design of a number of related card tables. Like card tables, tea tables were central to enter-taining and socializing, so they were subject to a high level of development and made to embody the most fashionable trends in design. A similar aesthetic goal was expressed in different ways in other regions. A number of turret-top tea tables were made in the Boston area, patterned after a 14-turret table of Philadelphia origin. Portsmouth's highest develop-ment of the Chippendale tea-table form is best represented by the China tables associated with Robert Harrold. The Connecticut area followed the Philadelphia preference toward high-style, round tea tables, led by the stylistic trends of the Chapin school.

STRUCTURAL NOTES

The Newport tea table is of mortise-and-tenon construction, with the aprons tenoned into the leg blocks. No pins or pegs are visible from the outside of the piece, and their presence is not discernible from inside because of the later addition of large corner blocks. The need for these corner blocks suggests that the mortise-and-tenon joints were originally glued but not pegged. The knee blocks are glued and nailed to the legs. The thin, half-round bead under the tabletop is a thin piece of mahogany applied to the top of the frame. The top is dished from the solid and is fastened in place with 18 triangular pine glue blocks. Shrinkage of the top has resulted in a crack in one end of the top and the failure of the glue blocks along one side. The underside of the top and the inside of the aprons were planed with a toothed plane to increase the adherence of glue blocks.

RECTANGULAR TEA TABLE

NEWPORT, 1760–1775

Mahogany; pine

H 26¾ in.   W 33¾ in. *(top)*   D 19½ in.

Courtesy Rhode Island Historical Society

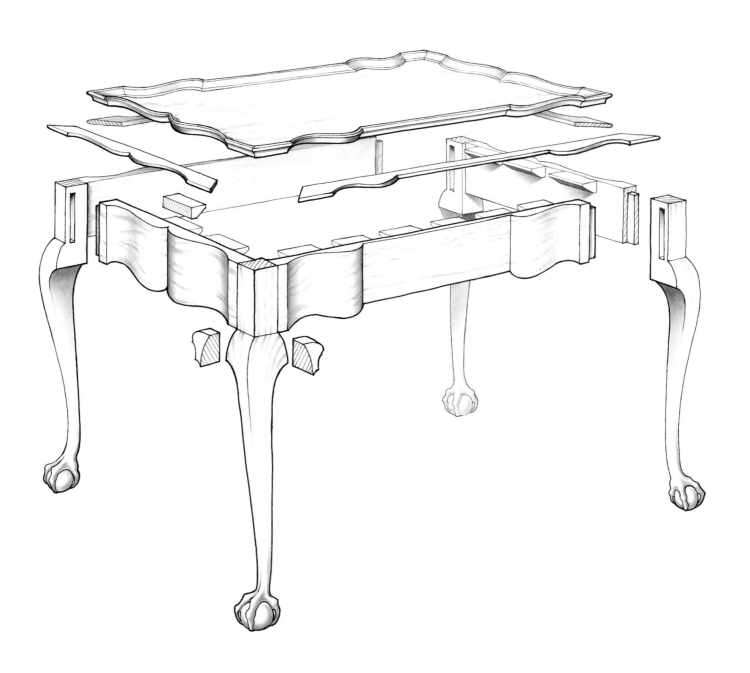

ROUND TEA TABLE

HISTORICAL NOTES

The distinctive, downward-flaring turning, sculptural legs and characteristically angular ball and claw feet of Historic Deerfield's round tea table are indicative of the Chapin school of Connecticut furniture. The Chapin school was a small group of shops working in the manner of Eliphalet Chapin (1741–1807), who had trained in Enfield, Connecticut, and in Philadelphia. Chapin's Philadelphia training and innate skill as a designer and builder combined the sophistication of urban design elements and structure with the restraint of New England tastes. The result was a unique, regional school of furniture design with a high level of aesthetic and technical development.

Round tea tables such as this Deerfield example first appeared in America during the Queen Anne period in furniture design and were based on English "pillar and claw" or "snap tables" of the 1730s. The form reached its peak of development after mid-century with Chippendale-era styling, and included elaborately shaped pillars, ball and claw feet, and dished and shaped tops.

ANALYSIS

This example shows the continuation of Queen Anne–era structure with the detailing in the Chippendale style. The large diameter of the base of the pillar and the mass of the three legs that radiate from it give the base a solidity and strength not seen in weaker examples. The dramatic, downward taper of the pillar and the stately cyma-based curve of the legs draw the eye downward. The legs themselves, void of carving but fully sculptural in their shape, terminate in powerful feet and exude a strong presence. This example has substituted opulently shaped surfaces for richly carved ones.

The bird cage, the mechanism by which the top tips and turns, while intended to be functional, also offers a visual balance to the complexity of the base and serves as a transition to the large tabletop. The top itself is dished with a delicate molded edge. Its form is simple but its ample size counters the visual complexity of the base. A smaller top would need to be more ornate to achieve the same balance.

RELATED FORMS

The Chapin-school table represents the center of the range of development for round tea tables. Such tables were the predominant form of tea table in Philadelphia, where, as important focal pieces, they were subject to the full complement of Rococo carving and ornament. New Englanders opted for rectangular, four-legged tables for their most important tea tables, but round tea tables and related candlestands were still nearly ubiquitous. As one would expect, the New England forms are generally more reliant on shape than ornament for their appeal.

The bird-cage mechanism and the dished top are significant features by which to judge both the sophistication and price of these tables. The inclusion of the bird cage added about 50% to the price of a table, and the addition of a dished or turned top roughly doubled it.

STRUCTURAL NOTES

The three legs are attached to the turned pillar with large sliding dovetails. They are reinforced with a three-lobed iron plate nailed to the base. The bird cage consists of four baluster-shaped turnings with turned tenons connecting upper and lower plates. The bird cage, which slides over the shaft of the pillar, is held in place by a tapered wedge that passes through the pillar, holding a turned ring against the lower plate. The top tilts on two pintles, or pivot pins, that extend from the sides of the upper bird-cage plate into the two battens screwed to the underside of the tabletop. A brass catch locks the top in the horizontal position.

ROUND TEA TABLE

CONNECTICUT RIVER VALLEY, 1770–1800

Cherry

H 29 in.

Top
36¾ in. dia.

Courtesy Historic Deerfield

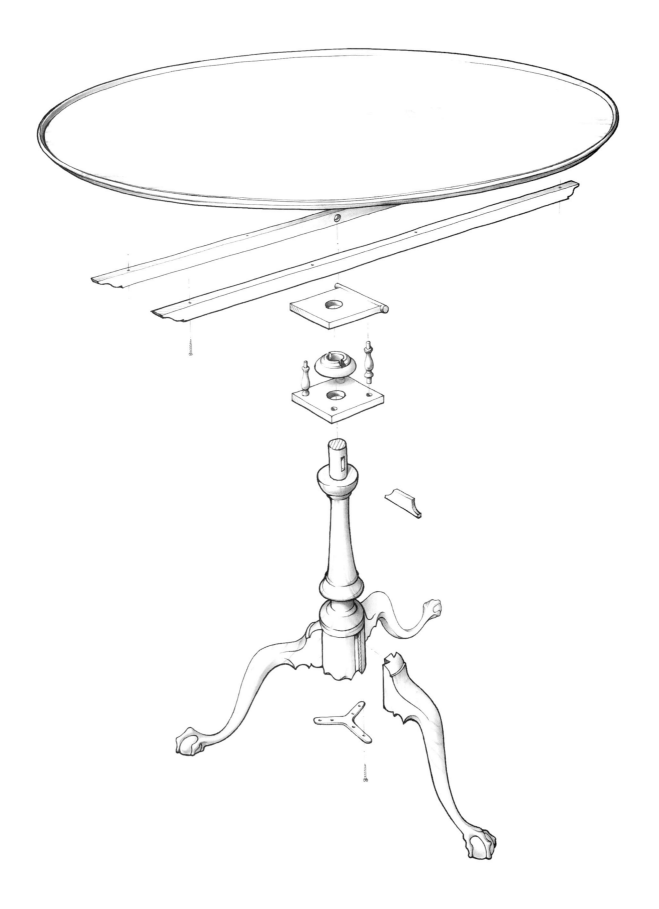

DROP-LEAF DINING TABLE

HISTORICAL NOTES

Drop-leaf dining tables came into widespread use with the William and Mary gateleg tables late in the 17th century. The form proved practical in American homes because of its ability to seat many people for dining and fold neatly to one-third its width when not in use. The table, made to conform to Queen Anne–period ideals, dropped the frenzied base of the William and Mary designs for the simple elegance of four cabriole legs. Two were stationary and were made to swing on a hinged rail to support the leaves. Period refinements in apron shapes, edge molding, and the use of rule joints to conceal the leaf hinges were part of the new styling. The Chippendale era continued most of the features of the Queen Anne tables with only stylistic changes.

ANALYSIS

The aesthetics of dining tables are severely limited by their functional requirements, but, nonetheless, the styling of the times is evident. The continuation of the Queen Anne style is clear in this example. With the exception of the ball and claw feet, the cabriole legs appear much as they had previously, but with a curved profile that exudes more strength.

The mass of the piece is made more evident by the stronger legs and the ball and claw feet, both of which command more attention than demure Queen Anne legs with pad feet. The feet on this example show the swept-back side talons indicative of Massachusetts origins. The nature of the frame of the table limits the amount of ornament that can be included, and here it is limited to the aprons on the end. This example has interestingly scrolled knee blocks, akin to those on Salem pieces, and a cyma-curved apron profile to enliven the visible portion of the frame.

RELATED FORMS

Other drop-leaf tables of the Chippendale era were built with square or rectangular tops, in keeping with the increase in rectilinear forms during this period. A variety of structural details were employed, the most recognizable being the Newport method of dovetailing cross-braces to the frame, with three on the top and two underneath. Screws through the top braces were used to attach the tabletop. This table is representative of the majority of tables of the era, in that the top is attached with glue blocks and it has a simple, functional hinge design and frame structure.

STRUCTURAL NOTES

The rails are joined to the legs with mortise-and-tenon joints, each double-pegged. The inner rails are dovetailed to the end rails with half-blind dovetails. The inner rails are spaced away from the hinged rails with pine blocks, an arrangement that allows the square ends of the hinge to rotate freely. The inner rails are nailed through the pine blocks to the outer rails. The knee blocks are applied over the apron and are separate from the swinging legs. The top is attached to the frame with glue blocks, and a single cross-brace is screwed to the underside of the top.

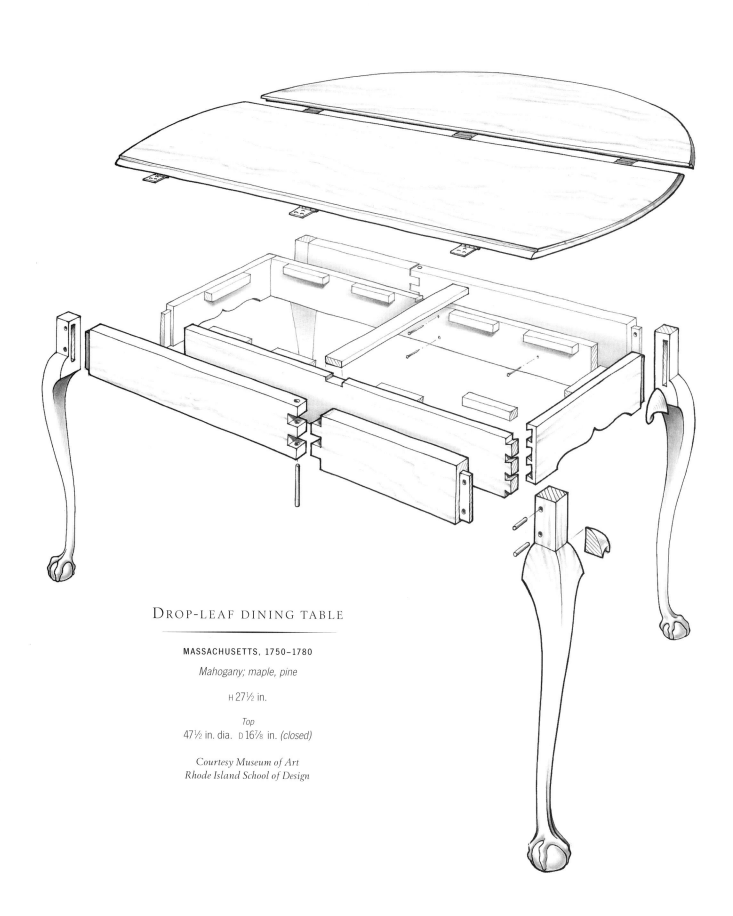

Drop-leaf dining table

MASSACHUSETTS, 1750–1780

Mahogany; maple, pine

H 27½ in.

Top
47½ in. dia. D 16⅞ in. *(closed)*

Courtesy Museum of Art
Rhode Island School of Design

ARMCHAIR

HISTORICAL NOTES

A Connecticut Chippendale-style armchair of the Chapin school, the example on p. 280 was purchased by Francis P. Garvan in 1924 from Harry Arons of Ansonia, Connecticut, one of the early wholesale dealers of American antique furniture. The Chapin school was a small group of shops working in the manner of Eliphalet Chapin (1741–1807). Chapin had trained as a cabinet-maker in Enfield, Connecticut, and spent four years training in Philadelphia, as well. He opened a shop in East Windsor, Connecticut, in 1771 at the then-seasoned age of 30 years. His Philadelphia training brought an infusion of high-level, Chippendale-era develop-ment to the central Connecticut area. The shops of the Chapin school were those of relatives, journeyman cabinetmakers who had trained with family members, and even imitators who perpetuated the distinctive Chapin style.

ANALYSIS

American Chippendale-style chairs followed English trends and were markedly different from the earlier Queen Anne designs. They are one of the few Chippendale forms that represented a sharp departure from, rather than a modified continuance of, earlier styles. Most noticeable is the simple curve in the profile of the back, replacing the cyma-based shape of Queen Anne designs. Also, the rear stiles are splayed outward toward the top, meeting the crest rail in outward-facing ears, rather than arching inward toward the splat.

The Chippendale style sheds the restraint of the Queen Anne design. While the design cannot exude the mass of the era's case pieces, it does display an opulence in its carved features. The aesthetics of the period called for bringing a focus to the details more than the outline. The ball and claw feet, carved crest-rail shell, and crest-rail ears are integral to the design, not simply added embellishments. Having shed its stretchers, the stance of the piece is bold and confident, giving the chair a commanding presence. Curved shapes are used extensively, but the design includes more rectilinear elements than earlier chairs. Just as case pieces were made to exude the Chippendale aesthetic by stressing their mass and rich surface, so do Chippendale chairs through their solid stance and intricately carved or shaped details.

RELATED FORMS

American Chippendale chairs show a wide variation in regional preferences for carved ornament and splat design. Those of the Chapin school are among the American chairs least fettered by carved detail. In the English tradition, high-style Philadelphia chairs show a preponderance of carving on the knees, feet, seat rail, splat, stiles and crest rail. Boston chairs are generally more delicate, giving more attention to form than carving, but they too often show extensive, though restrained, carving on the knees and back. Newport cabinetmakers diverged to explore the Chippendale designs of Chinese influence, which were of rectilinear form with a minimum of carved ornament.

STRUCTURAL NOTES

The seat rails are tenoned into mortises in the front and rear legs. They are double-pegged on the back of the chair only and reinforced with large glue blocks in each corner. The side rails are tenoned through the rear legs and are flush with the rear surface. Each through-tenon has a small wedge at the top and bottom to lock it into the mortise. The method of attachment of the crest rail to the stiles is not apparent, but X-ray analysis has indicated the use of dowels in blind-drilled holes. The splat is curved to follow the shape of the stiles and is tenoned into the crest rail and shoe. The shoe is nailed to the rear seat rail.

No pegs are visible, except those on the back that secure the tenons of the rear seat rail. The arm support is screwed to the front leg post and side rail with two screws from inside the seat rabbet and one screw from the outside of the support. The support is tenoned into a mortise in the underside of the arm. The rear of the arm is secured by a screw through the stile. The screws on the stile and outside of the arm support are countersunk and plugged. The frame of the loose seat is of mortise-and-tenon construction.

EAST WINDSOR, CONNECTICUT, C. 1780

Cherry; white pine

H 40½ in.   W 27½ in.

seat
H 16¼ in.   W 22¾ in.   D 18 in.

Courtesy
Yale University Art Gallery

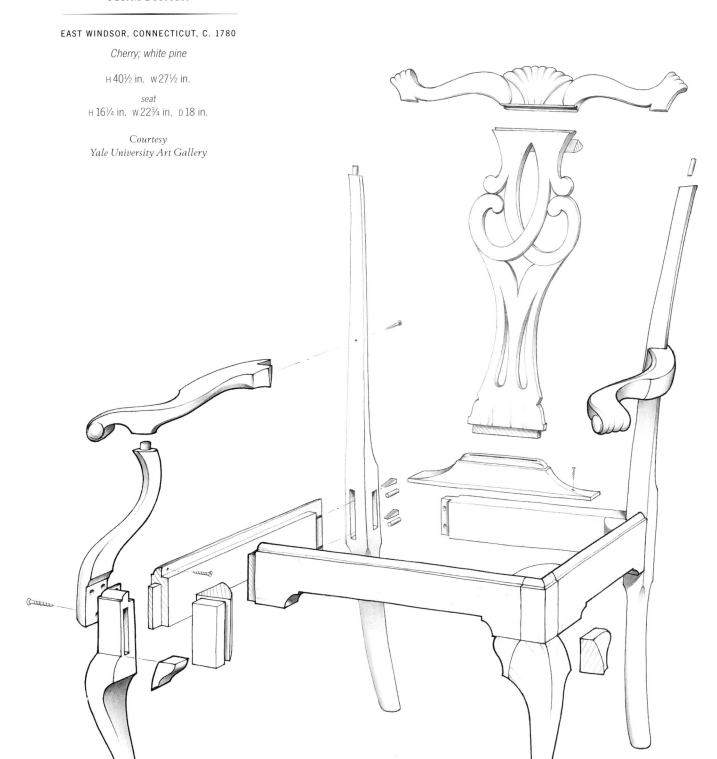

FEDERAL

Hepplewhite sideboard

HISTORICAL NOTES

The sideboard shown on p. 284 has a history of ownership in Maine and the Boston area. Its design and details indicate an eastern New England origin, but its simplicity rules out its having been made in the major urban shops of Boston. The tapered feet are often associated with the North Shore or Salem, and given the high quality of craftsmanship, such an attribution is possible. Sideboards were new to the American furniture with the Neoclassical period, during which they combined the roles of side tables and bureaus to become an important piece of dining-room furniture. As the focus of attention in the Federal dining room, sideboards were subject to a high level of development in their design and ornamentation.

ANALYSIS

As important case pieces, sideboards usually embody well the aesthetics of the Federal era. Most notable is the simple geometric aspect of the design. Like other case pieces, it is rectilinear in elevation, and curved in plan. The piece has a spare and sophisticated appearance unfettered by the detail of carved ornament or intricate shapes. The long, thin, tapered legs lift the mass of the case far above the ground. The length and slimness of the legs, and their resulting small footprint, minimize the visual mass of the piece. The ornament is limited to string inlays and small quarter fans, which highlight the simple geometric lines of the piece. The smooth surfaces are enlivened by a high grade of mahogany and mahogany crotch veneers, bringing attention to the surface material itself. The net result is a design of clean and rectilinear elegance with a light and delicate stance.

RELATED FORMS

Curved-front sideboards of this type are directly related to a design presented in Hepplewhite's *Guide* of 1788. From this starting point, the design of American sideboards diverged into both simpler and more elaborate designs. Providence cabinetmakers, Thomas Howard (1774–1833) foremost among them, developed smaller, flat-fronted sideboards with no curves except in the apron profile. Boston, New York and Baltimore, the larger urban centers of furniture making, produced sideboards of imposing lengths and complexity. Some of these were *tours de force* of Federal cabinetmaking, with great sweeping curves and extensive and elaborate veneering and inlay. This example is representative of the mainstream of very good design and craftsmanship and is indicative of an upper middle class client's tastes and price range.

STRUCTURAL NOTES

The sides and back are joined to the legs with mortise-and-tenon joints, a series of four along each joint. The vertical interior case dividers are similarly tenoned into the front center legs and through the back. The tenons through the back are locked in place with wedges driven into the mortises adjacent to the tenons. The tenons and wedges are trimmed flush with the case. The bottom rails and drawer dividers are maple, faced with mahogany veneer, and doubled tenoned to the front legs. The veneered top rail is dovetailed to the top of the legs.

The mortise-and-tenon joints throughout are glued but not pegged. The case bottom is glued to the front rails and the joint is reinforced with glue blocks. It is nailed to the underside of the case back and to nailed-in guides at the sides. The drawer runners and guides are nailed to the case sides and rabbeted to receive dustboards below the two outer top drawers. A longitudinal cross-piece is dovetailed between the top of the case back and the front rail.

The top is thin (3/8-in.) bookmatched mahogany, with pine strips glued around the perimeter to increase its edge thickness. The edge is veneered with a cross-banding and inlaid band. The top is attached by screws through the front rails and from pockets in the sides and back. The drawers and door fronts are mahogany veneer over pine with applied cockbeading. The drawer components are finely dovetailed with narrow, closely spaced pins. The drawer bottoms slide into grooves in the fronts and sides and are nailed to the drawer backs. The lower right drawer contains bottle partitions let into dadoes in the drawer sides and back as illustrated in Hepplewhite's *Guide* (see p. 84). The doors are veneered over curved pine panels made with breadboard ends to minimize warping.

Hepplewhite Sideboard

NORTH SHORE, MASSACHUSETTS, 1790–1800

Mahogany; pine, inlays of holly, maple, ebony and walnut

H 39¾ in.   W 57¾ in.   D 24¾

case
W 56 in.   D 23½ in.   D *(at side)* 15½ in.

Private collection

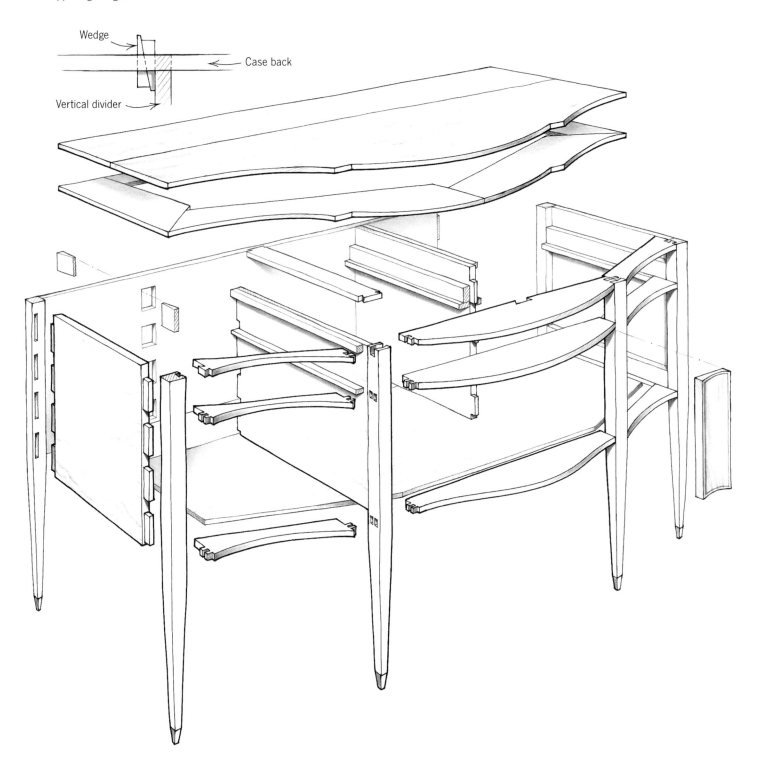

Tenons on end of vertical case divider are locked in place with opposing wedges.

Wedge

Case back

Vertical divider

SHERATON CARD TABLE

HISTORICAL NOTES

This card table is one of a pair on display at the Rhode Island Historical Society's John Brown House, and bears the label of Joseph Rawson and Sons, Providence. After the Revolutionary War, Providence emerged as a new center of commerce and furniture making, since many residents of Newport had fled during the British occupation. Joseph Rawson and Sons became one of the leading cabinetmaking firms in the city, catering to the needs of an increasingly prosperous merchant class and offering pieces of the most fashionable Neoclassical designs. Their work showed the same amount of sophistication as that from other, more established furniture-making centers of the day, such as Baltimore, New York and Boston.

A nearly identical table bearing the Rawson label, but made some two decades later, features the aprons veneered in bird's-eye maple with painted borders and central floral designs, reflecting the increased popularity of painted furniture in the first half of the 19th century.

ANALYSIS

This table illustrates the use of relatively simple lines with bold veneering that is such a prominent element of the design and ornament in the Federal styles. The front apron and sides have flowing serpentine shapes, which are continued in the shape of the top. In elevation, however, the shape of the apron is not as apparent. There is no other shaping of the apron to distract from the purity of the lines of the piece.

The Sheraton influence is manifested in the slender turned legs, which are reeded over much of their length, but fluted for a short length near the top. The legs form turrets on the front corners, which are veneered to become an integral part of the aprons and whose shape is continued in the ovolo corners of the top. The legs taper downward to terminate at the floor with a light footprint. By keeping the apron long and thin, and by using widely spaced but delicate legs, the desired appearance of delicacy and lightness with stability was achieved. The level of sophistication is heightened by the refined detail of the turned legs and the extraordinary effect of the veneered front.

RELATED FORMS

By the end of the 18th century, travel and communication between cities, a proliferation of explicit design books and an increase in the number of mobile journeyman cabinetmakers were tending to blur the distinctions between the regional styles of furniture centers and homogenize much of American furniture. Forms similar to this table were made in every sizable city, with only minor differences in construction details and decoration to differentiate them. With the increased specialization of various aspects of the trade, some parts of the veneer, like patterned stringing, inlaid patterns or highly figured panels, were purchased from local inlay makers. In the absence of labels or markings, these patterns of stringing and inlay are often the best clues to the origin of a piece from this period.

STRUCTURAL NOTES

The curved front and side aprons are veneered over solid pine and are tenoned into the legs. These joints are not pegged, but instead reinforced with large, angled pine glue blocks, a method commonly used during the Federal period. The left rear leg swings on a hardwood rail, which is hinged near the center to support the tabletop when it is fully open. An inner rail is dovetailed to the rear of the left side apron and extends across the back to the right rear leg. The swinging fly leg is rabbeted to overlap the side apron when it is closed, thus concealing any gap between the leg and apron. The top is joined to the base by screws extending at an angle through pockets in the aprons into the underside of the top. The top leaf opens on brass hinges let into the sides of the top and leaf.

SHERATON CARD TABLE

PROVIDENCE, RHODE ISLAND, 1795–1810

*Mahogany; cherry, pine, figured satinwood,
holly, and mahogany veneers*

H 28½ in.　W 37 in.　D 18 in. *(closed)*

Courtesy Rhode Island Historical Society

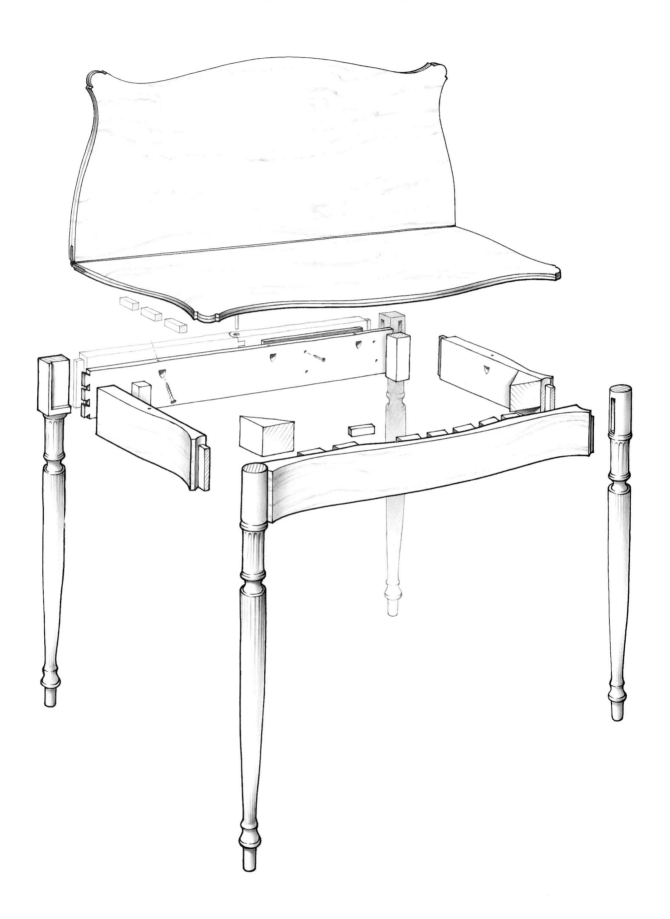

SHIELD-BACK SIDE CHAIR

HISTORICAL NOTES

One of a pair of shield-back side chairs, Rhode Island School of Design's example shares many similarities in construction and ornament with other chairs bearing the label of the firm of John Carlile (1727–1796) and Sons. It is likely the work of John Carlile, Jr. (1762–1832), one of six sons, who was active in the business from the early 1780s. Similar chairs were made by other Providence makers as well as by craftsmen in Boston, Salem and Newport. The design of this chair derives from those presented in Hepplewhite's *Guide* of 1788.

ANALYSIS

Shield-back chairs differ greatly in appearance from Chippendale-era chairs and embody a different set of design ideals. Whereas the earlier chairs exhibited a bold, masculine stance, those of the Federal period are delicate and composed of thin elements throughout. In addition to using tapered legs, the rear legs converge sharply, reducing the overall footprint. With the visual mass reduced to a minimum, the design appears tall and light.

Federal-era chairs have more curved elements than other forms of the period, but they do not include the cyma-based reverse curves that had formed the basis for Queen Anne and early Georgian shapes. More often than not, the curves are part of Neoclassical design elements, in this case the shield shape of the chair back. With the exception of the back, the design adheres to the Neoclassical scheme of using straight structural members and curved fronts. In contrast to tables and case pieces, most Federal-era chairs rely on delicate and shallow carved detail to enhance the Neoclassical elements shown in silhouette, in this case the kylix (a shallow bowl on a pedestal), swag and plume of the splat. The use of limited carving stems from the original designs shown in Hepplewhite's *Guide* and Sheraton's *Drawing Book* and the fact that veneering and inlay work is better suited to the flat surfaces of case pieces.

RELATED FORMS

This chair back is just one of many popularized by the design books of the Neoclassical period. Among the many English designs that were published, some saw widespread acceptance in the American market while others did not suit American tastes. In the family of shield-back chairs, splat designs varied widely in shape and detail and were subject to regional variations and preferences.

A variation on the shield back was the urn back, a Rhode Island and Connecticut favorite that dispensed with the lower back rail of the shield and, like earlier chairs, extended the bottom of the splat to a shoe on the rear seat rail. The wheel back was another variation of the shield back, where a round wheel shape with spokes was substituted for the shield. Square-back chairs, consisting mostly of rectilinear elements and more closely associated with the Sheraton designs, came into widespread use later in the Neoclassical period.

STRUCTURAL NOTES

The chair is of mortise-and-tenon construction throughout, using thin $\frac{1}{4}$-in. wide tenons on the delicate joints of the stretchers and back. The rear legs and stiles are continuous from the floor to the underside of the crest rail. The rear stretcher, rear seat rail, and lower rail of the shield are tenoned to the leg and stile. The top of the stile is tenoned into the crest rail with a shouldered tenon. The splat is tenoned to the top and bottom rail of the shield with a continuous, thin tenon.

The side seat rails are tenoned through the back legs. Corner glue blocks have been added to the back inside corners and are original to the front inside corners. The tenoned joint of the rear seat rail is the only joint in the chair that is pegged. The front joints are concealed under upholstery, but the presence of large corner glue blocks suggests they are not pegged. The stretchers are tenoned to the legs and the medial stretcher is tenoned to the side stretchers. The upholstery is tacked over the rail on the front and sides but it is attached to the top of the rear seat rail, where the tacks are covered by a thin strip of wood. Above the seat, the stiles and rails that comprise the shield are semi-elliptical in cross section.

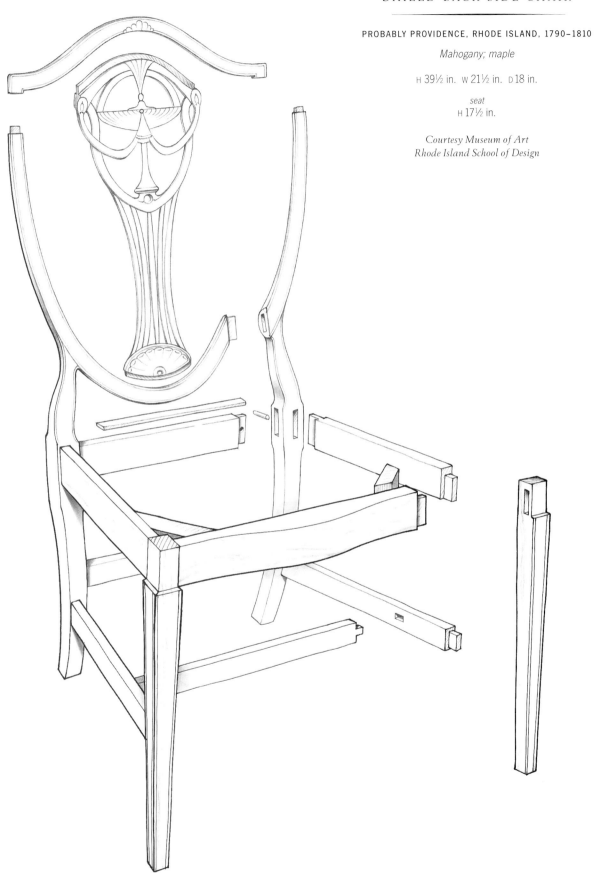

SHIELD-BACK SIDE CHAIR

PROBABLY PROVIDENCE, RHODE ISLAND, 1790–1810

Mahogany; maple

H 39½ in. W 21½ in. D 18 in.

seat
H 17½ in.

Courtesy Museum of Art
Rhode Island School of Design

WOOD AND WOOD MOVEMENT

All wood, regardless of its age or how well it has been dried in the past, has a moisture content that is in equilibrium with the humidity of the surrounding air. As the humidity changes, the wood expands or contracts.

The *moisture content* is defined as the ratio of the weight of water present in a sample of wood to the weight of the wood with no water present. This can be determined with an electronic moisture meter or by weighing the sample before and after thoroughly drying it in an oven. The calculation is then:

moisture content
$$= \frac{(\text{wet weight} - \text{dry weight})}{\text{dry weight}}$$

The ever-present moisture content in wood should not be confused with *green*, or unseasoned, wood. When a tree is first cut and sawn into boards, it is full of water in the form of sap. Most of this water is held in the cells and pores of the wood and is known as *free water*. Once the tree has been cut, the free water begins to evaporate, and eventually the only water left in the wood is that which saturates the cell walls. This is known as the *fiber saturation point* and averages 28% moisture content, though this figure varies slightly among species. Any wood with free water present, and therefore a moisture content above 28%, is considered green.

Drying the wood is intended to further reduce the moisture content. As the wood continues to dry and leave the cell walls, the wood, like a sponge, changes from damp and soft to dry and hard. As it dries and hardens, it also shrinks considerably. The wood can be only as dry as the surrounding air, so air-drying, outdoors but under cover, will allow the moisture content to drop to about 14%. Kiln-drying or storing the wood

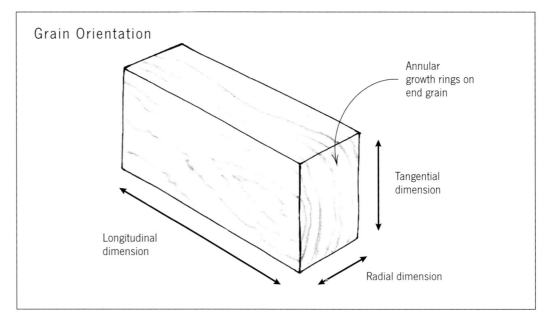

Grain Orientation

Annular growth rings on end grain

Tangential dimension

Longitudinal dimension

Radial dimension

indoors during the heating season can reduce the moisture content to 6% or less.

Even after having been thoroughly dried, wood continues to expand and contract with changes in humidity. The amount of this movement depends on the orientation of the grain and growth rings. The expansion or contraction takes place across the grain nearly twice as much in the tangential direction of the growth rings as in the radial direction across them. Changes in length are negligible. The amount of wood movement may be calculated as follows:

$\Delta D = DS \,(\Delta MC \,/\, FSP)$
where ΔD is the change in dimension,
D is the original dimension,
S is the empirically derived shrinkage percentage,
ΔMC is the change in moisture content, and
FSP is the fiber saturation point 28% (0.28)

Due to the seasonal extremes of humidity, bare wood can vary from 5% to 14% moisture content from winter to summer, which for hard maple (S tangential = 9.9%) can mean an annual expansion and contraction of ³⁄₈ in. for each foot of width in the tangential direction. Sealing the wood with a protective finish reduces the transfer of moisture in and out of the wood, and can reduce the variation of moisture content to 7% to 10%, thereby reducing seasonal movement to ⅛ in. (For more detailed information on wood movement see R. Bruce Hoadley, *Understanding Wood,* The Taunton Press, 1980.)

The primary point to remember is that all wood continually expands and contracts with changes in the humidity of the surrounding air. By knowing the principles by which it behaves, its future movement may be anticipated and calculated with accuracy. In addition, the shrinkage of original pieces, as evidenced by

cracks or the out-of-round dimensions of turnings or circular tops, may be measured and the original moisture content of the wood may be determined. Given the speed with which the moisture content of wood reaches equilibrium with the surrounding air, most large cracks on original pieces likely occurred within a year of their completion.

WOOD SHRINKAGE

WOOD	TANGENTIAL	RADIAL
Ash, white	7.8%	4.9%
Birch	9.2	7.2
Cherry	7.1	3.7
Mahogany	5.1	3.7
Maple, hard	9.9	4.8
Maple, soft	8.2	4.0
Oak, white	10.5	5.6
Pine, white	6.1	2.1
Poplar	8.2	4.6
Walnut	7.8	5.5

CHRONOLOGY OF ILLUSTRATED PUBLICATIONS

(Published in London unless otherwise noted.)

1688
JOHN STALKER & GEORGE PARKER
A Treatise of Japanning and Varnishing (Oxford)

1711
JEAN LOUIS BÉRAIN
Oeuvre de J. Bérain
Oeuvre de J. Bérain contenant des ornaments d'architecture
Ornaments Inventé par J. Bérain (Paris)

1712
DANIEL MAROT
Oeuvres du Sieur D. Marot, Architecte de Guillaume III, Roi de la Grange Bretagne
Receuil des Plances des Sieurs Marot, père et fils (Amsterdam)

1715
ANDREA PALLADIO
Four Books of Architecture, 4 volumes translated from the Venetian original of 1570

1728
JAMES GIBBS
A Book of Architecture

1734
JUSTE AURÈLE MEISSONNIER
Oeuvre de Juste Aurèle Meissonnier (Paris)

1737–1738
JACQUES FRANCOIS BLONDEL
De la Distribution des Maisons de Plaisance (Paris)

1740
MATTHIAS LOCK & HENRY COPELAND
A New Drawing Book of Ornaments

1740
BATTY LANGLEY
The City and Country Builder's and Workman's Treasury of Designs, reissued in 1745, 1750, 1756 and 1770

1742
BATTY LANGLEY
Gothic Architecture Improved by Rules and Proportions

1742
BATTY & THOMAS LANGLEY
Ancient Architecture

1744
JOHN VARDY
Some Designs of Inigo Jones and William Kent

1744
MATTHIAS LOCK
Six Sconces

1746
HENRY COPELAND
A New Book of Ornaments, 2nd edition issued c.1750

1746
MATTHIAS LOCK
A Book of Shields

1746
MATTHIAS LOCK
Six Tables

1746
MATTHIAS LOCK
The Principles of Ornament, or the Youth's Guide to Drawing of Foliage, reissued in 1768

1750–1752
WM. & JOHN HALFPENNY
New Designs for Chinese Temples, Garden Seats, etc., published in parts

1751
MATTHIAS DARLY
A New Book of Chinese, Gothic, and Chinese Chairs

1752
MATTHIAS LOCK & HENRY COPELAND
A New Book of Ornaments with Twelve Leaves

1753
WILLIAM HOGARTH
Analysis of Beauty

1754
MATTHIAS DARLY & GEORGE EDWARDS
A New Book of Chinese Designs

1754
THOMAS CHIPPENDALE
The Gentleman and Cabinet-Maker's Director

1755
THOMAS CHIPPENDALE
The Gentleman and Cabinet-Maker's Director, 2nd edition

1755
THOMAS JOHNSON
Twelve Girandoles

1756–1758
THOMAS JOHNSON
One Hundred and Fifty New Designs, published in monthly parts and in 1758 as a bound volume

1757
SIR WILLIAM CHAMBERS
Designs for Chinese Buildings and Furniture

1758
THOMAS JOHNSON
Designs for Picture Frames

1759–1763
WILLIAM INCE & JOHN MAYHEW
The Universal System of Household Furniture, published in shilling weekly installments

1759–1762
THOMAS CHIPPENDALE
The Gentleman and Cabinet-Maker's Director, published in shilling weekly installments

1760
SOCIETY OF UPHOLSTERERS AND CABINET-MAKERS
Household Furniture in Genteel Taste, Chippendale, Ince & Mayhew, and Johnson contributed, reissued 1762

C.1760
ROBERT SAYER
The Ladies' Amusement or Whole Art of Japanning made easy

1761
THOMAS JOHNSON
One Hundred and Fifty New Designs, 2nd edition

1762
P. BARETTI
A New Book of Ornaments on 16 Leaves for the Year 1762, reissued in 1766

1762
THOMAS CHIPPENDALE
The Gentleman and Cabinet-Maker's Director, 3rd edition

1762

THOMAS JOHNSON
A New Book of Ornaments

1764

ROBERT ADAM
The Ruins of the Palace of the Emperor Diocletian at Spalatro in Dalmatia

1765

J. CRUNDEN
The Carpenter's Companion for Chinese Railings and Gates

1765

J. CRUNDEN
The Joyner and Cabinet-Maker's Darling

1765

ROBERT MANWARING
The Cabinet and Chair-Maker's Real Friend and Companion

1766

ROBERT MANWARING
The Chair-Maker's Guide

1768

MATTHIAS LOCK &
HENRY COPELAND
A New Book of Ornaments, Consisting of Tables, Chimnies, Sconces, Clock Cases, etc.

1769

MATTHIAS LOCK &
HENRY COPELAND
A New Book of Foliage

1769

MATTHIAS LOCK &
HENRY COPELAND
A New Book of Pier Frames

1773–1778

ROBERT ADAM & JAMES ADAM
The Works in Architecture, published in parts

1777–1791

MICHELE ANGELO PERGOLESI
Original Designs on Various Ornaments

1779

THOMAS CHIPPENDALE, JR.
Sketches of Ornament

1788

A. HEPPLEWHITE & CO.
The Cabinet-Maker and Upholsterer's Guide

1788

THOMAS SHEARER
Designs for Househould Furniture

1788

THOMAS SHEARER,
GEO. HEPPLEWHITE, ET AL.
The Cabinet-Makers' London Book of Prices and Designs of Cabinet Work

1789

A. HEPPLEWHITE & CO.
The Cabinet-Maker and Upholsterer's Guide, 2nd edition

1791–1794

THOMAS SHERATON
The Cabinet-Maker and Upholsterer's Drawing Book, published in four parts

1793

THOMAS SHEARER,
GEO. HEPPLEWHITE, ET AL.
The Cabinet-Makers' London Book of Prices and Designs of Cabinet Work, 2nd edition

1794

A. HEPPLEWHITE & CO.
The Cabinet-Maker and Upholsterer's Guide, 3rd edition

1800–1835

PIERRE DE LA MÉSANGÈRE
Meubles et Objets de Goût, periodical (Paris)

1802

THOMAS SHERATON
The Cabinet-Maker and Upholsterer's Drawing Book, expanded edition

1802

The London Chair-Makers' and Carvers' Book of Prices for Workmanship, supplement added in 1808

1803

THOMAS SHERATON
The Cabinet Dictionary

1805

THOMAS SHERATON
The Cabinet-Maker, Upholsterer and General Artist's Encyclopaedia, unfinished, part 1

1807

THOMAS HOPE
Household Furniture and Interior Decoration

1808

GEORGE SMITH
A Collection of Designs for Household Furniture and Interior Decoration

1809–1828

RUDOLPH ACKERMAN
Repository of Arts, Literature, Commerce, Manufactures, Fashions and Politics, periodical

1812

PIERRE F. L. FONTAINE &
CHARLES PERCIER
Recueil de Décorations Intérieures, serialized since 1801, published as a bound volume in 1812 (Paris)

1812

GEORGE SMITH
A Collection of Ornamental Designs after the Manner of the Antique

1812

THOMAS SHERATON
Designs for Household Furniture...on eighty-four plates

1820

RICHARD BROWN
The Rudiments of Drawing Cabinet and Upholstery Furniture...after the manner of the antique

1826

GEORGE SMITH
The Cabinet-Makers' and Upholsterers' Guide, Drawing Book and Repository of New and Original Designs for Household Furniture

1828

P. & M. NICHOLSON
The Practical Cabinet-Maker, Upholsterer and Complete Decorator

PERIOD VARNISH RESINS

AMBER
Any of many varieties of fossil resin of vegetable origin, mined or gathered from the ground. The Baltic region is particularly rich in amber. Amber is a yellow to red-brown fossil resin, very hard like fossil copals. It is soluble in hot oil after having been heated to high temperatures to liquefy the resin.

ANIME
Also called animé or animi. Resins from the tropical American tree Hymenaea courbaril and possibly Zanzibar's *Trachylobium mossambicense.* Zanzibar animi was a rare fossilized resin used in drying-oil varnishes, soluble in hot oil only after having been liquefied. Soft resins by this name are soluble in alcohol and may have been classified as a variety of soft copal.

BENZOIN
Also called benjamin. Resin of trees of genus *Styrax*, especially S. *Benzoin* of Southeast Asia. A red-brown aromatic balsamic resin with a vanilla-like odor. Used as a primary varnish resin in the 17th and 18th centuries and as an additive to reduce brittleness in varnishes with harder resins. Also mentioned in formulae for some polishes to impart a high gloss. Soluble in alcohol.

COPAL, HARD
Includes Hard Manila copal, Kauri copal (New Zealand), Belgian Congo copal and Benguela copal. Fossil resins from a variety of trees of Africa, Australia, New Zealand and Southeast Asia. Hard copals include a wide variety of fossil resins from trees of different species. They are all very hard and generally insoluble in alcohol or turpentine. They must be liquefied by heating to about 500°F before becoming soluble in hot oil.

COPAL, SOFT
Includes Manila gum copal, Brazilian copal. Resins from Southeast Asian tree *Agathis dammara* and American sumac *Rhus copallinum* among others. Soft copals include a number of soft resins from various unrelated trees. As soft resins, they can be used in spirit varnishes and are often included in drying-oil varnishes. They are generally soluble in alcohol and turpentine, though the percentage of solubility varies among types.

DAMMAR
Resin of pinaceous trees of genus *Dammara* and dipterocarpaceous trees of Southeast Asia, Australia and New Zealand. A copal-like resin, harder than rosin but softer than most copals. Very clear as a spirit varnish. Soluble in spirits of turpentine, but only 71% soluble in alcohol.

ELEMI
Also called allemy. Resin of gumbo limbo tree *Canarium commune* or American burseraceous tree *Bursera simaruba*. Elemi includes soft resins from several trees that were added to varnishes to counter the brittle characteristics of harder resins. Soluble in alcohol and turpentine.

MASTIC
Also called pistachia galls. Resin from Mediterranean pistacia or lentix tree (*Pistacia lentiscus*). Soft pale yellow to light green, aromatic and astringent resin. Makes a clear varnish and adds elasticity and gloss to other resins. Mixed with pigment and boiled linseed oil to add luster to paints. Chewed as gum by the Turkish. Soluble in turpentine, 64% soluble in alcohol.

ROSIN
Also called colophony or turpentine. Resin from the sap of conifers including pine, fir, balsam, spruce and larch trees. Rosin is a translucent yellow to amber, brittle and fragmented resin left after the distillation of spirits of turpentine from conifer sap. It is a poor and inexpensive primary resin for varnish, but helps harder resins to flow more smoothly. In modern usage it is heated with glycerin to make synthetic ester resins. Soluble in both alcohol and turpentine. Different varieties are made from various species of tree:
- Chio turpentine: Mediterranean pines
- Venice turpentine: European larch
- Strasbourg turpentine: German fir (*Abies excelsa*)
- French rosin: maritime or cluster pine (*Pinus maritima or pinaster*)

SANDARAC
A resin from cypress or juniper-like tree of northwest Africa Tetraclinis articulata (*Callitris quadrivalvis*). A brittle, pale yellow aromatic resin; hardest of the soft, spirit-soluble resins. Makes a colorless spirit varnish greatly favored during the 18th century. Also used for incense. Soluble in alcohol.

SHELLAC
Excretion of Indian and Southeast Asian insects *Coccus lacca, Laccifer lacca, Tachardia lacca* or *Carteria lacca* on ficus and other trees, after ingestion of the sap. As deposited on branches, it contains 66% lac resin, the rest being wax, gluten and lac dye. The grades of shellac depend on its level of refinement. The lac resin is soluble only in alcohol.
- Stick lac is as found on branches.
- Seed-lac has been scraped from branches and crushed, with water soluble dye washed out.
- Button lac is the least refined shellac and is brown in color. It has been melted and filtered through fabric. Often 10%–20% rosin has been added.
- Garnet lac is a dark amber color and has had the shellac waxes, which are insoluble in alcohol, removed. Sometimes also includes 10%–20% rosin.
- Orange shellac is a light amber color and has most impurities removed. It is the best of the shellac film finishes, as it is more stable and elastic than all others.
- Blonde shellac has been bleached to remove the remaining amber color.

PERIOD COLORANTS

ALKANET ROOT: red
Red dye from the root of the European and American plant *Alkanna tinctoria* and related plants. Used to color oil and turpentine.

BARBERRY ROOT: yellow
European and American shrub of genus *Berberis,* especially *B. vulgaris.* Bark and roots yield yellow dye when boiled in water.

BRAZILWOOD: red and purple
Dyewood from various tropical trees of genus *Caesalpinia,* especially American *C. Echinata* and Indian *C. sappan.* The sawdust of the heartwood was an important dyestuff in the 17th and 18th centuries. The color is extracted from the dust by boiling in water.

DRAGON'S BLOOD: red
A dark red resin from various species of the tropical plant *Dracaena,* or the fruit of the Malaysian and East African palm *Daemonorops draco.* The resin is soluble in alcohol, but not in water.

FRENCH BERRIES: yellow
Also called Avignon berries. Small berries of prickly shrub of the buckthorn family, *Rhamnus infectoria,* which grows along the northern Mediterranean coast. Yield a yellow dye when boiled in water.

IRON LIQUOR: grey-brown to black
A grey-brown, water-based dye stain produced by soaking rusted iron scraps in water with the addition of acetic acid (vinegar) and tannic acid (nut galls). Could be used in conjunction with logwood dye to yield a black color.

LOGWOOD: red
Also called campeachy wood. Dense dyewood from tropical Indian and Central American tree *Haematoxylon campeachianum.* The color is extracted from the dust by boiling in water. The addition of other chemicals can turn the red to a purple, brown or black.

NUT GALLS: yellow-brown to brown
Nut galls are abnormal growths or excrescences on plants caused by insects, damage, disease or other injuries. They contain concentrated sap and bark constituents. Most references refer to oak nut galls, which are a source of tannic acid used in conjunction with other colorants.

OCHRE: yellow to red-brown
Any of a class of natural earth pigments composed of silica or clay with hydrated iron oxides. Usually ground with linseed oil to produce paint or pigmented stain.

ORCHIL: red to purple
Also called archil and orseille. A water-based dye derived from the Mediterranean lichen, especially the species *Rocella.* It is purple in its natural state, but can be turned more red or blue with alkali treatment.

SIENNA: yellow-brown to red-brown
A class of natural earth pigments like ochre with a yellow-brown color. Sienna may be roasted to produce burnt sienna and deepen its color to a red-brown. Ground with linseed oil to produce paint or pigmented stain.

TURMERIC: yellow
Aromatic, ground rootlike stem of Indian plant *Curcuma longa.* Also used as a cooking spice to make curry. Yields a yellow dye when boiled in water.

UMBER: red-brown to brown
Natural earth pigments like ochre and sienna but with manganese dioxide. Raw umber is brown, burnt umber is red-brown. Ground with linseed oil for paint or pigmented stain.

VANDYKE BROWN: medium to dark brown
Also called Cassel earth or Cologne earth. An organic brown pigment derived from peat. Substitutes use red iron oxide and lamp black to achieve the same color. Usually ground with linseed oil for paint or pigmented stain but also used as colorant for water-based dye.

WALNUT PEELINGS: brown-black
The peelings and shells of walnuts are called for in formulae for black ebonizing stains. They are boiled in water with logwood and vinegar, sometimes with a wash of an iron sulfate solution to deepen the color.

PERIOD FINISHING FORMULAE

Original methods of making stains and finishes are nearly as numerous as the shops that used them. Many have been published repeatedly, with slight variations, since the late 18th and early 19th centuries, and their true origins are not clear. Some of the more representative formulae, using materials that are known to have been available, are listed here. Specific sources are noted, but most of these formulae are among those that appeared in *The Cabinet-Maker's Guide* (London, 1809), its many subsequent editions, and a host of similar guide books that proliferated into the early 20th century. These are not intended to be definitive 18th-century recipes, since there were none that could be considered true standards, but they do represent a general description of finishing formulae that were used during the period.

Caution: Any of these formulae that involve the use of heat or acids are exceptionally dangerous to make or use. Alcohol, spirits of turpentine, linseed oil and their vapors are all combustible and should never be used near fire or flame or without adequate ventilation. The authors of the 1688 *A Treatise of Japanning and Varnishing* warned:

Some artists...scruple not to strain...varnish by fire or candle-light: but certainly day-light is much more proper, and less dangerous; for should your varnish...take fire, value not that loss, but rather thank your stars that your self and work-house have escaped....It would almost excite ones pitty, to see [one] perish thus in the beginning of his Enterprise; ...his beginning and his end are of the same date; his hopes vanish, and his mischance shall be registered in doggrel Ballad, or be frightfully represented in a Puppet-show or on a Sign-post.

These finishing formulae are presented for study and are not intended as recipes to be followed; most are quite inferior to their modern counterparts.

STAINS
Brown Stain:
   1 lb. Vandyke brown
   4 qt. water
   2 oz. potash
Boil the Vandyke brown in the water until the volume is reduced to $2^2/_3$ qt. Add just enough water to the potash to dissolve it and add it to the reduced liquid. Apply two or three coats with a brush.

Aquafortis (nitric acid) is credited in many books as imparting a nice brown color to a variety of woods. It is mentioned as being used in a dilute solution of one part acid to ten parts water, and full strength, though that strength in the 18th century is uncertain.

Red Stain:
   2 oz. dragon's blood
   1 qt. rectified spirits of wine (alcohol)
Break the dragon's blood into small pieces and mix with the spirits of wine. Allow the bottle to stand in a warm place and shake occasionally until the colorant is dissolved.

   8 oz. logwood chips
   3 pt. water
   $1/_2$ oz. salt of tartar (potassium carbonate, a potash)
Boil the logwood chips in water until a very dark red is obtained. Add the salt of tartar and apply to the wood with a brush while boiling hot. Two or three coats with drying between may be required.

Black Stain:
   1 lb. logwood chips
   4 qt. water
   2 handfuls walnut peelings
   1 pt. vinegar
Boil the logwood in water; add the walnut peelings and boil it again. Strain out the chips and add the vinegar. Apply the stain boiling hot. Black stain is improved by a coat of 1 oz. copperas (ferrous sulfate) dissolved in 1 qt. water, applied hot after the logwood solution has dried.

   1 lb. logwood chips
   4 qt. water
   2 oz. iron filings
   1 pint vinegar
Boil the logwood in water, and apply the liquid to the wood three or four times, allowing it to dry in between. Dissolve the iron filings in the vinegar and apply it to the wood.

In addition to these methods, linseed oil, made to dry by boiling and the addition of lead-oxide dryers, could be colored by adding pigments such as burnt sienna, burnt umber or Vandyke brown. It could also be tinted red with alkanet root. Spirits of turpentine were added to thin the oil.

VARNISHES
Sandarac Spirit Varnishes:
   1 lb. sandarac
   1 oz. mastic
   3 oz. Venice turpentine
   $1^1/_2$ oz. copal
   $1/_2$ oz. elemi
   $1/_2$ oz. benzoin
   $1^1/_2$ oz. anime
   $1/_2$ oz. rosin
   3 to 6 pt. spirits of wine (alcohol)
The anime, benzoin, copal and rosin must be crushed to a powder. Dissolve in separate bottles: the copal and rosin in $1/_2$ pt. spirits; the anime, benzoin and Venice turpentine in $3/_4$ pt.; the sandarac and mastic in $1^1/_2$ pt; and the elemi in $1/_4$ pt. Allow to dissolve for two or three days, shaking each occasionally. Strain the contents of each bottle through linen into a larger bottle. Stalker and Parker, *A Treatise of Japanning and Varnishing* (Oxford, 1688)

   5 oz. sandarac
   2 oz. mastic
   1 oz. elemi
   1 oz. oil of lavender
   1 or 2 lb. (pt.) spirits of wine
Dissolve the ingredients in the top of a double-boiler, not allowing the alcohol to boil. When cool, filter through cotton. André-Jacques Roubo, *L'art du menuisier* ("The art of the joiner," 3 vols., Paris, 1769–1774)

   5 lb. sandarac
   1 lb. mastic
   4 oz. anime
   2 gal. spirits of wine
Add the resins to the alcohol and keep the mixture in a warm place, shaking occasionally, until the resins are dissolved. Strain out any remaining solids. *The Cabinet-Maker's Guide* (London, 1809; Concord, N. H., 1827)

Seed-Lac Varnish:
   $1^1/_2$ lb. seed-lac (unrefined shellac resin granules, water-soluble dye washed out)
   1 gal. spirits of wine
Add the seed-lac to the spirits and let stand for 24 hours or more. Shake and strain into bottles through flannel, squeezing out all the liquid. Allow to stand undisturbed for two or three days. Pour off the clear top part of the liquid into another bottle, allow the remainder to settle for a day or two, and repeat. This is said to have clarity, but a "reddish tawny color." (*A Treatise of Japanning and Varnishing,* 1688)

Shell-Lac Varnish:

$1\frac{1}{2}$ lb. shell-lac (shellac resin flakes, which have been melted, filtered, stretched into sheets, and broken into flakes)

1 gal. spirits of wine

Stir and shake the ingredients together, allow to stand for 24 hours, and strain. This has little sediment, but lacks clarity. It is described as being dull and foggy but commonly used for varnishing olive wood and walnut. The authors state, "Whosoever designs a neat, glossy piece of work must banish this as unservicable for, and inconsistent with the rarities of our art." This formula is identical to that of seed-lac varnish, but without the more elaborate filtering and decanting procedure. (*A Treatise of Japanning and Varnishing,* 1688)

Copal Spirit Varnish:

5 oz. copal

3 oz. shellac flakes

1 qt. alcohol

Grind the resins to powder and mix with alcohol. Bottle the mixture and put it in a warm place, with occasional shaking until the resins are dissolved.

Turpentine Varnish:

20 oz. rosin

1 qt. spirits of turpentine

Boil the rosin in the turpentine for 30 minutes; allow to cool before using. (This was also called common brown varnish. It was inexpensive, brittle and of poor quality.)

Oil Varnish:

1 qt. linseed oil

$\frac{1}{2}$ lb. rosin

2 oz. spirits of turpentine

Boil the linseed oil for an hour and then add the rosin, stirring until it is dissolved. Then add the turpentine. Upon cooling, strain the mixture and bottle it for use.

Vernis Martin (Martin's Copal Varnish):

8 oz. Chio turpentine

8 oz. amber, crushed

1 lb. copal, crushed

3 pt. 4 oz. spirits of turpentine

2 oz. colophony

24 oz. oil, linseed, poppy or nut oil, boiled with dryers added

Warm the melting pot and melt 4 oz. Chio turpentine. Add the 8 oz. of amber, mix well and leave on the heat for 15 minutes. Remove from heat; add the 1 lb. copal, the remaining 4 oz. Chio turpentine, and 4 oz. of warm spirits of turpentine. Return the mixture to the heat for about 30 minutes, stir well and add the 2 oz. colophony while stirring. Keep it on the heat until all the solid resins are dissolved. Boil the 24 oz. of oil and combine it with the resins, stirring it with a long stick. Return it to the heat and bring the whole to a boil again. Remove it from the heat and add 1 qt. of hot spirits of turpentine. Bring this to a boil, remove it from the heat and add 1 pt. more of hot spirits of turpentine. (This is the famous drying-oil varnish made by the Parisian varnishmaking Martin family and was a much sought-after formula in its day. It sounds exceptionally dangerous to make.) *Genuine Receipt for making the Famous Vernis Martin...* (Paris and Dublin, 1776)

True French Polish:

1 pt. spirits of wine (alcohol)

$\frac{1}{4}$ oz. copal

$\frac{1}{4}$ oz. gum arabic

1 oz. shellac flakes

Crush the resins and mix them with the spirits of wine. Place them in a closed vessel and keep them near a warm stove, shake occasionally, and in two or three days the resins will have dissolved. Strain through muslin and keep tightly corked for use.

Wax Finish:

1 part beeswax

1 part spirits of turpentine

1 part linseed oil

Mix the ingredients with the aid of heat until well dissolved. Two drams of alkanet root infused into the turpentine will give the finish a red color. Apply with a brush or cloth, allow to dry and buff the wax film. (Wax was also applied as a paste, shaved and just softened with turpentine.)

POLISHES

Beeswax Polish:

4 oz. beeswax

1 pt. spirits of turpentine

$\frac{1}{4}$ oz. rosin

1 oz. alkanet root

Boil the turpentine with the alkanet root to extract as much of the color as possible. Scrape the beeswax into a pot and add just enough of the turpentine to moisten it. Add the rosin and mix. Cover and let stand for six hours. Apply to the surface, let dry and buff.

For Spiriting-Off and Polishing French Polish:

1 pt. alcohol

$\frac{1}{4}$ oz. benzoin

$\frac{1}{4}$ oz. shellac

4 tsp. poppy oil

Mix the resins with the alcohol. Keep the mixture in a warm place, with occasional shaking, until all the resins are dissolved. Upon cooling, add the poppy oil, shake well, and it is ready for use. Apply in a light and quick circular motion with a cloth just slightly dampened with the polish.

Linseed-Oil Polish:

$\frac{1}{2}$ pt. spirits of turpentine

$\frac{1}{2}$ pt. boiled linseed oil

$\frac{1}{2}$ pt. strong vinegar

1 to 3 oz. rottenstone (optional)

Combine the turpentine, linseed oil and vinegar and shake well. Apply to the surface, rub well and remove the excess. Buff later to remove all traces of oil. Add rottenstone to the mixture to cut through accumulated grime and wax. The linseed oil in this formula will darken wood, so this polish should only be used on the intact surfaces of new furniture.

ANTHEMION
An ornament of flowers or buds arranged in a linear string pattern; usually associated with the Neoclassical style. Also a radiating pattern of Greek origin suggesting a honeysuckle bud.

BANDING
See Crossbanding. Feather banding.

BANDY LEG
Short cabriole leg used on case pieces such as chests or desks that would otherwise have bracket feet.

BLOCK FRONT
A design treatment for case pieces where the front surface is divided into three vertical sections; the outer two are raised forward and the center section is recessed.

BOMBÉ
A case shape in which the vertical lines of the case side and front are swelled outward; from the French for "bulged" or "swelled."

BOSS
A half turning, often oval in shape, applied as a decorative surface ornament; most often used on case pieces of the Jacobean style.

BOULLEWORK
Intricate marquetry of tortoiseshell, brass, silver, horn, ivory and mother-of-pearl as practiced by André-Charles Boulle (1642–1732); sometimes *buhlwork.*

BRACKET FOOT
A foot for case furniture, consisting of two pieces shaped in profile and joined at right angles, that is affixed to the corner of the case below the base molding.

CABOCHON
A smooth, convex panel, oval or round in shape.

CARTOUCHE
A smooth, flat or convex panel surrounded by scrolled carving, as would hold an inscription or initials.

CARYATID
A decorative support column in the form of a female figure.

CHINOISERIE
Any of a number of European decorative techniques in imitation of Chinese design and ornament.

COCKBEADING
Small astragal molding, half-round in cross section, used to surround drawer fronts or drawer openings.

COMPASS SEAT
A chair seat that is curved in plan, with a convex shape at the front corners and across the front and a concave shape at the two sides; sometimes called a *balloon* or *horseshoe* seat.

COVE MOLDING
A concave molding profile; also called a *cavetto* molding.

CREST RAIL
The uppermost horizontal rail, usually of a chair back; often carved or shaped.

CROSSBANDING
A narrow band of veneer applied to the edge of a drawer front or surface in which the grain of the veneer is oriented perpendicular to the length of the banding. *See also* Feather banding.

CURULE
An ancient Roman chair design with an X-shaped base, which in its original form could be folded.

CYMA CURVE
An S-shaped curve, sweeping in one direction and then the opposite. Originally seen in the molding profiles of classical architecture but adapted as a basis of curved furniture elements in the late Baroque period.

DUSTBOARD
A horizontal panel built into a case to separate one drawer opening from those above and below it.

DUTCH FOOT
A flat, disclike foot, usually for cabriole legs, most of which is shaped on the lathe to include a small-diameter cylindrical pad at the floor; also called a *pad* foot.

EBONIZING
Application of black pigment to wood to simulate the appearance of ebony.

FEATHER BANDING
Two narrow bands of veneer applied to the edge of a drawer front or surface in which the grain of each strip is oriented at 45° to the length of the banding and at 90° to each other. The banding has the appearance of the structure of a bird's feather. *See also* Crossbanding.

FEATHER EDGE
An edge tapered in thickness to a point or to a thin dimension.

FORM
A joined bench with rails, stretchers and a flat board for the top. An elongated version of a *joint stool.*

FRENCH FOOT
A thin, tapered foot for case pieces, characterized by a gentle outward curve.

FRENCH POLISHING
A method for applying a finish wherein a ball of cloth, moistened with shellac spirit varnish, is rubbed lightly over the wood surface in either a repeated series of quick passes or in a tight circular motion.

GIRANDOLE
An elaborately ornamented wall-hung mirror frame, often with candleholders; frequently of Chinese or Rococo design.

HALLUX
The rear digit in the claws of raptorial birds of prey and the claws of ball and claw feet.

HUSK AND DROP
A linear inlay of flowers and buds used in Neoclassical designs.

JAPANNING
An imitation of Oriental lacquer consisting of raised gilded figures on a black or mottled background.

JOINT STOOL
A small stool with turned legs joined by rails and stretchers with a flat board for the top.

KICKER
A rail within a case positioned above a drawer to prevent the drawer from tipping downward when opened.

KLISMOS
An ancient Greek chair design notable for tapered curved legs sweeping forward and backward below the seat.

LOPER
A sliding rail that extends to support a leaf or lid.

MARLBOROUGH LEG
A straight leg, sometimes with a molded shape along its length, often ending in a square plinth of slightly greater width.

OGEE FOOT
A bracket foot with a cyma-shaped surface profile.

ORMOLU
A gilded bronze decorative mount.

OVOLO
A convex molding profile approximating a quarter section of an ellipse.

PATERAE
Ornaments in the shape of circles or ovals, usually seen in Neoclassical designs.

PATINA
The accumulation of marks, encrustations and grime and a degradation of the surface usually associated with great age or use.

PEDIMENT
An architectural term for a peaked feature atop the cornice molding that is either triangular in shape or broken at the center with straight or cyma-shaped segments rising on either side.

PEMBROKE TABLE
Any of a number of small drop-leaf tables approximately 3 ft. in length and width when open; also called a *breakfast* table.

PIECRUST TOP
A decorative edge treatment primarily used on pedestal tables where the raised molded edge is shaped in a series of connected cyma curves.

PINTLE
A cylindrical protrusion extending from the top block or bird-cage of a pedestal table into a hole in the batten on the underside of the top about which the top pivots to tilt.

PLINTH
A square or rectangular block, usually serving as a base for a leg or a finial.

PULVINATED
A slightly convex molding profile, usually used in a frieze; from the Latin *pulvinus,* or cushion.

PUMICE
A powdered form of volcanic glass used as a mild abrasive for rubbing out a finish.

ROTTENSTONE
Decomposed siliceous limestone, usually more finely powdered than pumice, used for polishing a finish to a higher luster than that possible with pumice.

RULE JOINT
A joint used in drop-leaf tables where the profile of a quarter-round and fillet in the top fit into a cove and fillet in the leaf, thereby concealing the hinge and eliminating a gap.

RUNNER
A rail within a case on which a drawer slides.

SERPENTINE FRONT
A shape for the front of case pieces that is reverse-curved in plan, with concave sections flanking a convex center. Reverse-serpentine fronts have convex sections flanking a concave center.

SHOE
A horizontal element, often with a concave profile on the front and sides, that joins the vertical splat of a chair with the back seat rail.

SLIPPER FOOT
A foot for cabriole legs that has a teardrop-shaped footprint, being rounded at the heel and pointed at the front.

SPADE FOOT
A tapered plinth foot, smaller at the bottom than the top, usually used to terminate a square-tapered leg.

SPANISH FOOT
A brushlike, outwardly swept foot seen in post-Restoration furniture through the William and Mary period.

SPLAT
The central vertical element of a chair back rising from the seat or lower cross-rail to the upper crest rail.

STRINGING
A narrow linear inlay of one or more strips of veneer.

TESTER
The frame of a tall-post bed from which hangs the canopy or bed hangings.

TIP-TOP TABLE
A pedestal table on which the top is hinged to tip to the vertical position.

TORUS MOLDING
A large convex molding, nearly semicircular in profile.

TRIFID FOOT
A foot of three connected lobes for cabriole legs; also called a *drake* foot.

VASIFORM
A form resembling a classical vase shape, similar to an inverted baluster shape.

VOLUTE
A spiral or scroll-shaped ornament.

WHORL FOOT
A foot in a spiral, volute form.

BIBLIOGRAPHY

Barquist, David L.
American Tables and Looking Glasses in the Mabel Brady Garvan and Other Collections at Yale University. New Haven, Conn.: Yale University Art Gallery, 1992.

Bjerkoe, Ethel Hall, with John Arthur Bjerkoe.
The Cabinetmakers of America. New York: Bonanza Books, 1957.

Blow, Michael, ed.
The American Heritage History of the Thirteen Colonies. New York: American Heritage Publishing Co., 1967.

Boger, Louise Ade.
The Complete Guide to Furniture Styles. Enlarged ed. New York: Charles Scribner's Sons, 1969.

Bridenbaugh, Carl.
Cities in the Wilderness: The First Century of Urban Life in America, 1652–1752. New York: The Ronald Press Co., 1938.

Bushman, Richard L.
The Refinement of America: Persons, Houses, Cities. New York: Alfred A. Knopf, 1992.

Carpenter, Ralph E.
The Arts and Crafts of Newport, Rhode Island, 1640–1820. Newport, R. I.: The Preservation Society of Newport County, 1954.

Carter, Isaac Newton, and H. Loren Thompson.
Engineering Drawing: Practice and Theory. 2nd ed. Scranton, Penn.: International Textbook Co., 1943.

Cescinsky, Herbert.
English Furniture from Gothic to Sheraton. 3rd ed. New York: Bonanza Books, 1967.

Cescinsky, Herbert, and George Leland Hunter.
English and American Furniture. Garden City, N. Y.: Garden City Publishing Co., 1929.

Chase, A. W.
Dr. Chase's Recipes or Information for Everybody. Ann Arbor, Mich.: R. A. Beal, 1876.

Chippendale, Thomas.
The Gentleman and Cabinet-Maker's Director. 3rd ed. London, 1762. Reprint. New York: Dover Publications, 1966.

Christie's.
The Collection of Mr. And Mrs. Eddy Nicholson. New York: Christie, Manson & Woods International, Inc., 1994.

Comstock, Helen.
American Furniture: Seventeenth, Eighteenth, and Nineteenth Century Styles. New York: Bonanza Books, 1962.

Davidson, Marshall B., ed.
The American Heritage History of American Antiques from the Revolution to the Civil War. New York: American Heritage Publishing Co., 1967.

Davidson, Marshall B., ed.
The American Heritage History of Colonial Antiques. New York: American Heritage Publishing Co., 1967.

Davidson, Marshall B., and Elizabeth Stillinger.
The American Wing at the Metropolitan Museum of Art. New York: The Metropolitan Museum of Art, Alfred A. Knopf, 1985.

de la Croix, Horst, and Richard G. Tansey.
Gardner's Art Through the Ages. 5th ed. New York: Harcourt, Brace and World, 1970.

Durant, Will and Ariel.
The Story of Civilization. Vols. 7–9: *The Age of Reason Begins, The Age of Louis XIV, The Age of Voltaire.* 11 vols. New York: Simon and Schuster, 1961–1965.

Ecke, Gustave.
Chinese Domestic Furniture in Photographs and Measured Drawings. Peking, 1944. Reprint. New York: Dover Publications, 1986.

Edwards, Ralph, and Margaret Jourdain.
Georgian Cabinetmakers. Rev. ed. London: Country Life Ltd., 1946.

Fairbanks, Jonathan L., and Elizabeth Bidwell Bates.
American Furniture: 1620 to the Present. New York: Richard Marek Publishers, 1981.

Fales, Dean A., Jr.
The Furniture of Historic Deerfield. 2nd ed. Deerfield, Mass.: Historic Deerfield, Inc., 1981.

Forman, Benno M.
American Seating Furniture 1630–1730: An Interpretive Catalog. New York: The Winterthur Museum, W. W. Norton & Co., 1988.

Gaynor, James M., and Nancy L. Hagedorn.
Tools: Working Wood in Eighteenth-Century America. Williamsburg, Va.: The Colonial Williamsburg Foundation, 1993.

Gilbert, Christopher.
The Life and Work of Thomas Chippendale. Bristol, England: Artlines (UK) Ltd., 1978.

Gloag, John.
A Complete Dictionary of Furniture. Rev. ed. Woodstock, N. Y.: The Overlook Press, 1991.

Godfrey, C., comp. & ed.
The Hardwood Finisher. New York: The Industrial Publication Co., 1908.

Greenlaw, Barry A.
New England Furniture at Williamsburg. Williamsburg, Va.: The Colonial Williamsburg Foundation, 1974.

Gregory, E. W.
The Furniture Collector: Old English Furniture of the XVII & XVIII Centuries. London: Herbert Jenkins, Ltd., n. d., c.1915.

Harris, Nathaniel.
Chippendale. Secaucus, N. J.: Chartwell Books, 1989.

Hayward, Charles H.
Antique or Fake?: The Making of Old Furniture. New York: Van Nostrand Reinhold, 1970.

Heckscher, Morrison H.
American Furniture in the Metropolitan Museum of Art. Vol. 2: *Late Colonial Period: the Queen Anne and Chippendale Styles.* New York: The Metropolitan Museum of Art, Random House, 1985.

Heckscher, Morrison H., and Leslie Greene Bowman.
American Rococo, 1750–1775: Elegance in Ornament. New York: The Metropolitan Museum of Art, Los Angeles County Museum of Art, Harry N. Abrams, 1992.

Hepplewhite, A., & Co. (George).
The Cabinet-Maker and Upholsterer's Guide. 3rd ed. London, 1794. Reprint. New York: Dover Publications, 1969.

Hinckley, F. Lewis.
A Directory of American Furniture. New York: Bonanza Books, 1953.

Hinckley, F. Lewis.
Directory of the Historic Cabinet Woods. New York: Bonanza Books, 1960.

Hiscox, Gardner D.
Henley's Formulas for Home and Workshop. Enlarged ed. New York: Avenal Books, 1979.

Hoadley, R. Bruce.
Understanding Wood: A Craftsman's Guide to Wood Technology. Newtown, Conn.: The Taunton Press, 1980.

Hope, Thomas.
Household Furniture and Interior Decoration. London, 1807. Reprinted as *Regency Furniture and Interior Decoration.* Dover Publications, 1971.

Jobe, Brock, ed.
Portsmouth Furniture: Masterworks from the New Hampshire Seacoast. Boston: Society for the Preservation of New England Antiquities, 1993.

Jobe, Brock, and Myrna Kaye.
New England Furniture: The Colonial Era. Boston: Houghton Mifflin Co., 1984.

Kane, Patricia E.
300 Years of American Seating Furniture: Chairs and Beds from the Mabel Brady Garvan and Other Collections at Yale University. Boston: New York Graphic Society, 1976.

Kates, George N.
Chinese Household Furniture. Toronto & London, 1948. Reprint. New York: Dover Publications, 1962.

Kaye, Myrna.
Fake, Fraud, or Genuine?: Identifying Authentic American Antique Furniture. Boston: Little, Brown & Co., 1987.

Keno, Leigh, Joan Barzalay Freund and Alan Miller.
"The Very Pink of the Mode: Boston Georgian Chairs, their Export and Influence." *American Furniture 1996.* Milwaukee, Wis.: Chipstone Foundation, 1996.

Ketchum, William C., Jr., with The Museum of American Folk Art.
American Cabinetmakers: Marked American Furniture, 1640–1940. New York: Crown Publishers, 1995.

Kettell, Russell Hawes.
The Pine Furniture of Early New England.
New York: Dover Publications, 1929.

Kirk, John T.
*American Chairs: Queen Anne and
Chippendale.* New York: Alfred A.
Knopf, 1972.

Kirk, John T.
*American Furniture and the British
Tradition to 1830.* New York: Alfred A.
Knopf, 1982.

Kirk, John T.
*Early American Furniture: How to
Recognize, Evaluate, Buy and Care for the
Most Beautiful Pieces–High Style,
Country, Primitive and Rustic.* New York:
Alfred A. Knopf, 1970.

Landrey, Gregory J.
"The Finish Crack'd: Conservator's fix
for a fractured film." *Fine Woodworking,*
No. 49 (November/December 1984):
pp. 74-76.

Lockwood, Luke Vincent.
Colonial Furniture in America. 3rd ed.
2 vols. New York: Charles Scribner's
Sons, 1926.

**Madigan, Mary Jean, and
Susan Colgan, ed.**
*Early American Furniture from Settlement
to City: Aspects of Form, Style and
Regional Design from 1620 to 1830.* New
York: An Art and Antiques Book,
Billboard Publications, 1983.

Main, Jackson Turner.
*The Social Structure of Revolutionary
America.* Princeton, N. J.: Princeton
University Press, 1965.

**Mayhew, Edgar de N., and
Minor Myers, Jr.**
*A Documentary History of American
Interiors: From the Colonial Era to 1915.*
New York: Charles Scribner's Sons,
1980.

McLoughlin, William G.
Rhode Island, A History. New York:
W. W. Norton & Co., 1978.

Miller, Edgar G., Jr.
*American Antique Furniture: A Book for
Amateurs.* 2 vols. New York: M. Barrows
& Co., 1937.

**Monkhouse, Christopher P., and
Thomas S. Michie.**
American Furniture in Pendleton House.
Providence, R. I.: Museum of Art,
Rhode Island School of Design, 1986.

Montgomery, Charles F.
*American Furniture: The Federal Period,
in the Henry Francis duPont Winterthur
Museum.* New York, Viking Press, 1966.

Morse, Frances Clary.
Furniture of the Olden Time. New York:
Macmillan Co., 1902.

**Moses, Michael, and
Israel Sack, Inc.**
*Master Craftsmen of Newport: The
Townsends and Goddards.* Tenafly, N. J.:
MMI Americana Press, 1984.

Moxon, Joseph.
*Mechanick Exercises or the Doctrine of
Handy-Works.* London, 1703. Reprint.
Mendham, N. J.: The Astragal Press,
1994.

Mussey, Robert D.
"Early Varnishes: The 18th century's
search for the perfect film finish." *Fine
Woodworking,* No. 35 (July/August
1982): pp. 54-57.

Mussey, Robert D.
"Old Finishes: What put the shine on
furniture's Golden Age." *Fine
Woodworking,* No. 33 (March/April
1982): pp. 71-75.

Mussey, Robert D., Jr., ed.
*The First American Furniture Finisher's
Manual.* Originally *The Cabinet-Maker's
Guide.* Concord, N. H.: Jacob B. Moore,
1827. Reprint. New York: Dover
Publications, 1987.

**Newell, Adnah Clifton, and
William F. Holtrop.**
Coloring, Finishing and Painting Wood.
Rev. ed. Peoria, Ill.: Charles A. Bennett
Co., 1972.

Nutting, Wallace.
*Furniture of the Pilgrim Century (of
American Origin) 1620-1720.* 2 vols.
Framingham Mass., 1924. Reprint. New
York: Dover Publications, 1965.

Nutting, Wallace.
*Furniture Treasury (Mostly of American
Origin).* 3 vols. New York: Macmillan
Publishing Co., 1928, 1933.

Oates, Phyllis Bennett.
The Story of Western Furniture. London:
The Herbert Press, 1981.

Ott, Joseph K., et al.
*The John Brown House Loan Exhibition of
Rhode Island Furniture.* Providence, R. I.:
The Rhode Island Historical Society,
1965.

Palladio, Andrea.
The Four Books of Architecture. London,
1738. Reprint. New York: Dover
Publications, 1965.

Payne, Christopher, ed.
*Sotheby's Concise Encyclopedia of
Furniture.* London: Conran Octopus,
1989.

Randall, Richard H.
*American Furniture in the Museum of
Fine Arts Boston.* Boston: Museum of
Fine Arts, 1965.

Reich, Jerome R.
Colonial America. Englewood Cliffs,
N.J.: Prentice Hall, 1989.

Sack, Albert.
Fine Points of Furniture, Early American.
New York: Crown Publishers, 1950.

Sack, Albert.
*The New Fine Points of Furniture: Early
American, Good, Better, Best, Superior,
Masterpiece.* New York: Crown
Publishers, 1993.

Sack, Harold, and Max Wilk.
American Treasure Hunt. New York:
DKB Publishing, 1986.

Sack, Israel, Inc.
*American Furniture from the Israel Sack
Collection.* 10 vols. Alexandria, Va.:
Highland Press Publishers, 1957–1991.

Salaman, R. A.
*Dictionary of Woodworking Tools
c. 1700-1970.* Rev. ed. Newtown,
Conn.: The Taunton Press, 1990.

Salomonsky, Verna Cook.
*Masterpieces of Furniture in Photographs
and Measured Drawings.* Grand Rapids,
Mich., 1931. New York: Dover
Publications, 1953.

Santore, Charles.
The Windsor Style in America. Vol. 1 & 2.
Philadelphia: Running Press, 1992.

Sellens, Alvin.
*Woodworking Planes: A Descriptive
Register of Wooden Planes.* Augusta,
Kansas: Alvin Sellens, 1978.

Sheraton, Thomas.
*The Cabinet-Maker and Upholsterer's
Drawing Book.* London, 1793–1802.
Reprint. New York: Dover Publications,
1972.

Sloane, Eric.
A Museum of Early American Tools. New
York: Funk and Wagnalls, 1964.

Smith, Page.
*The Shaping of America: A People's
History of the Young Republic.* New York:
McGraw-Hill Book Co., 1980.

Stair, Alastair A.,
"Claw and Ball Feet: Where they came
from." *Fine Woodworking,* No. 10
(Spring 1978): pp. 55-57.

Stalker, John, and George Parker.
A Treatise of Japanning and Varnishing.
Oxford, 1688. Reprint. London: Alec
Tiranti, 1960.

Stoneman, Vernon C.
*John and Thomas Seymour,
Cabinetmakers in Boston, 1794-1816.*
Boston: Special Publications, 1959.

Trent, Robert F.
*Hearts and Crowns: Folk Chairs of the
Connecticut Coast.* New Haven, Conn.:
New Haven Historical Society, 1977.

Venable, Charles L.
*American Furniture in the Bybee
Collection.* Austin, Tex.: University of
Texas Press, Dallas Museum of Art,
1989.

Wadsworth Atheneum.
*Connecticut Furniture: Seventeenth and
Eighteenth Centuries.* Hartford, Conn.:
Wadsworth Atheneum, 1967.

Ward, Gerald W. R.
*American Case Furniture in the Mabel
Brady Garvan and Other Collections at
Yale University.* New Haven, Conn.: Yale
University Art Gallery, 1988.

Ward, Gerald W. R., ed.
Perspectives on American Furniture. New
York: A Winterthur Book, W. W.
Norton & Co., 1988.

Wertenbaker, Thomas J.
The Golden Age of Colonial Culture.
Ithaca, N. Y.: Cornell University Press,
1975.

Zea, Philip, and Suzanne L. Flynt.
Hadley Chests. Deerfield, Mass.:
Pocumtuck Valley Memorial
Association, 1992.

CREDITS

British Museum, London, England
(© p. 16)

Brooklyn Museum, New York (pgs. 37 right [Henry L. Batterman Fund], 252)

Collections of Henry Ford Museum and Greenfield Village, Dearborn, Michigan (pgs. 21 bottom left, 42 bottom, 107 bottom)

Colonial Williamsburg Foundation (pgs. 11 top right, 21 top, 24 right, 46 top, 47 bottom, 76 bottom, 77 bottom, 177)

Connecticut Historical Society, Hartford, Connecticut (pgs. 11 top left, 70 top)

Dallas Museum of Art (pgs. 67 top [Faith P. and Charles L. Bybee Collection, gift of Mr. and Mrs. Charles Sharp], 91 bottom [Faith P. and Charles L. Bybee Collection, gift of Effie and Wofford Cain Foundation], 95 bottom right [Faith P. and Charles L. Bybee Collection, gift of Cecil and Ida Green])

Detroit Institute of Arts, Founders Society Purchase, Eleanor Clay Ford Fund, General Membership Fund, Endowment Income Fund and Special Activities Fund (p. 6)

Dover Publications (pgs. 35 bottom [*Chinese Domestic Furniture,* 1986 reprint]; 62, 63, 64, 66 left, 71 left, 77 top [*Gentleman and Cabinetmaker's Director,* 1966 reprint]; 80, 83, 84 [*Cabinet-Maker and Upholsterer's Guide,* 1969 reprint]; 85, 86, 95 top right [*Cabinet-Maker and Upholsterer's Drawing Book,* 1972 reprint]; 105 [*Household Furniture and Interior Decoration,* 1971 reprint]; 115 [*Little Book of Early American Crafts and Trades,* 1976 reprint])

Zack Gaulkin (pgs. 41, 229)

Christopher Gilbert and Artlines (UK) Ltd. (p. 81)

Jeffrey P. Greene (pgs. 29 top right, 42 top right, 51, 67 bottom, 120, 122, 148, 154, 164 bottom left)

Historic Deerfield, Inc., Deerfield, Massachusetts (pgs. 14 top, 20 left, 22 bottom, 24 center, 79 bottom [Amanda Merullo photo], 222 [Amanda Merullo photo], 235 [Amanda Merullo photo], 242 [Amanda Merullo photo], 256 [Amanda Merullo photo], 274 [Amanda Merullo photo])

Susan Kahn (pgs. 29 bottom, 39 bottom, 53, 66 right, 93 bottom, 100, 116, 130 bottom left, bottom right, 133-137, 150-153, 157-163, 164 top, bottom right, 165-167, 169, 172-175, 178,180-183, 186-189, 191-196, 198, 207 top, 245, 271, 284, 287)

Nathan Liverant and Son, Colchester, Connecticut (p. 42 top left)

Metropolitan Museum of Art, New York (pgs. 11 top center [gift of Mrs. J. Insley Blair, 1951, 51.12.2], bottom left [bequest of Mrs. J. Insley Blair, 1952, 52.77.51], 39 top [gift of Mrs. Russell Sage, 1909, 10.125.135], 56 [purchase, Joseph Pulitzer Bequest, 1940, 40.37.3], 58 [gift of Samuel P. Avery, 1897, Geoffrey Clements photo], 59 [Harris Brisbane Dick Fund, 1925, 25.20], 60 [gift of J. Pierpont Morgan, 1906, 07.225.34a, b], 75 bottom [Friends of the American Wing Fund, 1967, 67.114.2], 82 [Fletcher Fund, 1945], 103 [gift of Capt. and Mrs. W.G. Fitch, 1910, in memory of Clyde Fitch], 107 top [funds from various donors, 1966], 108 top [gift of Francis Hartman Markoe, 1960], 251 [bequest of Flora E. Whiting, 1971, 1971.180.31])

Museum of Art, Rhode Island School of Design, Providence, Rhode Island (pgs. 18 [gift of Mrs. Gustav Radeke, American Furniture catalog #22], 23 top [gift of the estate of Mrs. Gustav Radeke], 44 center [gift of Mrs. Gustav Radeke], 45 top, 48 right [bequest of Charles L. Pendleton, by exchange American Furniture catalog #106], 69 right [bequest of Charles L. Pendleton], 72 top [bequest of Leila P. Bowen; Del Bogart photo], 72 bottom [bequest of Charles L. Pendleton], 73 bottom [Museum Works of Art, American Furniture catalog #64], 75 top right [bequest of Charles L. Pendleton], 79 top [bequest of Charles L. Pendleton], 259 [bequest of Charles L. Pendleton, 04.079], 265 [bequest of Martha B. Lisle, 67.166], 277 [Museum Works of Art, American Furniture catalog #64], 290 [bequest of Miss Emily Spaulding])

Museum of Fine Arts, Boston (pgs. 9 top [gift of Maurice Geeraerts in memory of Mr. and Mrs. William H. Robeson], 12, 20 right [gift of Hollis French], 24 left [gift of Mr. and Mrs. Dudley Leavitt Pickman], 25 top [gift of Robert L. Parker and Margaret S. Parker in memory of Winnifred Franklin Jones], 25 bottom [bequest of Charles Hitchcock Tyler], 28 [gift of Mr. and Mrs. Dudley Leavitt Pickman], 31 [gift of Hollis French], 37 left [bequest of Charles Hitchcock Tyler], 38 [M. & M. Karolik Collection of Eighteenth Century American Arts], 40 top [gift of Mrs. Jean Frederic Wagniere in memory of her mother Henrietta Slade Warner], 45 bottom [gift of Hollis French], 47 top [anonymous contribution and William E. Nickerson Fund], 54 [Julie Knight Fox Fund], 71 bottom [M. & M. Karolik Collection], 89 right [gift of Mrs. David R. McIlwaine in memory of Margaret Lander Pierce], 91 top [Charles H. Tyler Fund], 96 top [bequest of Miss Hannah Marcy Edwards for the Juliana Cheney Edwards Collection], 102 [gift of Mrs. Horatio A. Lamb in memory of Mr. and Mrs. Winthrop Sargent], 219 [gift of Hollis French], 224 [gift of Mr. and Mrs. Dudley Leavitt Pickman], 248])

The Newport Historical Society (pgs. 68 center, 69 left [John Corbett photo])

Rhode Island Historical Society, Providence, Rhode Island (pgs. 66 right [Susan Kahn photo], 93 bottom [Susan Kahn photo], 94 top, 271 [Susan Kahn photo], 287 [Susan Kahn photo])

Israel Sack, Inc., New York City (pgs. 22 top, 42 top center [American Antiques], 43, 232, 239)

Smithsonian Institution (pgs. 9 bottom, 71 top right)

Society for the Preservation of New England Antiquities, Boston (pgs. 44 left [gift of Caroline Barr Wade; David Bohl photo], 48 left [bequest of Frances S. Marrett; Richard Cheek photo],48 center [bequest of Ellen M. and Alice E. Jones; Richard Cheek photo], 55 [bequest of Ellen M. and Alice E. Jones; David Bohl photo], 66 top right [gift of Virginia L. Hodge and Katherine D. Perry; Richard Cheek photo], 75 top left [bequest of Julia Crocker; Richard Cheek photo])

Bud Steere Collection (pgs. 117, 118, 121)

Toledo Museum of Art, purchased with funds from the Florence Scott Libbey Bequest in memory of her father, Maurice A. Scott (p. 17)

Wadsworth Atheneum, Hartford, Connecticut (pgs. 23 bottom [gift of Mr. and Mrs. Robert P. Butler], 29 top left [Wallace Nutting Collection, gift of J. Pierpont], 68 right [gift of Mr. and Mrs. Robert P. Butler])

Wallace Collection, London, England (p. 35)

Wethersfield Historical Society, Wethersfield, Connecticut (pgs. 14 bottom [Scott Phillips photo], 130 top [Jeffrey Greene photo])

Winterthur Museum (pgs. 10 top, 11 bottom right, 27, 36, 44 right, 50, 70 bottom, 73 center, 74, 75 top center, 76 top, 78 bottom, 87, 88, 89 left [funds for purchase gift of Lammot duPont Copeland], 90 left, 93 top, 94 bottom, 95 left, 96 bottom, 97 [top, gift of Henry F. duPont, February 1958], 98, 106 top left, top right, 207 bottom [purchase funds gift of Henry Belin duPont])

Yale Center for British Art, Paul Mellon Collection, New Haven, Connecticut (p. 33)

Yale University Art Gallery, bequest of Olive Louise Dann (p. 46 bottom)

Yale University Art Gallery, Mabel Brady Garvan Collection (pgs. 8, 10 bottom, 15, 19, 21 bottom right, 49, 68 left, 69 center, 73 top, 78 top, 90 right, 99, 106 bottom, 108 bottom, 212, 216, 262, 280)

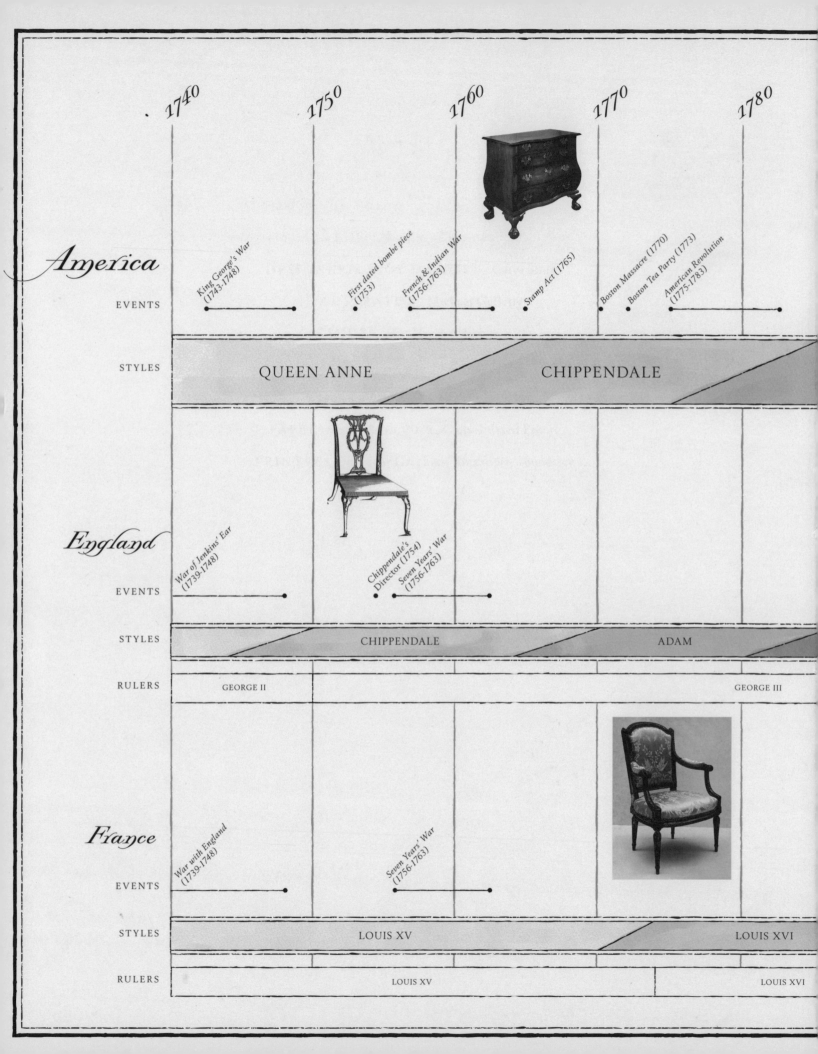

1740 *1750* *1760* *1770* *1780*

America

EVENTS

King George's War
(1743-1748)

First dated bombé piece
(1753)

French & Indian War
(1756-1763)

Stamp Act (1765)

Boston Massacre (1770)

Boston Tea Party (1773)

American Revolution
(1775-1783)

STYLES

QUEEN ANNE   CHIPPENDALE

England

EVENTS

War of Jenkins' Ear
(1739-1748)

Chippendale's
Director (1754)

Seven Years' War
(1756-1763)

STYLES

CHIPPENDALE   ADAM

RULERS

GEORGE II   GEORGE III

France

EVENTS

War with England
(1739-1748)

Seven Years' War
(1756-1763)

STYLES

LOUIS XV   LOUIS XVI

RULERS

LOUIS XV   LOUIS XVI